FEAR & MEMORY

in the Brazilian Army and Society, 1889–1954

SHAWN C. SMALLMAN

FEAR &
MEMORY

in the Brazilian Army and Society,

1889–1954

The University of North Carolina Press
Chapel Hill and London

Designed by Heidi Perov
Set in Cycles, Charter and Flightcase
by Keystone Typesetting, Inc.

Manufactured in the United States of America

The paper in this book meets the guidelines for
permanence and durability of the Committee on
Production Guidelines for Book Longevity of the
Council on Library Resources.

Library of Congress Cataloging-in-Publication Data

Smallman, Shawn C.
    Fear and memory in the Brazilian army and society,
1889–1954 / Shawn C. Smallman.
        p. cm.
    Includes bibliographical references and index.
ISBN 0-8078-2691-X (cloth: alk. paper)
ISBN 0-8078-5359-3 (pbk.: alk. paper)
        1. Brazil—History—1889– 2. Brazil. Exârcito—
Political activity. 3. Civil-military relations—Brazil—
History. 4. Sociology, Military—Brazil. I. Title.
F2537 .S65   2002
981.06'4—dc   2001052576

cloth   06 05 04 03 02   5 4 3 2 1
paper   06 05 04 03 02   5 4 3 2 1

For Margaret, Paige, and Jack

CONTENTS

ACKNOWLEDGMENTS

I would like to thank Emilia Viotti da Costa. No advisor ever gave more freely of her time and energy. I also owe a great debt to my other advisors at Yale, Gil Joseph and Daniel James. Frank McCann kindly answered a letter from a graduate student who needed to understand the Brazilian archival system. José Murilo de Carvalho gave graciously of his time to discuss the historiography and current trends in the armed forces. Maria Cecília Spina Forjaz helped to introduce me to Fundaçao Getúlio Vargas. The late Gerson Moura explained the issues involved in the petroleum debate.

I wish to thank the staffs of the Clube Militar, Biblioteca Nacional, Serviço de Documentação Nacional da Marinha, Instituto Historico e Cultural da Aeronautica, and the Arquivo Nacional. Without the aid of Professor Ivan Rodrigues de Faria and the staff at the Arquivo do Exército, this book could never have been written. I owe a special debt of gratitude to the staff of the Centro de Pesquisa e Documentação Contemporânea do Brasil (Fundação Getúlio Vargas), where Marie Ignez Niedu tracked down countless items over many months. The staff at the U.S. National Archive were patient and helpful. This project was made possible with grants from the MacArthur Foundation and the Henry Hart Rice advanced research fellowship given by the Yale Center for International and Area Studies. I also received travel money from Portland State University. Most of all I wish to thank the Smith Richardson Foundation, which funded the one-year sabbatical that enabled me to complete this manuscript.

I owe thanks to many soldiers, but I would like to make special mention of Colonel Asdrubel Esteves, for both his aid and his humor. My friends Jacques Buxbaum and Milton helped me through a thousand crises. Paulo Henrique Machado took me to Petrópolis when the heat became unbearable. Luis Vitor Tavares shared many lunches with me at La Mole. Jean Marcel Fontes de Alencar shared Mercado Sao José, the apartment, and the ghost. Daryle Williams gave good advice, improved my Portuguese, mixed good drinks, and made Brazil fun.

Henrik Kraay, Michelle Gamburd, and Friedrich Schuler read sections of the manuscript. I also wish to give particular thanks to Frederick Nunn, who has served as a mentor to guide this project to completion.

Finally, I wish to thank my parents Lee and Phyllis, as well as my sister Ellen. Most of all, I wish to thank Margaret Everett, who could be trapped in a Volkswagen bug floating down the street and still make our time together fun.

FEAR & MEMORY

in the Brazilian Army and Society, 1889–1954

Introduction

This book explores the informal structures of power that shaped civil-military relations in Brazil from 1889 to 1954, and provided the foundations for authoritarian rule after 1964. It also considers the military's construction of historical memory as part of an official history of nation building and nationality that has shaped both popular and scholarly memory. This work challenges conventional Brazilian history, collective memory, and, most fundamentally, the Brazilian military's account of its own experience and its role in national development. In so doing, it undermines the armed forces' narrative of unity and examines the internal conflicts that military versions of Brazilian history have chosen to forget.

Between 1964 and 1973 a wave of military coups swept across Latin America. They differed from previous military interventions in that armed forces not only chose to retain power, but also to transform their societies. In nations like Argentina the armed forces did not limit their ambitions to altering the national economy, political system, and social structure. They wished to change even the way people thought.[1] To understand these authoritarian regimes, scholars have paid great attention to the coups and the events that led to them. Some authors have depicted the Brazilian military as an institution forced to act by urgent circumstances such as the infiltration of the enlisted ranks by unions, the irresponsible appeals of populist politicians, and the desperate sense that a polarized political system was breaking down.[2] While accurate enough, this narrative represents an insufficiently historical perspective, one that does not examine the deep roots of the military's political actions, which laid the groundwork for later authoritarian rule. Attention needs to be paid not only to particular events and individual actors, but also to the long-term trends that shaped the military's behavior once the coup took place.

The Brazilian military's decision to retain power and to impose a particular political program resulted from its historical experience. Structures that supported authoritarianism in Brazil did not suddenly appear during the coup but rather evolved over decades. By carefully examining factional conflicts within the Brazilian military until 1954, this book emphasizes the major changes that reshaped the institution long before the coups took place and that the military has since sought to conceal.

Brazil's Importance and History

While Spanish America fractured into many republics after independence, Portuguese-speaking Brazil remained intact. Brazil's current position as the most powerful nation in Latin America is due partially to its common language as well as its size, population, military, and economy. The fifth largest nation in the world, it occupies nearly half of South America, an area larger than Europe, and it borders all South American nations except Chile and Ecuador. According to the 2000 census Brazil has over 169 million people; the Brazilian state of São Paulo alone has nearly twice the population of Guatemala. In terms of both manpower and expenditure, Brazil has the largest armed forces in South America, with four times the enlistment of the Argentine military. The Brazilian economy—the ninth largest in the world—is much larger than Russia's. In 1996 the gross domestic product (GDP) of Brazil was larger than that of all Spanish South America combined. The Brazilian economy acts as the financial linchpin for the rest of Latin America.[3]

Until recently, historians have generally argued that Brazil's political history has been characterized by greater political stability than many of its neighbors. It is true that Brazil achieved independence from Portugal in 1822 without war, largely because the monarch's son, Pedro I, became the new emperor. But this political continuity did not stop Brazil from experiencing a series of uprisings, rebellions, and racially inspired revolts at the local and regional level throughout the nineteenth century, as recent scholarship has emphasized.[4] The government suppressed many of these uprisings with great brutality. Still, at the national level the figure of the emperor provided a sense of continuity and stability lacking in Spanish America, until a military coup ended imperial government in 1889. Between the foundation of the republic and the 1964 coup, Brazil ostensibly remained a democracy for all but nine years (the *Estado Novo* or New State, 1937–45).

The armed forces did frequently intervene in politics. In 1889, 1930, 1937,

1945, and 1954, the military (or factions within it) helped either to change the structure of government or to replace the nation's leader. Even so, during the twentieth century the military never retained power after intervening in politics but rather transferred power to civilians. In Brazil this changed with the 1964 coup, after which the armed forces dominated the political system for twenty-one years (1964–85). The military first engineered "the Brazilian miracle"—six years of explosive growth—then oversaw an equally remarkable period of debt and decay.

New Opportunities for Scholarship

The Brazilian military withdrew from power in 1985 as authoritarian regimes crumbled throughout the continent. Although it retained great influence, the play of democratic politics gradually eroded the military's power.[5] This situation has created a unique opportunity for scholars of Brazil. The military no longer formally censors books and newspapers, and it has lost its ability to control academic courses and offerings. Equally important, the legacy of fear has begun to erode, as memories of political torture fade. In this environment, many new sources have become available.[6]

During military rule the armed forces banned many books and pamphlets, which disappeared from libraries and bookstores. These works are now emerging from private collections, or are accessible at the archive of the social and political police, Delegacion Especial de Segurança Política e Social/ Departamento de Ordem Política e Social (DESP/DOPS). Officers, including military dissidents, have placed their papers and memoirs in such centers as Fundação Getúlio Vargas. Much like scholars studying Eastern Europe and the former Soviet Union, specialists in Latin American history now have access to resources that they never expected to see.[7] This situation permits a scholarly reappraisal of the military's own collective memory.

The Military's Influence over Historical Memory

Until the start of the democratization, the military's dominance over the political system inevitably shaped studies of the military, not only in Brazil but also in many other South American countries. These militaries have long possessed allies in civilian society, regulations to discipline retired officers, authority over military archives, and a legacy of fear. Military leaders controlled access to their archives and granted interviews to historians, as part of an effort to create an "impartial" account of their past. By this means officers promoted an official history that emphasized military unity and that focused solely on events and topics that the armed forces deemed acceptable.

In this official narrative, the military explained all institutional changes by referring only to common, public experiences, that is, formal structures sanctioned by the institution's hierarchy. Officers spoke at length about new schools, famous officers, combat experiences, and foreign missions. The resulting narrative is characterized more by what was omitted than by what it included. For example, officers produced countless works on their ideology, a safe topic.[8] As a result, specialists have been able to study carefully how military ideology shaped everything from coups to the authoritarian regimes that followed.[9] Yet other important issues—such as terror, race, and corruption—received little attention. Of course, some authors have challenged the military's hegemony. Nelson Werneck Sodré and Stanley Hilton—to name but two of the best-known writers—have critically examined the military's history.[10] Yet in some respects the armed forces' hegemony has endured; "official" army concerns permeate the work of even some distinguished authors.

The extent of the military's influence can be seen by considering specific works. Edmundo Campos Coelho wrote an insightful book that emphasized the military's autonomy in the mid-1970s.[11] Yet a lack of primary sources hampered his study. During authoritarian rule Coelho had difficulty viewing the complex social and political forces that shaped military politics. As a result, his work depicted the army as a monolith. Coelho argued that the army suffered from an "identity crisis" and became increasingly alienated from society. By overlooking the factions and struggles that shaped military policy, Coelho adopted the army's depiction of itself as a united institution that based its actions on its ideals.

Other scholars have also tended to reify the military. Robert Hayes's study, *The Armed Nation*, adopts the rhetoric of the Brazilian military itself. According to Hayes, the Brazilian military has become imbued throughout its history with a "military corporate mystique." The armed forces conceived of themselves as the nation's saviors, which led them to search for a "military messiah." Although Hayes does refer to the military's factional conflicts, he does not carefully examine the slow process through which army factions created and manipulated doctrine. Instead, he adopts a psychological explanation for the armed forces' behavior that emphasized enduring military beliefs. While potentially useful, Hayes's work contains no critique of the military's creed. Because of this approach, his work omits discussion of events the military wished to ignore, such as political terror.[12]

Even authors with access to new sources have not completely escaped the armed forces' hegemony. For example, William Waack and Paulo Sérgio Pinheiro carefully studied the 1935 "communist" uprising within the Brazilian military. William Waack had access to new sources available in Moscow, while Sérgio Pinheiro had access to over 90,000 documents from the archive of former president Artur da Silva Bernardes.[13] Yet neither author traced the origins of the conspiracy back to the army's senior leadership although disgruntled commanders formed an alliance with civilian elites under the leadership of Artur Bernardes. In this case, the interests of a wide range of parties supported the military's version of the past. Nor was this example unique. In many instances, the military has succeeded in shaping both popular and scholarly memory.

Informal Structures and Conflict

To escape the military's influence, this work uses new sources to emphasize the informal structures that shaped the institution's political behavior. Informal structures are the unwritten rules, organizations, and beliefs that shape power without official sanction or government funding. Examples of these structures would be corruption networks, civil-military alliances, army factions, racial beliefs, family ties, and regional allegiances. These structures exist without government endorsement. A chart of the army's official hierarchy would ignore them, yet these factors define power within the institution to such an extent that an alternative hierarchy predicts officers' authority nearly as much as their official rank. Often, informal structures shape the military's relationship with civilian society more than its official organization.

To understand these informal structures, this work gives considerable attention to military factions and the internal conflicts they generate. Officers indicated the issues that mattered to the army by fighting over them. During moments of struggle, military factions or parties often turned to civilians for support. This situation shattered the army's image of unity and left documents that reveal military politics with unusual clarity. Like bolts of lightning, factional conflicts allowed observers to view the military landscape.

Few subjects have been studied so carefully as military factions in Latin America, a topic on which there is a rich regional and theoretical literature.[14] This scholarship, however, has sometimes been weakened by a lack of discourse between historians and political scientists. For example, political scientists Alain Rouquié and Antonio Carlos Peixoto correctly argue that military factions resembled political parties, in that they served as a means to aggregate and express political interests.[15] Yet this only became a dominant characteristic of military factions in Brazil after World War II, as the military responded to trends in the international arena and Brazilian society (the Cold

War, the rising power of nationalism, and the polarization of Brazilian society). Historians have carefully studied factional conflicts throughout Latin America, but they have not always placed these contests within a broader context of social and political change. For example, the work of Robert Potash and John Foster Dulles describes military factions and their conflicts in (respectively) Argentina and Brazil, but does not always tie these contests to larger historical issues. Without this context, history becomes chronicle, that is, a record of events lacking interpretation.[16] Military conflicts mattered because they formed part of larger historical processes as officers debated essential choices during times of rapid change.

The armed forces have wanted to conceal these struggles in part because they suggested that nations such as Brazil could have taken different social, political, and economic paths. For this reason, the armed forces have used violence and terror to shape the memory of the past. In 1910, for example, a naval rebellion with racial overtones rocked Brazil. The armed forces went to extreme lengths over the course of half a century to erase the public memory of this event—imprisoning a sane witness in a mental hospital, kidnapping one journalist, terrifying another, and stripping scholars who studied this topic of their rights.[17] Selective amnesia has remained the military's official policy toward painful questions ever since. In 1952, General Alcides Etchegoyen won the presidency of a military social club, after a campaign marked by terror. Meeting with reporters the next day, Etchegoyen said: "I am ready to answer only the questions that are about subjects after the election. I forget everything before the vote. I have a poor memory."[18]

This work examines the conflicts that officers sought to forget. In adopting this approach, this work does not seek to sensationalize the past, but rather to come to a more thorough understanding of military behavior. This effort does not entail explaining the 1964 coup, an event that took place because many political actors combined to undermine democracy in South America, the military being only one actor among many.[19] Instead, this work examines the informal structures that shaped the military's involvement in politics. Throughout Latin America, profound changes took place within national militaries long before the wave of coups drew attention to these institutions in the 1960s and 1970s. In Brazil, for example, many structures that later bolstered military rule—the existence of a powerful military party, with a system of intelligence and terror to repress dissent, strong civil-military alliances, a network of corruption to provide rewards, and a clear program for the nation—existed by 1954. These informal structures acquired critical importance when broad changes in Latin American politics and society undermined democratic government. This context shaped how officers perceived the army's role in politics after the coup and provided the framework that defined military government. Yet these networks, alliances, and organizations have remained hidden because of the military's efforts to shape historical memory.

Organization

While all three branches of the armed forces must be considered to understand military politics, the army has held the most weight in civil-military affairs. This history focuses on the Brazilian army and society during this period. Following McCann's example, this work conflates the terms military and army where this approach does not lead to confusion.[20] Chapter 1 examines the army's conflict with traditional elites during the Old Republic (1889–1930). During this period, the institution remained fractured between competing personalities and bound to an ostensibly democratic government by a system of corruption. Despite the army's conflicts with rural elites, it also shared many attitudes with them, such as a firm belief in Brazil's racial hierarchy and a concern with the growing power of the working class.

Chapter 2 (1930–37) examines how traditional elites sought to regain control over the institution after their defeat in 1930. This chapter also looks at how the army created myths in response to this challenge in order to exclude civilians from the institution and to justify the army's involvement in civilian affairs. Chapter 3 (1937–45) discusses how contending military factions sought to impose their project onto the institution. The vision of development—and of the army's role in national life—that these factions created laid the groundwork for the armed forces' bitter conflict in the postwar period. Chapter 4 (1945–48) explores how the rising power of the United States in the region after World War II created a profound division within the military, which split into two parties with diametrically opposed projects. The issue of petroleum development began a bitter conflict between these two blocs. Chapter 5 (1949) examines the manner in which the conflict led both military parties to create a clearly organized ideology. Chapter 6 (1949–51) studies the changing nature of the conflict and the manner in which it reshaped the army's informal structures of power. Chapter 7 (1951–52) examines the defeat of dissident officers in 1952. Their collapse allowed one military party to impose its vision of the army's role, and a wave of terror then purged the institution of many nationalist officers. While the defeat of one military party did not end the divisions within the army, the victors subsequently set its agenda.

Chapter 8 discusses the 1964 coup and the informal structures that laid the groundwork for military rule. Finally, a brief epilogue discusses the current state of civil-military relations in Brazil. Recent democratization has created a mood of optimism about civil-military relations in Latin America.[21] But regional armies continue to influence civilian policy through the legacy of fear, military violence, paramilitary organizations, and civil-military alliances.[22] In this context, it is crucial to critically examine these armies' history and the complex factors shaping their involvement in politics.

1

Officers versus Politicians
1889–1930

Throughout the Empire (1822–89) a paradox troubled Brazilian politics. The army was designed to serve as an instrument of order. In other words, civilian leaders wished the army to defend the power and privilege of the slaveholding elites who dominated the political system. Yet the landholding class did not trust the army and sought to counterbalance its power. In this contradiction lay the origins of the tension between the Brazilian military and political elites.

The army was a strange instrument to uphold a slave society defined by a racial hierarchy because Brazilians viewed military service as a punishment. Soldiers hunted the poor and the unemployed in the streets to fill the ranks. In the countryside, some poor men entered the army when they were run down by horsemen with lassos. Officers maintained discipline with physical punishment, which they justified by arguing that a large portion of their men were criminals. Joining the ranks did not appeal to whites with the opportunity or resources to avoid service, and conscripts were largely black or mixed-race.[1] Many officers came from poorer provinces, and it was not uncommon for them to come from families of declining fortune seeking to ensure that their sons would not sink into poverty and disgrace. Traditional elites therefore wondered how the army could ensure social stability when its men were drawn from the lowest strata of society and its officers (especially after 1850) often had weak ties to the upper class.[2]

The elites' lack of confidence in the army manifested itself in different ways. Most importantly, in 1831 the government created the National Guard, a military organization that excluded the poor, to serve as a check on the army. It existed under the authority of the minister of justice, and its officers were the most powerful local civilians. To army officers it represented a challenge that they would resent until the end of the Empire. To serve his own political ends, the emperor sometimes encouraged the army's mistrust of the elites. For example, in 1823 Pedro I accused the delegates to the Constituent Assembly of wishing to abolish the army, a lie he promoted to ensure the military's support when he closed this body.[3] But the emperor at times also lacked confidence in the army, which sometimes caused officers to question his commitment to them. This situation gradually created an army riddled by resentment.

The Paraguayan War (also called the War of the Triple Alliance, 1864–70) proved to be the turning point in civil-military relations during the Empire. In alliance with Argentina and Uruguay, the Brazilian Empire entered into a war with Paraguay. Brazil proved to be completely unprepared to defeat its opponent, which, although much smaller, had begun to industrialize under a strong central government. The National Guard could not deal with such a challenge, and the army quickly grew in size, funding, and power. After the war, elites wished to strip the army of the influence it had gained.

Officers believed that they had saved the nation from disaster despite the cowardice and treason of the elites, whom they perceived as having been more concerned with defending their privileges than with protecting their country. This tension was heightened in the late 1870s and early 1880s, as an influential minority of officers began to articulate a vision of the nation's future that included policies that rural elites opposed, such as abolitionism. The army's role in abolition (1888) was much more complex than the military's own version of its history indicates.[4] But the army's unwillingness to support this institution exacerbated a relationship of mutual mistrust between the elites and the military, with roots that stretched far back into the imperial period. This tension would shape the military's involvement in society throughout the First Republic (1889–1930).[5] The army's perception of itself as the nation's savior, its fear of competing institutions, and its difficult relationship with civilian elites, all had their roots in this period.

Independence

Brazil began its road to independence in November 1807, when Napoleon invaded the Iberian peninsula. To avoid capture, the Portuguese monarch and his court sought British protection and fled across the Atlantic to Brazil. The monarchy found Brazil to be so inviting that after Napoleon's defeat it was only with great pressure from the Portuguese parliament that Dom João VI returned home in April 1821. He left his son, prince regent Pedro, behind. Brazilians, reluctant to lose the privileges they had enjoyed during the emperor's presence, supported Dom Pedro I as he declared Brazil's independence on September 7, 1822 and became the first Brazilian emperor.

The new emperor was determined to retain considerable power. Even before declaring Brazil's independence he had convoked a constituent assembly. Displeased with the assembly's work, he dissolved it on November 12, 1823 with the army's support. This decision sparked a rebellion in the northeast, where a series of provinces came together to found the "Confederation of the Equator." The emperor successfully put down this uprising by November 1824. The rebellion did not prevent him from issuing the first Brazilian constitution on March 25, 1824, which (with amendments) existed until the end of the Empire. It created a monarchical government with considerable power, despite the existence of a chamber of deputies and a senate. The emperor appointed senators, called elections, and had the right to veto legislation. He also had the ability to grant nonhereditary titles of nobility.

Dom Pedro I proved to be an unpopular ruler. He plunged his country into debt with Britain, led Brazil into a disastrous war with Argentina, and scandalized Brazilians with an open extramarital affair. By 1831 there were street demonstrations against his rule. On April 7, 1831 he abdicated his throne and returned to Portugal. His son, Dom Pedro II, was only five years old. The ensuing period (1831–40) is known as the Regency because leaders acting in Pedro II's name governed Brazil. It was a time of political turmoil and regional rebellion, which sometimes acquired a class or racial character that threatened the elites.

The Elites and the Army

Throughout the Empire, Brazilian politics were governed by a small population of social and political elites. Its members controlled land and slaves, the main means of measuring wealth during the empire. This class also controlled the agricultural production (mostly sugar and coffee), which dominated Brazil's economy. These elites, however, were defined not only by their wealth but also by their social and political influence. Patriarchical relationships, family allegiances, and regional loyalties, gave a small number of individuals—almost entirely male—immense power, which the imperial government could sanction by granting nonhereditary titles of nobility. While new groups (such as industrialists) could attain wealth, they could not join Brazil's dominant class based on this measure alone.[6]

While Brazil's traditional elites fought among themselves for power and prestige, they nonetheless shared an essentially conservative worldview. Despite their fascination with Europe and modernity, traditional elites defined this vision in terms of the nation's past. They wanted to ensure the autonomy of the state governments that they dominated, to keep the central state weak, to exclude the masses from politics, and to maintain slavery. While they wished the army to defend their authority, they also wished to limit its strength because it was an agent of the central state outside their control.

At independence, the army was an unprofessional institution in which many soldiers were conscripts, while its officers often won their rank through service rather than schooling. Its key role was to serve as a bulwark of the social order, although it did not always prove to be effective at this task. Some idea of the elites' concerns about the army can be gained from the report that the minister of war, Manoel da Fonseca Lima e Silva, sent to the chamber of deputies in 1832. The minister of war was appalled by the number of officers in the army and deeply concerned about the military's expense, from which he saw little public benefit.[7] He was also very disturbed by the indiscipline and rebelliousness of the troops. He pointed to the "calamitous days of the past July which filled the inhabitants of this capital with horror, because of the anarchy that rapidly and terrifyingly took command of part of the troops stationed here."[8] The government responded to military unrest by sending troops back to the provinces. This measure did not resolve the situation, as the minister of war described in a passage that gives insight into the character of the troops:

> By an ill-fated and flawed system of recruitment, adopted and fol-
> lowed by the last administration, appropriate only to purge from the
> provinces the most abominable men noted for their vices, of mercurial
> temperament and horrifying crimes, people always dangerous to public
> tranquility; by this flawed system of recruitment, there passed into the
> corps of the army almost everything that was the worst in the population,
> and they have been converted into the deposit of moral blindness. These
> were the same men, who arriving at the beaches of their provinces, gradu-
> ally there reproduced, and with greater atrocity, the same terrible scenes
> that happened in this capital. The government, strengthened by legisla-
> tive measures, did not hesitate to extinguish some corps, which appeared
> to be forgetful of their sacred oaths."[9]

The minister concluded by noting approvingly that the army had been signifi-
cantly reduced in size. Indeed the army was cut from approximately 30,000 members in 1830, to 14,342 the following year; government spending on the

military was also sharply cut.[10] The elites found the army to be a poor tool to uphold the social order, as many of its troops came from the poorest section of the population.

The National Guard

The inadequacy of the army led the Regency to create the National Guard in 1831. This body, under the control of the minister of justice, was intended not only to defend the elites against the masses, but also to check the power of the army. All adult men who met a minimum income requirement were compelled to serve. Its officers were always the men who had the greatest social power in a locality. Indeed, well into the twentieth century, "colonel" would be an honorary term for a powerful landholder in the northeast. In effect, this organization was a tool of the landholding class.

The army bitterly resented the creation of the National Guard as an insult to its honor. Officers thought that the army was treated as a poor stepchild of the National Guard and that for this reason it often lacked funding and supplies. The army also deplored the fact that it was forced to impress poor men (usually Afro-Brazilians) into the ranks, whereas the National Guard recruited the wealthy and the educated. This inequity led to a racial division between the two organizations, much like the racial differences between the army and the navy, which also had an officer corps with an aristocratic character. While some people of color did serve in the National Guard, they faced great discrimination, as the black newspaper *O Homem de Cor* complained in its inaugural issue. All these factors heightened the mutual mistrust between the elites and the army.[11]

The Regency and the Sabinada

One might have expected the army to gain political power during the Regency, a period of political turmoil that required the imperial government to use force to maintain its authority. Until recently, historians have argued that Brazil was far different from Spanish America in that independence did not bring the social chaos and political unrest that plagued Brazil's neighbors. More recent evaluations have questioned this old belief. In 1824 northeastern provinces had rebelled in the Confederation of the Equator. A subsequent rebellion in the Banda Oriental (Uruguay) in 1825 had been followed by war with Argentina in 1827. Foreign mercenaries rebelled in Rio de Janeiro in

July 1828. All this had taken place before Pedro I abdicated the throne in 1831, and the years that followed saw Brazil brought to the edge of dissolution.

Between 1832 and 1845 Brazil endured five major rebellions, some of which had a strongly regional character: the Cabanos War in Pernambuco (1832–35), the Cabanagem War in Pará (1835–40), the Sabinada in Bahia (1837–38), the Balaiada in Maranhão (1838–41), and the Farrapos War in Rio Grande do Sul (1836–45). During these conflicts three provinces—Bahia, Pará, and Rio Grande do Sul—flirted with independence.[12] It is true that these revolts were all defeated, that they did not bring about profound social or economic changes, that Brazil remained a unified nation, and that power remained in the imperial family's hands. In part because Brazil was a slave society, the elites had a profound distrust of popular mobilization, which they feared might lead to a successful slave rebellion such as had already occurred in Haiti.[13] The elites' fears helped to prevent Brazil from undergoing the chaos that washed over Spanish America after independence. However, for the political leaders who lived through this period, the rebellions were a terrifying experience that led to a period of conservatism after Pedro II came to the throne in 1840.

Despite the military's role in ensuring the government's survival, old patterns of mutual mistrust endured. The army did not benefit from this period of turmoil, in part because military officials had participated in many of the uprisings.[14] For example, the Bahian Sabinada (November 1837–March 1838) was led by both radical liberals and "army officers who resented the military reforms of the 1830s and, for a time, found allies in the numerous colored militia officers and men whose venerable organizations had been abolished in 1831."[15] Officers of all ranks had joined the rebellion, from cadets to a lieutenant general. They were angered by cuts in the number of troops, which had also left some officers unemployed. They were equally furious that the government had replaced the "army controlled militias with the civilian National Guard in 1831."[16]

Until 1831 the city of Salvador had possessed four militia regiments under the army's authority, one of which had been composed of free blacks, while a second regiment had been made up of mulattoes. When the National Guard was founded, these regiments were extinguished. Militiamen could join the National Guard if they had sufficient income, but they faced bitter discrimination, and militia officers were banned from joining the National Guard. The rebels gained strength from this perceived injustice. Black and mulatto troops joined the uprising, as did some of their officers.

The rebels abolished the National Guard, whose members fled the city. Yet it was the National Guard that the imperial government relied upon to retake

Salvador, at one time the capital of the former colony: "With the retreat of the police force on November 13, the military lines had been drawn. The police and the National Guard, creations of the previous six years, would face army units and Salvador's old militia across the trenches."[17] Because this struggle acquired a racial character, it frightened the elites.

The rebels' leadership gradually lost control of the movement, which came to be dominated by Afro-Brazilians. Faced with little other choice, the rebel leadership declared freedom for all Brazilian-born slaves as they fled their owners to join the uprising. This situation in the heart of a major slaveholding region threatened Brazil's social system and may explain the extreme brutality of government forces, who killed over a thousand people when the rebels' lines collapsed in March 1838.[18] Twelve officers who had joined the rebellion received death sentences, although they were later given amnesty.

Understandably, the elites did not believe that they could rely on the army to maintain order and enacted reforms during the Regency that were intended to limit the military's power.[19] The creation of the National Guard was but one manifestation of the growing distance between the army and the planter class. Elite families were increasingly unlikely to send their sons to become officers. More and more officers were themselves children of military men, which increased the social distance between the army and the elites, and fewer officers served in the government.[20] The army did not increase its size, funding, or power with time. Indeed, by 1850 the army had only 1,400 officers and 16,000 troops, nearly half the level of 1830. The relative weakness of the army—not only during the Recency, but also during the following quarter century—encouraged lingering military resentment.[21] Indeed, the military later remembered the Regency as a period when the elites sought to destroy the armed forces, as military historian Nelson Werneck Sodré described: "The Regency, little by little, concretely undertook the destruction of the army."[22]

The Paraguayan War

The turning point in civil-military relations during the Empire came in 1864 with the onset of the Paraguayan War. Although the war's origins are complex, the Paraguayan dictator Francisco Solano López began the fighting by invading Brazilian and Argentine territory.[23] The ensuing conflict pitted Brazil, Uruguay, and Argentina against Paraguay, in a hopeless struggle that cost the lives of 60 to 69 percent of Paraguay's population. The Paraguayans fought so fanatically that at war's end there were four to five women in Paraguay for every man.[24] By the time that López was run down and killed by Brazilian cavalry on March 1, 1870, the Brazilian army had profoundly changed.

Paraguay had benefited during the war from a strong central government, which had begun to industrialize the nation. The Paraguayan military also had three to four times as many troops as Brazil did. To meet this challenge, the Brazilian government had been compelled to vastly increase the size of the military, a task it accomplished in part by forcibly recruiting large numbers of the poor, usually Afro-Brazilians. Some Brazilian slaveowners voluntarily sent their slaves to fight during the Paraguayan War, while worrying that the lack of troops at home might encourage a slave uprising.[25] In the army's own memory, the wartime experience led the army to favor abolitionism, an argument that supported the army's myth that it has always had good race relations in its ranks. In fact, most officers did not come to support abolitionism for another decade, when positivism (a French philosophy that stressed the importance of science and reason) acquired a strong military following. Only a fraction of Brazilian slaves (less than 1 percent) were freed to fight. Most soldiers were free men of color or poor whites.[26] But the war did shift the racial balance in the army somewhat, as Afro-Brazilian sergeants managed to enter the officer corps. This shift did not concern the elites as much, however, as the army's unprecedented influence and new ideals.

The army had grown in size and its leaders—especially the Duke of Caxias, Luiz Alves de Lima e Silva—had acquired great power. Some officers had also begun to favor policies, such as industrialization, that supported military goals but not elite interests.[27] For this reason, with the end of the conflict the elites in the legislature rapidly cut the military's budget and enlistment. This policy outraged military leaders, who had blamed their difficulties during the war on the unpatriotic and incompetent leadership of civilians.[28] To army leaders, the rapid cuts in their organization appeared to be a betrayal.[29] The army doubted both the willingness and the capability of traditional elites to solve Brazil's problems. It was during this period that Brazilian officers began to think of the army as the "nation's savior," which became an important aspect of the military's depiction of itself.[30]

The Overthrow of the Empire

Despite the efforts of civilian leaders, the army remained a powerful political actor that could challenge elite interests. Civilian politicians criticized army commanders who expressed opinions on political issues, which led to a political crisis called the "Military Question" in the 1880s. This conflict began with a series of perceived insults to army commanders which officers and civilians hostile to the status quo seized upon as a reason to attack the government.[31] Behind this conflict lay a number of different factors. The army's lack of funds and a patronage system that advanced incompetent officers infuriated commanders who wanted the army to possess a measure of autonomy from the nation's political leadership. The army resented the power that elites had over military promotions and within the institution in general; an officer's advancement could rely more on civilian allies than personal merit.[32] Resentful officers also blamed the politics of regional elites for what they perceived as Brazil's political and economic backwardness, and they were exasperated by evidence of civilian corruption.[33]

The army also refused to support slavery any longer, in large part because of the growing power of positivist thought within the institution. Officers' public statements on this issue angered the planter class. In 1887 Deodoro da Fonseca, the army's most influential commander and first president of the Military Club, wrote Princess Isabel (Pedro II's daughter) to request that the army not be used to capture fleeing slaves. His appeal was movingly written and doomed slavery in Brazil because the institution could only be maintained by force. Princess Isabel abolished slavery in her father's name on May 13, 1888.[34] Until that time, military abolitionism only served to exacerbate the difficult relationship between the army and civilian leaders from the planter class.

By 1889 Pedro II was in a dangerous position. Social and economic trends had significantly eroded his power since 1870. A powerful planter elite, not allied to the monarchy, had arisen in southern Brazil. The northeastern planters, long the core of the monarchy's support, had lost influence. The emperor repeatedly clashed with the Church. A growing urban population believed that the government ignored its interests. Republican ideals had gained power within Brazil, while some of the emperor's supporters were angered by abolition.[35] Although most senior officers remained staunchly monarchist, republicans had even attracted a very small but significant following within the army, where positivist officers preached republicanism.

The government's actions during the Military Question had angered some officers. Many commanders believed that under imperial rule the army had long suffered neglect and mistreatment. (Military grievances included provisions of the 1824 constitution, the Regency's reforms, Caxias's treatment during the Paraguayan War, meddling in promotions, and chronic insufficient funding.)[36] For these reasons, the head of the government, Viscount Ouro Preto (Afonso Celso de Assis Figueiredo), and his liberal cabinet were concerned, when he assumed the position of prime minister on June 7, 1889.

Ouro Preto's cabinet wished to balance the army's power by strengthening the National Guard and the police in an effort to reduce the risk that civilian opponents might try to use factions within the army against the monarchy. The military perceived the cabinet's intentions in a more sinister light. During the "Military Question" army general Deodoro da Fonseca referred to a widespread belief that the Brazilian government wished to replace the army with the National Guard.[37] A French journalist reported that the government intended to disperse military units to the countryside before dissolving the military. The government's chronic neglect of the military, combined with political resentments, helped to make this accusation believable to powerful military leaders. Members of the republican press skillfully manipulated these deeply rooted fears to push the military to overthrow the government.[38]

Attacks by civilian leaders created the necessary conditions for a military movement against the monarchy, as Edmundo Campos Coelho has noted. On November 14, 1889, false rumors circulated that the government intended to arrest Deodoro da Fonseca, and the army's leading republican, Benjamin Constant.[39] Because of the political tension, officers believed these rumors and feared that the government planned to destroy the army. Although a monarchist, Deodoro da Fonseca led the coup that overthrew the government.[40]

Given the turmoil within the army, both officers and civilians found it difficult to understand the significance of the coup. A faction of junior officers, influenced by positivist ideals, wished to found a republic.[41] Yet republicans represented perhaps no more than a fifth of the officer corps. The army was divided into factions, and the rebels had not consulted the navy.[42] There was no strong leadership for the coup. Both Deodoro da Fonseca and Benjamin Constant Botelho de Magalhães, the head of the positivist faction, proved to be in poor health and soon died. Moreover, Deodoro da Fonseca himself probably only wished to change the government, not to overthrow the emperor, a vision he shared with many officers.[43] Military leaders shared outrage over civilian politics, to be sure, but they lacked a consensus on a clear political program. The army founded a republic less because of the numbers and power of the republican officers than the disunion and confusion among their opponents. On November 15, 1889, Deodoro da Fonseca responded to the wishes of his most ardent supporters and declared Brazil a republic. Few army leaders, apart from a republican faction of junior officers, had a clear vision of this new polity.[44]

Military Rule

Despite a democratic facade, the army created what at times resembled a military government. Deodoro (Brazilian leaders are often referred to by their first names) first controlled the provisional government that replaced imperial rule, then ensured his election as president by threatening to send troops to dissolve Congress.[45] Unable to prevent his accession to the presidency, civilians selected another army officer, Floriano Peixoto (who disliked Deodoro) as vice-president on February 25, 1891. Officers made up one-quarter of the constituent assembly that Deodoro convened, and soldiers moved into many posts previously held by civilians.[46] Deodoro included civilians in his ministry, but a "civilian clothed with authority either submitted to the direction delineated by the military milieu in which he lived, or he retired from his office."[47] Deodoro thought of his regime as a military government, and he quickly moved to double the size of the armed forces and to increase their pay.[48]

Yet neither Deodoro's prestige nor the rewards that he showered upon the institution could conceal the profound disunity within the armed forces. Officers had united during the coup only because they believed that civilian leaders were attacking the military. As June Hahner has stated, the removal of this perceived danger led the army to collapse into internecine rivalries: "They were basically protesters without programs."[49] The army lacked international support because most foreign nations believed that the collapse of the old regime threatened their financial interests.[50] The army sought to form civil-military alliances, but these proved to be difficult to maintain. Deodoro tried to forge alliances with northeastern planters, a group whose political power was on the wane. Younger officers favored republican politicians, yet republicans wished to decentralize political power, which most officers ardently opposed.[51] Moreover, the political interests of the northeastern landholders and the republicans were irreconcilable. Consequently, the army failed to rally a powerful group of civilians around a political project. The army as a whole never did develop a clear political program, an official ideology, powerful civil-military alliances, a system to repress dissent, strong international support, or a dominant military party to shape the institution's politics. What is remarkable is that the military shaped politics for the next five years despite its weaknesses.

Because of these problems, Deodoro's perception of his strength was exaggerated. Officers could not ignore the wishes of powerful civilian leaders, as the provisions of Brazil's new constitution illustrated. Civilians had pushed for the rapid adoption of a constitution because they feared prolonged military rule. The constitution enacted in February 1891 created a federative republic with a presidential system of government modeled on the United States. Church and state were separated. All male citizens could vote, regardless of their wealth. The constitution also addressed key military interests, from the military's character as a permanent institution, to the question of centralism versus federalism.

The army was pleased by one constitutional provision that stated that the "forces of land and sea are permanent national institutions, destined to the defense of the homeland in the exterior, and the maintenance of our laws internally."[52] This statement reassured officers who feared that civilian leaders might wish to disband the armed forces. Yet the constitution also gave great autonomy to the states, which could seek foreign loans and set up their own military forces. While this measure pleased the planter class, which wished to keep the central state weak, it deeply concerned officers who favored strong executive control: "Brazil at the time was a federation of twenty nations, to the disgust of the military defenders of the state who were hostile to centrifugal forces."[53] The constitution did specify that the central state had the right to intervene in the local states to maintain order, yet many officers believed that this was not enough. Some political observers wondered if Brazil could continue to exist as a united nation.[54] This uncertainty quickly set the stage for a civil-military contest.

Deodoro's efforts to strengthen the executive's power led him to clash with civilian leaders at a time when he was politically weak. Even before Deodoro became the first president of the new regime, the army had been fractured by competing factions and personalities.[55] The navy had played little part in the coup and resented the army's dominance of the new regime. These tensions created an atmosphere of political chaos, which led Deodoro to decide to close Congress on November 3, 1891, an act without any legal basis. He wished to revise the constitution so as to reduce the states' autonomy, while strengthening the executive office. Three weeks later Deodoro's actions led to a naval uprising. Positivist army officers led by Floriano Peixoto refused to back Deodoro, who suffered a heart attack and left the government on November 23, 1891.[56] Power shifted to his rival, another soldier.

In his address to Congress in 1894, Floriano Peixoto condemned Deodoro for abandoning democracy and establishing a dictatorship.[57] But Floriano Peixoto proved to be a man of authoritarian temper who also sought to centralize the political system. Indeed, Floriano Peixoto has remained an important symbol for the Brazilian army because he fought to advance the institution's vision of the nation. Floriano Peixoto favored industrialization and nationalism as a means to weaken the power regional elites held over the government. Even the term "florianismo" came to mean the desire for a strong central state. To this end, Floriano allied with a small group of radical civilians, called Jacobins:

The interests of florianista officers and Jacobins overlapped on the issues of strong government and republicanism, and industrialization. They sought a strong republican government that would maintain the national armed forces (as opposed to state militias) as a leading power, and dominate both the country's agricultural oligarchy and the foreign commercial community that had grown out of the export-oriented economy. Such a government could concentrate on industrialization which would undercut planter power, open new economic opportunities to the bourgeoisie, and realize military aspirations by developing Brazil into a more modern state.[58]

This policy quickly led Floriano Peixoto into open conflict with rural elites, who seized upon divisions within the armed forces to regain control of the political system.

On September 6, 1893 the navy rebelled against the government. The navy had close ties to the monarchy and had not been consulted about the coup that founded the republic. The navy's relationship with the army had been difficult after the coup, in part because this institution had long ties with the traditional elites with whom the army sometimes clashed. The navy also was aware of its political power, for it had overthrown Deodoro with the support of disgruntled army officers. In September 1893, Adm. Custódio José de Mello, perhaps encouraged by a growing rebellion in Rio Grande do Sul, believed that the navy could also overthrow Deodoro's successor.

Floriano Peixoto refused to go into exile without a fight. As Stephen Topik has described, Floriano Peixoto turned to an American businessman to raise a mercenary fleet in the United States to crush the uprising.[59] While the government created this force, the rebels exhausted their public support by bombarding Rio de Janeiro and its sister city Niteroi, attacks which failed to cow the government. Equally problematic was the fact that the rebels lacked a common ideology. Naval officers devoted to the monarchy found it difficult to create a program in alliance with southern rebels devoted to extreme federalism. When finally faced with the government's new fleet, the naval rebels sought protection on Portuguese ships, which transported them to Rio Grande do Sul. The federal government managed to overcome its opposition in this state in August 1894.

Despite Floriano's ultimate success in defeating the navy, this strange episode—in which a xenophobic officer used foreign forces to crush a military rebellion—also showed the limits to the army's power. Floriano Peixoto had wished to turn power over to his protege, Lt. Col. Lauro Sodré, who favored a military dictatorship.[60] But he lacked the power to enforce his will. To end the political chaos, Floriano Peixoto reluctantly turned the government over to Prudente de Moraes on November 15, 1894.[61] This civilian politician represented the interests of powerful São Paulo planters, members of Brazil's landholding class. Their backing had allowed Floriano to overcome both the uprising in Rio Grande do Sul and the naval rebellion, but they had exacted the presidency as their price.

Besides encouraging the army to return power to civilians, the naval uprising had a number of other results. This experience drove a wedge between the two branches of the armed forces. In 1894 Floriano Peixoto announced a number of measures to weaken the navy, which he cheerfully noted would result in a "notable economy for the public coffers."[62] It demoralized Brazil's monarchist forces because the public did not rally to monarchist leaders within the revolt (such as Adm. Saldanha da Gama). They realized that no uprising would undo the new republic. But to officers it seemed that Brazil might break into different states or succumb to monarchical forces unless the army used violence to overcome the republic's political and regional enemies. This belief led to tragedy and bloodshed three years later at Canudos.

From Canudos to the 1904 Uprising

In 1893 a lay preacher in the remote backlands (sertão) of Brazil's northeast founded a religious community called Canudos. This preacher, Antonio Vicente Mendes Maciel (also known as Antonio Conselheiro), refused to recognize the authority of the republic. His community attracted over 20,000 converts, draining the labor supply that rural landholders depended upon. The Catholic Church feared his growing power. These factors led him into conflict with the state and local government. Two expeditions sent against his community by state police and infantry both failed. At this point, the state of Bahia called on the federal government for help. The army proved eager to intervene because they feared a monarchist conspiracy in the hinterlands. Officers could not believe that sertanejos (backlanders) could have defeated two expeditions on their own. Col. Moreira César took command of the third expedition. On March 3, 1897, his 1,300 men attacked Canudos and were routed. Moreira César died during the retreat. The army then launched a massive expedition with more than 5,000 men. Despite the army's overwhelming resources, the lightly armed sertanejos held out for four months without any outside aid before Canudos finally fell on October 5, 1897. Thousands of people had died in the conflict.[63]

The events at Canudos became part of Brazil's popular memory. Few events have been as exhaustively studied, and this event inspired literary and scholarly masterpieces, such as Euclides da Cunha's *Os sertões* (the Backlands). This work by a journalist who witnessed events (and later scholarship such as Robert Levine's definitive study, *Vale of Tears: Revisiting the Canudos Massacre in Northeastern Brazil, 1893–1897*) made clear that Canudos was a complex religious and social phenomenon. While Canudos's leader, Antonio Consel-heiro, condemned the republic, he had no firm ties with outside monarchists.

To republican army officers, angered by the existence of monarchist news-papers, the idea that foreign conspirators had not inspired Canudos seemed implausible. They believed that they had saved the republic from disaster. From this experience they drew the lesson that the army was the nation's savior; it would keep the nation united despite the appeal of regional senti-ments or the conspiracies of monarchists. Accordingly, the army put down another millenarian movement in southern Brazil (the Contestado, 1915–16) with similar violence.[64] This perception of the army as savior also encouraged military resentments against the nation's civilian leadership, which they be-lieved sometimes sought to undermine the army.

In 1897 a powerful florianista faction still rejected the idea that the mili-tary should withdraw from politics. This faction, however, was temporarily discredited when a soldier who favored their cause attempted to murder President Prudente de Moraes. He failed only because Marshal Machado Bit-tencourt (returning from his command of the fourth expedition against Canu-dos) was stabbed to death while protecting the president. The backlash that followed dashed some officers' hopes of regaining control of the political system for a number of years.[65]

Nevertheless, this faction again sought to overthrow the government in 1904. As Jeffrey Needell's careful work has shown, these officers broke most of the rules of military politics. Throughout its history, the army has opposed mass politics and feared the power of trade unions. Col. Lauro Sodré broke this mold. An army officer and senator, Sodré had been Floriano Peixoto's fa-vorite. He knew that the army needed civilian support to overthrow the politi-cal system. Sodré founded the Centro de Classes Operárias, which joined "industrial artisan, railroad, and dockworkers unions into one umbrella or-ganization."[66] The army faction he represented (which included among its members Gen. Olímpio de Silveira and Gen. Silvestre Travassos) also formed an alliance with the leaders of the urban poor, many of whom were black. This was remarkable because in general most army officers shared the social-Darwinist racist views of Brazil's civilian leadership. As late as the 1940s, the army's leadership sought to exclude blacks from the officer corps.[67] At this moment, however, a military faction sought allies to create a popular chal-lenge to the government.

Republican officers planned to take advantage of popular protest over mandatory vaccinations. The origins of the rebellion lay not only within the army but also in urban discontent caused by the government's disregard for the needs of the poor. As Theresa Meade has described, around the turn of the century the government launched a major effort to beautify Rio de Janeiro.

This effort had entailed the destruction of many slum communities and created widespread popular distrust of all government programs. For example, government health inspectors might be trying to fight epidemics, but the poor noted that their visits often were followed by demolition teams, who destroyed the only homes the working class possessed because they were "unhealthy."[68] The resentments this created led to an explosive situation in 1904, when the government ordered mass vaccinations against smallpox. Positivist officers seized upon this issue to fan the fears of the poor, who were already bitterly angry against the government. They were being hypocritical, as Theresa Meade has pointed out, for the positivists exalted the power of science and modern medicine. Lauro Sodré condemned mandatory vaccinations but had his own children vaccinated.[69] Still, dissident officers realized that popular resentment offered them an opportunity. They intended for their civilian allies to foment chaos in the capital in order to create the conditions for a coup.

When the uprising began, civilian rebels clearly viewed themselves as being in alliance with the military. They succeeded only too well, however, because in the confusion the government canceled a military parade that was to have marked the beginning of the coup. Forced to rely on military cadets, army conspirators tried to overthrow the government on November 14 but failed. The government first defeated military rebels, then loyal army units stormed Saúde, a largely Afro-Brazilian slum community. Hundreds of people were sent into internal exile (in what Hélio Leônicio Martins called an "Equatorial Siberia") in Brazil's remote interior.[70]

The popular uprising clearly had roots within the armed forces, as Needell argued: "The roots of the revolt of 1904, centering on the coup of November 14, thus lie in the ongoing attempts of jacobino military elements to retake power and destroy the regime of the Paulista-led oligarchies."[71] To this extent, this uprising can be linked to the ongoing efforts of republican officers to challenge the political status quo. Yet this uprising was remarkable in that the military formed an alliance with civilian groups outside of the elites. In this respect, the 1904 uprising foreshadowed events to take place during the 1950s. Indeed, as many military officers who fought the army's leadership in the 1940s and early 1950s were positivists; it is possible that they were inspired by the memory of Lauro Sodré's civil-military alliance.

In the short-term, however, the uprising marked the last effort by the florianistas, who never again challenged the government. In his 1904 report to the president, the minister of war condemned the political forces that sought to make the army an "object of mistrust and fear to the conservative classes in society, of whose interests they must be the greatest and most solid guarantee."[72] The minister also condemned the "theoretical studies" and "purely abstract speculations" to which officers had become prone.[73] This comment was directed at the positivist instructors who dominated the Escola Militar (Military School) at Praia Vermelha. In the aftermath of the rebellion, the government closed the school, rapidly weakening the positivist faction.[74] While this tended to remove the army from politics, it did not end civil-military tensions.

Some common themes emerged during this period, as patterns were established that would endure until well after World War II. Military leaders stressed the importance of solidarity and unity within the institution they controlled, a policy that they justified with nationalist rhetoric. They feared that the army's weakness endangered the nation's integrity, and they carefully watched for signs of regional rebellion. At the same time, military dissidents (often angered by their superior's perceived corruption) formed factions to challenge the army's leadership. Many of these officers were willing to form social alliances to promote their agendas, even with the local leaders, the working class, and the Afro-Brazilians whom senior generals most distrusted. The army high command responded to these challenges in the same manner it did regional rebellions, that is, with massive repression, torture, and censorship, whether of military dissidents or civilian rebels. The military then crafted its historical memory—its official story—to conceal this violence and to justify the army's actions. This account had power because it generally had the support of national elites, who shared certain key interests with the army leadership because both parties wished to preserve the racial and political status quo. Despite these common interests, however, the most enduring theme during this period remained the antagonism between the military and civilian elites, a tension that colored most aspects of Brazilian politics.

Civilian Rule

Civilian presidents and their allies regarded the army with justified concern. In return, the army believed that civilian elites still sought to destroy it, a belief that has since found some sympathy among scholars. Edmundo Campos Coelho has argued that after 1889 the elites renewed their efforts to weaken the army: "What Huntington called the policy of eradication accurately describes the basic attitudes and behavior of Brazil's civilian political elite in relation to the army until the revolution of 1930."[75] But this statement reflected the army's perception of elite actions, rather than the reality. It is true that the army had benefited more from military administrations than from the civilian governments that followed. Between 1889 and 1894, while the military dominated government, the army's share of federal spending more than doubled from 10 percent of the budget to 23 percent. After civilians returned to power, this rate slowly declined until it reached 17 percent of the budget in 1910.[76] Yet this decline reflected the fact that military governments faced more armed rebellions than later civilian administrations. Despite real shortages of weaponry and equipment, the military grew in power throughout the Old Republic. For example, the army had approximately 13,500 members in 1888; by 1900, only twelve years later, it had more than doubled its enlistment to 28,000 men.[77] But the army still resented the political victory of agricultural elites over the army which the inauguration of Prudente de Morais represented.

What lay behind the army's anger were efforts by civilian elites to impose policies that challenged the army's vision for the nation. Brazil remained putatively democratic. After 1906, however, a gentleman's agreement between traditional elites alternated the presidency between the two powerful southern states of São Paulo and Minas Gerais. Elections usually acted as a facade to legitimate elites' power.[78] Power devolved to the local level. Successive presidents adopted the "politics of the governors," in which governors supported the president's policy in Congress in return for which they ran their states' affairs without interference. Political bosses, called colonels because of their position in the National Guard, dominated local politics. The government reversed Floriano Peixoto's support for industry in favor of programs to expand coffee production. To ensure regional independence state political leaders also created militias that were better trained, equipped, and funded than the central army. São Paulo received a French military mission (a group of French officers sent to train Brazilian soldiers) in 1906, thirteen years before the federal military.[79] While the central army grew in absolute numbers, its relative power declined. Upper-class Brazilians viewed military service as the preserve of men too poor to have another choice. The military had not only lost the prestige and power it briefly held after 1889 but also the ability to block policies it opposed.

The Army as the Nation's School

The army responded to its perceived marginalization by trying to redefine a role for itself as the nation's "school." Many armies throughout the hemisphere wished to bring about long-term social change to strengthen the state. In Argentina and Chile, the military believed that the formation of the working class and the arrival of European immigrants had undermined a sense of national identity; in Peru officers worried that the native peoples had no sense that a central state existed; in Brazil officers believed that the political power of regional elites undermined citizens' loyalty to their nation. Officers in all these countries believed that mandatory conscription would not only swell the army's enlistment, but also create a sense of national identity.[80]

Between 1900 and 1907 the governments of Chile, Peru, Ecuador, Argentina, and Bolivia all began mandatory conscription. Brazil remained an exception to this hemispheric trend. The 1891 constitution had made military service mandatory, but civilian governments had failed to implement this inconvenient article. In 1908 Congress finally passed legislation to enforce conscription, but the elite-dominated government then chose to disregard its own legislation. Only with World War I did mandatory conscription become a major political issue. In 1915 and 1916 the army launched a major campaign for mandatory conscription which gained the support of Brazil's middle class. In 1916 the government began a national lottery to conscript young men.[81]

Despite this lottery, however, the army failed to become the nation's school. The same legislation that created the lottery exempted members of shooting clubs from the draft. Although the clubs were ostensibly intended to promote shooting ability, membership in these organizations allowed wealthy elites to avoid service. Equally problematic, many Brazilians simply did not appear when conscripted. Mandatory conscription did allow the army to swell its enlistment, but it failed to create any of the social changes the army wanted because the upper and middle class refused to do their duty.[82] Most people feared military service as the reserve of the urban poor, northeastern refugees, and convicted criminals.[83] Despite the army's efforts to attract Brazilians to military service, it remained the option of the desperately poor.[84] The army also had no desire for a meaningful encounter with the Brazilian masses which might have changed how both groups thought about the nation. Despite the example of the 1904 rebellion, most army officers maintained a profound distrust of mass politics, the urban poor, and nonwhites. Some officers viewed mandatory service as a means to mix different classes and races to create a Brazilian identity.[85] Most officers, however, proved not to hold this view, a fact that doomed the army's efforts to failure.

The Revolt of the Whip

One event revealed the racial beliefs and social conservatism that divided the armed forces from the Brazilian people. Although Brazilians have taken pride since the 1940s in what Gilberto Freyre called their nation's "racial democracy," race long influenced all aspects of Brazilian society.[86] Racial discrimination was not institutionalized and legalized by the government as in the United States. Nonetheless, race served as a marker for political power in Brazil. Like Brazilian society, the armed forces had long been divided along racial lines.[87] The officer corps was largely white, while the soldiers were either black or mixed race. In the army, one faction had allied with the black, urban poor during the 1904 rebellion, but the florianistas had lost power after this movement failed. The army never was a monolith, even on the question of race. For example, during the 1930s, Gen. Pedro Aurelio de Góes Monteiro spoke out against racist views. But as a whole, so-called "scientific racism" dominated the army's thought until the 1950s. Indeed, as late as the 1940s army regulations prevented people of color and Jews from entering the schools that trained officers.[88] The situation was far worse in the navy, however, where many officers were descended from slaveholders. In 1910 this racism contributed to a major naval rebellion called the "Revolt of the Whip."[89]

Brazilians perceived the navy as an aristocratic institution, governed by the sons of traditional elites.[90] Most sailors were ex-slaves, or the sons of slaves, who entered the navy against their will. Officers used leather whips tipped with metal balls to whip sailors for even the most minor infractions.[91] Unable to leave the service until they completed fifteen years in the ranks, sailors endured racial abuse and physical violence.[92] As officers tried to control their men with terror on isolated ships, racial tensions became extreme.

The Revolt of the Whip began in 1910 when black sailors, unhappy at their treatment, carefully planned an uprising within the navy. They chose as their leader first class helmsman João Candido Felisberto, an experienced sailor who became known as the "Black Admiral."[93] In November 1910, officers had a sailor (Marcelino Rodrigues Meneses) whipped into unconsciousness with more than two hundred blows before his fellow sailors. The whipping continued well after he fainted.[94] A wave of anger caused conspirators to advance their plans. On November 22, 1910, thousands of sailors seized navy ships, killed white officers who resisted, imprisoned the rest, and trained their guns on Rio de Janeiro.[95] The government quickly moved army troops to the presidential palace and the coastline, but they could do little to overpower the fleet.[96] Both the president, Marshal Hermes Rodriguez da Fonseca (a military officer and nephew of Deodoro da Fonseca), and Congress had to accede to the rebels' demands in order to save the capital itself from bombardment. The government issued official statements of regret and pardoned all sailors involved.[97] The government may also have reassured sailors that it would end capital punishment. On Saturday, November 26, 1910, the sailors returned control of the ships to their commanders. Both naval and army officers were furious with the amnesty; they asked that the national flag be flown at half-mast for eight days.[98]

The government's amnesty did not end the crisis. On November 28, 1910, President Hermes da Fonseca passed a decree that allowed the minister of the navy to expel without trial any sailors undermining discipline.[99] Sailors perceived this law as an effort to reverse the amnesty, and the attitude of naval commanders also angered sailors. White officers believed that their men were racially inferior and that they could control them only by force. A book published the following year by an anonymous white officer captured these attitudes. This work, *Política versus marinha*, described Afro-Brazilians as a primitive race incapable of advancement. Its author argued that Brazilian sailors needed to be controlled by the whip, as slaves had been.[100] Naval commanders deliberately provoked a second uprising by brutal treatment that included whippings.[101] Because most sailors remained loyal to the government, loyal forces quickly suffocated the uprising.[102] The navy then used terror to repress all dissent.

The navy brought the prisoners (some of whom had remained loyal to the government during the second uprising) to a naval base called Ilha das Cobras (Snake Island).[103] On December 24, 1910, eighteen prisoners were placed in an underground cell on the orders of the island's commander, Frigate Capt. Francisco José Marques da Rocha.[104] The men had been beaten and were suffering from both hunger and thirst.[105] Later that evening naval officers poured buckets of quicklime (some sources say whitewash, which is water mixed with quicklime) into their cell to "disinfect" it.[106] This form of violence may have held racial symbolism, in that racist officers ostensibly sought to cleanse the cell.[107] When the jailor opened the cell on Christmas morning, sixteen men were dead.[108]

The navy directed symbolic violence against other sailors. On December 24, 1910, the steamship Satélite set sail for the Brazilian state of Acre, with ninety-seven former sailors aboard.[109] Without any legal proceeding, the navy had condemned these men to slave labor in Santo Antônio da Madeira, an area famous for its death rate from malaria.[110] Seven of the men had red crosses next to their names on the list of prisoners when the ship sailed on Christmas day, 1910.[111] The ship's leader (Second Lt. Francisco de Melo) chose these men and two other sailors to be shot during the trip. Before their deaths, Francisco de Melo ordered that they first be whipped.[112]

These actions did not result from the attitudes of isolated commanders but rather from military policy, as illustrated by the careers of the officers involved. Frigate Capt. Francisco José Marques da Rocha, the author of the massacre in the underground cells, was charged in the men's death, but he was absolved in June 1911. President Hermes da Fonseca invited him to a private dinner, and a few days later he was promoted.[113] The government also never punished Second Lt. Francisco de Melo. Instead, he received a promotion.[114] The minister of war commended him in a military bulletin for his service on the Satélite. President Hermes da Fonseca defended his decision to shoot these sailors. Although seventy-nine armed soldiers were aboard, and the officers kept the unarmed prisoners locked below deck, the president argued that the soldiers grew too seasick to control the prisoners, leaving no choice but "measures of supreme energy."[115] Both branches of the armed forces defended the navy's violence because they shared its racial views.

Despite the navy's efforts to conceal events, newspapers soon made the story public.[116] Rui Barbosa, a distinguished senator, loudly denounced the navy's abuse of its men.[117] The navy believed that it was being mistreated by "politicians."[118] Despite a public outcry, however, this case did not bring the armed forces into conflict with Brazilian elites. Instead, most Brazilian elites wished to ignore the navy's use of violence, as the progovernment newspaper *O Paiz* made clear: "If we were the only ones who knew this monstrous fact, we would certainly not divulge it, judging the terror and revulsion it would cause."[119]

Brazilian elites perceived the uprising not only as a military rebellion, but also as a challenge to Brazil's racial order. Edmar Morel reprinted a political cartoon on the cover of the Brazilian magazine *Careta* on December 10, 1910. The cartoon showed two thin, white officers saluting an obese black sailor. The caption read "The Discipline of the Future," implying what would happen if white officers ceased to use the whip. The satire captured elites' fears that without violence they would lose their privileged social position.[120] The cartoon also reflected the views of naval officers, who believed in the racial inferiority of their men.[121] It was no coincidence that João Candido became known as the Black Admiral, while Hermes da Fonseca came to be called "President Very White."[122] The debate over corporal punishment was really about a vision of race and citizenship. Other military rebellions—such as that of the tenentes during the 1920s—did not meet with equal violence, because they did not similarly challenge the social order.[123] Race defined class lines in Brazil, and racial views bound even the most radical officers to Brazilian elites. The contest between the military and the elites took place within an arena confined by strict lines, and both sides refused to mobilize the masses.

This refusal explains the armed forces' efforts to silence all discussion of this history. On April 11, 1911, a team of naval doctors examined João Candido and declared that he was mentally ill.[124] Expelled from the navy, he was committed to a mental hospital, even though he was so lucid that his nurses let him go home every night, providing he returned in the morning.[125] By this means the navy ensured that a government inquiry would not hear his account of events.[126] For more than the next half century, the navy and the government used terror against journalists and scholars to suppress all memory of the revolt, with amazing success. In 1934 the journalist Aparício Torelly announced plans to publish ten articles on the rebellion by Adão Pereira

Nunes in the paper *Folha do Povo*. He published two articles before naval officers kidnapped and beat him. The paper halted the series.[127] The secret police censored all mention of the rebellion during the Estado Novo (New State, 1937–45). Authors such as Adão Manuel Pereira Nunes were forced to use pseudonyms to write on the topic.[128] Nunes and civilian author Edmar Morel had their political rights suspended after the 1964 coup.[129] The question of military terror was explosive because it was tied to the question of race. For this reason, both the armed forces (including the army) and the elites wished to silence all discussion of the 1910 rebellion.

Because of these efforts, English language works on military history largely ignore this rebellion.[130] Yet the uprising had an enduring effect on the Brazilian armed forces. At the same time that the army wished to make the military into the nation's school, the navy undermined this doctrine by questioning the idea of obligatory service.[131] Equally important, the elites had long viewed the navy as a check on the power of the army. In the aftermath of this rebellion, the navy was weakened, and the army's influence increased.[132] Long after 1910 this uprising with racial overtones continued to influence the armed forces and the elites.

Military Salvations

The racial views shared by most civilian leaders and military officers did not dampen the bitterness of the struggle between the two groups. As the army sought to weaken the power of regional leaders, it decided to seize upon interelite disputes in its own interests. The landholding class never acted as a strong unit, but rather fought over social, economic, and family issues, as its members contested political positions. Given the rampant fraud that characterized local elections, democratic means could not determine the transfer of power. In November 1911, for example, contending cliques both declared victory in Salvador's municipal elections, and both created their own city council. Officers viewed these conflicts as an opportunity to break the power of local elites and to foster political centralization. After Gen. Hermes da Fonseca had won the presidential election in May 1910, he had begun a policy of appointing men loyal to the government (usually army officers) to govern states where civilian politicians contested control. If the army had succeeded in centralizing power through these interventions, it would have changed the entire dynamic of Brazilian politics, by reversing the Politics of the Governors. Officers called these interventions salvações (salvations) because officers viewed them as part of the army's duty of national salvation. By this, officers understood that the policy would strengthen the state.[133]

The original interventions all took place in Brazil's northeast, far from the new center of Brazil's political power in the south. The nation's most powerful landowners did not perceive that these actions threatened their authority. But when the interventions began to occur at the behest of local garrisons outside the control of Hermes's civilian allies, the army's agenda for the salvations became apparent. In 1911 rumors circulated that Hermes's administration intended to intervene in São Paulo, Brazil's economic heartland. Frightened elites quickly organized Patriotic Brigades to defeat any federal intervention. The army officially abandoned its plans to intervene, but Gen. Mena Barreto announced his candidacy for the governorship of Rio Grande do Sul, a powerful southern state. Before resigning as minister of war, he appointed men he trusted to posts in that state.[134]

The elites understood that the army's agenda for the salvations represented an open challenge to their power. Pinheiro Machado, Hermes' civilian mentor, issued an ultimatum to the president on their behalf. Hermes could either abandon military salvations, or he could lose the support of the civilians who supported him. The army had not placed Hermes in power; rather the civilian politicians who controlled the electoral machine had supported him. Hermes da Fonseca knew that the army by itself lacked the power to impose its agenda on the nation, as Floriano Peixoto's experience had proven.

In March 1912 Hermes appointed Gen. Vaspasiano de Albuquerque—who opposed military salvations—to replace Gen. Mena Barreto as minister of war. By this means, Hermes signaled that he was abandoning the policy of military salvations, a policy change that infuriated many radical officers. These commanders controlled the Military Club (Clube Militar), a social body that provided officers a forum to express political views. Throughout 1913 the Military Club continued to advocate military salvations and to manipulate the army's involvement in northeastern politics. In 1914, Hermes responded by closing the club, arresting twenty-eight officers, and declaring a state of siege. Among the officers arrested was Gen. Mena Barreto, the most prominent advocate of military interventions. By doing this, Hermes satisfied the powerful São Paulo planters who were the most important force in civilian politics.[135]

This class retained considerable military force apart from the army. It is true that the National Guard was dissolved in 1918. World War I had proved the need for a professionally trained and equipped force that the National Guard could not provide. In addition, the elites realized that with the army's modernization, National Guard units could no longer provide a check on the army's power. Instead, the elites relied on state military forces created under the provisions of the 1891 constitution. These state forces were sometimes true armies with their own artillery and air forces. Their combined troop strength outnumbered the central army. São Paulo received a military mission from France in 1906, thirteen years before the national army welcomed a similar mission.[136] The dissolution of the National Guard did not end the elites' efforts to counterbalance the army's power. In some respects, the army's relative strength had not changed greatly since the latter years of the Empire, as many officers must have understood.

The Young Turks

The army's efforts to impose its vision onto the nation had failed, and the long struggle with rural elites appeared sterile. This conflict had absorbed a great deal of energy and resources that the army might have used for strictly military ends. Even before the failure of national conscription to achieve its goals and the defeat of military salvations, some officers had questioned the wisdom of involving the army in society. Warfare had become increasingly sophisticated, and officers perceived a clear need to modernize the army. The outbreak of World War I in 1914 encouraged this perception, as officers realized how unprepared their nation was for modern conflict.

Before becoming president, Hermes da Fonseca had sent a few young officers to train in Germany. These officers returned to Brazil committed to remaking the army into an apolitical instrument of external defense. These officers—called Young Turks because of their dedication to military reform—believed that the army's participation in politics had weakened it. In 1913 they founded a military journal, *A defesa nacional*, to decry the army's entrapment in civilian affairs. While these junior officers (such as Estevão Leitão de Carvalho and Bertholdo Klinger) still argued that the army could act as a model for society, they remained dedicated to creating an apolitical institution.[137]

Like the Young Turks, the rural elites who dominated the government also wished to create an army dedicated to external defense. Against considerable military opposition (mainly from senior officers with wounded pride) the government contracted a French military mission, which arrived in March 1919.[138] The French commanders sought to reorganize the military on European lines, which entailed a clear political philosophy. In the famous phrase of one French commander, the army should be a "great mute" that remained silent on national issues. To this end, the French altered military instruction to emphasize the army's "military" duties. The French founded military schools, drafted war plans, oversaw military maneuvers, and enacted new rules for promotion. The French mission also encouraged a program of military modernization that gave the army heavy artillery, light tanks, and fighter planes. To some observers, it seemed that the French mission had transformed the army into an apolitical force dedicated to external defense.[139]

Yet the French mission's successes were more apparent than real. Military education and modern equipment could not alter Brazilian political reality. The army was far more likely to face an internal rebellion (such as the religious movement of Canudos) than a foreign enemy. No amount of weaponry could change the nation's economic dependence on foreign powers. Nor could the army decide to withdraw from politics by an act of will. An intricate network of civil-military alliances, regional affiliations, and business arrangements now bound the army to society. Civilian elites had helped to create these informal structures to control the military's ambitions, while seeking to use the army in their own struggles. The Young Turks sought to reorganize the army without paying attention to the society and economy that supported it, and their failures encouraged the army to return its attention to society. Officers' anger over the military's alliances with civilians soon proved so powerful as to threaten senior officers' authority.

Military Corruption

One informal structure that civilian elites had helped to create was a system of military corruption that bound the military to the government. Back when civilian politicians had first struggled to reassert control over the army in 1894, they realized that they could ensure commanders' loyalty by ignoring their wrongdoing. A disorganized system of political loyalty and military corruption soon evolved, as one dissident officer complained: "Advantages of all sorts (lucrative commissions, anticipated promotions, the transfer of garrisons and staff, impunity from justice, etc., etc.) are used by powerful politicians in order to deflect the soldier with few scruples from the principles of good morality, in order to place him in the service of an unpatriotic cause."[140] While effective, by the 1920s this structure created dangerous resentments within the institution, thereby drawing the army into politics.

Corruption became so widespread that it discredited the senior officers with the junior ranks.[141] Some army commanders came to view their positions more as vehicles to personal wealth than as a means of national service. In 1922, when the government ordered Marshal Hermes da Fonseca (president of the Military Club) arrested, military corruption helped define the institution's loyalties. Senior officers who were profiting from the system supported the government, while their subordinates denounced civilian leaders. The government's plans to arrest Hermes so angered officers that they met at the

Military Club to discuss rebellion. Although outraged, senior officers coun-
seled patience. This advice forced them to confront junior officers intent on
rebellion, who reminded their superiors of the corruption that had guaranteed their loyalty.

One young firebrand, Lt. Asdrúbal Gwaier de Azevedo, took the lead
among the young officers denouncing corruption at this meeting. He accused
commanders of sins so petty that they now seem humorous. For example,
Azevedo claimed that Gen. Francisco Ramos de Andrade had used funds to
pay for concubines.[142] Azevedo also sparked heated confrontations by accusing military leaders of everything from stealing coal intended for navy ships
to embezzling public funds to pay for gambling debts. Junior officers were
particularly angered by instances of corruption during the Contestado Rebellion (1915–16), when the institution battled another religious movement in
the south of Brazil (in Paraná and Santa Catarina). Displaced landholders and
unemployed railway workers had fought the state in the name of their dead
leader, José Maria, whose imminent resurrection they anticipated.

During this contest, one of the army's most corrupt officers, Gen. Fernando Setembrino de Carvalho, had entered a partnership with speculators.
By granting merchants false receipts for provisions, Setembrino embezzled
large amounts of money. Capt, Tertuliano Potiguara also purchased nonexis-
tent goods for the battlefield. Junior officers found thirty packs labeled "gre-
nades" filled with rocks and fifteen railway cars stuffed with straw instead
of uniforms. General Setembrino and Captain Potiguara together purchased
twenty thousand pairs of boots that no soldier ever wore. According to Lieutenant Azevedo, soldiers had even faced hunger during the fighting because of
their commanders' corruption.[143] The army overcame the rebels in 1915, but
the resentment of young officers endured.

The moral bankruptcy of the high command undermined its authority to
deter a faction of junior officers from their planned rebellion.[144] Young officers
wished to prevent the elites from using the army as a pawn in their disputes.
When conflict over this issue led to the arrest of Marshal Hermes and the
closing of the Military Club, they rose against the government. On July 22,
1922, junior officers, some of whom were Hermes's relatives, rebelled at Copa-
cabana fortress in Rio de Janeiro.[145] Senior officers remained loyal to the
government and quickly suffocated the uprising.

The government's victory failed to end the turmoil within the military.
Junior officers believed that the government had gravely insulted their institution's honor. When Artur da Silva Bernardes became president in November
1922, he ruthlessly sought to eradicate military dissent and to weaken the
army's power. During Bernardes's administration the government cut the
army's enlistment by a quarter, although the president lived in a legal state of

siege throughout his administration.[146] Bernardes also appointed General Setembrino de Carvalho to be minister of war (1922–26).[147] In 1924 junior officers
(the lieutenants or tenentes, which gave their movement its name, tenentismo) launched a guerrilla war to overthrow the government. As loyal as he
was corrupt, Setembrino led the army against this uprising.

The Tenentes

It took General Setembrino two years to suffocate the tenentes'
movement, in large part because the senior commanders had little wish to
shed their subordinates' blood. Loyal army forces attacked the tenentes' column when it entered their area, but showed little interest in pursuing the
group once it had passed by. The tenentes began a war of movement. Between
April 1925 and February 1927, the tenentes marched from Brazil's southern
borders to the Amazon, from there on to northeastern Brazil, and then returned south to Bolivia and exile. They fought over fifty battles and marched
24,000 kilometers, but they failed to rally the mass support for their ideals
that they needed to challenge the elite politics of the Old Republic.

It has proved almost impossible to characterize the tenentes' program, a
question that has caused almost endless debate. João Quartim de Moraes
views the tenentes as part of a longstanding leftist tradition within the military. Joseph Comblin believes that they were political conservatives, influenced by European critiques of liberalism. In frustration, Vavy Pacheco
Borges even denies that tenentismo existed as an organized political movement. She believes that civilians created tenentismo as a term only during the
1930s and that the tenentes never united around a clear political program.[148]
These contradictions arose because tenentismo contained a multiplicity of
political projects. The tenentes rebelled because of challenges to the military
as an institution, rather than because they represented a political party with a
clear program. It can be dangerous to use political labels such as "conservative" or "liberal" to define army factions because they are influenced by military ideals without exact counterparts in civilian politics.

Tenentismo represented the survival of an old military vision for the nation.[149] Conservative tenentes wanted to guarantee a secret ballot, create a
free press, end political corruption, and halt patronage. More radical tenentes
believed that the government should recognize unions, enact labor legislation, provide free education, and promote industry. While they disagreed
over the necessary means, both wings of the movement had a common goal.
The tenentes wanted political centralization, an autonomous state, and an
end to the elites' control of politics.

The tenentes' movement failed because most of its members had a profound distrust of popular mobilization. Despite the later historiography, which has depicted them as the servants of the new urban class, officers such as Juarez Távora feared nothing so much as a popular revolt. Távora embodied the paradoxes created by the military's social conservatism and racial views. More than any other tenente, Távora tried to articulate his group's vision of legal and political change.[150] But in his social vision Távora remained a man of another century. In a letter to the former leader of the tenentes, Luis Carlos Prestes, Távora later argued that the abolition of slavery had represented a violent seizure of private property by the state. A "true statesman" would not have supported the "radical humanitarianism" of the abolitionists, but would instead have fought for a more "equitable" and "wise" solution. Instead of abolishing slavery overnight, the government should have reformed its abuses in order to gradually eliminate it over five to fifteen years: "This would have avoided, in the same way, the ugliness of life in the slave quarters; it would have better prepared blacks for the duties of future citizenship; it would have avoided the economic disorganization that with a sudden blow destroyed many 'lords' and considerably upset our own national economy. Whomever travels today through the various parts of the state of Rio (de Janeiro), and compares its current economic misery with the vitality of other times, can evaluate well the total result caused by the extremism of the law of May 13."[151] On May 13, 1888, Brazil had become the last state in the western hemisphere to abolish slavery. Nonetheless, Távora clearly believed that abolition arrived too soon and thereby caused an economic and social disaster. In 1904 some officers had been willing to reach across the lines of race to form a popular alliance, but the tenentes were not ready to follow their example.

These racial attitudes help to explain why the tenentes neither sought nor succeeded in rallying the mass support they needed to achieve victory. Without addressing social issues, they could not create a convincing program of political change. The frustration this situation engendered caused some tenentes to become so radicalized that they later joined the Communist Party. To these commanders, it seemed that the army could not reinvent itself unless it first remade Brazilian society. The tenentes had always believed that because of officers' technical skills they could offer a dispassionate vision that could serve as a basis to modernize the nation. The tenentes thought that regional elites had coopted military superiors, who had been too willing to have the army serve as a tool of special political interests. The tenentes would be different. Despite their disdain for politics, however, the tenentes became caught up in the major political currents sweeping Brazil at the time. The more that the army became involved in civilian affairs, the more politicized the institution became.

The Twilight of the Old Republic

To the end, the tenentes remained the most ardent opponents of the Old Republic. A division within the elites gave them the opportunity they needed. In 1929, President Washington Luís chose another Paulista (person from São Paulo), Júlio Prestes, to succeed him. This violated the alliance between the two populous southern states of São Paulo and Minas Gerais, which had alternated the presidency between them. This system had prevented interelite disputes from escalating into a crisis. In 1929, the collapse of this system united the elites of Minas Gerais and Rio Grande do Sul in support of the candidacy of Getúlio Vargas, who governed the latter state. Vargas made a clear break with previous elite politicians, by promising social reforms to improve the lives of urban workers. This promise proved attractive in October 1929, as the world slid into economic crisis during the midst of the campaign. Blatant fraud marred the elections on March 1, 1930, in which the official candidate emerged victorious.

Vargas began to conspire. He turned to the tenentes, who viewed him as an instrument to launch their revolution. During the 1920s, the tenentes had remained isolated from the military as a whole. Like the positivists and the Young Turks, their ideals never had the support of most army officers, let alone senior commanders. The tenentes had sought to achieve victory on the battlefield. They had not conspired to undermine the bonds of rank and hierarchy by more subtle means.

By 1930, the tenentes realized that to succeed, they would have to challenge the army's leadership from within. Unlike during their previous uprisings, therefore, they first sought carefully to create informal structures of power within the army by reaching across the lines of rank. This entailed careful organization and propaganda as they subverted Brazilian troops to their movement. Aided by a faction of civilian elites, the tenentes enjoyed great success in their effort. Of course, the most powerful generals in the army were aware of their conspiracies and rallied the institution to meet the challenge. This time, however, the army's leaders would face a movement that not only rallied widespread support within the institution, but also had powerful civilian allies.

Conclusion

The army remained trapped in an enduring contest with rural elites throughout the Old Republic. The history of the military's struggle with traditional elites is complex and marked by collusion as well as conflict. Both informal ties (such as corruption) and shared beliefs (the racial hierarchy) bound the two groups together. Although the army's political vision differed from that of the elites, in many respects its social vision was similar. The army was also divided between warring factions defined by competing personalities; often a particular faction was named after its commander. These generals sought to form alliances with influential civilians in order to advance their interests. At the other extreme, the Young Turks wished to create an apolitical military and to modernize the institution. To this end, they wished to withdraw the army from civilian affairs. These divisions within the army colored the institution's relationship with civilian elites. The two groups had struggled to impose their visions onto the nation ever since the foundation of the republic. By manipulating the military's currents and sentiments, civilian leaders successfully bound the institution to the government, despite frequent conflicts over political issues.

By the 1920s, social changes had altered this relationship. Rapid urbanization led to the creation of a middle class that wished to contest the power of older social and political elites. Large-scale immigration and foreign investment contributed to a new Brazilian identity; nationalism became an increasingly powerful political discourse. The rise of trade unions gave a new working class the means to challenge elite policies. These organizations, however, still did not have legal protections, which meant that they frequently clashed with the government. The Great Depression greatly curbed Brazil's agricultural exports, even as industrialization reshaped the Brazilian economy. The emergence of a modern infrastructure improved communication within Brazil, encouraging internal migration. These changes undermined the regional interests, the agricultural economy, and the traditional relationships that shaped the elites' power. In this situation, elite divisions and popular discontent made the government vulnerable to a civil-military alliance.

2

Chaos, Communism, and Terror
1930–1937

When a civil-military alliance overthrew the government in 1930, it marked a clear defeat for the traditional elites who had dominated the Old Republic (1889–1930). As part of this transformation, old elites lost influence within the army as the revolutionaries retired senior generals to ensure the military's allegiance. Previous mechanisms to control the institution (such as corruption) broke down. Civilian politicians responded with an intense effort to create new informal structures of power within the institution, based on personal ties, regional affiliations, and ideological appeals. Given the atmosphere of uncertainty and unrest within the military, these endeavors met with considerable success. The history of the period between 1930 and 1937 is the story of how the army's leadership fought civilian elites for control of the military.

Army leaders viewed civilians' efforts to acquire influence within the military as a most dangerous threat. They carefully watched as civilian politicians worked to build military followings. Senior generals viewed these efforts through the prism of the army's experience since the nineteenth century. During the waning years of the Empire, officers had feared that traditional elites intended to dissolve the army as a means to weaken or even destroy the state. In the 1930s, influential army generals (such as Pedro Aurélio de Goés Monteiro) believed that the Brazilian nation was in danger of disappearing. By this, they meant that without the support of a strong military, the central state might collapse. If that occurred, they feared that Brazil would disintegrate into warring regions. The fear that Brazil might repeat Spanish America's experience after independence haunted Brazilian officers and colored their bitter conflict with regional elites.[1]

For a period of seven years, the army hierarchy (led by Gen. Goés Monteiro and Gen. Eurico Gaspar Dutra) sought to end challenges to its control and to exclude civilians from influence within the institution. Given that enlisted men frequently rebelled, that rebel officers (tenentes) sought new power within the state, that senior commanders conspired, and that civilian politicians had their own plots, this proved difficult to achieve. In this atmosphere of unrest, officers seized upon a communist rebellion within the army as a means to reassert their control. Army leaders concealed the true origins of the rebellion among senior generals and powerful politicians. Instead, they carefully constructed a mythology around this event. This narrative helped the military to seize power in 1937, in alliance with a civilian dictator, Getúlio Vargas. This moment represented the army's triumph over regional leaders.

The Revolution and Its Aftermath

By September 1930 Getúlio Vargas had been plotting a rebellion for months. He had chosen Lt. Col. Góes Monteiro to lead the uprising, in part because his relatives held key positions in important garrisons. Together, the two men had created an insurgent army of tenentes, gauchos (southerners from Rio Grande do Sul), and revolutionaries. Throughout Brazil, conspirators infiltrated the barracks to prepare for the coming uprising. When the revolt began on October 3, 1930, many troops refused to obey their commanders. Before the fighting ended, the revolutionaries removed perhaps three-quarters of the officers in Rio Grande do Sul and the northeast from their posts.[2] Some army units fought bravely only to be overrun by the rebels. Many other companies either had been seized by their men or lacked the will to fight. Collapsing from within, the army prevented a bloody civil war only by turning power over to Vargas on November 3, 1930. The Old Republic had disintegrated.

Although the army had transferred power to Vargas before his followers could seize it on the battlefield, the revolution represented a major defeat for the military. Despite the previous efforts at reform, a civilian rebellion had overcome the general staff. Officers in the capital had watched in horror as Vargas prepared the rebellion.[3] The military as an institution had remained outside the revolutionary forces. Not one general had joined the revolt that a lieutenant colonel had led. The army's weakness could not be hidden by a quick transfer of power. To officers betrayed by their sergeants, or outgunned in combat, the army's weakness was apparent.

The military suffered not only a humiliating defeat but also a serious collapse of discipline.[4] Contemporary observers feared the army might disintegrate after the revolution because of internal unrest, which was particularly dangerous among the enlisted men. During the revolution tenentes had persuaded sergeants to overthrow their commanding officers.[5] As men arrested their officers at gunpoint, the result has been called an "internal betrayal." These rebellions continued after the overthrow of the government. Tenentes manipulated promotions to reward supporters and to settle old scores. Sergeants became officers overnight, challenging the social standing of higher ranks. To defend their followers' position, the army general staff progressively restricted sergeants' careers throughout the 1930s. The Escola de Sargentos (Sergeant's School) was closed in 1931. Over 500 of its graduates had become officers during its fourteen years of operation. In 1934 the army stopped promoting sergeants. In 1939, military regulations banned sergeants for serving for more than nine years. With their time in service limited and their opportunities for promotion restricted, the sergeants saw few rewards for their sacrifices. Rebellions by enlisted men plagued the army during the 1930s.[6]

These rebellions were particularly bitter because the controversy had a racial character. People of color were more likely to be poor, and therefore to have joined the ranks by necessity. One of the few opportunities that poor black men had for social advancement was to enter the army and work their way into the officer corps. When this avenue was closed, it contributed to a "whitening" of the officer corps that continued throughout the 1930s and 1940s. This discrimination helps to explain the unusual violence and frequency of the revolts led by sergeants during this period.[7]

Struggles among junior officers exacerbated the conflict among troops. Most tenentes rejoined the armed forces, and they demanded the rank they believed they ought to have held had they not left the army to rebel against the government. Because the tenentes returned to the ranks before the high command had settled the issue of seniority, this issue divided junior officers between "popsicles" (the tenentes) and "radishes" (loyalist officers). These blocs fought so bitterly over rank that the general staff had to create separate units to segregate these factions.[8] In addition, tenentes exercised more political power than their rank suggested, which drew them into conflict with senior commanders.[9] Vargas placed some tenentes in charge of state governments to ensure both their loyalty and his control. The tenentes also tried to increase their political influence by founding the October 3 Club in May 1931.[10] This organization sought to create a plan for the revolution and to advance the tenentes' political beliefs.[11] In the end, the tenentes proved to be too divided to represent a strong political force, and they also alienated their peers by criticizing their commanders and manipulating promotions.[12] Both the October 3 Club and the tenentes lost power after April 1932.[13] Nonetheless, the army's leadership continued to fear the power they exercised.

Conflicts among senior generals also undermined army discipline.[14] The revolution divided the institution among generals whose prestige attracted their followers.[15] Military factions generally did not struggle over ideological questions but rather personal allegiances. These rifts weakened the military's power within the state, even as officers became increasingly involved in politics. A former naval officer explained: "Yes, they acted more, but it was in personal terms, and they came into conflict. So they canceled each other out."[16] This situation not only lessened the army's political influence, but also undermined discipline at the highest levels of the institution.

Bruce Farcau has argued that military factions tend to form around what he calls the charismatic leader, who has the "nebulous quality of a magnetic personality."[17] He believes that in Latin America this quality is much more important to an officer's success than in British or American armies.[18] Consequently, Farcau argues that in military politics "ideology is largely determined by that of the charismatic leader of that faction."[19] He also argues that factions formed around ideological issues tend to be weaker and shorter lived, yet the Brazilian example contradicts this assessment.

In Brazil most powerful military factions have had an ideological basis. As the military professionalized during the twentieth century, military factions became increasingly powerful, in part because they tended to become increasingly defined in ideological terms. As part of this process, ideological appeals came to create what Farcau calls "vertical ties" across the lines of rank.[20] For example, in the early years of the Old Republic the positivists and Young Turks were important factions defined by ideology, but they tended to be much more successful amongst junior officers than senior commanders. By the 1950s, however, factions appeared that were more effective than their predecessors at attracting officers from all ranks. This process, in which ideology became increasingly important to the army's factional politics, was not linear. In the aftermath of the 1930 revolution, a host of factions appeared defined by their individual leaders. The result was a chaotic period in which short-lived factions appeared and faded with the fortunes of a few key individuals, a circumstance that badly undermined the army's unity, power, and discipline.

The situation was desperate. The army devoted much of its energy to fighting conspiracies and rumors. Some officers even wished to resign because of the atmosphere of confusion.[21] Gen. Góes Monteiro stated that the Brazilian army resembled the Russian armed forces before the revolution.[22] Until 1932 he worried that General José Fernandes Leite de Castro and other dissatisfied generals might launch a coup. In turn, other leaders warned Getúlio Vargas that Gen. Goés Monteiro conspired against him.[23] If Vargas needed Goés Monteiro to control the military, he needed other generals to control Goés Monteiro.[24] Rumors of an impending military coup troubled Vargas's allies.[25] They had good reason to mistrust the loyalty of army commanders, many of whom had opposed the revolution.[26] The revolution had purged many "reactionary" officers or reduced their influence. Military divisions created opportunities for these commanders to challenge the army's new leadership. For example, the question of promotions caused serious resentment, as revolutionary officers quickly entered positions that gave them power over the peers. In the case of Goés Monteiro, his rapid rise to power led to an explosion of anger within the army that kept him from becoming minister of war in 1931.[27] Despite the success of the revolution, Vargas and his military allies had difficulty commanding the army's loyalty.

In this situation, it became difficult to know who conspired against whom, as one example illustrates. Gen. Pantaleão Telles Ferreira—whom young officers perceived to be a reactionary—commanded the military police. One night in 1931 a rumor began that the military police planned to rebel. Revolutionary officers rushed to mobilize the navy to protect Vargas. Batista Luzardo, a police chief, soon appeared at the naval arsenal where junior officers promptly placed him under arrest. When officers interrogated their prisoner, Luzardo said: "Getúlio ordered me to see what was happening, because there is news that you here in the navy are placing forces in the arsenal patio to attack the MPs. The army is also mobilizing, and the military police are entirely tranquil."[28] It took a direct order from Vargas to free the imprisoned police chief. He had been trapped not only by loyal officers, but also by the atmosphere of the time.

The Rebellion of São Paulo

In this situation, commanders such as Goés Monteiro feared that regional leaders might seize upon the army's weakness to challenge the authority of the central state. Events soon persuaded officers that their fears were justified. No group had lost as much power with the revolution as the traditional elites in São Paulo, who had dominated the Old Republic. In some respects, the revolution marked the shift of power from agricultural and rural elites to a new industrial and urban class.[29] The Paulistas feared the mobilization of the urban masses and changes to Brazil's social system. They hated the reforms proposed by the tenentes and believed that their state deserved special consideration.[30] To limit the government's power, they called for elections and a new constitution. In their anger over their loss of power, the Paulistas prepared finally to overthrow the federal government.

Army leaders learned that not only did São Paulo plan to rebel, but also other powerful states, particularly Rio Grande do Sul.[31] Given the power of state militias, the army took this challenge seriously. Rio Grande do Sul already had a better armed brigade than any in the army.[32] São Paulo rose in rebellion on July 9, 1932.[33] But when the moment arrived, other states failed to join São Paulo, in part because of Vargas's astute political maneuvering, and in part because the movement had clearly separatist goals. As Thomas Skidmore has described, the Paulistas remained divided over many political issues, but they all rallied around a sense of regional identity. This helped to mobilize the populace: "Middle-class housewives contributed their jewelry in a 'Campaign of Gold' to finance the war effort, while their sons volunteered for duty in the trenches."[34] The contest was not only a struggle between the federal army and the state militias, but also a civil war supported by an enthusiastic populace. But this same rhetoric cost the movement any broader support: "As was perhaps inevitable, they allowed demands for constitutional reform to become mixed, and finally identified, with regional separatism. This meant that the liberal constitutionalists forfeited any support for their principles which might well have been forthcoming from urban centers in other parts of Brazil, especially in the states of Minas Gerais and Rio Grande do Sul. Such aid was essential if they were to have any hope of success, and its absence dealt a death blow to the 'constitutionalist' movement."[35] The army proved determined to crush the resistance and launched an air bombardment of enemy forces in the encircled city.[36] After a two month siege, with sometimes heavy fighting, São Paulo surrendered.[37]

The federal government's victory had a number of important effects. It not only assured the survival of Vargas's government, but also pulled his government back to the political center. The tenentes had wished to see radical reforms carried out before a new constitution could be implemented, but in the aftermath of São Paulo's rebellion Vargas promised to hold elections for a constituent assembly. He also abandoned some of the more radical ideals of his followers. This experience had proved that the government needed to be conciliatory in its treatment of civilian elites. At the same time, the rebellion had a major impact within the army, where it reestablished the bonds of discipline that had been gravely weakened after the 1930 revolution. Power tended to return from the tenentes to the generals.[38] The army also came to believe that it could no longer permit state militias to exist outside its authority, given the danger of regional separatism.

The Army's Fear of National Collapse

This experience also strengthened the army's perception that it was under attack from civilian elites. General Góes Monteiro stressed this point in his writings. He believed that the postrevolutionary period was characterized by the military's struggle against regional strongmen, called caudilhos. These figures wished to either dominate the federal government or to secede from it.[39] Given this reality, he argued, only the army could guarantee the nation's survival: "The signs of national decomposition are already perceptible and visible, so much so that we cannot have doubts that if other paths are not taken in our affairs, national politics and our destinies, we will have to watch, as will the generations to come, the disappearance of Brazil. All the elements of the army must dedicate themselves to the most high expression of sacrifice . . . avoiding interference in factional struggles that only lead to the demoralization and indiscipline of the armed forces."[40] Several trends encouraged this perspective. During the revolution, army officers had formed dangerous ties with civilians. After the overthrow of the Old Republic, regional leaders created followers within the military with promises of positions in political commissions or army promotions.[41] By this means, civilian elites sought to regain the influence over the army that they had enjoyed during the Old Republic. Army leaders, however, believed that civilians were infiltrating the army in order to destroy it.[42] Góes Monteiro claimed that the followers of one regional politician did "not want anything other than the reduction or absorption of the armed forces."[43] Much as in the closing years of the Empire, officers believed that civilian politicians wished to undermine the central state, so as to further their regions' independence.[44]

One example of the civil-military conflict this belief created can be seen in the struggle between the governor of Rio Grande do Sul, José Antônio Flores da Cunha, and the army's leadership, especially General Góes Monteiro. Flores da Cunha aspired to the presidency and sought to create a body of followers within the military. During the period before São Paulo's rebellion in 1932, the army hierarchy believed that Flores da Cunha had allied with the Paulistas to plot a larger rebellion. The army received reports that Governor Flores da Cunha was moving military material into his state and infiltrating provisional troops (not only soldiers from the state militia, but also armed civilians loyal to Flores da Cunha) into neighboring Santa Catarina. Góes Monteiro thought that Flores da Cunha sought to weaken the army, perhaps to break his state apart from Brazil.[45]

This situation led to a bitter confrontation between the two men. Góes Monteiro believed that Flores da Cunha had coopted many officers, including generals, who waited only for his signal to rebel. One night in June 1932, he learned from a family member (Capt. Cicero Augusto de Góes Monteiro) that Flores da Cunha was plotting rebellion with many high officers in a nearby apartment. Accompanied by Cicero and several officers, Monteiro forced his way into the building and past the soldiers waiting inside the doorway. Góes Monteiro rushed to the governor's apartment, where he caught Flores da Cunha speaking to high commanders in Góes Monteiro's division. Góes Monteiro later claimed that in the ensuing confrontation Flores da Cunha attacked the federal government. Revolution was inevitable, Flores said, and Rio Grande do Sul would take part, as would Minas Gerais, São Paulo, and the armed forces. Furthermore, Flores stated that "he was organizing the garrison of Rio de Janeiro, to avoid any reaction, in face of an irresistible movement."[46]

According to Góes Monteiro, he challenged Flores da Cunha to accompany him to see President Vargas. While Góes Monteiro drove him to the palace, Flores da Cunha criticized the army's lack of discipline. Upon arriving, Flores da Cunha was ushered in to see the president, while General Monteiro waited outside. When the meeting finished, the governor muttered complaints but promised to support the government. Flores da Cunha had little choice because a variety of factors worked against a successful uprising by the southern states.[47] Flores da Cunha's refusal to join São Paulo's rebellion in July 1932 helped to ensure the rebellion's failure.

Góes Monteiro's Term as Minister of War

The confrontation between the general and Flores da Cunha only intensified after this encounter, especially after Góes Monteiro became minister of war. In January 1934, Góes Monteiro refused Vargas's offer to become minister of war because he believed that the president had rejected his program.[48] Vargas then met with Monteiro, pointed to his letter on his desk, and said: "Your program is approved and the government will execute it at any cost."[49] During his first months as minister of war, Góes Monteiro sought to make legal changes to the army's structure in order to isolate officers from civilian politics. Góes Monteiro tried to reshape the military judiciary. He used his influence to ensure that the 1934 constitution denied soldiers the right to vote, but the general became frustrated as his efforts met with outside opposition.[50] When he tried to limit Flores da Cunha's influence by introducing new laws governing promotions, the governor's pressure forced him to modify the statute. By the spring of 1934 the tension between Flores da Cunha and the armed forces threatened to break into open warfare.[51] In this environment, the minister of war found it impossible to reorganize the military.[52]

In frustration, Góes Monteiro sought to increase the army's influence within the state. In May 1934, Góes read and approved a memorandum written by Gen. Valdomiro Castilho Lima which he then circulated among high commanders.[53] This document proposed creating a "council of generals." Valdomiro's main goal was to create an institution that could strengthen the military in relation to regional elites. In the memorandum's conclusion, Valdomiro asked Góes Monteiro to prepare to fight Flores da Cunha, to prevent another humiliating defeat like that of 1930.

Other army leaders quickly protested against what they perceived as a challenge to the government. For example, Gen. José Maria Franco Ferreira found the memorandum confusing, but he believed its author suggested overthrowing Vargas if the president opposed the council's plans. General Franco Ferreira was horrified by what he perceived as a move towards military dictatorship. He also argued that such a council would destroy military unity because colonels might create similar bodies. Other generals rejected the proposal for identical reasons. During this period, General Monteiro secretly planned to run for the presidency.[54] Other generals knew this fact, feared his ambition, and rejected his proposal.

Góes Monteiro did not abandon his efforts as minister of war. Indeed, he became even more ambitious in his plans because he decided that the only way to save the army was to alter the nation. General Góes Monteiro used his 1935 annual report to the president to propose a new mission for the military. In the study's introduction, Góes Monteiro stated that throughout the army's history the military had always come under attack from outside forces. The problem, he argued, was the lack of a "national political idea" to unite all Brazilians.[55] The army had to be "immunized" against civilian politicians, a step that required changing society. Góes Monteiro proposed, among other suggestions, to return the army to the educational program it had considered earlier in the century.[56]

Unlike his predecessors, Góes Monteiro understood that any discussion of social reform in Brazil entailed a discussion of race. If officers believed that blacks were inherently inferior (as a navy officer had asserted after the 1910 rebellion), then it followed that no effort to change the Brazilian masses could succeed.[57] But recent changes in Brazilian society helped Góes Monteiro to argue against this view.[58] Economic trends undermined the old system of patronage based on class and race. Urban groups had acquired new influence. The rise of mass politics made it dangerous to ignore popular issues. The new power of nationalism led Brazilian thinkers to question racist ideals advanced by European thinkers. In this context, Góes Monteiro explicitly challenged old racial ideals within his institution. In doing so, Góes Monteiro went against the dominant trend within the army over the next decade, which excluded people of color from the officers ranks.

In his report to the president, Góes Monteiro discussed the question of race in a serious manner.[59] He began by condemning the racism of various nineteenth-century thinkers, which he stated lacked any scientific basis. In Brazil, he argued, with so much racial mixing, it was impossible to talk of truly different races. Brazil had failed to develop not because of the racial makeup of its people, but rather because of the populace's lack of education. The minister of war believed that this realization was important to the army's future.

Góes Monteiro suggested that the government force all young male Brazilians to receive military instruction in "recruitment reserves." Participants would meet in barracks, where army officers could teach citizens every day outside of work hours. In essence, he proposed to make the military into the nation's tutor, with officers teaching young males in their free time.[60] In so doing, the minister of war wished to avoid the errors the army had committed earlier in the century. The army would not separate itself from the populace with its racism. Instead, it would seek to create a sense of national unity, which would strengthen both the army and the state.

Many historians have described Góes Monteiro as the author of the military's new role during the late 1930s.[61] In this case, however, his proposal had little support within the military. The army had failed to create an educational role earlier in the century, and the officer corps had no desire to return to this ideal. The minister of war never clearly explained how this mission could have ended civilian influence within the military, and most officers wished to exclude people of color from the army, as later policies revealed.[62] A new program needed broad support within the military, which entailed a consensus amongst army factions. It could not be imposed upon the army from above, as General Góes Monteiro wished to do. It was impossible for a military leader to change the institution until the army had closed itself to society.

Góes Monteiro was shocked by the intense plotting within the military, by civilians, by officers, and by communists.[63] An atmosphere of chaos existed that made it impossible for any minister of war to retain his position for long. Góes Monteiro himself became caught up in the conspiracies swirling around him when he attempted to force Congress to increase military salaries. Flores da Cunha seized upon his blunder to press for Góes Monteiro's removal.[64] On May 1, 1935, General Monteiro wrote Vargas his letter of resignation. The contest between the general and the politician proved that the army could not ensure discipline based on military reforms alone. Only a profound change in Brazil's political climate could enable the army to defeat its civilian challengers. Then, because of a terrifying rebellion, the army began to increase its power only a few months after Góes Monteiro's resignation. The military carefully used this rebellion both to strengthen its political power and to attack its civilian opponents.

The Communist Intentona

In 1934 military commanders began to plot against the government.[65] Their plan to overthrow the federal government was driven as much by humiliation as by ideology. Some officers had left the armed forces after 1930; others had lost the prestige they had enjoyed before the revolution. These officers allied with civilian politicians who desired a revolution, under the nominal leadership of former president Artur da Silva Bernardes. The nation was divided into zones, each of which had a military commander. Army and naval officers infiltrated police forces and collected military weapons. The conspirators successfully targeted the sergeants and the lower ranks to create their combat force. They created ties with almost every garrison in the country and worked with state police forces. By late April 1935, the extent of the conspiracy deeply concerned Getúlio Vargas.[66]

Their conspiracy, however, was quickly infiltrated by the police in the federal district, led by an army officer named Filinto Muller. By the end of the year, Muller had a clear picture of the conspirators' entire plan. Perhaps even worse for the conspirators, between October 1934 and January 1935 the Brazilian Communist Party (PCB) began to take part in the plot. As General Góes Monteiro described, the conspirators were divided among three factions: one linked to São Paulo, which involved both officers and civilians; a second current that was purely military, composed of generals and admirals who shared authoritarian ideals; and a third group made up of officers and enlisted men, to whom communism seemed an attractive ideology.[67] The latter faction attracted the attention of the Soviet Union. In particular, communist agents noted the profound division between officers, who were loyal to former president Artur Bernardes, and the sergeants who wished to make a social revolution.[68] These ideological divisions made Bernardes' conspiracy susceptible to an external take-over.

As Moscow followed the conspiracy, it became convinced that this uprising could succeed. The Communist International (Comintern) sent to Brazil its best leaders from Germany, the Soviet Union, and the United States. In addition, the Comintern was able to build upon the earlier work of military rebels (tenentes) during the 1920s. Luís Carlos Prestes, the former head of the tenente movement, had converted to communism while in exile in Bolivia. He left Moscow that winter and arrived in Brazil in April 1935 to take over the conspiracy. He was accompanied by Olga Benario, a member of the Soviet military's secret service, who was responsible for Prestes's safety.[69]

The communists rapidly gained influence over the conspiracy by winning the enlisted men to their cause. Their success came very quickly. The first organized leftist elements began to penetrate the conspiracy only in January 1935. By March 1935, the communists dominated the movement. This horrified many commanders who had been uncertain whether to take advantage of the strength of the Communist Party for their own ends.[70] After July 1935, most officers who remained in the conspiracy either chose to leave or were forced out by Prestes.[71] A revolutionary political party had seized the conspiracy the officers had created.

In July 1935 Vargas outlawed the National Liberation Alliance (ALN), the front organization for the conspirators. This step cost the movement any remaining support among the original military conspirators.[72] In the face of government repression, Prestes found that he was also unable to rally widespread support for his uprising from civilians. However, Prestes had considerable experience plotting a military rebellion. His agents continued to fan throughout the army, winning over soldiers to their cause. By November 1935, the communists' plans were fully laid. From the northern city of Natal, to the nation's capital of Rio de Janeiro, soldiers suddenly rose up to seize control of the military from their commanders.

Nevertheless, the rebellion ended in disaster because of the communists' disorganization and the workers' apathy. In addition, the secret police, Departamento de Ordem Política e Social (DOPS) proved to be efficient, and British intelligence warned the Brazilian government that an uprising appeared imminent.[73] The rebels never had a chance. In the aftermath, all branches of the armed forces responded with a program of political terror. Army generals believed that they were under attack from external agents and that they had to respond ruthlessly. They targeted not only communists, but also all those they perceived as a threat. The army pushed for legislation to strengthen the state and its repressive apparatus. Its leaders also seized upon the incident to warn of the danger the army faced from outside infiltrators. For this reason, the army and navy shaped the memory of the uprising so as to conceal its origins within the armed forces. They succeeded in this effort, in part because of the culture of fear that they created.

Political Terror in Brazil

In the aftermath of the uprising, military commanders were in no mood for mercy.[74] The minister of the navy, Henrique Aristides Guilhem, and the minister of war, João Gomes Ribeiro Filho, were terrified by the revolt and recognized their colleagues' desire to purge the armed forces and society. As naval officer Ernâni do Amaral Peixoto noted, the memory of the 1910 rebellion remained fresh within the navy, where it created a special horror of rebellion. Navy captain Lúcio Meira wrote that the conspirators were seeking to repeat the Revolt of the Whip.[75] With naval officers' worst fears realized, commanders were willing to repress dissent with terror. Capt. Lúcio Meira personally supervised (and participated in) the beatings of sailors by the special police.[76] Admiral Guilhem expressed his institution's outlook: "Cleansing and punishment are needed."[77] Similar sentiments existed within the army. During the fighting, minister of war João Gomes Ribeiro Filho told Gen. Eurico Gaspar Dutra: "Let's bomb everything, because I don't want any of that rabble to come out of there alive."[78] After the rebels laid down their arms, Gomes wanted to have them summarily shot. President Vargas had to give him a direct order that this was not to take place.[79]

Given this climate within the armed forces, it is unsurprising that minister of war Gomes denounced the "liberalism" of legislation that restricted the "kind of repression required."[80] In fact, Brazilian laws did little to curb the military's use of terror because neither the president nor Congress had the will to see them enforced. The army and navy as institutions played a crucial role in this repression, which went far beyond arresting officers, transporting them to their torture, legitimating their suffering, and influencing the military officers who commanded civilian police. Because the uprising had taken the form of an attack on the armed forces, officers believed that they had to take an active role in the movement's repression. Many of the people torturing prisoners were army and naval officers, as in the cases of Elise Saborowski and Victor Allen Barron, two members of the Comintern.[81]

The German Arthur Ernst Ewert (alias Harry Berger) was tortured with electric shocks.[82] Brazilian officer Nelson Werneck Sodré alleges that Ewert also watched soldiers repeatedly rape his wife, Elise Saborowski (Elise Ewert), until he lost his reason.[83] Minna Ewert wrote a heartbreaking description of her brother and sister-in-law's torture: "In my brother's presence they beat my sister-in-law's naked body till she fainted. They burned my brother with lighted cigarettes till he had two hundred burns. He was hit on the head till he lost consciousness and then was given an injection in the arm which revived him and the torturers began again. Another torture consisted in [sic] choking him, six times in the course of the night. Furthermore, both of them were tortured with electric shocks, and one of his wife's ears was badly burnt."[84] Minna Ewert's efforts to save her family proved futile. Vargas ultimately sent Saborowski to Germany, where she met her death in a concentration camp.[85]

Victor Allan Barron, an American who had formerly been a member of the Communist Youth, underwent horrible tortures after his arrest.[86] Although most of these tortures took place at the police station, there was no question about who controlled this process. A naval captain (and doctor) supervised Barron's torture, as he was beaten, shocked, and had his testicles squeezed until he fainted.[87] U.S. ambassador Hugh Gibson visited him and protested his torture to Filinto Muller, but there was no saving him. Indeed, U.S. secretary of state Cordell Hull ordered Gibson not to involve himself any further in the case.[88] According to Brazilian authorities, Barron committed suicide by jumping from the second floor of the central police station. It is unclear if he was dead before he went through the window or if he died in the hospital after the fall.[89] In the U.S., Congressman Vito Marcantonio denounced Barron's torture and murder before the house of representatives. He read a statement from Joseph R. Brodsky, Barron's lawyer, who claimed personal knowledge of his client's torture: "They beat him with belts and rubber hose; they burned and shocked him with live electric wires; they punched and kicked him around constantly and did not let him sleep for days."[90] Neither this publicity nor mass protests in the United States ended the terror in Brazil, because the military perceived that its survival was at stake.[91]

On the day Barron died, March 5, 1936, the police found Prestes and Olga Benario in a suburb of Rio de Janeiro. Prestes survived, although he endured long imprisonment. Olga—pregnant with Prestes's child—was not so fortunate. A German Jew, she was deported to her home country in August 1936, and was received by the Gestapo. She died in a gas chamber at Páscoa in 1942.[92]

It is difficult to overstate the savagery of state terror. The special police and military officers tortured not only their prisoners, but also their victims' wives and children.[93] Prisoners had sharp objects forced under their fingernails until their hands were maimed, as happened with José Romero.[94] The head of the Brazilian Communist Party was beaten and tortured for a week. Some prisoners simply disappeared.[95] Nobody was exempt. The armed forces insisted that the government arrest specific individuals, and even Vargas feared to resist their demands.[96] Many people unconnected to the conspiracy suffered. The state and the military seized upon this opportunity to repress not only communists, but also anarchists, union leaders, "socialists, progressives, and reformers of all stripes."[97] The military reserved some of the worst violence for soldiers and sailors.[98] Muller arrested 1,300 soldiers, who were taken to an isolated island for "safe-keeping."[99] These men did not find safety in their seclusion.

The Creation of a Myth

What is remarkable about this list of horrors is not only its brutality, but also who was exempt. The military largely ignored the officers and civilians who had initiated the plot, though the government knew of their role. By the end of 1934, Filinto Muller had known everything about the conspirators' plans: the names of the participants, their motivation for rebellion, the names of their messengers, and the sites where they stored arms.[100] But these individuals remained concealed not only immediately after the rebellion, but also in the military's "official" account of the uprising. The military has collectively remembered the rebellion every year, by having senior officers visit a cemetery where the remains of loyalist soldiers were interred. This ceremony served a political purpose—to remind the armed forces and the nation of the need for permanent vigilance against the communists.[101]

In this context, the military could not have admitted that a former president led the initial movement, that conspirators met at his house, and that his son (Artur Bernardes Filho, a federal congressman) was involved. It would have been too disturbing to acknowledge that Arthur Bernardes stored munitions and other supplies at his property in Viçosa.[102] The list of military officers involved included many highly respected men. Important civilians participated in the initial plotting, such as João Neves da Fontoura and Christiano Machado.[103] These revelations would not only have made military terror unacceptable, but also would have prevented the military from using the uprising as a political tool. Instead, the rebellion served to rally frightened Brazilian elites behind the state and the military. It also justified a radical purge of the political left.[104] For this reason, the armed forces concealed the roots of the uprising among its commanders, and instead argued that the rebellion had come from outside the institution, from a still dangerous enemy.[105]

It is not that the military's account of the revolt was false, but rather that it was incomplete. There was a communist rebellion within the army, which had taken place upon orders from Moscow. (In asserting this the military was in fact more honest than the Brazilian communists, such as Prestes, who untruthfully denied that Moscow had ordered the uprising.) The communists so completely subverted the original plot within the army that many officers found the official account of the rebellion to be convincing, but the true record of events was more complex than the official myth that the state promulgated. The original military plotters unintentionally laid much of the groundwork for the later rebellion by organizing the sergeants, subverting officers, and stockpiling weapons. Yet the government did not seize upon this history to warn about the danger of conservative generals and their civilian allies. Instead, the state and the military chose to simplify this complex history in a major effort to reshape political memory.

This censorship has affected even the best scholarship on the 1935 rebellion. Even careful authors (such as William Waack and Paulo Sérgio Pinheiro) have failed to uncover the roots of the rebellion within the military itself. In writing his study, Sérgio Pinheiro had access to over 90,000 documents of former president Artur da Silva Bernardes, then in the possession of his son.[106] Both father and son had taken part in the conspiracy. Yet the origins of the rebellion remained obscure because the former president's family and the military both shared an interest in concealing the truth.

That the military succeeded in concealing the truth for so long is a testament to the power of censorship at the time. In a climate in which accurate information was impossible to obtain, silence permitted the armed forces to rewrite history in its interest. Senior commanders such as Gen. Eurico Gaspar Dutra reduced the complex history of the uprising into a useful myth, which illustrated the dangers "foreign" ideologies posed to Brazil. Official accounts described how communist soldiers had murdered sleeping officers in their beds, although this atrocity never occurred.[107] These accounts served to dehumanize the rebels and to justify the terror that followed. Censorship also enabled the armed forces to manipulate the rebels' identities in other respects. For example, after the rebellion Gen. Pedro Aurelio de Goés Monteiro demanded the creation of a fascist state on the nationalist-socialist model to purge Brazil of "Semitic internationalism."[108] By linking dissent with ethnic identity, the armed forces defined the victims of military terror as "others" who were not true Brazilians. It became common to refer to the uprising as the "Jewish-Communist conspiracy."[109] In using rhetoric that defined the victims of military terror as "aliens," the Brazilian military adopted a discourse (usually anti-Semitic) often used by Latin American militaries to justify repression.[110] In the Brazilian case, this enabled the military to justify the coup that made Getúlio Vargas dictator in 1937.

The Foundation of the Estado Novo

By early 1937 the government had enacted repressive legislation, silenced political opponents, and eliminated the communists. But these steps did not satisfy the military. It wished to close itself to political society, as José Murilo de Carvalho has argued.[111] A minority of officers also desired the power to intervene more directly in the economy, but the army was too weak to implement this role without outside support. The army hierarchy may have considered seizing power, even without Vargas.[112] However, a military dictatorship threatened to create dangerous rivalries within the armed forces, and Brazil lacked a history to give such a government legitimacy. Instead, senior officers created "a military coup in civilian clothing" with the aid of President Vargas.[113]

By May 1937 many observers worried that the government planned to annul the upcoming elections and to seize power for itself. On June 1, 1937, newspapers reported that generals had contacted the minister of war, Gen. Eurico Gaspar Dutra, to condemn the army's intervention in politics. In the political struggle that followed, some of these generals were arrested.[114] In August 1937 the president spoke with General Góes Monteiro, then head of the general staff, to ask what he should do if the Congress obstructed reforms. He replied that Vargas had to dissolve it.[115] By late September 1937 the plans for the coup had been well laid. In the last week of September 1937 the army General Staff "found" a communist plan to take over the country, the Cohen plan. In reality, a member of Goés Monteiro's staff (Capt. Olímpio Mourão Filho, a member of the Brazilian fascist party, the integralistas) likely wrote this document, based on an article in a French military magazine.[116] He deliberately chose a Jewish name for his work. Góes Monteiro seized upon it as a tool to advance military interests.[117] General Góes Monteiro sent this document to the president, to military leaders, and to journalists. It created a state of hysteria that forced Congress to once again renew the state of emergency.

In the aftermath of the Cohen plan's publication, events unfolded with an air of inevitability. Vargas knew he could count on the support of Plínio Salgado, the leader of the integralistas, a powerful civilian party modeled after fascism.[118] After the government took control of the state militia in Rio Grande do Sul, Flores da Cunha realized that he could not halt the oncoming coup. On October 17, 1937 he fled Brazil. On November 10, military police closed Congress. Vargas signed a new constitution in the presidential palace that same morning. The coup met with almost no civilian resistance. As Aspásia Camargo has argued, the government had already neutralized the opposition.[119]

One institution that might have had the power to challenge Vargas at this point was the Catholic Church. Throughout the nineteenth century, the Brazilian Church was a weak institution by Latin American standards. Still, the Church had worked successfully to strengthen itself after the turn of the century. At moments of political crisis, the Catholic Church has played an important role in twentieth century Brazilian history. For example, when Vargas's forces advanced on Rio de Janeiro in 1930, it was Cardinal Leme who persuaded President Washington Luís to resign so as to prevent bloodshed.[120]

What is strange then is the relative lack of interest that most senior army officers showed for the Church until the 1960s.[121]

The papers and memoirs of senior army leaders such as Góes Monteiro only rarely mention the Church. Relations between the Church and the army had been strained after the foundation of the republic because its military founders had separated church from state. Military positivists, a powerful faction within the armed forces during the early years of the Republic, disdained Catholicism.[122] But in the long run, despite factional divisions within both bodies, the Church and the military shared a similar perspective on social issues. Both were authoritarian, paternalistic institutions that favored social order, opposed communism, and distrusted the masses. Accordingly, military officers could pay little attention to the Church for decades because they assumed that the Church either supported their positions or would remain silent. No major military faction formed an important alliance with the Church between the 1920s and the 1950s; specific references to the Church (apart from formulaic statements about the threat from "godless" anticommunism) were infrequent in the military's internal debates. As the Church changed, so would its relationship with the armed forces, but the Catholic Church did not seriously challenge Vargas or the military as they founded the Estado Novo. If a serious challenge did emerge to this authoritarian government, it could only come from within the military itself.

Some military leaders, such as Gen. Eduardo Gomes and Gen. Juarez Távora, protested against the coup. Like other tenentes, they opposed the foundation of the Estado Novo because they supported José Américo de Almeida, then a presidential candidate. Still, most officers accepted events, in their surprise at the sudden closure of Congress.[123] Dutra ordered those officers who opposed the coup to remote postings or to positions that did not involve the command of troops.[124] But this step was taken from caution and not from need, for the army remained calm.

There were a number of reasons for the army's unity. The minister of war, Eurico Gaspar Dutra, proved to be a skilled leader who wrested control of the institution not only from civilian parties, but even from Vargas himself.[125] Legislative changes gave the state the necessary power to fight military conspirators; article 177 of the Brazilian constitution of 1937 allowed the government to retire officers to the reserve at its discretion. Many military dissidents were purged in this manner.[126] Perhaps equally important, however, was Dutra's creation of a powerful system of internal espionage to ensure officers' loyalty.

This system was not entirely new. Dutra's ally, General Góes Monteiro, had created an intelligence service before the foundation of the Estado Novo.

One observer said that "the most important element that General Góes relies upon is Colonel Gustavo Cordeiro de Faria, who directs a perfect secret service within and without the army under the watchful eye of General Góes, and with the support of Captain Filinto Muller, Chief of Police."[127] Muller had proved to be unpopular within the army; he aligned himself with Góes Monteiro to improve his standing. After November 1937 Dutra continued to rely upon Muller, who warned Dutra of complaints against him.[128] Dutra also created a systematic intelligence organization within the army, which worked under his strict control.

Repression and Memory

This military service, which quickly ended all open opposition to the army's leadership, was divided into two sections. Subunits of the general staff kept files on officers, many of which would also be forwarded to the secret police (DOPS), the chiefs of police, and the commanders of state police forces, all of which the military effectively dominated during the Estado Novo. Officers' promotions and assignments depended upon the evaluation of these bodies within the general staff. Equally important, Dutra created a special division within the cabinet of the minister of war, within which military officers carefully screened all those who wished to join the general staff or to enter its school. They also vetted all young men entering schools that prepared them to be officers, based not only on their ideological reliability, but also on their religious and racial purity. One former officer, Nelson Werneck Sodré, described how this worked: "The entrance of young men into the Military School, and the preparatory schools that then began to appear, were submitted in a secret manner to a rigorous inquiry. A document created in the cabinet of the ministry, and sent down to commanders, categorically prohibited the entrance or enrollment of the sons of Jews, people of color, those of humble origins, and the sons of couples separated for any reason; the commands were authorized to cooperate with police authorities to investigate their class or nature, and naturally, their ideological character."[129] This process helped to "whiten" and "Christianize" the officer corps. (In public ceremonies, the army has long sought to present white troops to the public.)[130]

As José Murilo de Carvalho has argued, these instructions represented a culmination of a process. Mass military service had "whitened" the ranks after World War I. With new regulations preventing sergeants from entering the officer corps in the 1930s, people of color had become yet more marginalized within the army. Even after these regulations were revoked, discrimination endured. At the foundation of the Republic, there had been a considerable number of nonwhite officers within the army, in part a legacy of the Paraguayan War. By the 1950s photographs of officers at gatherings and social events often revealed people who looked as though they had emigrated en masse from Portugal. This process, which had longlasting effects upon the institution, accelerated with Dutra's efforts to reshape the officer corps.[131]

This vetting of all officers ensured not only Dutra's absolute control over the military, but also the authority of other army leaders. The army's power was further strengthened by its ability to use political terror against its civilian opponents. The army did not have a permanent organization within the military dedicated to state terror, but it had considerable influence over the state's repressive apparatus. Political torture by civilian police became common.[132] Throughout the Estado Novo (1937–45), repression generally took place either under the aegis of the social and political police (DOPS), which was led by an army officer named Capt. Afonso Miranda Correia, or by civilian police under the authority of another army officer, Filinto Muller. (The chief of police in the federal district, he controlled civilian police throughout Brazil.)[133] The military also ruled the military police, which had previously been governed by the states.[134] This structure was important politically within the armed forces. According to Gen. Umberto Peregrino Seabra Fagundes (the minister of war's aide during 1944–45), the use of torture did not trouble officers because it was carried out by the police, and it seemed less frequent than it would after Brazilian democracy collapsed in 1964.[135] Nonetheless, the links between the armed forces and the police were intricate and multifaceted. For example, Filinto Muller used police funds to strengthen the capabilities of military intelligence services, rather than expending his money on his own institution.[136] Although Brazil was ruled by a civilian dictator, Vargas relied on the armed forces as the basis of his regime. In this context, the lines between civilian agencies and the armed forces became blurred.

The close link between the armed forces and civilian agencies responsible for security also can be seen in terms of personnel. When Muller resigned his position in July 1942, Vargas replaced him with an army colonel, Alcides Etchegoyen. Muller promptly returned to the army, to serve as a cabinet official on Minister of War Dutra's staff.[137] When Etchegoyen resigned as police chief in August 1943, Vargas replaced him with another army officer, Lieutenant Colonel Nelson de Mello.[138] These appointments reflected the extent to which the military had acquired influence within the state apparatus dedicated to intelligence and repression. The military maintained a distance from the instruments of terror, while retaining a measure of control over them.

The army also controlled that part of the state dedicated to censorship. Minister of War Dutra had long opposed freedom of the press.[139] When the head of the Departamento de Imprensa e Propaganda (DIP) resigned, Vargas replaced him with an army major who had served as the head of the army's secret service.[140] As Elizabeth Cancelli has noted, propaganda always forms part of the apparatus of terror.[141] The army used its influence to defend its "official story." The military could not accept any challenge to its version of its past, because that would have challenged the legitimacy of the regime itself.[142]

Accordingly, the military used its power to enforce silence. The state censored all discussion of the 1910 rebellion.[143] When Gustavo Barroso wrote about the naval rebellion for the newspaper *A Manhã* during the Estado Novo, he was called to the DIP, the agency responsible for censorship. Maj. Amilcar Dutra de Menezes told him that he was not to write any further on this topic, on the orders of the minister of the navy, Adm. Aristides Guilhem.[144] The military also sought to conceal the true history of the 1935 uprising. The military did not only rely on state censorship to accomplish this goal, but also the culture of fear. Even before the coup, Gen. Newton de Andrade Cavalcanti had ordered the kidnapping of a newspaper editor who published an article that angered him. Cavalcanti refused to release him until he had read and reflected upon the Cohen plan.[145] After the coup, free thought became even more dangerous. Both army and navy officers pushed to ensure that books that displeased the military would be confiscated by the police and their authors arrested.[146] The military placed great faith in its ability to reshape history through these efforts. During a later military government, the armed forces appointed Filinto Muller to be head of the Human Rights Council— Conselho de Defesa dos Direitos da Pessoa Humana—of the Ministry of Justice.[147] This action indicated not only the depths of military cynicism but also the extent to which the armed forces believed they could manipulate the popular memory of the past.

Conclusion

Between 1935 and 1937 the Brazilian army underwent a remarkable transformation. To justify measures they desired, generals such as Góes Monteiro had exaggerated the chaos and confusion within the military after the 1930 revolution. Still, the revolution had gravely weakened the bonds of discipline and hierarchy. Army generals fought among themselves, and they also had to deal with rebellions by enlisted officers and the new-found power of the tenentes. Both the far Right and far Left sought to build followings within the armed forces. In desperation, senior commanders, such as General Góes Monteiro, even spoke of the "disappearance" of Brazil. This rhetoric captured officers' fears that the nation faced a serious crisis because of the army's weakness. Army leaders blamed civilian politicians for this crisis, much as they had blamed imperial politicians for the army's weakness under the empire.

With the establishment of the Estado Novo, Eurico Gaspar Dutra and General Góes Monteiro acquired positions of unquestioned authority within the army, and they smashed their political enemies. Civilian politicians lost their ability to award or punish military officers. The government enacted military-supported policies that centralized political power and industrialized the economy. The army achieved unrivaled power within the state. To some extent, the establishment of the Estado Novo marked the army's final victory over the traditional elites, which brought to a close a conflict that had lasted for more than half a century.

The army could not have achieved this success without the mythology that it created around the 1935 uprising. This event did more than frighten Congress into declaring a state of siege. It enabled the army to legitimate its seizure of power among civilians. It also served to rally officers as senior commanders, in alliance with Vargas, overthrew Brazilian democracy. For this reason, strict censorship and political terror throughout the Estado Novo preserved the military's version of its past. The army has continued its efforts to define a specific historical memory of this event, by such means as an annual ceremony at São João Batista cemetery, to honor the "martyrs" of 1935. At this ceremony no mention is made of the origins of the conspiracy or of how army leaders created a myth around this event to end Brazilian democracy.

3

The Meaning of Independence
1937–1945

With the foundation of the Estado Novo, the army had acquired a position of immense power in the political system. It no longer needed to fear challenges from regional leaders and traditional elites. In this context, army leaders had the opportunity to think about the army's role in society in a sustained fashion. Many Latin American armies had difficulty defining their missions, since the armed forces proved more likely to intervene in internal conflicts than to fight a foreign foe. Nonetheless, there was a strong memory throughout Latin America of European imperialism in the nineteenth century. In the 1930s, Germany, Italy, and Japan all followed expansionist policies that exacerbated Latin fears. Many Latin Americans worried equally about the influence of the United States. During the early twentieth century, this nation had intervened militarily in the small and less developed states of Central America and the Caribbean. South American nations also had not proved immune to U.S. pressure, as Colombia had learned with the loss of Panama.

An overt military intervention in South America by the United States seemed unlikely. Yet many Latin elites worried that their economic dependency made them vulnerable to foreign pressure. In particular, Latin Americans feared the power of multinational corporations. United Fruit Company had impressive power in Central America. Although Standard Oil had great influence in all of South America, it had particular influence in Venezuela. U.S. companies had endorsed challenges to the Mexican government when they supported corporate interests. This atmosphere led to a fear of imperialism and a concern with the economic influence of foreign powers which seemed exaggerated to outsiders, but which made sense in historical context. All Latin American countries were keenly aware that foreign powers could use economic influence as readily as military power to inhibit national sovereignty.

Every Latin American military had to determine what it meant to defend a nation defined by its position of dependency in the world economy. In the twentieth century this meant defining their countries' relationship with the United States, the dominant power in the hemisphere. During the 1930s, the Brazilian army favored economic nationalism because of the international context. The political and military power of Germany created an American rival. The United States proved willing to sacrifice some commercial interests for reasons of international politics. For a short period, Argentina, Brazil, and other nations followed a state-led approach to development that engaged the military in society in profound new ways. No sooner had these militaries adopted these roles than international pressures undermined the armed forces's vision. This history defined the issues at stake in military politics for the next three decades. Indeed, in the post–Cold War period many Latin American militaries are forced once again to wrestle with this problem.

The Army's New Power

After the coup, the only remaining threat within the army were the integralistas (Brazilian fascists), who believed that the foundation of the Estado Novo gave them an opportunity to seize power. The integralistas had become a powerful force within the army after 1934, as officers searched for an anticommunist ideology to rally their men. Vargas had formed a tacit alliance with the integralistas, which had helped to ensure the army's support for Vargas's coup. Yet Vargas had no intention of sharing power. To the horror of Plínio Salgado, the integralistas' leader, Vargas outlawed the party shortly after he ended democratic rule. Integralistas responded by rising against the government on May 10, 1938. Despite a fierce assault upon the palace, loyal units overcame the rebellion. The integralistas' defeat marked the exclusion of the last group within the military capable of challenging the power of either Vargas or Dutra.[1]

The Estado Novo was a quasi-military regime. Vargas relied on the army as the key pillar of his government. His administration used terror to silence public dissent, particularly any criticism of the army. He also carried out army-supported policies that dampened regional sentiment and strengthened industrial interests. Vargas's right hand man, Gen. Eurico Gaspar Dutra, had firm control over the army. No longer could officers readily conspire against the army's leadership. This unity bolstered the army's authority. The army's presence within the state expanded rapidly, as officers filled many posts that were not strictly military. With its old enemies neutralized, the army rethought its role.

Anticommunism was a powerful strain in military thought. The Brazilian state had fostered anticommunist sentiments since the 1920s.[2] In the aftermath of the 1935 uprising within the armed forces, army leaders had seized upon anticommunism as a means to legitimate policies they desired. Yet the military's ideology during the 1930s and early 1940s could not be characterized by anticommunism alone. The army's main concern was the maintenance of the hierarchy and the exclusion of the military from political conflict. Thus leaders such as General Góes Monteiro worried about the influence of the floristas (followers of Flores da Cunha) as the main threat to the army, while other commanders feared the power of the integralistas. The government had smashed the Communist Party, and in a climate of political terror its influence was limited. Moreover, some senior generals clearly understood that the Cohen plan was a forgery. When Eurico Gaspar Dutra declared the foundation of the Estado Novo in a proclamation to the army on November 10, 1937, he made no reference to communism.[3] Brazilian officers founded the Estado Novo to protect the army from an array of opponents, of which the communists were not necessarily the most powerful. In the aftermath of the coup anticommunism proved a useful tool to rally civilian support. However, anticommunism was a negative philosophy which did not provide a clear program for the army's role in development and defense. In later years, officers throughout Latin America would develop a far more sophisticated vision of anticommunism called National Security Ideology, which would fill this intellectual gap. But during the 1930s the Brazilian army looked to another doctrine then powerful in Latin America to define the army's role in society.

The Argentine Ideal of Defense

After World War I, many Latin American officers reconsidered the meaning of defense. Rapid industrialization altered not only national economies, but also the character of warfare. Technological advances meant that no nation could prosper without adequate supplies of petroleum, steel, and similar industrial goods. Officers feared that these trends made their nations even more dependent on major world powers. In Argentina, many officers argued that the nation was threatened less by foreign armies than by the economic dominance of international trusts.[4] Standard Oil, for example, could have strangled both industry and the military by halting petroleum sales. The head of the Argentine army engineers, General Mosconi, frequently told Brazilian officers of his experience in an air force regiment. His unit had been late paying its fuel bill, and a foreign oil company then halted a military exercise by refusing to sell further fuel to the air force. Even if apocryphal this story symbolized officers' fears, and it became known far outside Argentina.[5] These concerns encouraged first the Argentine military (and later other Latin American forces) to adopt a particular vision of defense and development.

This particular vision of defense defined the main threat to the Argentine nation as the imperialism of the foreign nations. This imperialism was as much economic as political, for these powers kept Argentina in a state of dependency. To defeat this challenge the state had to develop key sectors of the economy in order to reduce the reliance of Argentina and its military on foreign powers. What use were pilots without foreign-made planes? And what good were planes without the fuel to fly them? Security and development were inextricably linked.[6] This belief quickly came to shape Argentine military policy. The engineering corps advocated state intervention in the economy to free the nation from its state of dependency. General Mosconi became the head of the state oil company, a position he viewed as a means to defeat the power of foreign trusts. International trends in the 1930s made Mosconi's program appear attractive to officers in other Latin American militaries.[7]

Many Latin American officers worried about the renewed danger of imperialism, embodied in the policies of Germany, Italy, and Japan. Yet this fear was also shaped by South America's past experience with the British Empire, which led most commanders to believe that imperial powers were as likely to act through economic intimidation as armed force. Because warfare had come to rely upon technology, South American armies depended upon developed countries for the arms they needed. In this situation, many officers pressured for state-led industrialization in order to make the nation self-sufficient in case of war. Equally important, officers desired to make their nation independent by enabling it to create the key products controlled by developed nations. Military interests encouraged officers to adopt Mosconi's program.[8]

The 1930s also presented Latin American armies with a brief window of opportunity during which they could adopt these policies without severe retribution. With the onset of the Great Depression, liberalism lost its legitimacy as an economic and political philosophy. The economic crisis forced the state to intervene in the economy in developed countries, which made it more difficult for major powers to condemn state intervention in Latin American economies. Moreover, the growing strength of the Axis powers encouraged the United States and Britain to seek allies in Latin America. For a brief period, these two countries proved less beholden to private interests than to the demands of national security. Not only did Mosconi's program prove attractive to officers in many Latin American countries, the international context made it appear feasible.

The military in Latin American countries such as Argentina and Uruguay encouraged a state role in development. In Bolivia the military government expropriated Standard Oil's holdings and created a government owned corporation "modeled on the already famous state corporation in Argentina."[9] But as John Wirth has argued, no military adopted Mosconi's ideas with greater enthusiasm than Brazil's.[10] The army created an intricate bureaucracy that dominated the steel and petroleum industries. The Brazilian general staff created economic plans that Vargas's government promulgated. General João Mendonça Lima was Vargas's minister of transport and had to oversee Brazilian railroads. Army officers served in a host of government regulatory agencies, such as the Foreign Trade Council (CFCE), which was completed dominated by the military. The CFCE's special commission on steel was led by Gen. Amaro Soares Bittencourt and Adm. Ary Parreiras. The army also shaped the transportation, electrical, and mining sectors of the economy.[11] Its concern with development involved the army in an enduring manner in what had once been civilian affairs. As late as 1951, six generals and seventy-nine officers were serving in "civilian capacities."[12] From the 1930s to the 1950s there was extensive militarization of public administration in Brazil.

Brazil's Adoption of a New Military Role

Numerous academics have studied how Brazil's army became involved in state-led development.[13] Some authors have argued that the army adopted a civilian ideology. Other specialists have argued that the army created the program to meet strictly institutional interests. Thus John Wirth argued that the Brazilian military followed an ambitious policy of economic nationalism, while Edmundo Campos Coelho believed that the army mainly wished to produce needed weaponry.[14] All scholars have had difficulty defining the military's program because the armed forces never organized it into a coherent ideology.[15] A military ideology is a system of thought that pervades the entire institution, defines the military's mission, is taught in a systematic fashion to officers, has a paper or journal that expounds it, can be organized into a coherent program, and is supported by the hierarchy. Because the Brazilian army's new role emerged more as a convergence of interests than as a product of struggle, no faction was ever compelled to articulate it in a persuasive fashion. The Brazilian army adopted this approach to defense because it met the interests of different groups within the armed forces, rather than because of a process of intellectual persuasion.

The military's new role emerged as a consensus among many military factions, which used a common program for different ends. For example, the army's high leadership liked equating security with development. Doing so allowed a wide range of issues to be considered military concerns, and this definition of defense expanded the army's influence within the state. It also legitimated favorite military policies such as centralization, nationalism, and industrialization.[16] The latter policy particularly concerned high commanders, who believed that they could never create a strong army in a weak state.[17] Industrial development formed a prerequisite for military success. Finally, leaders such as Eurico Gaspar Dutra and Góes Monteiro wished to rally the army around a national project to unite the army so that it presented a united front to civilian society, regardless of the program's details. This meant that army leaders welcomed a military role in development less from a doctrinaire approach to economic growth than from a pragmatic calculation of military interests.

The people who proved to be the chief intellectual proponents of the military's new mission were the army engineers.[18] These officers were influenced by their peers in Argentina, where the army had been involved in national development for over a decade. This new role promised not only to increase engineers' influence within the military but also to give them positions commanding state industries. However, engineers turned to this program less from corporate interests than from ideological affinity. Army engineers had long been influenced by positivism, a French doctrine that described war as an irrational enterprise that humanity would abandon after scientific advancement. These beliefs attracted many engineers, such as Gen. Júlio Caetano Horta Barbosa, to a nonviolent mission in development.[19] Horta Barbosa was the director of the army engineers in 1936, when General Góes Monteiro chose him to be subchief of the army general staff. From this position he advocated the army's involvement in economic development. The difference between the engineers and the general staff lay in the fact that for the army leadership, such as Góes Monteiro, the role was the means to an end, a way to create a united military with its own arms supply. For the army engineers, industrialization became an end in itself—the emancipation of the nation from "economic imperialism."

Although some tenentes had not favored the establishment of the Estado Novo, they continued to hold a measure of power within the new regime. An army role in development attracted these officers because it promised to increase the power of technocrats. Because of their distaste for politics, which they associated with regional elites, the tenentes had proposed changes to limit politicians' power. In particular, the October 3 Club (as mentioned in the last chapter, the tenentes had created this organization with their allies to construct a program for the 1930 revolution) had debated creating a "technical council" with the power to veto some of the executive's acts. In addition, the club had proposed dividing the legislature between two bodies, a technical chamber and a "professional" chamber, to be dominated by politicians. Only the technical chamber would have been able to decide upon technical matters. The technical representatives were to be appointed by "recognized class organs," such as the Engineering Club.[20] The tenentes failed to gain support for their proposals in the early 1930s, but the engineers' program seemed to accomplish many of the same goals by guaranteeing a technocratic approach to development.

Finally, the remaining integralistas still had influence, even after Vargas banned their party. The Green Shirts dreamed of "a utopia in which Brazil would be independent of the hegemonic nationalist powers."[21] Their fear of economic imperialism gave them a xenophobic hatred of Britain, and the term they used for their ideology implied Brazilian resistance to foreign powers. The integralistas also wished to increase the central state's power so as to enable it to eliminate the political interests and economic parties that divided society. These officers favored involving the army in state-led development as a means not only to limit foreign influence, but also to increase the state's authority.

From this perspective, this doctrine emerged not only due to the influence of foreign military leaders but also to a confluence of interests within the Brazilian army itself.[22] All these factions could unite around this program because it promised to increase the army's power. It built upon the old idea of the military as the nation's savior in such a manner that a wide array of opponents could be defined as the enemy: corrupt politicians, foreign trusts, or disloyal capitalists. It blurred the line between internal security and external defense, so that the armed forces could justify a role in previously internal affairs.[23] At a time when the military had captured considerable power within the political system, it also promised to increase the military's power within the economy.

This ideology also had a number of contradictions that would later shape the army's internal conflicts. At the time, nationalism was a political tool of Brazilian elites who used it not only to advocate industrialization but also to criticize the working class.[24] Populist politicians and the political left had not yet adopted it as a discourse to advance their policies. As army officers adopted a role in development, their discourse became increasingly xenophobic. Nationalism was not only a powerful belief that many officers held but also a tool that some commanders pragmatically adopted to justify military interests. They believed that a nationalist program of development could increase the military's authority by involving the army in state enterprises. There were also contradictions within the nationalist philosophies of certain officers. For example, positivist engineers (like General Horta Barbosa) despised nationalism as a political philosophy but used nationalist rhetoric to support state-led development. Many officers were sincere nationalists. But the contradictory or calculated nationalism of some army leaders helps to explain later changes within military thought, as individual officers known for their nationalism seemed to take antinationalist positions.[25]

The army's perception of its interests shaped its adoption of this new role. In the early 1930s the ideal of national development had not been important within the armed forces. Horta Barbosa had not opposed land concessions to foreign corporations as a means to develop the steel industry. Although the military had wanted to develop war materials, it had not envisioned a larger role for itself defending the national economy. Yet after the 1935 rebellion a vision of state-led development soon shaped military planning. Military studies began to criticize the power of "foreign trusts" in key sectors of the economy. During his term as the head of the general staff, from March 1936 to May 1937, Gen. Arnaldo de Souz Paes de Andrade described the army's duty: "We must not delude ourselves because, observing Brazil's political life, the army alone represents the profound sentiment of national cohesion. Working for the solution of the great national problems (steel, fuel, etc.) the General Staff tries to contest for our economic emancipation, the only means for us to have an efficient armed forces."[26] After the foundation of the Estado Novo, the popularity of this sentiment fostered military unity.

Even officers who opposed the coup, such as Horta Barbosa, reconciled themselves to the Estado Novo because it not only strengthened the army but also gave the military the tools to regulate development. The 1937 Brazilian constitution created the means for the state to intervene in development through the Council of the National Economy.[27] The government had already created a number of "defense institutes" to organize economic activities, such as the Federal Council of Foreign Commerce. The government greatly augmented the power of these bodies after the coup.[28] And new agencies appeared to regulate the economy, such as the National Council of Waters and Electric Energy, the National Council of Mines and Metallurgy, and the National Council of Industrial and Commercial Policy. A complex web of government organizations came to dominate key sectors of Brazil's economy. By managing this bureaucracy the military largely controlled the section of the state that controlled development.

The Military and Petroleum

The relationship between these organizations and the army can be seen from one key example, that of the National Petroleum Council. South American militaries had long worried about their nation's petroleum supply because it was essential both to modern warfare and civilian industry. Its production was controlled by a small group of powerful corporations, such as Standard Oil, which had an unpleasant reputation in Latin America. The petroleum trusts often worked closely with their home countries of Britain and the United States which upheld their business interests.[29] During the 1930s there was a glut of petroleum upon the world market; thus companies were discouraged from finding new reserves. Many officers believed that corporate interests did not match their national needs.

Army engineers had worked to address this concern in military policy even before the establishment of the Estado Novo. In January 1936 Horta Barbosa wrote the minister of war, Eurico Gaspar Dutra, a memo describing the danger that foreign trusts posed to Brazil. Because modern warfare depended upon fuel, Horta Barbosa argued that Brazil had to free itself from its dependency upon the petroleum corporations. He asked that the army participate in petroleum exploration.[30] After the foundation of the Estado Novo, Góes Monteiro chose Horta Barbosa to be second-in-command of the general staff. From this position, Horta Barbosa worked to gain the support of Dutra and Góes Monteiro for his ideas.[31] As war approached in 1938, Brazil had a fuel supply sufficient for only a few days of ordinary usage. Horta Barbosa managed to persuade Dutra and Góes Monteiro that the army had to take steps to defend Brazil's economy. Once their backing was assured, Horta Barbosa used their authority to force the civilian bureaucracy to advocate creating an agency to regulate petroleum development.[32]

On April 29, 1938, the government created the National Petroleum Council (CNP) based on Argentine legislation.[33] Góes Monteiro had approved the decree creating this organization without even reading it. This organization had ample powers to regulate all aspects of the petroleum industry, and its charter guaranteed that the Brazilian military controlled it. The CNP's leadership was composed of a president and eight councillors, with one representative for each branch of the armed forces. The councillors acting for the navy and the army (though not the air force) had the right to appeal decisions to the president, if they believed that national security was involved. Effectively, this regulation gave the armed forces control over the organization, but the military's dominance of the CNP was guaranteed less by legislation than by political practice. General Horta Barbosa became the organization's first president, which set a lasting precedent. Capt. Ibá Meirelles became his chief of cabinet. According to Col. Artur Levy, a member of the council during this period, the military's privileged position meant that officers never needed to use their veto. Organized as a "special organ of the Presidency," the CNP remained under military control.[34] Through the creation of similar state agencies, the army managed Brazilian development during the Estado Novo in accord with its new vision of its role. The Brazilian armed forces shaped not only the political system, but also key sectors of the Brazilian economy.

Unintended Consequences

This effort had a number of unexpected effects upon the military as an institution. Since the foundation of the Old Republic, the government had ensured the loyalty of key officers by turning a blind eye to their malfeasance. While widespread, military corruption had generally involved the wrongdoing of isolated commanders who used their authority to misuse military funds and supplies in a way that bound the army to the administration. With the army's involvement in economic development, however, new opportunities for thievery and fraud presented themselves. Army officers now had control over far greater financial resources, so corruption tended to involve networks of officers, who used their control over the state for financial benefit. Graft allowed powerful officers to build followings within the institution. Corruption reached the highest levels of the armed forces; in the 1940s it involved even the minister of war, Gen. Canrobert Pereira da Costa. During the censorship of the Estado Novo, this corruption remained concealed, and records of its existence only survive in sources such as officer's diaries. With the end of authoritarian rule, however, the military would be swamped by scandals that had their origin in the army's newfound economic power.[35]

The army's involvement in economic development also led it to form new ties with groups in civilian society. While in the past corruption had bound the army to the government, during the Estado Novo army officers formed ties with conservative businessmen. (After the return to democracy in 1945, many of these civilian allies would prove harshly critical of subsequent governments.) Now officers were linked to the regime's opponents, but officers did not only form alliances because of corruption. In their new posts they created bonds with civilian bureaucrats, local entrepreneurs, foreign diplomats, and state leaders. These ties later shaped military politics.

The International Context

The military was also affected by changing international pressures. Brazil's army, like those of other South American countries, adopted a role in economic defense at a uniquely favorable time in terms of international affairs. Yet the approaching threat of war changed this situation even as the army increased its control over the Brazilian economy. Some army leaders had the foresight to see this problem. In a memo written in December 1936, General Góes Monteiro stated that Brazil could not remain neutral in the event of war. He argued that Brazil would lose its political independence as it came to rely on the only power able to meet its needs, the United States. He reiterated this belief in a secret memorandum he sent to General Dutra, the minister of war, on September 23, 1939. Planned arms purchases from Germany were unrealistic, Góes Monteiro argued. Only the United States had the funds, expertise, and weaponry to meet Brazil's requirements. Dutra ignored his arguments, only to be infuriated when the British intercepted German arms shipped to Brazil during the war.[36]

Brazil became a target of U.S. influence because the Allies could not afford to let Brazil remain neutral during the conflict. As Hitler overran Europe, the U.S. army became concerned by the strategic position of Brazil's northeast. If the western hemisphere faced an extracontinental invasion, U.S. planners believed that Brazil was the logical place for an attack because of its proximity to French West Africa. In 1940 this incredible scenario appeared plausible to U.S. officers, who feared that Germany might soon conquer England. Brazil's coastal defenses were pitiful. On President Franklin Roosevelt's orders, the U.S. army drew up plans in May 1940 to rush 100,000 men to the Brazilian coast. The United States also studied how to acquire Brazil's strategic materials, to create air bases in the northeast, and to patrol the South Atlantic. To prepare for war, the United States required Brazil's cooperation.[37]

Brazilian officers had no interest in a national alliance with either Britain or the United States, which many perceived as the main dangers to Brazil's economic independence. At a social gathering in 1940, some of General Dutra's staff officers argued that a British defeat would further Brazilian interests because England had kept Brazil as a virtual colony.[38] General Góes Monteiro spoke critically of those officers who wished to ally with Britain (as opposed to Germany) saying that they preferred "the 'British slavery' because they consider it to be more agreeable and only economic and they have already experienced it."[39] When a Brazilian newspaper ran an advertisement in January 1941 that stressed Britain's ties with Brazil, Góes Monteiro and Dutra unsuccessfully pressured President Vargas to suspend its publication. The newspaper had earlier refused to run anti-British articles as the army requested.[40] Many officers in the army had an equal dislike for the United States. Dutra argued that the United States treated Brazil like an "Asian possession" as it attempted to force the nation to take part in hemispheric defense: "They want, under the appearance of an alliance, dominion."[41] Even after Brazil declared war on Germany in August 1942, Dutra continued to speak of the danger of the "voracious interests of foreign capitalism, allied to the imperialism of its governments, and the impatriotism of many of our countrymen."[42] The army's role in economic defense led it to view the Anglo-American alliance as the greatest threat to Brazil.

State department analysts in the United States clearly understood why Brazil's army had anti-American sentiments. These officers cautioned that senior Brazilian officers were not "pro-Nazi." Instead, U.S. analysts stressed the nationalist character of officers' thought and the tendency to equate the army's needs with those of the nation. Brazilian officers particularly feared the economic power of the United States and Britain "as much as, if not more than, domination by Axis powers."[43] U.S. analysts believed that the United States had to address economic concerns to gain support within the Brazilian military: "If the Brazilian army could be given clear-cut evidence of the German invasion or even that German economic domination would be more detrimental to Brazil than economic domination by Britain and the United States, then the attitude of the army . . . might change rapidly."[44] The United States began a calculated effort to persuade Brazil that its interests lay in a U.S.–Brazilian alliance.

An authoritarian ruler, President Vargas did not have a powerful ideological bond with the major Western democracies. He had made some sympathetic overtures to the Axis powers, but wished to remain neutral in the war. A shrewd politician, however, he soon seized upon the advantages that the U.S. need for support presented. Vargas wished to make a deal. Brazil would contribute to hemispheric defense if the United States would fund Brazilian development. For Vargas, the key to national development was a major steel mill to provide an essential resource for modern industry. The United States proved reluctant to make the major investments that Vargas requested. Disappointed, in June 1940, Vargas gave a speech stating that Brazil might have to look to "strong nations" to promote its industrialization. Washington changed its terms, and in September 1940 the two nations signed an accord to create a major steel-production facility called Volta Redonda. Over the following two years similar negotiations continued between Brazil and the

United States, as Vargas acquired U.S. resources for Brazilian development.[45]

The army did not favor Vargas's bargain. Powerful army leaders (such as General Góes Monteiro, General Dutra, Gen. Canrobert Pereira da Costa, and Gen. Euclydes Zenóbio da Costa) opposed any alliance with Britain and the United States.[46] When Dutra and his family heard that Paris had fallen to the Germans, they cheered. As Gen. Nelson de Mello stated many years later: "The hierarchy of the army was Germanophile. There is no debating this."[47] Yet officers soon found that the army gained significant rewards from the Vargas's alliance.

In the short-term, the U.S.-Brazilian alliance may have actually reinforced the army's role in development. The army benefited from U.S. funding for a major Brazilian steel mill. Many generals even envied Col. Macedo Soares, who headed this project, because he had more men under his command than they did. So many army engineers went to Volta Redonda that students in the army engineering school feared that they would lack professors.[48] Nonetheless, the United States shaped the army's developmental project. The Brazilian government not only found its political decisions constrained, as General Góes Monteiro had warned, but also found its economic independence limited. The army had formed its role largely to defend against U.S. and English influence, but it could develop the steel industry in a "nationalist" fashion only as part of a bargain with the United States. This same agreement may have doomed Horta Barbosa's dream to create a state petroleum refinery. During the war, the United States alone had the cash to fund this investment, but Vargas had to choose between steel and petroleum because the United States could not afford to fund both industries.[49] Horta Barbosa's planned refinery, the key to his plans to develop the entire industry, was never built.

The military learned that to create the industrial base necessary to free the nation from its reliance on foreign powers, it required both the capital and the technology of developed nations. As quickly as Brazil developed its war industry, technological changes and military expansion outdated its factories. The policy of import-substitute industrialization continued, but the country also took advantage of the huge U.S. demand for Brazilian raw materials. Although Brazil used these exports as a bargaining tool, international trends no longer allowed it to follow a policy of economic nationalism without retribution. Brazil faced intense pressures to gear its economic development to meet the needs of the United States. The army as a whole did not abandon its policy of state-led development. But some army leaders, who had adopted this policy for pragmatic reasons, began to turn away from policies they had earlier advocated.[50]

Wartime constraints illustrated the limitations of Brazil's economic independence. The CNP found it difficult to meet Brazil's petroleum needs, and gasoline rationing began in April 1942. The military worried that submarine warfare might block oil tankers from reaching Brazil. By July 1942 the shortage of petroleum had become so severe that the largest concrete company in Brazil threatened to stop production because it lacked fuel. The government had to consider turning to Argentina to ensure its concrete supply.[51] The cost of living rose quickly during the war, creating popular discontent, and the shortage of petroleum was one factor blamed for this problem. Army leaders saw that their policies had not overcome Brazil's developmental challenges. In November 1942 General Góes Monteiro argued that if he calculated Brazil's development against that of other nations, Brazil was actually losing ground.[52]

Brazil's Participation in the War

Despite these concerns, Vargas was pleased with the United States' economic support. In May 1942 Vargas signed a military agreement with the United States, allowing it to use air bases in northeast Brazil. Although this document remained secret, Brazilian support for the allied war effort became obvious. German U-boats launched savage attacks against Brazilian shipping. These losses, combined with popular sentiment, encouraged Vargas's decision to declare war upon the Axis in August 1942. He had already made the decision that led to Brazil's participation in the war months earlier. After the United States had entered the war late in 1941, Vargas believed that the Allies would emerge victorious. Their victory threatened to destroy his own authoritarian regime unless he joined their cause. His advisors believed that by participating in the war, Brazil could increase its power within South America. Furthermore, the army reluctantly overcame its fear of economic imperialism because only the United States could supply both arms for the troops and the goods needed to develop the nation.[53] The most powerful groups within Brazilian politics believed that Brazil would benefit by participating in the war.

Vargas intended to seal his wartime alliance with the United States by sending Brazilian troops to fight in Europe. To accomplish this Vargas had to overcome opposition from the Brazilian public and the British government (which believed that resources devoted to equipping Brazilian forces would be better spent on U.S. troops).[54] More importantly, by 1942 Vargas defeated opposition within the army, which reluctantly agreed to plan for an expeditionary force (Força Expedicionária Brasileira or FEB) to fight Germany. By this time, the army realized that Germany's defeat was inevitable, and officers wished to favor the winning side.[55] Even so, Minister of War Dutra had to organize the FEB with little support from the general staff (Estado Maior do

Exército), whose commander, General Góes Monteiro, remained staunchly opposed to creating this force. Dutra himself showed little enthusiasm for the project and even delayed creating the FEB, perhaps hoping that the war would end before Brazilian troops could depart. As late as the end of 1943, it appeared that Brazilian troops would never serve overseas.[56]

Besides the hostility of these high-level commanders, there were other factors that led to the long delay in the creation of the FEB. Both Vargas and the army were worried about the political implications of this new organization, and many officers did not wish to join.[57] As in every war, however, there were some officers (such as Brigadier Gen. Oswaldo Cordeiro de Farias, who became the commander of the FEB's artillery) who volunteered in the hope of furthering their ambitions.[58] Accordingly, Dutra and Góes Monteiro carefully scrutinized all selected officers to ensure that no communists joined the expedition and that no rivals would profit from a commission within this glamorous new force.[59]

The potential benefits from participating in the FEB were such that despite his initial opposition to its creation, Dutra eventually campaigned to enhance and ensure his authority by personally leading the FEB. His fellow officers, however, tried to persuade him that Vargas was plotting to remove him from the country.[60] This argument may have swayed Dutra to remain in Brazil, but the fact that the FEB was to be smaller than initially planned was probably a more important reason. In August 1943, Dutra agreed to appoint Gen. João Batista Mascarenhas de Morais to lead the FEB. Mascarenhas was selected because he was Vargas's friend, a competent officer, and a terrible politician. Given his lack of political ambition and charisma, neither the president nor military leaders feared his future influence.[61]

Nevertheless, Dutra left little to chance and acted carefully to curtail Mascarenhas's power; for example, he ensured that Mascarenhas did not select the men he took with him. Dutra exercised that power, and he chose men for their loyalty to himself and the government, not their ability. The chief of Vargas's coterie of military advisors later alleged that the most capable officers never joined the FEB.[62] This assertion was probably unjust, but it pointed to the importance placed on political loyalty when Dutra selected the officers to go to Europe. Ricardo Banalume Neto has argued that Vargas's government forced some opponents into the FEB.[63] Yet the president also kept military opponents from leaving the country to prevent them from gaining prestige in combat. These political machinations and the conflicting interests of the men responsible for creating the FEB shaped its character and contributed to the tension that later developed between the ideals its soldiers professed and the policies its commanders advocated.[64]

On July 2, 1944, the FEB finally set sail for Italy. Ever since, the Brazilian army has celebrated the fact that 25,000 soldiers fought the German army in Italy. Countless works by Brazilian officers have emphasized the expedition's military successes and its friendship with the United States.[65] According to Brazilian officers, this experience led the FEB to adopt democratic and liberal ideals, which they acquired from their contact with U.S. troops in Italy. Historians have generally agreed that the FEB had a profound impact on the Brazilian army.[66] Many authors have argued that these sentiments contributed to Vargas's downfall in 1945.[67] Scholars have also invoked the FEB to explain not only the collapse of the Estado Novo but also the coup of 1964 and the military regime that followed.[68] That is, the FEB's democratic and liberal ideals supposedly laid the basis for the end of Brazilian democracy, as well as the authoritarian regime and political terror that followed. The best authors in the field (Frank McCann and Alfred Stepan) have emphasized the "liberal" and internationalist ideals of the FEB, but the FEB never played the role ascribed to it by these specialists.

The FEB serves as a cautionary tale that illustrates the continuing influence that South American militaries have over their own memory. In this case, the high command promulgated a historical myth in its own interests, but this myth had no foundation in fact, which meant that it could be sustained only by the use of terror to silence dissident voices. In reality, the FEB formed a nationalist force sympathetic to Vargas. These officers and soldiers spent years struggling against the army's high command before their political influence was smashed by violence in 1952. In the aftermath of their defeat, the army high command then ascribed its own views to the very men they had repressed, as a means to legitimate their beliefs.[69]

The war experience did not imbue veterans with pro-U.S. and democratic ideals. Regular contact between U.S. and Brazilian forces took place only at the highest levels. Mascarenhas succeeded in limiting the number of American officers communicating with his men. Moreover, not many Brazilian commanders spoke English; nor did members of the two armies engage in ideological discussion. Given the language barrier and infrequent contacts, most officers, let alone soldiers, remained isolated from their U.S. counterparts.[70] United States officers found that Brazilian troops did not meet their expectations, and they voiced their opinions. Some febianos (expedition members), including Col. Floriano de Lima Brayner, chief of the FEB's general staff, resented their dependency on the United States. At times, a sense of animosity between Brazilian and American officers was fed by many small insults to Brazilian pride.[71] As one FEB commander stated (Col. Nelson de Mello, who during the war headed the Sixth Infantry Regiment from Caçapava, São Paulo), the Americans had little influence upon the febianos at all.[72]

Instead, the febianos were shielded from any information that could undermine their loyalty to Vargas's regime. General Mascarenhas strove to keep his troops from participating in any political activity or discussion.[73] Indeed, all but a few high commanders remained ignorant of political events in Brazil, let alone the ideals of American democracy. Most febianos even had to rely on German propaganda broadcasts to learn of events at home.[74] As a result, the FEB remained isolated from a growing political current in Brazil, where democratic rhetoric was undermining Vargas's authority. In Brazil, FEB victories became the excuse for rallies, where civilians denounced their authoritarian government.[75] But there has been a tendency to conflate the rhetoric surrounding the FEB with the thought of its members.[76] The junior officers and soldiers of the FEB never held the prodemocratic and liberal views that historians have ascribed to them. Such views might have led them to challenge the Vargas regime; instead, they remained politically disengaged.

Military opposition to the Estado Novo and its founders began within Brazil. There had doubtless been some earlier plotting among old tenentes such as Juraci Magalhães. Nonetheless, these military conspiracies were neither serious nor effective. Only in late 1944 did important opposition to Dutra's control appear, as the case of the Military Club demonstrated. The Military Club was a social organization of officers with a long history of opposition to the government. An elected body within a hierarchical institution, its elections allowed officers to challenge the army's leadership. During the 1930s, Góes Monteiro and Dutra both served as presidents of the club. After the foundation of the Estado Novo, candidates tightly linked to these leaders continued to control the institution. But in 1944 a commission of officers asked Gen. José Pessoa to run for the club's presidency. Pessoa loathed both Góes Monteiro and Dutra, as all officers knew.[77] By approaching Pessoa, this committee openly challenged the army hierarchy. With the aid of his former students at a military school, Pessoa won the election. His victory symbolized the growing resistance within the military to both the Estado Novo and the officers who had created it.[78] This situation posed a dangerous threat to Vargas.

The Veterans' Return

Vargas did not have to fear the return of the FEB. Alzira Vargas, the president's daughter, has claimed that accounts depicting the FEB as part of a "wave of democracy" were nonsense. Instead, the return of the FEB bolstered Vargas's popularity; he even viewed the force as a means to prop up his regime.[79] From July to October 1945 there was immense excitement as thousands of Brazilians turned out to greet the returning troops. As General Góes Monteiro noted, Vargas made a point of welcoming all the febianos in mass parades designed to build support for his regime. Vargas's military allies seized upon these rallies to make pro-Vargas statements that frightened their fellow officers. According to Nero Moura, a pro-Vargas officer who served in the Brazilian air force in Italy, army leaders such as Dutra and Góes Monteiro feared that Vargas might use the FEB to retain power. For this reason, Moura argued, these leaders disbanded the FEB.[80]

Senior commanders (such as General Góes Monteiro and Gen. Valentim Benício da Silva) also worried about communist infiltration of the armed forces, a concern that shaped how powerful generals viewed the FEB.[81] Despite Dutra's efforts, he had failed to create a staunchly anticommunist force. Communists had joined the FEB to fight against the Soviet Union's enemies.[82] In Italy the febianos had begun a fund-raising campaign to aid the daughter of the imprisoned communist leader Luís Carlos Prestes.[83] Upon their return, a minority of febianos also threw their support to the Communist Party. According to a secret report prepared by the Brazilian Ministry of War, the communists enjoyed great success in recruiting FEB officers to their cause. The report argued that the FEB should be disbanded as rapidly as possible: "And the more rapidly the demobilization is made, the more efficient will be the results obtained from this fitting and opportune recommendation."[84] The report also warned that the communists were receiving armament from returning soldiers. The FEB's leaders did what they could to stop the loss of this weaponry, with little success: "We know that wherever [Communist] meetings take place there is hidden armament acquired from veterans. To prevent this arms trade FEB officers decided to inspect the luggage [of returning veterans]. But even so, many arms have entered [Brazil] hidden in vehicles, the equipment of particular army units, etc., and by this means the Communists have even acquired the small machine guns of the S.S."[85] This situation deeply troubled Dutra and Góes Monteiro.

On June 6, 1945, Dutra demobilized the FEB well before the first troop ships arrived back in Rio de Janeiro. He also outlawed "[the formation] of veterans groups, commenting on the campaign, or even reading the poetry the men had written."[86] Army leaders viewed veterans with such distrust that war service was often more of a liability than an asset.[87] A climate of political crisis gripped Brazil at the war's end. In this atmosphere, army commanders did not protest the disbanding of the FEB despite powerful military reasons to maintain it as a fighting force.[88] Most of the FEB's members then returned to their professional tasks and abstained from military politics.[89] It would be inaccurate to say that the FEB returned with democratic ideals that undermined the Estado Novo. Instead, the Brazilian army reconsidered both its support for the Estado Novo and its role in development because of social and geopolitical change.

The Army Reconsiders Development

Even before the departure of the FEB, the army's leadership had weakened its commitment to economic defense. In 1942 the minister of agriculture had approached Vargas about altering Brazil's petroleum policy. These pressures forced Horta Barbosa to resign on July 30, 1943. Vargas replaced him as the head of the CNP with Gen. João Barreto, who believed that the door to foreign investment had to be left open for pragmatic reasons.[90] As the war continued, senior army leaders wondered if the army could benefit more from cooperation with the United States than from continued reliance on state involvement in the economy.

The army's changing perception of its interests became clear in a series of secret meetings held between August 10 and late October 1945.[91] On August 9, the day before the first meeting, Góes Monteiro returned to his old post as minister of war. Upon this occasion, Góes Monteiro gave a speech in which he argued that the army had to integrate itself into a system of continental defense. This role, he stated, had replaced the old ideal of national security. In his first meeting with the generals, Góes Monteiro built upon this point. He stated that he wanted to restructure the army in order to adapt it to a return to "constitutional" government. As part of this effort, the army had to respond to the international situation because all the military's hopes to improve itself depended upon the victorious powers, specifically the United States.[92] In a sense, Góes Monteiro's speech fulfilled his earlier prediction that war would make Brazil dependent upon the United States. In the aftermath of the conflict, the United States held unquestioned predominance in the hemisphere. Because of U.S. pressures, at the Chapultepec conference in February and March 1945 Brazil had agreed to accept the principles of Bretton Woods: nondiscrimination against foreign capital, the abolition of restrictive commercial practices, and the elimination of economic nationalism. In the postwar context, the army's older role in economic development had become problematic.[93]

The rhetoric of economic nationalism also changed in a manner that troubled army leaders. Each Thursday throughout the late summer and early fall, the generals met and discussed reform proposals. But their meetings increasingly came to be dominated by discussion of the political situation. With the defeat of the Axis powers, democratic ideals were in ascension throughout the hemisphere. Everyone realized the Estado Novo could not endure. Vargas had promised to allow free and fair elections to take place in December, but the army doubted his commitment.

Vargas had carefully promoted labor legislation during the Estado Novo as a means to gain the support of the urban working class. As his position became increasingly uncertain, Vargas tried to stall political change with social reform. Vargas also began a series of intricate political maneuvers. He reluctantly made General Dutra "his" presidential candidate, while intending to betray him. This move divided the armed forces between two officer candidates because the old tenente Eduardo Gomes had already announced his candidacy. At the same time, Vargas legalized the Communist Party, released its members from jail, and allied himself with Prestes. In return, the communists supported maintaining Vargas in power—and postponing elections—until a constituent assembly could be convened. The army, which collectively and officially remembered the 1935 uprising, believed that Vargas had betrayed it.[94]

The army also began to fear Vargas—and the power of economic nationalism—because of events in Argentina. On October 9, 1945, the Argentine military had arrested Juan Perón, an army officer who had acquired dangerous support outside the armed forces. On October 17, 1945, a massive labor demonstration forced the military to free him. Whether Vargas was influenced by Peron or acted from his own experience, the military perceived him to be following the Argentine path. Economic nationalism had acquired a new connotation throughout the hemisphere. Far from being a tool of the elites, it had become a means of popular mobilization. Whereas nationalist rhetoric had been a means to exclude politics from economic decisions, civilian leaders now used it to politicize developmental choices. The army had an enduring hatred of the Communist Party in the aftermath of the 1935 uprising. The growing power of unions therefore disturbed officers, particularly because (as in many Latin American countries at this time) the Communist Party had many followers among labor leaders. The very real linkages between these groups encouraged officers to conflate the two bodies, which they viewed as demagogic challenges to the state. In allying with them, Vargas seemed to be challenging the army.[95]

These concerns shaped the army's thought as generals discussed the military's role. Powerful army leaders, such as Gen. Heitor Borges and Gen. Cristóvão Barcelos, expressed their concern that the elections take place as planned. The pressures upon the minister of war were so intense that Góes Monterio was sleeping only four hours a night.[96] In this environment, Gen. Newton Cavalcanti presented a proposal to restructure the army so that it could meet its "international commitments." General Góes Monteiro supported his arguments by noting that the army served as an instrument of foreign policy that should support the promises Brazil made at international conferences. At Chapultepec, Góes Monteiro argued, Brazil had accepted a role in hemispheric defense. In addition, Brazil had joined talks about a worldwide system of security while discussing the foundation of the United Nations in San Francisco. Góes Monteiro referred to Brazil's May 1942 agreement with the United States in order to explain his vision of military interests: "We have to maintain, then, our military structures based on this accord . . . and if the peace is broken again, they will have to ask our military cooperation, and we in turn will have to solicit them for our preparation."[97] In essence, Góes Monteiro wished to continue the wartime bargain that Brazil had struck with the United States. The accord that Vargas had forced upon the army, over its fierce opposition, now became the justification to reshape the army's role.

General Newton Cavalcanti made it clear that the army should abandon its old role in economic development. He argued that the army had to remove itself from economic issues: "I judge it indispensable, therefore, to carry out a complete restructuring, because all questions related to industrial and agricultural mobilization are not the work of the Ministry [of War], but rather of the government."[98] Cavalcanti proposed that the government create a ministry of production, independent of the military, to take over this task. Senior generals wished to withdraw the army from its involvement in development.

The international trends that had fostered the armed forces' role in development no longer existed. The military's old fear of imperialism waned with the defeat of the fascist states and Britain's near bankruptcy. At the same time, the renewed influence of the United States meant that South American countries could not expect to follow a policy of economic nationalism without financial and political retribution. The army's experience in steel and petroleum had persuaded some commanders that the state needed outside aid to develop the economy. In the postwar world, only the United States had the funds to help Brazil develop economically. As economic nationalism acquired a new meaning through the hemisphere, the military rethought its old role. Senior officers believed that the United States would continue to need Brazil. They wished to use U.S. interests to obtain what the army and the nation required.[99]

The End of the Vargas Administration

International trends also doomed the Estado Novo. With the exception of two generals, all senior commanders believed that Vargas had to go. Many civilians approached the military to ask the army to end the regime.

Both presidential candidates were soldiers, which ensured that Vargas could not launch another coup like that of 1937. The tenentes backed Eduardo Gomes, while senior army commanders favored Dutra. Even General Góes Monteiro may have had presidential ambitions. On October 26, 1945, the army published a proclamation declaring that the army guaranteed free elections. Getúlio Vargas then committed the inexplicable error of appointing his brother Benjamin Vargas to be the federal district chief of police, Filinto Muller's old post. The army did not learn of this decision until the morning of October 29, 1945. The military's sense of betrayal only made sense in the context of the political paranoia of the time. Some officers seriously believed that Benjamin Vargas might use his position to arrest high generals. The army overthrew Vargas that day.[100]

On October 30, 1945, the National Petroleum Council announced the results of bids to build a private refinery in the federal district, a decision that broke with the state's previous role in economic development.[101] Coming one day after the deposition of Getúlio Vargas, this event symbolized the new trends in the army leadership's thought. But the military as a whole had not changed its role. Although many senior generals wished to forge a new program of continental defense, most officers still believed that the army had to maintain the nation's economic independence. As the army general staff sought to form new ties with the United States and to remove the military from its involvement in the economy, serious tensions began to appear within the institution.

Conclusion

Military factions had changed during the Estado Novo. In 1945 many officers still belonged to factions defined by their allegiance to a powerful general. However, the welter of factions and cliques that had characterized the army during the early 1930s had disappeared. Eurico Gaspar Dutra had become unquestionably the most powerful man in the army. With great skill he had created alliances between different military factions, limited the power of civilians within the army, and created a sense of the military as a class.[102] Under his leadership, officers recovered the allegiance to the army as an institution that the 1930 revolution had destroyed, and many officers associated this sense of loyalty with a program of economic development.

The identity of many officers had become bound to an ideal. The rules of the game had changed for commanders who aspired to positions of power. In order to gain a powerful following, they had to appeal to officers on the basis of ideas, as well as the old ties of region, experience, and blood. But many generals failed to understand how the structures of power had changed within the institution. Before the war, the military had closed itself to society, but by intervening in the economy, it had played a role that ensured unprecedented contact with civilians. As they attempted to redefine the army's role, senior officers found that they could not command their units through the formal lines of authority alone. The fact that the army once again had opened to society made the situation even more dangerous because it allowed for "the emergence and radicalization of factions within the military organization."[103] Military struggles inevitably spread to civilian society and vice-versa. A dangerous period of conflict lay ahead, as ideology became an essential means to control the armed forces.

4

The Struggle over Petroleum
1945–1948

Although the Estado Novo ended in October 1945, the armed forces still retained immense power within the political system. Eurico Gaspar Dutra, the minister of war during the Estado Novo, became the nation's first president. He sought to shape national politics in the army's interests. This task proved to be difficult because the onset of the Cold War placed new limitations on Brazil's economic and political choices. Dutra and the army high command wished to ally their nation with the United States in exchange for developmental aid. Yet most officers disliked this policy and distrusted U.S. influence. For this reason, the question of petroleum development became a controversial issue during Dutra's administration. At stake was Brazil's position in the new Cold War order. As officers reacted to this situation, one military faction rallied civilians behind its program. This effort to challenge the army high command created a dangerous conflict within the military.

The Army's Political Power

Eurico Gaspar Dutra won the presidential elections on December 2, 1945. His presidency ensured that the army retained the influence it had enjoyed during the Estado Novo. Dutra was a powerful, ruthless, and effective leader. His bravery was legendary within the armed forces. Henrique Lott watched Dutra during the São Paulo rebellion in 1932, when he stood in front of terrified troops and yelled, "Advance! Advance! Advance!" Officers believed that during the 1935 uprising, Dutra's aide was shot and killed at his side. When the integralistas attacked the presidential palace in 1938, Dutra came to Vargas's aid with a handful of troops, and continued in command after a bullet grazed his ear.[1] Dutra ensured his authority over the army with equal ruthlessness. He not only removed from key posts those he distrusted, but he also tried to destroy his military opponents.[2] In April 1946 Dutra chose Gen. Canrobert Pereira da Costa to be his new minister of war. Although Canrobert had gained power as a member on the promotions committee from 1943 to 1945, his true authority came from Dutra's trust.[3] Dutra had the solid backing of the army, an important prerequisite for a president who had difficulty giving speeches and rallying public support.[4]

Dutra used his power to reshape Brazil's international relations. As historian Gerson Moura has stated, a new political alliance between Brazil and the United States had become the basis for the elites' hopes to develop the country. But a contradiction existed between the government's alliance with the United States and the nationalist legislation of the Estado Novo. Dutra had long warned about the dangers of U.S. influence. Now, however, Dutra began to liberalize Brazil's economy.[5] In part he did so by ensuring that the constituent assembly adopted clauses he favored. Dutra's political party, the Partido Social Democrático (PSD), and its ally the União Democrática Nacional (UDN) controlled the assembly. The state continued to censor the radio, and journalists remained cautious. The public found it difficult to pressure the assembly. This political environment allowed Dutra to shape the constitution as he desired.

Dutra consulted with the United States about Brazil's constitution. The U.S. chargé d'affaires furnished Dutra with a memo commenting on petroleum policy, and supplied a letter to Brazilian officials examining the clauses in the draft constitution that pertained to foreign investment.[6] In response to U.S. comments, Dutra ensured that the new constitution would permit a more open approach to petroleum development. While earlier laws had stated that petroleum research and production could only be carried out by native Brazilians, the new constitution restricted petroleum development to "companies organized in Brazil." This clause gave U.S. companies a means to participate in petroleum development through Brazilian subsidiaries.

After Brazil adopted its new constitution on September 18, 1948, Dutra used his influence to reshape petroleum legislation. To this end, Dutra appointed a commission to revise petroleum legislation under the leadership of an economic liberal, Odilon Braga. But the real power lay in two parallel commissions that Dutra created, on one of which Gen. Juarez do Nascimento Fernandes Távora served. The army general staff wished to control economic liberalization in order to guarantee that its interests were met. Far from public view, Távora shaped the work of Braga's committee. One member of Braga's commission, Col. Artur Levy, said that Távora met with him regularly to pass on orders: "He did not participate in the meetings, because he had a representative. He called the representative and gave him instructions."[7] Levy stated that he was Távora's spokesman. Through him, Távora (and the general staff) in effect had a veto over the committee's work.[8] The army high command wished to shape petroleum development so as to foster a better relationship with the United States.

The Debate over Petroleum

This effort entailed risks, which Dutra must have understood. As Gerson Moura and other authors have stated, petroleum entailed and embodied the issues that the army faced in the postwar era.[9] The issue of petroleum development embodied the contradiction between the national desire for economic independence and the need for capital and technology to develop the nation. As South American nations had to define their relationship with the United States, petroleum development became a litmus test for a particular set of economic and political relationships. At stake was whether Brazil would ally with the United States to gain developmental advantages or view the United States as the main threat to Brazilian sovereignty. As a canny politician who had demonstrated his ability to balance different currents within the army, Dutra doubtless weighed the implications of his decision. In the end, Dutra had to make some hard choices about internal policies and international relations to achieve his goals. By changing Brazil's nationalist policies he believed that he could forge an alliance that would benefit both Brazil's development and the army. This decision led to a bitter controversy within the army that even Dutra, a subtle and canny ex-general, found difficult to manage.

These military divisions became clear when the Military Club decided to hold a conference on petroleum in 1947. Gen. Juarez Távora acted as the spokesman for the general staff during this debate, as he emphasized: "During the elaboration of the proposed petroleum statute I spoke out on this point with the support of the General Staffs of the Army, the Air Force, and in general [of the armed forces]."[10] Távora's opponents so identified him with the general staff that they often referred to him by his function, rather than by his name.[11] As minister of agriculture in 1934, Távora had introduced a nationalist clause (that made subsoil riches belong to the state) into the constitution. This measure had provided the legal basis for state development of

petroleum. In May 1947, however, Távora argued against the state development of petroleum for pragmatic reasons. He declared that the general staff
did not care how Brazil obtained petroleum, so long as the nation obtained
enough petroleum to ensure its sovereignty in the briefest time possible.[12]
Távora even argued that in theory a state monopoly might be the best approach. But in practice, he said, Brazil lacked the capital to develop its own
resources. The West feared war with the Soviet Union. Brazil had to develop
its petroleum rapidly because the United States might need it to defend the
hemisphere.[13] The Estado Novo's petroleum legislation was the product of a
"rigid and intransigent nationalism."[14] He denounced his critics by referring
to the international situation. The general staff wished to liberalize petroleum
legislation as part of an alliance with the United States.[15]

Nationalist officers turned to General Horta Barbosa as their spokesman.
Horta Barbosa was the former head of the CNP, the former head of the army
engineers, and the former subchief of the general staff, a post he held from
1936 to 1938. If Távora was famous because he had fought as a tenente, Barbosa
commanded respect because he had been wounded while fighting the millenarian movement of Canudos. In a sense, he was a man of another age. John
Wirth describes him in a marvelous passage:

> Horta Barbosa was a respected senior officer whose years of service
> stringing telegraph lines in the Far West under General Cândido Ron-
> don, followed by hard duty on road and rail construction projects, had
> instilled in him a high regard for the Army's role in national integration
> and development. Having been wounded in the Canudos insurrection of
> 1897, and seasoned as a pathfinder, Horta Barbosa was deeply patriotic.
> His qualities of dedication, probity, and quiet competence, for which the
> old Brazilian army was famous, were reinforced by austere personal habits
> (he was a vegetarian) and a belief in the tenets of orthodox positivism. His
> small feet and hands, which moved in an economy of gesture, reinforced
> an impression of precision. Góes Monteiro, the ebullient Chief of Staff,
> liked to say of his taciturn deput: "I talk too much, but Horta talks too
> little."[16]

Horta Barbosa left retirement to enter the petroleum debate.

General Horta Barbosa was a man with influence for several reasons, not
the least of which was the web of kinship ties he enjoyed throughout the
government and the military. Even among well-connected senior officers,
Horta Barbosa's family ties were legendary. Speaking of one government official, Drault Ernanny said: "He has to be a relative of Júlio Caetano Horta
Barbosa, who is from a very large family here. Many members of this family
belong to the Bank of Brazil, many are in high councils, there are others in

Itamarati (the Brazilian foreign service). They are all, in a general manner, people of the first order, of a great tradition."[17] These connections reached into the army where his son, Luíz Augusto de Mattos Horta Barbosa, was a captain. In addition, Horta Barbosa's daughter married the younger brother of Col. Felicíssimo Cardoso, with whom he was allied in the army. These ties gave Horta Barbosa more power than his rank as a retired general might have suggested.

Between July and October 1947, Horta Barbosa gave speeches to the Military Club and other bodies, in which he articulated a powerful vision of economic defense. The development of warfare required radical modifications to national economies. The mechanization of combat entailed state participation in development. France had nearly collapsed from a lack of petroleum during the First World War because private companies had developed the nation's petroleum industry. The French state had been forced to intervene. As the duty to manage the nation's defense fell to the government, so did the duty to manage petroleum. Because modern armies required petroleum, British and U.S. trusts were struggling to control it. Without state aid, he argued, private capital could not defeat foreign trusts.[18] Horta Barbosa continually retold the old story of his Argentine mentor, Henrique Mosconi, whose air wing had been unable to purchase aviation fuel from Standard Oil because of late payments. This anecdote captured the fear of international trusts that characterized Horta Barbosa throughout his career. In later years his distrust of the United States clashed with the pervading anticommunism the Cold War created, but in 1947 his arguments convinced many fellow officers.[19]

Horta Barbosa's arguments evoked such a response within the military because he drew on old ideals long implicit in military planning. It was Horta Barbosa who first articulated a clear program based on these beliefs. His doctrine described the economic imperialism of foreign nations as the main threat to Brazilian sovereignty. It had a vision of Brazil's past, portrayed as a lengthy period of economic dependency, and a program for its future, characterized by state involvement in the economy. This ideology was not only nationalist but also characterized by a mistrust of private initiative. The nationalist officers did not want the economy to be developed by Brazilian entrepreneurs, who might not have at heart the interests of the nation. Rather the state, under the direction of the army, would organize the national economy to ensure national sovereignty defined in the broadest possible sense. A facet of this ideology which became more apparent as the conflict continued was its opposition to any alliance with the United States. Because the United States was the home of the most powerful trusts in the world, officers believed it was in Brazil's interest to remain neutral in international struggles that did not concern Brazil. These ideas were identical to those that Dutra had once promoted. But although other officers had made these points, nobody had united them as convincingly as Horta Barbosa did in 1947.[20]

Each branch of the armed forces responded differently to Horta Barbosa's ideological appeal. The situation in the navy was complicated. Some old integralistas and senior commanders (such as Adm. Juvenal Greenhalgh) supported Horta Barbosa's ideals. Many other naval officers did not. The situation was simpler in the air force, which was more reliant on U.S. technology. Most air force officers wanted an alliance in the United States, although many sergeants sympathized with the nationalists. But the army had the most power of any service, and its officers enthusiastically favored a state monopoly in petroleum. Telegrams poured into Rio de Janeiro from all over Brazil as officers praised Horta Barbosa's speeches. He even received a telegram of congratulations from Argentine army officers, who were pleased to see their ideals adopted by a neighboring military.[21]

The army high command attempted to silence voices of dissent. In July 1947 Dutra had tried to pass legislation that would have let the government retire officers to the reserve at its discretion. The opposition of Gen. José Pessoa—who denounced the proposal in public—ended this effort. But most officers lacked Pessoa's seniority, and army leaders had other means to repress opposition. The general staff pushed some officers into retirement; other officers chose to retire to escape the bonds of discipline and persecution for their views. Those officers who passed to the reserves lacked the power of their peers on active duty. Accordingly, some officers turned to civilians to seek allies to oppose the military hierarchy.[22] This decision gave birth to a popular movement.

The Reaction to the Debate

Nationalist officers could draw on popular distrust of the government as well as resentment toward the United States as they sought to build civilian support for their movement. During the 1930s a children's author and petroleum entrepreneur named Monteiro Lobato had written a series of inflammatory articles accusing the government of concealing Brazil's petroleum reserves from its citizens. People believed him in part because during the 1930s Juarez Távora (then the minister of agriculture) had discounted reports that petroleum had been discovered in the northeastern state of Bahia. Many people also resented the economic and political power of the United States, which led them to favor a nationalist position. In films and music, food and language, the cultural influence of the United States expanded during the 1940s. As Peter Seaborn Smith has stated, a sense of xenophobia drove the petroleum campaign—a reaction against the growing power of the United States.[23] For these reasons, Horta Barbosa's arguments attracted civilian support.

General Horta Barbosa decided to follow the example of Argentina's General Baldritch and created a public movement. The head of Argentina's army engineers during the late 1920s, Baldritch was "an effective public speaker who lectured in theaters, delivered addresses over the radio, and appeared before military groups such as the Naval Officers Club tirelessly repeating that the foreign oil companies endangered the Argentine economy, and were 'mortifying to the national honor.' "[24] In an open political environment, military dissidents in Brazil realized that they also needed civilian support to shape national policy. Commanders in the Military Club sent out "30,000 copies of the conferences of Horta Barbosa to the executive and federal legislature, state and municipal authorities, leaders of the armed forces, the means of mass communications (radio stations, newspapers, and magazines) unions, educators, libraries, etc."[25] Horta Barbosa even sent a copy of his speeches to the minister of war, Gen. Canrobert Pereira da Costa. These efforts succeeded in attracting popular support.

Students in particular responded to Horta Barbosa's appeal, perhaps because of their anti-Americanism. The leader of the Brazilian student's association, Roberto Gusmão, believed that the officers viewed the students' activism as a means to expand their political voice, as a "mega-phone."[26] The students were surprised to find that many army officers were staunch nationalists:

> They sought us out and we felt that they esteemed General Horta Barbosa. They had Colonel Carnaúba; they had other colonels who were also retired, others who were on active service, that they also esteemed. And the military appeared there (at a UNE [União Nacional de Estudantes] meeting), without their uniforms, evidently, and spoke with us, to give us the strength to continue the campaign, stimulating the campaign, and they made themselves public. And the followers of Juarez [Távora] were the minority; we perceived soon that they weren't the majority, although Juarez was a great figure in the army.[27]

Both Horta Barbosa and Juarez Távora spoke at conferences held by UNE, the student's association. Távora, always an authoritarian personality, became angry during the debate; he struck the table so hard that students feared it might break.[28] However, his passion failed to persuade the students, who formed a lasting alliance with Horta Barbosa and his followers. This mass mobilization infuriated the army high command, especially in the context of the early Cold War.

The Cold War and Brazilian Politics

In 1946 the Communist Party was legal, and the head of the party, Luís Carlos Prestes, was a member of Congress. On March 16, 1946, however, the communist journal *Tribuna Popular* quoted Prestes as saying that in the event of a war with Russia, he would organize a guerrilla movement to fight the Brazilian government. His comments made major news as far away as the United States. A wave of anticommunist sentiment swept Brazil, and the government began a systematic campaign to outlaw the Communist Party. Several important Brazilians asked that the party's electoral registration be cancelled. On May 7, 1947, the same month that Távora gave a speech on petroleum to the Military Club, the electoral tribunal revoked the Communist Party's registration. Early in 1948 Juraci Magalhães, a UDN senator from Bahia, asked Prestes in Congress what he would do if Brazil went to war with the Soviet Union. Prestes avoided the question. The next day, the chief of Dutra's military household, Gen. Alcio Souto, and the minister of war, General Canrobert, met with Magalhães to ask him to lead an effort to revoke the mandates of communist congressmen. Magalhães declined because he believed this effort had to be led by the president of the UDN.[29]

In January 1948 Congress revoked the mandates of its communist members. During the debate there were rumors, born of hysteria, that the communists had staged a revolt in the southern state of Rio Grande do Sul. The day of the vote, tensions ran high; most of the congressmen came armed, and the communists flashed their pistols. Magalhães's friends in the UDN had each been assigned a communist congressman to attack if violence began. Magalhães had chosen an old colleague, Gregorio Bezerra, for himself. If one shot had been fired, Magalhães later stated, there would have been a bloodbath. There was a considerable amount of fear until the communists quietly walked out of the building after the vote.[30]

As the government attempted to repress the Communist Party, fierce battles between police and communists raged throughout Brazil. On January 3, 1948, Brazilian police went to a communist newspaper. They told reporters they were searching for arms caches. A fight began, in which more than two hundred shots were fired. Forty people were arrested after a four-hour battle, among them a communist assemblyman. On January 8, the police attempted to close another communist paper, the *Tribuna Popular*. They were met with gunfire. When the police attempted to break down the iron doors, they found that they had been electrified. They gas-bombed the building. Nineteen people were arrested, and ten were injured.[31]

By mid-January of 1948 the violence had become organized. Gregorio Bezerra, a communist ex-congressman, was arrested on charges of sabotage, after the barracks of the Fifteenth Infantry Regiment in João Pessoa burned to the ground. There were reports that the fire had been set by army reservists who had recently completed their training, and the army stated that it had arrested the soldiers who had set the fires. These soldiers were held incommunicado. In April 1948 there were rumors of an impending communist revolt in São Paulo. On April 16, 1948, twenty-six "communists" were arrested after an explosion at the army's Deodoro arsenal, about fifty miles outside of Rio de Janeiro. The blast killed at least twenty-three people, twelve girls were missing at a nearby textile mill, and somewhere between one and two hundred people were injured. The plan, according to the government, had been to kill the minister of war, who had left the plant about fifty minutes before the explosion. The colonel in charge of the depot originally stated that he did not believe that the explosion had been caused by sabotage, but he later changed his mind.[32] Whether communists were responsible for the blast has remained unclear.

The government seized upon these events to justify still harsher repression of the Communist Party. On April 23, 1948, President Dutra asked the Congress for new legislation to fight communism. His argument was bolstered by the governments "discovery" of a plan to blow up oil tanks belonging to U.S. oil companies on Ilha Grande, an island in the bay of Rio de Janeiro. Troops were assigned to guard these properties and that of other foreign firms, such as the Canadian-owned Light and Power Company. Over a thousand people had been arrested in the anticommunist campaign. By April 24, 1948, Prestes had fled once again to Uruguay. The following month the government formed plans to remove communists from government employment. The Communist Party went underground, where it turned to community and neighborhood organizations to survive.[33]

It was in this political context that the government sent the petroleum statute to Congress on February 11, 1948. Although Odilon Braga had played a large role in drafting it, the proposed statute was not a strictly liberal document; it restricted foreign ownership of petroleum companies to 40 percent, it set royalties for petroleum sales at 10 to 14 percent the price of the crude oil extracted, and it permitted petroleum exports only after the internal needs of the country had been satisfied for three years. The latter provision would have effectively barred petroleum exports. Dutra's advisors, the U.S. lawyers Herbert Hoover Jr. and Arthur A. Curtice, said that no U.S. companies would invest in Brazil on such terms. Nonetheless, it outraged nationalist officers who organized a popular protest against this effort.[34]

A Civil-Military Alliance

In response to the proposed statute, the Center for the Study and Defense of Petroleum (CEDP) was founded in April 1948. Because the question of who created the center later became the subject of fierce debate, its early history can be told in detail. A number of groups came together to form this institute, under the aegis of army officers.[35] The idea for the center almost certainly began in the Positivist Club, as Estêvão Leitão de Carvalho has stated. The most prominent members of this body were army officers. On September 5, 1947, the Positivist Club had distributed a manifesto calling for the creation of a commission to organize a national petroleum campaign. Among those who signed this document was the club's president, Alfredo de Morais Filho, a naval commander who had escorted petroleum tankers during World War II. He later became the acting president of CEDP.[36]

The efforts of the Positivist Club merged with the work of another organization, the Anti-Fascist League of Tijuca. The leagues' secretary, an old communist named Henrique Miranda, later stated that this body had formed about three months after the Communist Party was banned. A number of senior army commanders participated in the league, including Gen. Euclides Figueredo (the organization's honorary president), Capt. Antônio José Fernandes e Manuel Melo, and Col. Felicíssimo Cardoso, a director in the Military Club. Both the Positivist Club and the Anti-Fascist League formed committees to study petroleum which advocated creating a state industry. The two organizations united to promote this view. The Military Club, the Positivists' Club, the Anti-Fascist League of Tijuca, and the students' organization, UNE, sponsored a meeting at the Brazilian press association on April 5, 1948. A number of military commanders were present, including Col. Artur Carnaúba, Col. Felicíssimo Cardoso, and Captain Antônio José Fernandes. The latter officer proposed the creation of CEDP, as did Henrique Miranda, to the acclaim of all those present. An engineer named Luíz Hildebrando de B. Horta Barbosa, the general's cousin, became the acting president of the club. Several important Brazilians received telegrams informing them that they had been chosen to be honorary presidents of CEDP. The most important recipient was General Horta Barbosa, who accepted the honor.[37]

Although the club was officially a civil organization, and the vast majority of its members were civilians, CEDP still resembled a paramilitary organization during the initial months of the campaign. The fact that the entire debate over petroleum was framed by the arguments of two officers illustrated how military leaders shaped popular discourse. The impetus for the club's foundation largely came from army officers, acting within the Anti-Fascist League of Tijuca and the Positivists Club. Army officers, such as Gen. Raimundo Sampaio, General Horta Barbosa, and Gen. Estevão Leitão de Carvalho, were its most important honorary presidents. Military men published articles on behalf of the center until early 1949. Col. Artur Levy and Col. Felicíssimo Cardoso were among its most active members. Family connections among officers may have helped to spread the organization. Although they formed only a fraction of the center's membership, the officers had a preponderance of power within the center. In some respects it resembled the October 3 Club, which army officers had used as a forum to discuss policy. A more accurate comparison, however, would be with the Alianza Popular that General Baldritch had founded in Argentina: "Founded to combat foreign—particularly US—imperialism, the Alianza proclaimed its intention to spark a movement throughout Latin America to protect the region's national resources from foreign investors. In fact, however this group composed primarily of students and intellectuals concentrated almost entirely on the Argentine petroleum question."[38] Like its counterpart, the Alianza Popular, the CEDP used nationalist rhetoric to attract civilian support.

The most important civilian to join the campaign was ex-president Artur Bernardes. He spoke about petroleum to officers in the Military Club during the first week in April 1948. When asked to speak, a surprised Bernardes had replied: "But me, in the Military Club?"[39] Yet Bernardes, once the tenentes' main enemy, received a standing ovation. Afterwards, he marched with officers through the streets of Rio de Janeiro to the shock of passersby. Many people in the petroleum campaign had wanted Bernardes to join the movement because, as Henrique Miranda said, he was an "ultra-reactionary" whose presence would end rumors that communists ran the petroleum campaign.[40]

Few politicians were more die-hard nationalists than Bernardes, whose xenophobia bordered on mania. On one occasion, Lobo Carneiro, a petroleum activist and relative of Horta Barbosa, was speaking with Bernardes. The former president began to warn of the dangers of a proposed canal linking the Amazon to the Orinoco river. When Lobo Carneiro stated that he did not see the threat, Bernardes began to scream at him: " 'No, you are completely mistaken! Look our ancestors pushed out our borders'—and here he pushed with his hand all the objects that were on the table, they all fell on the floor— 'thrust out our frontiers to the West and there our frontiers remain in places inaccessible and . . . unhealthy. Brazil has to have its closed frontiers in inaccessible and unhealthy places.' "[41] This paranoia did not prevent Bernardes from being a shrewd politician. According to one officer, Bernardes was convinced that the movement could only succeed with the military's leadership. He met with several officers at his house the night before he announced he was joining CEDP, and only after he had gained their approval did he proceed.[42]

Because of the strong pressures within the military not to participate in the petroleum campaign, officers retired to join the center. While a few officers had already begun to retire to the reserve in 1947, after the foundation of CEDP many officers followed their colleagues' example: "the active-duty military were impeded from participating. And so, as a measure they passed to the reserve—I won't say all, but a great majority, those that defended the national-ist current—there was even a phrase, in a joking tone: 'Pass to the petroleum reserve.' "[43] Another popular saying was that a colonel who retired from active duty became a "General of Petroleum." The number of officers who retired was considerable; by 1951 virtually no officer, of the dozens who had led the petroleum campaign, was on active duty. The future role these men would play was suggested by Estevão Leitao de Carvalho in the preface to the book he wrote on behalf of CEDP, in which he warned that retired officers would never ignore national questions.[44]

Nonetheless, the military hierarchy was reluctant to abandon a policy that it believed was essential to both the nation's development and the army's future. In June 1948 Juarez Távora spoke once again at the Military Club. He began by stating that he spoke on behalf of the general staffs of the armed forces. These branches disagreed with the petroleum statute on three points: they wished for greater restrictions on the export of crude petroleum, they thought the statute was too complicated, and they quibbled with the defini-tion of "public utility." Távora's statements indicated that the hierarchy re-mained committed to achieving its goals. But minor concessions and techni-cal changes could not gain support for the hierarchy's proposals, and Távora likely realized this. During the conference he condemned those who drove the masses to extremes of indignation and who accused their opponents of deliv-ering Brazil to foreigners.[45]

In the meantime, CEDP's organization flourished throughout the country. Its leadership declared June 1948 to be "Petroleum Month." Neighborhood organizations and women's unions quickly spread the movement. The latter groups held endless talks on the subject of petroleum. Most of these bodies were under the leadership of Alice Tibiriçá, whose daughter met and married Henrique Miranda during the campaign. Alice Tibiriçá's aid, and the great energy of her daughter, were important to the movement's success. The CEDP organizers also worked tirelessly to gain the allegiance of the middle and working class. They drew support from across party lines; Matias Olímpio, one of the center's honorary presidents, belonged to the elite-oriented UDN. The center also received support from a key figure in the press, Mattos Pimenta. He used his newspaper, the *Jornal de Debates*, to publicize the CEDP's activities. Indeed, the center operated out of his offices for some time. Municipal government proved to be a key instrument in the spread of the campaign from the industrial heartland to the rural interior. Strangely, CEDP had special success among small farmers in the remotest states. The officers succeeded in creating a truly national drive.

Yet two major groups remained outside of the movement. The officers made only a slight effort to reach out to unions, and it was not sustained. Many members of the working class joined the crusade, but only a few labor leaders committed themselves wholly to this issue. Although the campaign drew members from all parts of society, its leadership was strongly middle class.[46] Longstanding tension between the army and unions may have served to keep the two groups apart at this time. In many respects CEDP resembled a military-dominated political party during this period. But unlike Argentinians under Peron, the officers never formed an enduring alliance with labor leaders.

Equally important, officers failed to reach out to Afro-Brazilians and their organizations. The members of CEDP went to an unending series of rallies, but they did not travel to neighborhood associations in black areas, or incorporate Afro-Brazilian bodies into their movement. José Murilo de Carvalho has sought to explain a political clash between people of color and the army in Brazil during the 1980s by referring to the "internal whitening and the political whitening of the army."[47] Since the 1930s, army policies (such as restrictions on sergeants' promotion to the officers' rank and Dutra's policy of excluding Afro-Brazilians from military schools) had made it more difficult for blacks to enter the officer corps.

It is difficult to document the changing racial makeup of the army. While photographs of military functions during the 1940s and 1950s show officers who overwhelmingly appear to be white, racial categories in Brazil are fluid, and the manner in which people identify themselves is complex. Moreover, it is difficult to tell if different levels of the officer corps were more or less white. This question is still waiting for careful academic study. Still, given the well-documented military policies of the 1930s and 1940s which restricted non-whites from entering the officer corps, José Murilo de Carvalho is likely correct that the army had become more white.

This situation represented a change from circumstances in the army during the First Republic. When Col. Lauro Sodré had plotted his rebellion in 1904, he had been able to cross the divide of race, perhaps partly because the military as a whole had members who were not white. In the 1940s, the military leaders of CEDP were influenced by the "whitening" of the institution and did not reach out to Afro-Brazilians, which weakened their movement.

Even so, the participation of the army was a key reason for CEDP's success. Officers such as Artur Carnaúba and Col. Artur Levy worked tirelessly to spread CEDP's organization. From April to December of 1948, Carnaúba made over forty trips to the Brazilian interior to speak about petroleum. The influence of Horta Barbosa's followers could be seen at the foundation of a branch of CEDP in São Paulo on June 12, 1948. An observer from the American consulate viewed the event: "High ranking army officers have played an important role in the campaign and their active participation appears to be increasing rapidly. The fifth military region was officially represented at the foundation of the 'Centro Paulista de Estudos e Defesa do Petróleo' and speeches by army officers have been featured at all recent meetings."[48] The work of officers in the campaign influenced the entire movement. At the São Paulo meeting observed by the U.S. official, a city councilman stated that Brazil would avoid being drawn into the Cold War by nationalizing its resources.[49] Although a civilian, his speech represented the thought of many nationalist officers.

This rhetoric deeply concerned the military hierarchy, already convinced that communists led the movement. José Pessoa, who perceived himself as a nationalist, resented the communists' participation in the petroleum campaign. Pessoa bitterly described "certain generals in the directory of the Military Club, formerly orthodox positivists and today sympathetic to the Communists with whom they live embraced in our military society."[50] These men, he argued, manipulated the petroleum campaign to meet their political interests. In part, Pessoa's attitude reflected the new meaning nationalism had acquired within the military. Several important commanders distrusted nationalist rhetoric because it fostered popular mobilization that might challenge not only the state but also the army's influence within it. The army's leadership conflated nationalism with communism as a means to challenge new political organizations. As Gerson Moura stated, Dutra's government was marked by a fear of social conflict, always associated in Dutra's mind with communism.[51]

The military hierarchy was correct when it saw a close tie between the petroleum campaign and the Communist Party, as John Wirth has noted. The CEDP grew rapidly in part because it grafted itself onto the Communist Party. Politically isolated and facing government repression, the communists found in the campaign a means to work openly and to form alliances. Although communist leaders did not wish to take part in the struggle, the grass roots of the party ignored them. After petroleum became a major issue, therefore, the Communist Party reversed its prior opposition to a state monopoly in petroleum and joined the campaign. Important communists such as Lobo Carneiro and Henrique Miranda participated in the movement. The latter, with his political skills "knew how to discipline what might other-wise have been a short-lived campaign."[52] He also had contacts within the officer corps. Miranda himself stated that many officers who worked in the campaign were communists. The Communist Party was able to revitalize itself, despite government repression, because it could reach out to disparate groups concerned with petroleum.

Nonetheless, the communists' participation created tensions within CEDP. On July 17, 1948, Mattos Pimenta wrote a letter to Luíz Hildebrando de B. Horta Barbosa, the acting president of CEDP. Pimenta stated that the communists had penetrated the center and were using it for their own ends. Pimenta pointed out that the secretary of CEDP, Henrique Miranda, was a communist, as were most of the secretaries of the center at the state, municipal, and district levels. Pimenta declared that he sympathized with the communists. Nonetheless, he believed that the communists and the noncommunists in the movement had to come to a working arrangement. He wanted to create positions for two secretaries within the organization, one communist and the other noncommunist. He wanted to hold the latter position.

Pimenta had been an important member of CEDP since its inception. His paper, the *Jornal de Debates*, had supported the movement when the mainstream press had not.[53] In 1946 he published an article by Lobo Carneiro which discussed petroleum long before it became a public issue. In April 1948 Pimenta began to include a weekly section in his paper to present CEDP's news. He had helped found CEDP, he was an honorary president, and he allowed CEDP to use his offices. CEDP could not afford to estrange Pimenta during the struggle. Yet neither could it afford to alienate the communists, who were perhaps the most dedicated segment of its membership. On August 21, 1948, Luíz Hildebrando de B. Horta Barbosa replied to Pimenta's letter. He said that he was intransigently at Pimenta's side during the struggle. He supported all means that Pimenta found convenient to adopt, but he never once specifically mentioned the role of the communists in the campaign. Pimenta's suggestion had been side-stepped.[54] Members of CEDP were concerned by the communists' participation, but even the conservative Artur Bernardes realized that CEDP needed their support:

> Then he said to me (Henrique Miranda) there, in front of all the spectators: "Look Professor, it is so, and this is terrible, that you are even linked with Communists!" There was a general belly-laugh. Contained because no-one could belly laugh in front of Bernardes. But when we left, we were belly-laughing. This was the Bernardes, who later would personally come to defend, energetically, the presence of Communists

in the Petroleum Campaign, against the intrigues they (the Campaign's opponents) intended to carry out. He, General Leitao de Carvalho, and General Raimundo Sampiao argued with insistence, against the accusations of Matos [sic] Pimenta, for the continuation of the Communists, in quotations, in the Petroleum Center.[55]

To the army hierarchy, which saw fellow generals tolerating or even defending communists, there was a terrifying parallel with 1935. Once again a faction of the armed forces had allied with the Communist Party to challenge the government.

Government Repression and Its Failure

There was a certain degree of hypocrisy in the hierarchy's horror at this alliance. After all, Dutra had reached out to Prestes and the communists during the 1945 campaign, as had the UDN. Of course, the political moment had changed profoundly. But what really angered the general staff was the willingness of nationalist officers not only to reveal the military's divisions to the public but also to mobilize the masses against the hierarchy. The military leadership remained determined to break the campaign, and the label "communist" allowed it to legitimate its repression. During "Petroleum Week" in April 1948, the police moved to break up street rallies over petroleum. The federal police often were under military leadership, as was the case in Rio de Janeiro. The official violence increased during May 1948, although the following month the government began to waver in its policy. The campaign had gained too much support to be easily repressed. Still, incidents of state violence were not uncommon; the police dispersed a CEDP meeting in the interior state of Amazonas in July 1948. There was also economic repression. Activists risked their jobs. President Dutra phoned Professor Paulo Sá, the head of the Instituto de Tecnologia, to ask him to fire Lobo Carneiro for his work organizing the petroleum campaign. Professor Sá refused Dutra's request.[56]

The Brazilian government faced pressure from the United States and private companies to alter its petroleum legislation, which perhaps encouraged the government's repression. The United States government made it clear to President Dutra's cabinet that there would be a high price to pay if it did not liberalize its petroleum legislation. The Brazilian government had earlier applied to the Export-Import Bank for a loan to finance "petroleum activities" in Brazil. But the U.S. State Department argued that no loans should be granted until petroleum legislation had been changed. The State Department also worked to form ties directly with army officers. One U.S. official wrote that the State Department had to "continue to work in all feasible ways to get the Brazilian Army to see the importance of intelligent and constructive petroleum legislation."[57]

Nonetheless, the efforts of the State Department may have been less important than the work of private companies. There were contacts between Standard Oil and the general staff. General Távora told Gordon Michler of Standard Oil that he was convinced that Brazil was not prepared to nationalize petroleum because it lacked the "requisite capital, technical knowledge, and proven reserves to justify such a step."[58] Despite the unpleasant image of Standard Oil, these contacts were almost certainly not improper. But there was also corruption in the Brazilian military at the highest levels, and Brazilian corporations took advantage of this fact. For example, during the petroleum struggle, the Sampaio Refinery Group bribed some army officers to oppose the creation of a state monopoly in petroleum, according to the CIA.[59]

Despite foreign pressure, corporate lobbying, and army repression, the petroleum campaign grew at a rapid pace throughout the summer of 1948. Of key importance was the fact that army officers were enrolling in the movement by the hundreds. Fifty-four officers of the garrison of Santa Maria, in the state of Rio Grande do Sul, sent a telegram to Horta Barbosa to support his efforts. The head of this garrison was Gen. Estillac Leal, commander of the Third Military Region, and honorary president of that state's branch of CEDP. In August the *Jornal de Debates* published a petition in favor of a state monopoly of petroleum which over a hundred officers had signed. The issue had spread from the largest garrisons in the heartland to remote army outposts in the hinterland.[60]

The Attack at Peixoto's Statue

It was in this atmosphere of success that CEDP held a meeting on September 23, 1948 at the Brazilian Press Association (ABI). Gen. Estevão de Carvalho was in charge of events, but Gen. Raimundo Sampaio and Gen. Júlio Caetano Horta Barbosa also attended. In the words of Lobo Carneiro, even if not all these officer were positivists, these were men who had all been influenced by the great military positivist of the previous century, Benjamin Constant. The meeting went late, the speeches went on, and a sense of jubilation came over the participants. At the end, Col. Artur Carnaúba proposed to those present that they take the flowers off the tables and lay them at the feet of the statue of Floriano Peixoto in the nearby Plaza of Cinelândia. Everyone agreed, and the meeting flowed out into the public space, where Carvalho and Sampaio deposited flowers at the statue of the "Marshall of Iron." Colonel

Carnaúba then gave an impassioned speech in which he extolled the virtues that immortalized Peixoto. According to Henrique Miranda, Carnaúba was a communist. It may have been the image of a marxist praising Peixoto that triggered what followed. While Carnaúba spoke the police surged forward.[61]

Mattos Pimenta attempted to speak to the police in order to explain the improvised nature of the ceremony. The police continued moving towards Carnaúba, one officer aiming a firearm at Pimenta. Realizing that Pimenta was about to be shot, city councilman José Junqueira threw himself in front of the newspaper owner, whereupon the police shot him in the leg. The shot began a panic as everyone attempted to flee. Some CEDP delegates were clubbed. People fought back in self-defense. The policemen, frightened by the crowd, began firing their revolvers into the air, then at people. Not only protestors but even casual onlookers were injured. One policeman pointed his revolver at Euzébio Rocha but lacked the courage to fire. The next day a reporter from *Correio da Manhã* went to the plaza. He found it spattered with blood.

Capt. Luís Augusto Horta Barbosa, the son of the general, ran and called the army. According to Gen. Lima Câmara (who had not known the identity of the caller), Horta Barbosa's son claimed that three generals were being massacred in the plaza. Greatly upset, military commanders acted quickly, but the violence continued for fifteen minutes before the military police arrived. The crowd greeted them with cheers and applause. The MPs, who knew only that generals had been attacked, were in a grim mood. The shocked police broke and ran, but not all of them escaped. The military police held Laercio Gomes da Silva, a policeman whom they believed was "most responsible for events," at the Emergency Hospital. The soldiers did so on the orders of General Horta Barbosa.[62]

Seven policemen were injured; whether they were hurt by the crowd or the soldiers was unclear. They were taken to a local hospital, as were nine members of the crowd. One civilian had been shot in the leg; another man had been hit in the leg by a tear-gas grenade. The police circulated on the street corners around the hospital, perhaps trying to intimidate the wounded people entering the building. At the door to the emergency room two policemen stepped out of a car and threatened Euzébio Rocha. At this moment General Horta Barbosa approached and told the police to leave. If General Horta Barbosa had not acted firmly that night, similar confrontations might have resulted in a clash at the hospital.

Gen. Lima Câmara, the chief of police in the federal district, entered the hospital, accompanied by Gen. Zenóbio da Costa, the commander of the First Military Region. To onlookers, General Câmara appeared to be trying to mollify Zenóbio da Costa's anger. His policemen had nearly come into combat with the troops under Costa's command, and General Câmara seemed unsurprised at the state of the wounded. At one point he passed the actor Modesto Souza, who was lying injured on a bed. When the actor's wife attempted to speak to Câmara, he cut her off and screamed at the couple that they were communists. Souza claimed that he had only been listening to the speech of Carnaúba, at which point Zenóbio da Costa, beating his chest, yelled "I am General Zenóbio, Commander of the First Region; Colonel Carnaúba is a Communist."[63]

This explanation failed to satisfy the public. Estêvão Leitão de Carvalho later stated that Dutra had sanctioned the attack at Cinelandia. If so, Dutra had made a serious mistake. Brazilians were outraged, and telegrams flowed in to Horta Barbosa. The public wanted those guilty of the attack to be punished. The minister of justice argued that communist infiltrators were responsible for the violence. Gen. Lima Câmara also placed the blame upon the demonstrators, whom he said had meant to provoke a conflict. But Luíz Cantuária Dias Medronha resigned from the cabinet of the chief of police because he believed this accusation was untrue. Even more serious for the chief of police, General Câmara had to meet with Gen. Estêvão Leitão de Carvalho and General Horta Barbosa the next afternoon. We do not know what the commanders told Câmara, but after he left the meeting Câmara no longer wished to speak of the attack or to criticize the victims. He commented that only an inquiry could determine responsibility for events.

Although other street demonstrations had been broken up with violence in the past, this case was different. The public was outraged, and it cost Dutra military support. The emotional impact of an attack on officers paying homage to Floriano Peixoto, a major military hero, was immense. Even commanders who believed that communists ran the petroleum campaign were horrified that police had attacked a meeting patronized by generals. The dangers to the government were real. Two branches of the security forces had come into conflict, a clear warning of what could happen if the conflict continued.[64]

General Canrobert, the minister of war, attempted to halt officers' involvement in the petroleum question. On October 1, 1948, he addressed himself in a circular to division chiefs, the commanders of military zones and regions, and the secretary-general of the minister of war. In this document he advised "members of the army to remain aloof from public manifestations, as such, which involve the army in questions not directly related to its activities and which are dragging it into a field full of perils."[65] Henrique Miranda stated that the measure discouraged garrisons from publishing notes favoring the petroleum campaign, but many more officers retired to fight for a state monopoly in petroleum.[66]

The petroleum campaign could not be defeated with force or the control of formal structures of power. The military was in danger of disintegrating. Euzébio Rocha stated that 85 percent of the military garrison in Rio de Janeiro supported the petroleum campaign. He referred to a telegram sent to Horta Barbosa on October 15, 1948, by 248 officers of the First Military Region. These officers ignored the minister of war's circular and their fervently anti-communist commander, Zenóbio da Costa. There were other signs that the hierarchy's control was weakening. Febianos gave organized support to the campaign. The president of the Veterans' Association traveled to São Paulo on October 2, 1948 for a giant petroleum rally attended by nearly 40,000 people. However, it would be a mistake to focus on one particular group of officers; most commanders throughout Brazil supported a state monopoly in petroleum as part of a vision of economic defense.[67]

CEDP's Victory

Dutra had to give in. On September 30, 1948, shortly after the attack in Cinelandia Plaza, Dutra had proposed changes to the Salte plan for economic development in order to purchase goods for petroleum development. On October 7, 1948, Dutra signed a resolution that ordered that funds frozen in France during the war be used to purchase refinery equipment, petroleum tankers, and material for an oil pipeline. President Dutra then launched a well-organized public relations campaign that adopted his opponent's slogan with one twist. After Dutra's announcement, banners and wall posters appeared everywhere after Dutra's announcement, which said "the Petroleum is Ours, Thanks to Dutra." During Dutra's visit to the city of Salvador in December 1948, a plane dropped thousands of folders with this slogan over the city. One of the oil tankers Brazil purchased, the only one ready to sail, was renamed the Dutra.[68]

With his actions Dutra may have wished to strengthen the hand of Canrobert da Costa for the 1950 presidential elections, as U.S. officials believed. Canrobert's ambitions were an open secret, and Vargas kept a close watch on the activities of the minister of war. Duarte Anibal wrote Vargas that a list of men who supported Canrobert was circulating amongst officers. If Canrobert was to win, his allies had to end the popular mobilization around the petroleum issue. Canrobert's future, however, was less important than the army leadership's fear. The general staff needed to stop the struggle undermining its authority. Accordingly, the military hierarchy quickly moved to neutralize the issue of petroleum by appropriating its opponents' rhetoric.[69]

The CEDP had emerged victorious. The first National Petroleum Convention was held amid a mood of jubilation in mid-October, 1948. A faction of the military had defeated the hierarchy by mobilizing the masses. In a sense, the victory of the nationalist officers had been predictable. These men had benefited from the contacts they had formed with civilian elites during the Estado Novo, when high officers had led state regulatory agencies. As political society opened after 1945, civil-military alliances once again could form. With military support, the popular movement was a powerful force. The hierarchy, on the other hand, had ties to civilians through the União Democrática Nacional (UDN), but its distrust of mass mobilization prevented it from creating a broad campaign. Nor did it articulate a clear alternative to the arguments of Horta Barbosa. It failed to control either the civilian debate or the armed forces.

Conclusion

Peter Seaborn Smith has said that the petroleum debate in Brazil was shaped by two beliefs about oil, both of which were false. The first was that Brazil had oil, and the second was that the international trusts wanted to control this resource. From this perspective, the military's debate was ironic because Brazil has always lacked sufficient petroleum to support itself. But the conflict was less about oil than the army's role, which was why Dutra's decision could not end the conflict. Petroleum embodied the question of economic development. As Maria Augusta Tibiriçá Miranda noted: "This [economic development] was the great parting of the waters."[70] Although the two military factions' programs for petroleum development were not always dissimilar, what each policy represented for the military was radically different. Each vision of economic development, and hence of petroleum policy, matched a concept of the military's role in national defense policymaking. The armed forces were polarized less by petroleum itself than by what it symbolized.

As officers attempted to define the military's role in response to political and economic change, officers rallied around different visions of the institution. The resulting struggle altered the structure of factions that had previously controlled the armed forces. Officers and civilians who described the army at the time often used the phrase "the parting of the waters." This term signified the end of the old army and the birth of a new institution. It also described the division of the military into two groups that defined Brazil's armed forces until the 1964 coup. The petroleum struggle marked the moment at which the ideological fault lines appeared that later characterized military politics.

5

The Clash of Ideologies
1949

During the late 1940s armies and nations throughout the Third World had to wrestle with the international pressures created by the onset of the Cold War. This global partition profoundly impacted the military conflict in Brazil. Nationalist officers had begun their struggle in 1947 just as the world divided into two contending blocs. This situation undermined the nationalist party within the military. As the rhetoric of their civilian allies became increasingly radical, nationalist officers came to fear the movement they had unleashed, and they retreated to their base of support within the army. At the same time, the army general staff realized that to defeat military dissidents it needed to create a powerful ideology. Internationalist officers sought out institutions and allies to promote their vision, which they viewed as one battle in a global contest. The same ideological trends that threatened the nationalists' coalition strengthened their opponents. As a result the military underwent a bitter ideological struggle between two parties of roughly equal strength.

This struggle changed the role that ideology played within the armed forces. As Edmundo Campos Coelho has argued, the Brazilian army had never possessed an official ideology, that is, a system of thought that pervaded the institution, shaped its organization, and defined its mission.[1] In the past, officers had often adopted their ideology from civilians or embraced a vague rhetoric of national regeneration. But by 1949 both army factions had created sophisticated political programs with political and economic implications for society as a whole. As officers rallied behind two approaches to defense and development, the opposing ideological camps became clearly defined. Scholars such as Alfred Stepan have explained this period of ideological change by referring to factors such as U.S. influence, the experience of the Forca Expedicionária Brasileira (FEB), and the impact of the Escola Superior da Guerra (Senior War College).[2] Yet the army's ideology cannot be understood apart from the factional struggles that created it. Through this contest the ephemeral nature of factional ideals became embedded in the enduring traditions of army institutions. This period had an enduring impact upon the army and how its members viewed their involvement in politics and society.

The Destruction of a Civil-Military Alliance

Gen. Canrobert da Costa and other army leaders had learned that they could not defeat Horta Barbosa's faction with violence, as long as it formed part of a civil-military alliance. The general staff needed to undermine the public support this faction had gained during the petroleum debate. Early in 1949, therefore, senior officers not only espoused a state role in energy development but also launched a propaganda campaign against CEDP (Center for the Study and Defense of Petroleum). On January 28, 1949, the minister of war, Canrobert da Costa, met with journalist Mattos Pimenta. Afterwards, Pimenta wrote that Canrobert held a "nationalist" position on petroleum. The following month, Gen. Juarez Távora announced that the general staff did not oppose state exploration for oil. These statements formed one part of a strategy to defuse petroleum as a political issue and to change the terms of the debate. As another part of this effort, Dutra's government also began a propaganda campaign to attack the petroleum movement. In March 1949 the Department of Political and Social Order published a lengthy study to prove that communists led the petroleum campaign. Even before its release, however, government propaganda had convinced many people that CEDP was a radical organization.[3] As civilians and soldiers withdrew their support from CEDP, it was stripped of its protection against political repression. The government successfully changed the focus of the debate from petroleum to communism.

As the center became vulnerable, the government moved against its leadership. In January 1949 the municipal chamber of Fortaleza invited Alfredo de Moraes Filho to speak about petroleum. A naval commander and an active duty officer, Moraes Filho was the executive president of CEDP at the time. He traveled to Fortaleza on vacation but never had the chance to speak. Gen. Stêneo Albuquerque Lima, the military commander of the region, arrested him on Canrobert's orders. Moraes Filho was returned to Rio de Janeiro on the next plane. On January 29 and January 30, 1949, the Centro Cearense de Estudos e Defesa do Petróleo gathered to protest the arrest. Public anger still influenced government actions. The hierarchy quickly released Moraes Filho and ordered him to a remote outpost, but Moraes Filho no longer could be CEDP's president. The government attacks continued despite the public outcry.[4] On April 6, 1949, the acting president of CEDP gave a speech condemning the mounting police pressure upon his organization. Yet the repression continued, and the police killed people at later petroleum rallies. Despite the violence of these attacks, this repression harmed CEDP less than its internal problems did.[5] The destruction of the civil-military alliance can only be fully explained by the center's divisions and its loss of military patronage.

Divisions within the Petroleum Movement

The CEDP had always united diverse interests, but the conflicts at its center became public only after its victory in October 1948. Although failure generally creates discord, CEDP divided into warring factions at the height of its success. The center's policies became politically controversial as the Cold War shaped politics. The CEDP's anti–United States statements worried many of its members. During CEDP's national convention in October 1950, the secretary-general had lashed out at "U.S. imperialism." This speech angered a journalist, Rafael Correia de Oliveira, who wrote an article criticizing Miranda. Newspaper owner Mattos Pimenta and other civilians had long resented communist participation in CEDP.[6] In the context of the Cold War, the movement's rhetoric and membership became increasingly problematic.

The struggle between these journalists and CEDP's leadership became a conflict between moderate and radical (sometimes communist) members of the center. To moderate civilians, the radical leadership of the organization was at best opportunistic and at worst dangerous. The moderates believed that they had founded a popular campaign over communist opposition. According to them, the communists had joined CEDP only after it had become a success. Moderates resented what they perceived as their loss of power within the organization, and they were angered by the xenophobic and extremist rhetoric CEDP's leadership used, particularly Henrique Miranda's attacks upon the United States. To this faction, it seemed that the communists had found a popular campaign and made it a tool for leftist propaganda.

To radicals and communists, however, the moderates were at best naive and at worst foreign agents. The radicals believed that their dedication had enabled CEDP to survive repression, and they had worked to make CEDP a nonpartisan organization. Although they controlled key positions within the center, they welcomed people from all political parties. The campaign's opponents manipulated the label "communist" to damage the movement. Without discipline and unity, CEDP would fail. The radicals viewed their opponents as political zealots who might destroy the movement in their ignorance.

Petroleum had become a political issue because it attracted support from civilians with different interests who all believed that a state monopoly of petroleum was vital to Brazil's future. But the campaign's supporters soon realized that they had different reasons for advocating this program. They clashed over both the meaning and the conduct of the campaign. The moderates distrusted nationalist rhetoric and popular mobilization, while the radicals believed that only these tactics could succeed. Both sides looked to the center's military leadership to arbitrate the dispute. The generals decided to permit the mass rallies that disturbed the moderates, as Henrique Miranda described: "If we adopted the thesis of Matos Pimenta [sic] to come to hold exclusively conferences with technicians and specialists in petroleum affairs, the campaign, in our eyes, would die, because it would not attain the masses, and consequently it would not attain the parliamentarians who would decide about the Petroleum Statute. We took this problem to the generals and we opposed the thesis of Matos Pimenta. . . . The generals supported my, better said, our thesis."[7] But the center's military leadership could not resolve the argument among CEDP's civilian members. After the generals decided to continue mass protests, some civilians began to publicly criticize CEDP.

A struggle ensued between the center's radical and the moderate civilians. In January 1949 both factions published letters asserting that their supporters had founded CEDP.[8] Because a number of organizations had come together under the aegis of officers, both factions held an equal claim. Yet the debate continued because each faction wanted to portray itself as the legitimate voice of the center. Mattos Pimenta also published his earlier letter to CEDP's president, in which he suggested steps to limit the influence of communists within the organization. Pimenta believed that his recommendations had been ignored. Pimenta's ally, Oliveira, said that the crisis occured because "democrats" had prevented CEDP from becoming a weight in the balance of international competition.[9] To many observers, these statements seemed to confirm the government's allegations about the center. The officers' alliance with civilians—especially the extreme nationalists and communists—was becoming increasingly problematic.

To radicals within CEDP, it seemed that Mattos Pimenta was trying to divide their institution by adopting the government line. The center formed a commission to deal with Mattos Pimenta, headed by Alice Tibiriçá, Col. Artur Carnaúba, and Nilo da Silveira Werneck. They elaborated a dossier on Pimenta's statements and sent it to him as a warning. When Mattos Pimenta continued to criticize CEDP's leadership, they met at the student's center (UNE) on February 14, 1949, to discuss his accusations. The next day Pimenta and Oliveira learned that they had been expelled from CEDP when they read the news in a local paper. Their expulsion represented a turning point in the campaign because it marked CEDP's loss of moderate public opinion. Many other prominent figures resigned rather than endure a public struggle. Those civilians who remained in the campaign were more radical, nationalist, or socialist. The U.S. embassy noted that CEDP's division had weakened the petroleum campaign, and the officers who had created CEDP watched as conflict undermined their center.[10]

Nationalist officers struggled to overcome the problems created by the journalists' departure. The *Jornal de Debates*, Pimenta's paper, had given extensive coverage to the petroleum campaign. As it became clear in January 1949 that CEDP would lose this venue, officers needed a means not only to publish their views but also to regain public support. Artur Carnaúba and his fellow commanders, together with the leadership of CEDP, decided to found their own magazine *Emancipação* (Emancipation). Shortly after it was launched in February 1949, the magazine was sold throughout the nation. It reached perhaps 500 of Brazil's 2,000 municipalities and appeared in the newsstands of every state capital. Air force personnel helped to transport the magazine, which was funded with private contributions. Surprisingly, a patriotic refinery owner, Peixoto de Castro, contributed to the magazine even though it demanded the expropriation of private refineries.[11]

Emancipação was the official voice of CEDP, but it clearly spoke for the center's military leadership. The directors of the magazine were all military men: Col. Hildebrando Rodrigues, Col. Felicíssimo Cardoso, and Col. Artur Carnaúba. The magazine's secretary was Capt. J. L. Pessôa de Andrade, and the editor was General Horta Barbosa's cousin, Fernando Luís Lobo Carneiro. The first page of the first edition had articles by Gen. Raimundo Sampaio and Col. Arthur Carnaúba. The magazine reflected the views of an army faction.[12] The banner of *Emancipação* succinctly summed up these officers' beliefs: "There is no political independence without economic independence."

As the first edition of the magazine described, it was devoted to the study and defense of Brazil's resources, especially those goods necessary to economic and military defense. Only in this manner, it stated, could Brazil be freed from the economic dependency that prevented its industrialization. Artur Bernardes expanded on this doctrine in the magazines' second issue, in which he described a vision of national defense. Modern warfare, he argued, entailed the mobilization of all the nation's resources. The influence of foreign trusts had to be combated because the means of warfare had to be produced within the nation: "In a word, we need, before anything else, to defend our economy, because national defense is, before anything, the defense of the national economy."[13] Bernardes went on to say that a nation needed economic strength in order to have military power.

Emancipação was an interesting journal because it reflected the contradictions of the nationalist movement itself. Both sides in the contest had members who disagreed with some planks in their faction's political platform. Personalism, clientelism, friendships, and social alliances shaped military factions. Political concerns created ideological contradictions. For example, some officers who favored a nationalist approach to development allied with the hierarchy because they believed that the petroleum campaign was led by communists. Similarly, positivist army officers who deplored nationalism (and militarism) allied with the nationalists because they favored a larger role for the state in development.

Because of the latter officers' influence the magazine's tone initially was antiwar and antinationalist. For example, Luíz Hildebrando de B. Horta Barbosa wrote a series of articles that applied positivism to problems of national defense. In one article he argued that exaggerated nationalism threatened the true interests of humanity. Horta Barbosa believed that nationalism was an inevitable product of imperialism. Consequently, a true brotherhood of man could only be created after a complete reform of society at its economic base. To Horta Barbosa, this change appeared to be inevitable. The days of warfare were ending.[14] His articles suggested some of the private ideas that influenced the public doctrine of this army faction. But many of CEDP's civilian members disagreed with these positivist ideals and their critique of nationalism.

It is important to remember that the categories of "nationalist" and "internationalist" were constructed and artificial. The factions involved debated complex and controversial issues, and their members often disagreed over policy issues. For the nationalists, this created problems as officers' views diverged from those of their civilian allies.

Officers Lose Control of CEDP

Even as officers created a new voice for their beliefs, their influence within CEDP was waning. The center had represented the will of a military faction to project its vision of "economic emancipation" onto society as a whole, but within the organization the officers formed a minority whose interests differed from those of civilians. Army leaders had overlooked this fact to enable the center to achieve their goals. Yet as their authority came to be questioned, these differences could no longer be ignored. As moderate civilians left the center, both its rhetoric and its program became increasingly radical, and civilian leaders began to test the officers' control of the organization. At issue was not only the meaning of the campaign but also how it was to be conducted. Whoever decided this question could command the center. Although the military leaders had originally supported popular mobilization as a means to defeat the army hierarchy, they had never wished it to escape their control. Nevertheless, this began to occur. As early as October 1948 officers had been concerned by "unnecessary" public gatherings. The honorary presidents of CEDP met at Arthur Bernardes's house to discuss the problem. Oliveira later wrote that "the generals and Bernardes had decided to stop the numerous pointless meetings, the purpose of which was being perverted."[15] In future, they agreed, such meetings would only be held with their prior authorization. But it was not that simple, and the meetings continued after the generals forbade them.

On December 21, 1948, Gen. Raimundo Sampaio attended a meeting in the offices of Artur Bernardes. Gen. Estevão Leitão de Carvalho and Gen. Horta Barbosa listened grimly while Sampaio described his impressions of a recent trip to São Paulo. He had been horrified to hear more attacks upon the government than speeches for the cause. The rallies had escaped the control of officers, who no longer determined the center's agenda. The officers did not leave the organization, but they were marginalized within it. In February 1949 the executive presidency passed from Luíz Hildebrando de B. Horta Barbosa to a federal deputy, Domingo Vellasco. Although Luíz Horta Barbosa was a civilian, this moment began the transfer of power away from an army faction. Speaking in the salon of the socialist party, Vellasco said he accepted the presidency because of the "temporary impediment" of Luíz Horta Barbosa. His cousin, General Horta Barbosa, had sent his regrets at being unable to attend. During the ceremony Raimundo Sampaio criticized the role of communists in the campaign. Within the center, the break between civilian elites and army leaders was clear.[16]

In later years, officers downplayed their role in CEDP after 1948. Indeed, some scholars have even stated that prominent officers resigned from CEDP early in 1949. But CEDP's records show that Carvalho and other generals attended the center's meetings throughout the following year. Nonetheless, after July 1949 officers distanced themselves from the center. A year after army commanders founded *Emancipação* they seldom wrote articles for this publication (except for Felicíssimo Cardoso). *Emancipação* became increasingly radical. No longer did generals want their names to be associated with CEDP's policies. A few important officers remained in both CEDP and *Emancipação*. But senior officers, the engineers, and the positivists who had led this faction, no longer controlled these organizations. CEDP survived, but a civil-military alliance had been destroyed.[17] The remaining members of this military faction concentrated their efforts within the army and re-thought their goals.

The Factions Change

The nationalist faction underwent an ideological change, as many of its old members tired of the struggle.[18] As its base of support narrowed, this faction's agenda became broader. There were several reasons for this evolution. The general staff pressured nationalist officers so that those command-ers who remained politically active tended to be more militant. Even after the civil-military alliance was destroyed, the extremist ideas of some civilian leaders still influenced officers. As the faction's membership became increas-ingly xenophobic and radical, so did its program. Most importantly, political trends compelled army officers to rethink their ideals. The issue of petroleum had rallied the public to their cause. Once the government had nullified this issue, they needed to rephrase their program in the context of the Cold War.

Both the nationalist faction and the army's leadership underwent an ideo-logical evolution after 1948 as new political pressures changed the connota-tions of old ideas. The mounting tension in the international arena, the new influence of the United States, and the increasing power of nationalism influ-enced both factions. As officers attempted to redefine the army's mission, each faction formed a doctrine that characterized itself, and both factions attempted to form an institutional base within the military to promote their ideals. As they lost control of CEDP, the nationalist faction worked less with civilians and relied more on officers. At the same time, the army's leadership created a doctrine not only to regain support from officers but also to reach out to civilian elites.

The Escola Superior da Guerra

The changes within Horta Barbosa's faction were less dramatic than developments concerning the army leadership and internationalist of-ficers. In 1947 high commanders had lacked a clear ideology although they agreed on common military interests. They opposed Vargas because they feared his popular support, they distrusted nationalism, which they saw as a tool to mobilize the working class, and they favored foreign capital because it could fund Brazil's industrialization. The army hierarchy also believed that Brazil should maintain its alliance with the United States. The army had profited greatly from this policy during World War II; the Cold War provided an opportunity to continue this arrangement. By contributing to hemispheric defense, Brazil could remain useful to the United States. In return, the United States would fund Brazil's development. Despite the different interests of the United States and Brazil, the general staff and the internationalists believed that both the nation and the army could benefit from the Cold War.[19]

Yet this pragmatic calculation created neither a convincing world view nor a clear image of the military's role. The high command had lost in 1948, in part because its opponents had created a military ideology while it had not.[20] Most officers found a vision of the army's duty more persuasive than a description of military interests. Commanders needed an ideological basis to control the institution. As the general staff struggled to reassert its control over the army, its members began to create an alternative vision of the military. This concept of the army's role was defined by Brazil's participation in the Cold War. The army hierarchy used a new military school, the famous Escola Superior da Guerra (ESG), to justify its interests with a coherent doctrine.

After the outbreak of World War II, military leaders in the hemisphere worried that their schools taught irrelevant tactics. Many armies also decided that the sophistication of warfare entailed greater coordination among the services. Regional militaries, therefore, began overhauling their educational system by creating new military schools. Argentina founded a new war college in 1943, the United States itself established the National War College in 1947, and a series of schools were founded throughout South America in following years. For example, Peru created the Center of High Military Studies (CAEM) in 1950 and another military school, the Centro de Instrucción Militar del Perú (CIMP), in 1951. As part of this trend, the Brazilian military inaugurated the Escola Superior da Guerra on August 20, 1949.[21]

Scholars have written extensively about ESG. Much of this literature has described the school as the embodiment of foreign influence or the creation of the FEB.[22] Neither argument was accurate, although the school was modeled after the U.S. National War College, and its first leader was a former febiano. The school was unlike its U.S. counterpart. As Gen. Cordeiro de Farias said, "we are children of the War College. I admit with pride this paternity, but there does not exist anything more different from the War college than the Escola Superior da Guerra."[23] Nor did the school represent the influence of the FEB. Although febianos in ESG (such as General de Farias and Golberi do Couto e Silva) have attracted attention, their ideals were defined by their position in the army hierarchy rather than by their membership in the FEB. The army leadership has sought to shape the memory of the FEB as a pro-American and democratic force.[24] These were the views of some of the FEB's senior commanders, but most of the officers and men of the FEB held nationalist ideals and supported Vargas. In no way did their thought resemble that of ESG. Indeed, in the years to come, febianos risked their careers and lives to oppose the doctrine taught by ESG. By 1952, the army leadership would have imprisoned many former war heros (such as Maj. Leandro José de Figueiredo Junior and Capt. Joaquim Miranda Pessoa de Andrade) for their opposition to the general staff's policies.[25] The roots of the school did not lay in the United States or in the Italian campaign of the FEB but rather within the Brazilian army itself.

In his classic work, *The Military in Politics: Changing Patterns in Brazil*, Alfred Stepan argues that ESG profoundly affected not only the army's ideology but also its role. Instructors at this school created a doctrine, which he called the "new professionalism." This ideology redefined the military's mission so that the army focused less on conventional combat than on internal warfare. Stepan believes that this instruction gave officers not only the skills but also the sense of legitimacy to intervene in civilian politics. His belief was supported by Brazilian officers, who argued that ESG's foundation marked a watershed in military thought: "The Escola Superior da Guerra created a new mentality and politicized the Armed Forces. There is no doubt that they evolved enormously in this sense."[26] Despite these statements, however, Stepan's arguments are only partially correct.

As an isolated organization, ESG neither altered the military's ideology nor changed the army's role. Rather, the school contributed to changes that had already begun to take place within the army. Stepan's critics have pointed to a number of facts about ESG which undermine his arguments.[27] When officers decided to found ESG in 1946, they had not ascribed a particular ideological role to the college. No single school could have influenced an entire army in a few years, and not all of ESG's students accepted the doctrine they were taught. Their training at ESG marked only one part of a long military career during which they trained at other military institutions. Consequently, to assess how the school's training affected military ideology, the school cannot be considered in isolation. ESG's instructors reshaped military thought to the extent that they codified the ideas of an existing faction. Therefore, ESG's doctrine was the result of an ideological change rather than the cause of it. The history of the school and its influence within the army cannot be separated from the political struggle in which it was formed.

Although the men who had proposed creating ESG in 1946 had not ascribed an ideological role to the school, it nonetheless came to promote the views of a military faction. These men—Lt. Col. Golberi do Couto e Silva, Col. Ernesto Geisel, Col. Orlando Geisel, and Maj. Jurandir de Bizarria Mamede—were all internationalist officers with ties to the army hierarchy. But the most important figure in the school's early history was Gen. Cordeiro de Farias. In late 1948, Gen. César Obino sent Idálio Sardenburg to inform Cordeiro de Farias that he had been selected to head the school. Like Juarez Távora (who succeeded him as ESG's president) Cordeiro de Farias was a trusted representative of the general staff.[28] He was also a former member of the FEB. By appointing him to head the school, Canrobert da Costa could associate the general staff's program with the FEB, as a means to legitimate it. The febianos later fought against not only the liberal ideals that Cordeiro de Farias advanced but also Cordeiro de Farias's campaign to become the president of the Military Club. But they could not prevent ESG from acquiring an internationalist character.

Cordeiro de Farias shaped the schools' curriculum so as to persuade civilians and officers that a liberal economic program was necessary. The school brought together engineers, technicians, politicians, and economists to study national problems. During the first two months of the course, they traveled throughout Brazil to examine industrial plants, hydroelectric generators, and iron mines. The study program emphasized group projects upon which officers and civilians had to collaborate. Antonio Carlos Peixoto has called the resulting alliance an "anti-nationalist and anti-populist" coalition.[29]

The experience of Dutra and Canrobert da Costa during the petroleum campaign had taught high commanders the importance of civilian allies. Perhaps the worst crime of the nationalists, as far as the army's leadership had been concerned, was their willingness to mobilize the masses. While this step outraged leaders such as Gen. Canrobert da Costa, the army leadership soon learned that such civil-military alliances could be a powerful tool. Consequently, even before ESG had officially opened, the general staff had decided that the academy should also train civilians. Gen. Idálio Sardenburg stated that the school's purpose was to prepare civilians to promote development in order to improve national security:

> One way to aid the country to arrive to that point [economic independence] would be to create a mentality favorable to the promotion of development. And it was not enough that only the armed forces thought so. It was necessary that there be among civilians the same intention. I thought, then, that it would be interesting to form a mixed group of soldiers and civilians of different origins to exchange ideas and to create that mentality. My first idea to realize this was to create an institute of studies and afterwards it evolved into a school led by the Armed Forces. I have to clarify that I did not think of everything alone, isolated, but debating and talking with my friends. By means of this exchange of ideas there formed within the General Staff of the Armed Forces a group which shared that manner of seeing Brazil.[30]

While in charge of government agencies during the Estado Novo, nationalists such as Horta Barbosa had formed close bonds with civilians. The internationalists had not had the opportunity to have such sustained contact with civilians. Their civilian allies were largely UDN politicians. With the foundation of ESG, internationalist officers came to know newspaper owners who could give their concerns good press, businessmen who could donate money to their cause, and government officials who could favor their policies.

National Security Ideology

For this alliance to be successful, it needed to be based upon more than the shared interests of civilians and officers, and the army hierarchy needed to legitimate its views within the military. Commanders had learned during the petroleum struggle that they needed an ideological basis to validate their authority. As officers at ESG attempted to persuade both peers and civilians of their military program, they created National Security Ideology (NSI). This doctrine built upon the old ideal of the military as the nation's savior in order to adapt it to international constraints and social pressures. Edmundo Campos Coelho has argued that NSI was essentially identical to Góes Monteiro's views of the 1930s. However, old ideas acquired new meaning as the school's instructors applied them to the Cold War.[31]

The main idea of NSI was that development and security were linked. Speaking of ESG, General Sardenburg said that this idea "was written as much in the law that created the school as in its internal regulations."[32] Although this idea had roots in the early twentieth century, it had become so important that all other points revolved around it. This ideal was tied to another venerable military concept—the idea that the state embodied the nation. Gen. Nelson de Mello described this idea in flippant terms: "And the state is above everything, the national security is the state, It's a little like that."[33] Foreign enemies were attempting to infiltrate the nation and to undermine the populace's loyalty to the state. In part, this emphasis on "ideological frontiers" reflected the military's experience during the 1930s. Officers remembered how the army had nearly collapsed after the 1930 revolution because of its infiltration by civilian politicians. According to NSI, it was the military's duty to ensure the political integrity that the state's survival required.

These old ideals were placed into a new framework provided by the Cold War. The international contest enabled the hierarchy to create an ideology that attracted not only officers but also civilian elites. Anticommunism became the basis for an alliance with the United States. According to ESG's theoreticians, this role was not only a matter of political principle but also the inevitable result of geography. National Security Ideology used geopolitics to justify military interests, an approach that enabled officers to condemn "false" nationalism because it threatened hemispheric loyalty. Brazil needed to remain part of the international system in order to develop, and the army had the right to influence the nation's economic policy because Brazil had entered the age of "total warfare." In the contemporary world, clashes between armies were unlikely. Instead, foreign interests would attempt to undermine the nation's political system and economic development. The army's main struggle lay within Brazil itself.[34] As Frank McCann has noted, NSI resolved an old contradiction within the Brazilian military. Although officers long believed that the military's role should be external defense, the army had always been embroiled in internal struggles. National Security Ideology blurred the line between the two spheres.[35] The Cold War allowed the military to justify its participation in internal politics.

NSI throughout South America

A similar doctrine evolved throughout South America during this period. To some authors, such as Joseph Comblin, this common ideology reflected the influence of the United States.[36] But this new military doctrine actually evolved from old military roots, which influenced how regional armies adapted to the Cold War. The Brazilian army's creation of NSI must be considered as part of this experience. As regional armies responded to new political pressures that required them to reshape their role, their thought was shaped by an old perception of the army's duty. All these armies shared a commitment to defend the nation. As industry and technology became crucial to modern warfare, regional militaries came to recognize their nation's dependency. They found it impossible to defend a less-developed nation in a world with powerful capitalist powers. Consequently, defense became associated with development in military thought. At the same time, regional militaries shared a common perception that they acted as the nation's savior. This idea had several roots. The army had helped to consolidate nation-states after independence, the military was one of a few truly national institutions, the political system had been fraught with crises, and political parties had often been weak. As a result, the military perceived that it played a special role within the nation, and it carried this perception into the modern age, therefore affecting officers' concern with development.

As army factions debated development options, their struggles changed the significance of ideology within the institution. With the increased education of officers, the more technical nature of warfare, the expansion of regional militaries, and the influence of foreign missions, factions could no longer be based on personal loyalties. With the rise of the working class and the formation of trade unions, the military needed to justify its special role in the political system. Moreover, as the army became interested in development, it needed a program upon which to act. Even before the onset of the Cold War, the Argentine military had divided between what Martin Goldwert has termed "integral nationalists" and "liberal nationalists." The liberal nationalists saw the United States as a model and wanted a more open economic system. The integral nationalists, on the other hand, favored an authoritarian developmental model that could permit industrialization while limiting social dissent.[37] With the onset of the Cold War, the pressures to adopt a particular model of defense and development became even more intense.

As factions debated the army's role, the program armies adopted depended upon their institutional concerns and national interests. National Security Ideology was more of an agenda than a program, for its tenets could justify contradictory policies. In Peru and Ecuador, the army hierarchy defined defense as freedom from foreign (U.S.) influence, and the army encouraged state intervention in the economy.[38] In Brazil, Chile, and Argentina, the hierarchy used the Cold War to legitimate a military role in hemispheric defense and a liberal approach to development. Yet, despite these differences, in all these countries factions came to be defined in ideological terms. As Alain Rouquié has described, they no longer resembled factions as much as political parties, aggregating diverse interests around a single program. The dominant faction's program became the official ideology of the army. The foundation of ESG and the creation of Brazil's NSI must be viewed in this international context. During the period from 1948 to 1951, the Brazilian military underwent a profound evolution that polarized the army between contesting visions of the institution.

Conclusion

Scholars have carefully studied the creation of ideology within Latin American militaries, in part as a means to explain the wave of coups that swept across Latin America in the 1960s and 1970s. Something important had clearly changed within regional armies. These authors (such as Joseph Comblin, Maria Helena Moreira Alves, and Alfred Stepan) looked to a number of factors to explain the army's ideological change: the influence of the United States, the instruction provided by new schools, and, in the Brazilian case, the experience of the FEB.[39] Clearly, the international context did create ideological pressures that altered how officers perceived their role. But the Brazilian army's ideological evolution cannot be separated from the bitter factional conflict that wracked the army over a period of years. Ideology did not appear in a vacuum. It was contested and debated. Accordingly, the success and promulgation of a particular ideology was intimately connected to the fortunes of a military party that fought to advance its ideals.

Despite their internal divisions and ideological contradictions, during 1949 both military factions in Brazil sought to articulate a clear vision for the army and the nation. Nationalist officers largely abandoned a civil-military alliance after they began to lose control over its message. The general staff sought to find new civilian allies in order to promote a doctrine it had created. The army had divided between two ideological programs that defined the identity of the officers ascribing to them. Gen. Canrobert da Costa and other senior generals could not impose their vision onto the army by decree. If they wished their views to prevail, they would have to impose them onto the army by means of a political campaign. The years that followed saw the Brazilian military divided by a bitter contest that escalated even to the point of violence.

6

The Victory of the Nationalists
1949–1951

Although the military's internecine contest was fought over both political and economic issues, at its core was the army's effort to define Brazil's position in the Cold War. The centrality of this issue made for strange alliances within both factions. Although positivist commanders critiqued nationalism, xenophobic officers tolerated them because they supported a vision of state-led development that the nationalists believed would help secure Brazil's economic independence. Some officers who favored state-led development opposed the nationalists because they disliked their anti-American (and in their eyes possibly procommunist) rhetoric. As had always been the case, factions were also influenced by personal friendships and unit loyalties, political calculations and family ties. Nonetheless, by 1949, Brazil's need to define its position in the international order had polarized the army. The nationalists feared the economic power of the United States and its multinationalists. They wished to remain neutral in the Cold War and to have the army play an important role in economic defense. In contrast, the internationalist faction worried about the threat from communism and wished to ally with the United States in its global struggle. This faction believed that in return for its political backing in this contest, Brazil could win developmental support from the United States. In the eyes of both factions, their opponents appeared to be betraying Brazil.

In this context the two military factions had created competing visions of defense and development. To advance their views, both factions sought to win elections. Within the armed forces the Military Club, a social body with an elected leadership, represented an important prize. A victory in the club's elections would grant one group control of the club's journal, indicate which faction had the support of most officers, and strengthen that bloc's civilian allies. The latter consideration mattered because both factions sought to have their allies win the presidency. The nationalists allied with Getúlio Vargas, who had favored state-led development during the Estado Novo. Vargas represented their best hope to gain control of the military because the nationalists did not control the army's leadership. The internationalists favored the presidential candidacy of senior commanders such as minister of war Canrobert Pereira da Costa, or air-force brigadier-general Eduardo Gomes. In this manner, an intellectual division within the army became a wide-spread political contest, which involved most major actors in Brazilian politics.

A Military President?

In 1949 the Brazilian army divided not only over its role, but also over whether the next President would be a general. Within the officer corps, the plans of Gen. Canrobert Pereira da Costa to run for president created turmoil and rivalry. In March 1949 it appeared that President Dutra desired to launch Canrobert as a candidate. During a trip to Rio Grande do Sul, Minister of War Canrobert stated that he might run for the presidency if appealed to by a political party. This announcement worried nationalist officers, whom General Canrobert had long fought. General Canrobert also had other military enemies who feared his authoritarian tendencies. One of these opponents was Gen. José Pessoa Cavalcante de Albuquerque, who decided that he had to act. On March 22, 1949, he published a bulletin in which he ordered his commanders to remain out of politics. Pessoa also warned his officers to remember the Cohen plan and to distrust those who spoke of "communism" or "occult forces." Senator Salgado read Pessoa's proclamation in the senate, where it created a political crisis. General Góes Monteiro faced a firestorm of protest from his fellow senators, who believed he might be plotting a coup. Most people believed Pessoa had acted because the army planned to influence the elections, civilians also feared that Pessoa would suffer for his bravery: "That order of the day continues to be the subject of all the social groups, and already one waits for the firing of José, prison, the devil."[1] People had good reason for these fears. In a rage, Dutra ordered Gen. Mazza Ouvir to imprison General José Pessoa. But Mazza Ouvir refused, probably because of

José Pessoa's stature. In addition, Canrobert's position within the military was weakened by more than Pessoa's bulletin.

Behind the public statements lay a hidden tale of intrigue and corruption, which affected Canrobert's fate. The character of military corruption had undergone a profound change during the Estado Novo, when the army had not had to fear public opinion. The army had controlled the police, and the state and society had been unable to check military abuses. As a result, officers at the highest levels of the institution had allied with business leaders to reap profits. With the return to democracy in 1945, the papers disclosed many scandals involving officers. These scandals marked the army's newfound influence over the national economy.

For example, the army exercised considerable influence over CEXIM (Carteira de Exportação e Importação do Banco do Brasil). This was the branch of the national bank responsible for granting import and export licenses. An agency with immense influence, it came under constant political pressure, as shown by surviving letters from cities and municipalities. If CEXIM granted a license for a generator, it could bring electricity to an entire town. If CEXIM denied a request for railway equipment, a city in the interior could remain isolated. Although CEXIM theoretically prevented unnecessary purchases from weakening Brazil's balance of trade, it soon fell under the influence of powerful officers. These commanders wielded their power within the state for their personal benefit. For a price, officers would guarantee businessmen and municipalities that their foreign purchases would be approved and financed.

In June 1952, the police department covering robbery and fraud in Rio de Janeiro arrested a number of CEXIM functionaries. One of these bureaucrats, Domício de Oliveira Torres, confessed to having personally delivered 2.4 million cruzeiros (the Brazilian currency) to Gen. Antônio José de Lima Câmara, the former head of police in the federal district. According to Torres, General Lima Câmara had then divided the funds among military conspirators involved in CEXIM's business. General Lima Câmara denied facilitating the purchase of foreign material and swore to prosecute "the imposter Torres." Still, the situation was extremely awkward, especially as Lima Câmara was being investigated by police officers he had once commanded. The scandal involved so many officers that any convictions would have badly damaged the army's reputation. Furthermore, many other members of the army high command participated in similar schemes to benefit from the army's control of regulatory agencies. Lima Câmara's arrest could have set a dangerous precedent. Accordingly, in July 1952 when Brazilian papers revealed the names of people involved in the CEXIM scandal, the army acted decisively. Infuriated, Gen. Rio Pardense, who held Lima Câmara's old post commanding the Departamento Federal de Segurança Pública (the Federal Department of Public Safety) imposed censorship on police reporting. Because the military had controlled the police in the federal district since the Estado Novo, investigations into military corruption took place at the sufferance of the general staff. The investigation into General Lima Câmara's corruption was brought to a swift close.[2]

Sophisticated and organized forms of military corruption had become common as the Brazilian military became involved in economic development, and this change had affected military politics. No longer was corruption an isolated sin that civilian presidents tolerated to guarantee military loyalty. Instead, widespread military corruption bound officers to civilian elites, encouraged fund-raising for factional struggles, tied officers to their superiors, and united the army hierarchy in its struggle with dissident officers.[3]

Corruption reached to the very highest levels of the armed forces, where it even involved minister of war Canrobert da Costa. The funds this corruption generated had helped Canrobert to create a patronage network to ensure his military following. Yet this military corruption also made Canrobert vulnerable as he positioned himself for the presidency. Canrobert and other army leaders in the hierarchy had been selling arms to the dictator Trujillo in the Dominican Republic. This transaction had been kept secret from senior commanders outside the general staff because the minister of war and his supporters planned to profit from the sale, but information leaked out. In 1949 Gen. José Pessoa received a letter from a man who feared that Canrobert might become president.[4] He told Gen. José Pessoa that Canrobert had not sent the funds from the arms sale to the Bank of Brazil, the national bank. Instead, Canrobert had funneled them into a failing bank led by his personal friend, Machado de Oliveira. Canrobert had absorbed the difference between the official exchange and the black market rate, creating millions of cruzeiros in personal profit. The bank later failed, and the army had to pay a heavy indemnity to receive its funds.[5]

Gen. José Pessoa had long hated Canrobert, and he wished to block his political ambitions. José Pessoa was also furious because he believed that Brazil could not afford to lose any weaponry. General Pessoa launched his own investigation, which led him to write a series of blistering letters to Canrobert and other army leaders, whom he accused of endangering national security.[6] The scandal became public through an article in the newspaper *Diário de Notícias*. Pessoa wanted a government inquiry to prevent similar abuses by officers in the future, but this did not occur. Nonetheless, shortly afterwards the government launched an inquiry into irregular transactions at the Bank of Brazil. Although the investigation proceeded slowly, it ultimately uncovered Canrobert's involvement in an irregular wheat sale costing the Brazilian government twelve million cruzeiros.[7] The inquiry also found proof of Canrobert's illegal participation in the arms sale to Trujillo, although it chose to ignore this line of inquiry.[8]

Most of these facts became public only two years later, and Canrobert was never punished. Nonetheless, José Pessoa's attacks had cost Canrobert public trust and military prestige. By March 1949 it is likely that General Pessoa (and other army leaders) knew the scale of Canrobert's corruption. Even in 1950 Canrobert continued to aspire to the presidency, but he was not a viable candidate. On September 6, 1949, José Monteiro Ribeiro Junqueira wrote Vargas: "There is a great pessimism within the military regarding the future of Canrobert. Besides, to better explain it, the phenomenon is one of absolute indifference."[9] Junqueira had met with Gen. Zenóbio da Costa, who called it "absurd" to imagine Canrobert leading a political party. General Góes Monteiro still wished to make Canrobert the head of the UDN, but Dutra had changed his mind. He wanted to remove Canrobert from his post as minister of war, and to replace him with Góes Monteiro.[10] As the months passed, it became impossible for Canrobert to find a party. Other leaders (Brig. Eduardo Gomes for the União Democrática Nacional [UDN] and Christiano Machado for the Partido Social Democrática [PSD]) announced their candidacies. With the waning power of Canrobert, the danger that a united army might oppose Vargas ended. The general most identified with the internationalist faction had lost all credibility. This mistake by internationalist officers presented Getúlio Vargas with an opportunity.

Mounting Tension

The question of Vargas's return shaped the political climate. In December 1949 the government forbade political meetings without prior police approval. The police claimed that communists were taking advantage of these gatherings to cause riots.[11] In January 1950 there were persistent rumors of another military coup to prevent the upcoming presidential elections. The army hierarchy worked to ensure that its military opponents could not influence the presidential campaign. On January 28, 1950, the government passed a law retiring any officer who belonged to, collaborated with, or financially supported "illegal associations or political parties." Officers were to be tried in special military courts. If convicted, the officer was retired with the pay and allowances provided by law. This legislation effectively prevented active-duty officers from working with civilian organizations during the upcoming election.[12]

The senior officers who had deposed Vargas in 1945 worked desperately to prevent his return. They feared his vengeance should he again become president, and they opposed his economic policies. Many commanders had ties to the UDN, a right-wing political party which espoused a liberal economic program: "The UDN was rather passionate with regard to Vargas. When Vargas led the state-coup of 1937, it created a statist mentality, indisputably, and that conflicted with the doctrinaire thought of the UDN."[13] As Vargas prepared to campaign, he spoke out in favor of a state role in petroleum development. He also used nationalist rhetoric to lash out at foreign corporations within Brazil. He clearly sought to form an alliance with nationalist commanders. To senior officers, sometimes called the UDN in uniform, it seemed that Vargas's victory would be a disaster.

As early as April 1950, Góes Monteiro had threatened to plan a coup. One of Vargas's relatives in the army said that Dutra's total opposition to Vargas's return had led to plotting.[14] Canrobert tried to intimidate Vargas from entering the presidential campaign. He warned Ernâni do Amaral Peixoto that Vargas should not run: "I want you, sir, to say to him that he cannot be a candidate, because it could threaten the country with a conflagration. The problem is very difficult, I know the difficulties I have in the Ministry of War."[15] But Peixoto was not intimidated. He said that he would not give Vargas the message because it would only inspire him to be a candidate. A desperate Canrobert could only utter a plaintive explanation: "But I did not make a threat! You are understanding it incorrectly."[16] The hierarchy failed to coerce Vargas's allies.

Moreover, the army's leadership was trapped by a contradiction. Gen. Nelson de Mello has stated that most officers opposed Vargas, but only a minority opposed free elections. Internationalist officers wished to prevent Vargas's return but would not suspend the democratic process that opened the path to the presidency. Besides, Vargas still possessed great influence within the armed forces and the power to advance an officer's career. Any attempt to rig the election might lead to open conflict within the army. As the hierarchy realized that only a coup might prevent Vargas's return, its leadership fractured. Senior commanders plotted against Vargas, but they faced resistance within the officer corps. Dutra fought with Canrobert because the latter general had decided to guarantee the elections. Canrobert had announced on April 2, 1950 that he would not run for the presidency. He had then told Vargas's supporters that he would guarantee Vargas's inauguration, should the former president win the election. This decision infuriated Dutra, who was determined to prevent Vargas from returning to power at any cost. Dutra attempted to force Canrobert from his post as minister of war. Despite these divisions, however, some observers still believed that the army leadership might try a coup, regardless of the consequences, and that it all might end in revolution. But in May 1950 the hierarchy's position proved to be even weaker than it appeared.[17]

The Struggle to Control the Military Club

The nationalist faction supported Vargas because he advocated a policy of economic nationalism and because they hated Dutra. These commanders worked to acquire an institutional base within the army by winning elections in the Military Club. Between 1930 and 1964, Alain Rouquié argues, these elections were almost as important in Brazilian politics as their national counterparts, And the club's choice of president in 1950 received unprecedented attention. Between 1944 and 1950 the Club's membership had tripled because of the prestige it gained during the petroleum debate. As the military became polarized and it appeared Vargas might return, which faction controlled the club became critical. To nationalist officers this election represented an opportunity to acquire a military forum where the successful debate over petroleum had begun. They needed a new organization to present their views, now that they had lost control of CEDP (Center for the Study and Defense of Petroleum). But these elections were also seen by both officers and civilians as a military referendum on the presidential elections in October.[18]

The struggle within the Military Club was headed by Gen. Estillac Leal, who gradually became the leader of the nationalist officers. Estillac seemed to be an unlikely choice to lead a factional conflict. Nelson Werneck Sodré describes him as a simple man who led a rustic life. He lived in spartan accommodations and loved to hunt and fish. His home in Rio Grande do Sul was a paradise for dogs, who roamed at will throughout the rooms. Nonetheless, beneath Estillac's apparent simplicity lay a strong political will. Although Horta Barbosa had led the petroleum campaign, this faction needed the support of an active duty officer, and Horta Barbosa was retired. General Estillac had prestige, especially among officers from the influential state of Rio Grande do Sul. And Estillac was a fierce nationalist, whose extremist rhetoric reflected the new power of xenophobic and fanatically nationalist officers. In private, Estillac often referred to Dutra and Monteiro with the imaginary term "fascistoides." After meeting Estillac, the conservative da Fontoura said his "doctrinaire bases are characteristically leftist; he is anti-U.S., in the sense that he is anti-capitalist and anti-imperialist."[19] His fierce attacks on those whom he believed betrayed these principals caused him to be called a communist, but this accusation was false. Estillac, a former tenente and a Vargas supporter, represented the new face of an old military faction.[20]

In August 1949 fellow officers had asked Estillac Leal to run for the presidency of the Military Club. He chose General Horta Barbosa to be his running mate. Most officers perceived the election issue to be petroleum, but Estillac formed a campaign plan that also emphasized new regulations governing promotions and reforms favoring retired officers. Estillac expected to run unopposed. However, the general staff and internationalist officers worried that Estillac's victory might undermine their policies, as Gen. Francisco Teixeira described: "Naturally, given the importance of the campaign 'The Petroleum is Ours,' the military hierarchy , we will call it so, alerted itself to the problem of the importance of the Military Club, which for years had been unimportant. Then the hierarchy launched a candidate with weight in the army who was Cordeiro de Farias."[21] Much as Escola Superior da Guerra (ESG) gave the hierarchy a means to spread their doctrine, so too could the Military Club act as a political tool. The hierarchy could not allow this club to fall into the hands of Estillac and Horta Barbosa, who opposed their ideals. General Salvador César Obino approached General Oswaldo Cordeiro de Farias, the president of ESG, and asked him to run for the club's presidency. Two days before Estillac made public his campaign platform, Cordeiro de Farias announced his candidacy. According to Estillac Leal, both he and his friends were stunned. Estillac spoke with Cordeiro de Farias about fusing their campaigns to avoid a painful struggle, but even while they discussed this option the contest continued. Frustrated, Estillac Leal formally declared his candidacy.

Sadly, the campaign destroyed a real friendship between the two old tenentes. Both sides attempted to avoid an open conflict, even as the struggle intensified, and this effort led to contradictions. In one handbill Estillac denied that the military was divided, while in another pamphlet he claimed that its division was perfectly normal. Rafael Correâ de Oliveira, who had ties with officers, claimed that the appearance of a split within the army had been created by forces outside the army, but this was not true. The candidacies of Cordeiro de Farias and Estillac Leal had polarized the army.[22] Cordeiro represented the internationalist faction, which had the clear backing of the general staff. This faction wished to ally with the United States in the Cold War and to adopt a liberal approach to development. Estillac Leal represented the nationalist faction, which had widespread support within the officer corps. It viewed the economic influence of the United States as the greatest threat to Brazilian sovereignty, and it favored a state-led approach to development.

By February 1950 newspapers stated that the campaign had acquired the character of a national event. The army's struggle had become public, and it was possible to judge each faction's strength, as Nelson Werneck Sodré states:

"So I can say that the majority of military opinion was favorable to the thesis of a monopoly (in petroleum). But I already have said here that we did
not know the boundaries, and thus the quantitative dimension of one current
and the other current, because that division, the limits between one and
another were defined in the elections for the leadership of the Military Club
in 1950."[23] As Sodré notes, the conflict was shaped by the debate over petroleum development, which in turn symbolized larger issues. But the struggle was also influenced by the presidential elections. When an interviewer
tried to describe the conflict between Estillac Leal and Cordeiro de Farias as a
struggle over nationalism, Gen. Nelson de Mello replied that the real issue
was Vargas: "It was [nationalism]; but this was secondary, because we were
nationalists also, and the army was always more or less nationalist. The business was Getúlio."[24] At issue was not only a military program but also Vargas's
future.

Estillac Leal enjoyed many advantages. His supporters formed a broad
program and promised to work for the law for wages and privileges. Officers
were suffering from the nation's high inflation, which devalued their wages.
Estillac promised to lobby Congress for better salaries, thereby gaining crucial support. Estillac's campaign slate was anti-Dutra, which appealed to
officers disillusioned by his policies as president, and officers rallied to Horta
Barbosa, a hero from his role in the petroleum debate. On the other hand,
their opponent, Cordeiro de Farias, ran a weak campaign. Internationalist
officers were convinced that they could win on the basis of "an idea" without
any organization, but they never succeeded in communicating their platform
to the officer corps. In the end, Cordeiro de Farias had the backing of the
interior garrisons. However, in 1950, these officers were not able to vote. And
in the capital, Cordeiro de Farias found that his support was confined to
senior officers: "I won in Rio de Janeiro until the rank of captain. When I
arrived at the rank of lieutenant I was . . . defeated."[25] Cold War ideals rallied
the staff officers but not the rank and file. On May 17, 1950, the election was
held; nearly 80 percent of the Military Club's members voted, an unprecedented number. Estillac and Horta Barbosa received 3,932 votes; the Cordeiro
and Ribas slate won 2,707. The hierarchy had been defeated.[26]

The general staff was horrified. Internationalist officers blamed their defeat on the febianos. In his newspaper column, journalist Carlos Lacerda later
stated that the communist party had infiltrated the Veteran's association
(Associação dos Ex-combatentes) after the FEB's (Forca Expedicionária Brasileira) return. The communists had gained support in the military by pre-
tending to fight for the veteran's interests, which allowed them to spread
throughout the institution. He viewed the nationalists' rise to power in the

Military Club as part of this process.[27] In conflating nationalism with communism, Lacerda articulated a viewpoint shared by the conservative elites with whom the internationalist officers were allied. And Lacerda's protests suggested the extent to which war veterans supported the nationalists. Indeed, the febianos (such as Emygdio da Costa Miranda) had ensured the defeat of a FEB commander, Cordeiro de Farias.[28] Clearly their ideological devotion to the nationalist cause had outweighed any personal allegiance to a febiano. Their participation indicated the extent to which diverse groups within the army had rallied around the nationalist cause.

To Vargas this election proved that his return was possible. It boosted his supporters, some of whom had been reluctant to fight a hopeless battle. It seemed that Vargas had the military backing to guarantee his inauguration. General Estillac met with João Neves da Fontoura, who described the meeting to Vargas. The army, Estillac said, opposed a coup. The military leaders of Rio Grande do Sul would not interfere in the election. Dutra had lost most of his prestige, and Góes Monteiro had little influence. The day before, Estillac had said to Canrobert: "I, for four years, have been taking Dutra's crap; it seems that in the future you will have to take it from Getúlio."[29] Canrobert did not contradict him. In June 1950 Vargas officially declared that he was the presidential candidate of the labor party, the PTB (Partido Trabalhista Brasileiro).[30] The fate of Vargas and nationalist officers was closely linked.

Estillac Lobbies Officers and Sergeants

Although a major victory with implications for the presidential elections, the Military Club alone did not provide Estillac's faction with the support it needed. Most of these officers had retired and no longer commanded troops. They needed to use their new position to reach out to active-duty officers and to build a following in the ranks. To attract support, the Military Club portrayed itself as the proponent of officers' interests. A bill of wages and privileges for soldiers had been sent to Congress in 1948, but it had not passed. This bill now became associated with Estillac's faction. Many civilian elites believed that leftist elements within the military were manipulating the issue, as Ernâni do Amaral Peixoto described: "There was even a meeting at the Military Club, and they invited me to appear, as someone studying the law. You speak of the coloration of the left. In this meeting there were some thirty or forty officers, most of them retired, officers of the reserve, but visibly [sic] of the left. And that was the pretext to agitate! The government let it pass a long time; that law could have been approved in a month, but it waited two years."[31] But this same delay allowed Estillac's supporters to build on officers' frustration. The Military Club clashed with Congress as it pressured that body to pass this bill.

On August 31, 1950, Congress sent President Dutra a letter to complain of the "disrespectful" note they had received from the Military Club. Estillac's supporters had written to complain that deputies spent too much time in their home states dealing with local politics. This practice created problems for the officers who wanted to pass the bill. The Military Club also protested that a congressman had delayed a meeting to discuss the bill, which inconvenienced many officers who planned to attend this session. The officers warned Congress not to delay this meeting again: "If today there is a new delay to impede once again the progress of the project, then the officers will be invited to appear at the Military Club, in order to deliberate about the possible steps to take."[32] Although Estillac's faction often accused the hierarchy of intervening in politics, the Military Club did the same. These officers wished to dictate to Congress when it should debate issues affecting officers, and they did not refrain from using intimidation to obtain their goals. Their behavior infuriated the general staff, which believed its role had been usurped, and the army's image damaged.

To the general staff and Minister of War Canrobert, the Military Club's efforts to reach out to the sergeants appeared even more dangerous than its lobbying in Congress because this work broke an unwritten code. Since the early 1930s, officers had refused to draw enlisted men into their political struggles. Accordingly, the army's leadership acted quickly when the sergeants began to acquire a political voice under the influence of Estillac's faction. In August 1950 a sergeant, Carrion Roland da Silva, sent a telegram to the São Paulo branch of the Casa do Sargento, the enlisted man's equivalent of the Military Club: "I congratulate the directory of the social branch of that prestigious institution for having held a conference [with the] patriotic theme of [the] defense of mineral riches patronized [by the] Centro Estudos Defesa Petróleo [sic] in order to reveal the sinister plans of powerful trusts to embezzle our riches and strategic minerals to make a horrific atomic bomb for terror and for the struggle of working humanity to the detriment [of] world peace."[33] If this telegram was somewhat incoherent, Roland da Silva's sentiment was nonetheless clear. But he had taken a dangerous step. Minister of War Canrobert had twice warned him about such incidents. On August 28, 1950, Canrobert expelled Silva from the military. Within the Casa do Sargento, Canrobert's decision was met with revulsion and outrage.[34] In the coming year, retired generals who supported Estillac continued to hold gatherings in the Casa do Sargentos, to stress the need for a military role in development. But the army hierarchy continued to repress the sergeants' participation in politics.

The General Staff's View

To internationalist officers it seemed that the institution had been infiltrated by communists. Of course, their opponents were nationalists or positivists, who adopted a military role because of their experience and their beliefs. They had not been suborned by an outside party. But because of the memory of the 1930s and the fear of populist politicians, the hierarchy ascribed all internal divisions to outside forces. It was easier for commanders to describe their opponents as communists than it was to refute their arguments, and the Cold War influenced the political views of senior commanders. In November 1950 one member of ESG, General Honrato Pradel, spoke with Caio Miranda, who was representing Vargas as the ex-president attempted to learn his position in the army. Pradel said that a third world war was imminent, and the situation within the Military Club was dangerous. When the army was united, Pradel told Miranda, the politicians could not do anything. But when it was divided the situation became very bad. His thoughts were shared by Gen. Newton Cavalcanti, who believed that communists were behind every major Brazilian problem. Cavalcanti told Miranda that the army had been infiltrated by communists, as the situation in the Military Club proved. Gen. Cordeiro de Farias agreed.

Even some of Estillac's supporters accepted the idea that communists were attempting to destroy the Brazilian state. Gen. Octávio Ache clearly held statist ideals; he told Miranda that Brazil needed to create a ministry of production to resolve the chaotic condition of the national economy. And he wanted the government to found a series of collectives under the management of the state. Yet even this nationalist officer told Miranda that the communists wanted to create a "Bogotá in Brazil," a reference to the massive riots in Colombia in April 1948. Ache stated that only the army would keep Brazil from this disaster.[35] Caio Miranda's interviews with senior commanders illustrated how the Cold War had influenced officers' thought. Accordingly, Estillac created a fierce backlash when he criticized this conception of international politics.

The Journal of the Military Club

Estillac's victory gave his faction control over the Military Club's publication, *Revista do Clube Militar*. These officers had found it difficult to control organizations in which they had to ally with civilians, such as *Emancipação*. Their authority over a new publication presented them with an opportunity. As Peter Seaborn Smith has noted, the journal immediately adopted a tone of militant nationalism after Estillac's election.[36] It provided his faction with a means to transmit its views to the officer corps as a whole. Much as ESG had provided the army hierarchy with an institutional voice, the journal of the Military Club proved a means for Estillac's faction to articulate a coherent doctrine.

The July 1950 edition of the journal quoted Estillac's speech on assuming the presidency, during which he stated that the military combated "the imperialist pretensions of economic and political dominion."[37] In the same edition, retired general Raimundo Sampaio published an article arguing that Brazil needed to defend its radioactive minerals. In August, Artur Bernardes used the journal to criticize a UN commission created to study the Amazon, called Hiléia Amazônica. Nationalists such as Bernardes feared that this commission would help foreign nations and international trusts alienate Brazil's resources in the Amazon valley. In October 1950 the journal published an article by an anonymous author, who argued that the United States and France had lost the Vietnamese War.[38] Much like *Emancipação*, this magazine embodied the views of nationalist officers. But as the debate had increasingly shifted from petroleum to foreign policy, the political trends created by the Cold War exposed its arguments to attack.

On June 25, 1950, North Korean troops invaded the southern half of the peninsula. They reached the capital, Seoul, within three days. As the South Korean army was overrun, the U.S. military began a desperate rear-guard action. To many U.S. leaders, this attack formed part of a Soviet plan, and they called for international support. Many Brazilian officers had long believed that they would have to aid the United States in a future war with Russia, as one U.S. embassy member noted in 1949: "There is considerable opinion, particularly on the part of the military, that war between US [sic] and Russia is inevitable. In this connection, an officer high in the armed forces of Brazil, not so long ago remarked to me after several potions of John Barleycorn that his country would put two army corps in the field against the Soviets and not two divisions as was the case during the late unpleasantness."[39] But the army totally opposed involving Brazil in Korea. Gen. Henrique Lott later stated: "It was a war with which Brazil had nothing to do."[40] The conservative Gen. Nelson de Mello agreed: "What I know was that in the army there was a general repulsion. People don't like to go to war."[41] Although the sympathy of officers was with the United States, even the most conservative officers did not want Brazil to enter the Korean War.

Some of Estillac's supporters, however, not only argued that Brazil should remain neutral, but also criticized the U.S. intervention in the conflict. One officer anonymously wrote an article titled "Considerations about the War in Korea" in the journal's July edition. Because it was always published late, the issue came out in September, 1950. These five pages did more to undermine Estillac's faction than any other event. Even before publication, the article caused one member of the journal's committee to resign. This article clearly adopted the Soviet position in the Cold War, with devastating results.

In the essay, Colonel X argued that the origins of the Korean conflict were unclear, but he seemed to support North Korea's claim to be a victim. After two or three days of conflict, Colonel X stated, most of South Korea's troops had put down their arms and passed to the side of their brothers to the North. He described how the socialist leader of the south had refused to accompany President Syngman Rhee's retreat but rather had remained in Seoul to support the people's struggle. As soon as the United States intervened, according to the article, a process of national unification began as the populace rallied against the foreign invaders. The U.S. military fanned this hatred by massacring the civilian population as part of an inhuman strategy of total war.[42]

The situation on the Korean peninsular had been extremely complicated since the end of World War II. The South and North had repeatedly clashed in conflicts costing many Korean lives. Nonetheless, the accuracy of this article left much to be desired. At no point did the author suggest that the North bore some responsibility for the war. Despite the murky history of the war's origins, which left many details open to interpretation, the author's account was extremely biased. Nonetheless, his presentation of facts caused less outrage than his tone. The author wrote before MacArthur's landing at Inchon on September 15, 1950. At a time when the U.S. army was being driven into the sea, he launched a vitriolic attack on the U.S. intervention.[43]

As soon as the journal was published there was an explosion of anger within the officer corps. On September 26, 134 officers released a note to the press protesting the article.[44] But as quickly as the issue became public, it faded from public view. Nelson Werneck Sodré believes that this lull occurred because officers on both sides tried to reach an accommodation. The rapid U.S. advances after the Inchon landing also served to defuse the crisis. Most of all, however, the presidential elections on October 3, 1950 pushed other news into the background. High commanders were worried that Vargas might win.

Vargas's Return?

On October 3, 1950, Getúlio Vargas won the presidential elections. He received nearly 48 percent of the votes cast. Eduardo Gomes, his closest challenger, had received only a third of the popular vote. But some civilian elites and army commanders nonetheless wished to deny Vargas his victory. The army resented Vargas's return to power five years after he was deposed.

Gen. Cordeiro de Farias said in November 1950 that Vargas's victory constituted a revolution that "alarmed and frightened" the elites. Gen. Dimas Siqueira de Menezes, the commander of the First Armored Division, told Caio Miranda that Vargas's victory was a disaster for some generals. The commanders who had overthrown Vargas feared reprisals.[45] Immediately after the election, some civilian elites argued that Vargas had not yet won because he had failed to obtain an absolute majority. This argument was spurious because a three-way race made it nearly impossible for any candidate to win this mandate. Still, some officers seized upon this justification to prevent Vargas's return.

Vargas had the clear support of key groups within the military, such as the nationalists. In particular, the febianos had worked hard to secure his victory in the October elections.[46] But this was not enough to ensure Vargas's inauguration. Given the hierarchical nature of the military, Vargas needed the support of at least some senior commanders. Vargas was a wise politician who understood that he had to win more than the sympathy of most officers.

Within the armed forces Vargas had carefully cultivated powerful allies such as Gen. Estillac Leal and Gen. Zenóbio da Costa. He now turned to these leaders. Estillac fought hard to ensure Vargas's inauguration. On November 15, 1950, he gave a speech to the Military Club, on the sixty-first anniversary of the declaration of the Republic. Estillac used the opportunity to state that the presidential elections had been free and fair. He also emphasized that the armed forces would always be the guarantors of the Republic. Deputy César Costa read Estillac's speech in Congress, and it received considerable press coverage. Other generals also spoke out in favor of Vargas's inauguration, including Gen. Ciro Espírito Santo Cardoso. Vargas received crucial support because of his long work to create military allies; this labor had won Vargas the backing of the leader who did most to ensure his return, Gen. Zenóbio da Costa. He was important because he commanded the military region that included Rio de Janeiro. No coup could succeed unless the conspirators controlled the capitol.[47]

General Zenóbio was a brave man who had led the infantry in Italy and was twice promoted for courage. This disregard for danger had caused the febianos to hate him because they believed General Zenóbio spent lives needlessly during the war.[48] But it gave the general prestige among his peers. A powerful personality, Zenóbio was Canrobert's main opponent within the army. During late 1948 these two generals had attacked each other savagely as both men sought to build a following. Vargas used Zenóbio's hatred of Canrobert to gain his support.[49]

Vargas had sent friends to speak with Zenóbio more than a year before the election. On September 6, 1949, a Vargas supporter, José Monteiro Ribeiro

Junqueira, wrote the ex-president that he had Zenóbio's backing. This work was rewarded after the election, when army leaders planned a coup, and Vargas's allies prepared for a conflict. In late October, Gen. Euclides Figueiredo asked Zenóbio to help prevent Vargas's return. Zenóbio refused. Figueiredo grew angry and told Zenóbio that his decision could lead to civil war. Zenóbio calmly replied that "the war might have begun, if they had possessed sufficient courage."[50] On November 12, 1950, Zenóbio met with Dutra. The president told Zenóbio that if the electoral tribunal refused to validate the election, he would prevent Vargas from becoming president. When Zenóbio attacked his decision, Dutra flew into a rage and refused to change his mind. Zenóbio told Dutra that he could not rely on the troops.[51]

General Zenóbio met with Vargas's representative, Caio Miranda. There were rumors that Zenóbio was to be exonerated from his command, and Zenóbio declared that he was prepared to conspire. Not only was Zenóbio a brave man, but he had followers who were fanatically loyal, as Miranda had noted. Zenóbio would not hesitate to fight. Miranda regularly published articles for the magazine, *Radical*. He persuaded Zenóbio to allow this magazine to publish a statement in which Zenóbio expressed his belief that the electoral tribunal would validate the election. He also condemned those persons who involved the army in political issues. This pronouncement received great public attention because it indicated that a coup was unlikely. Internal rivalries within the army had weakened the hierarchy. Napoleão de Alencastro Guimarães wrote Vargas in December 1950 that "Zenóbio not only fulfilled, but also surpassed what was desired. Dutra helped us: he passed him over with the promotion of Canrobert. The results you can imagine."[52] General Zenóbio never shared the political views of Vargas as did Gen. Estillac Leal. Nor did he command a military faction; the officers who supported General Zenóbio were tied to him by bonds of personal loyalty, not a wider vision. Nonetheless, General Zenóbio had helped put to the test the hierarchy's commitment to permit Vargas's inauguration.

The army hierarchy lacked the will to create a civil war over the presidency. Even conservative officers such as Gen. Newton Cavalcanti and Gen. Dimas Siqueira de Menezes said that Vargas's victory should not be questioned. Gen. Álvaro Fiúza de Castro told Miranda that those generals who supported the absolute majority requirement had been poorly received by their peers. Equally important, those generals who opposed Vargas's inauguration were members of the general staff and did not command troops: "Officers of the General Staff. In the army they say officers of the bureau, that live seated in the great departments, in the General Staff, in the cabinets, but they don't have great contact with the troops. It was for this reason that they weren't able [to impede Vargas's inauguration], because the officers that were commanding the regions were almost all on the same side. They had the command of the high level, of the positions of eminence in the army, but they didn't have effective command of the troops."[53] By late December 1950 the army hierarchy realized that it could not prevent Vargas from becoming the next president of Brazil.

Renewed Conflict

At the same time that officers struggled over whether Vargas could return to the presidency, they also clashed over the article on Korea. The essay became the crux of a debate because it embodied several important questions. Colonel X had attacked Brazil's alliance with the United States, which the hierarchy believed would benefit both the nation and the military: "Our position in the Military Club, the position of the Estillac-Horta slate, was evidently anti-American. . . . But I am certain that the principal argument of the adversaries of the thesis of a monopoly [in petroleum] and of the adversaries of the Estillac-Horta leadership was exactly the necessity to maintain safe the alliance with the United States, that by destiny we had to follow the United States in everything that they wanted and it would be understood! Our opinion was completely different."[54] Of course, the Brazilian army did not share identical interests with the United States. There were contradictions in this alliance which Estillac's faction used to criticize the army's leadership. The general staff believed that these criticisms came from officers who sympathized with communism.[55] But the hierarchy did not attack the article for this reason alone. Although the debate was ostensibly over foreign policy, it also involved presidential politics. The essay enabled the hierarchy to attack Vargas's supporters within the army during the months before the inauguration. And this struggle must be understood not only as an ideological conflict but also as a clash over power. Would the general staff speak for the army or the directory of the Military Club? The involvement of the Military Club in political issues subverted the authority of the army hierarchy. The general staff believed that it had to remain the sole voice for the institution.

After a lull, while officers attempted to reach a compromise, the controversy reappeared. On October 15, 1950, a captain wrote the Military Club to express his solidarity with the journal's secretary, who had resigned in protest. According to Nelson Werneck Sodré, this letter marked the beginning of a renewed offensive against the Military Club. A steady stream of letters attacking the article flowed into the organization. One note had been signed by 124 officers. In response to this criticism, two officers resigned from the Military Club on October 24, 1950. On October 31, 1950, officers sent to the press a letter in which they demanded that the journal cease publishing anonymous articles. Throughout November, angry officers wrote press releases, petitions, and letters. Seldom had the army's divisions become so public. On November 10, 1950, Capt. Antônio Joaquim Figueiredo—the former secretary of the journal—published a letter explaining his reasons for resigning on September 25, 1950. He disagreed with the Korea essay because it addressed a political issue and countered Brazilian interests. On November 14, 1950, eight officers publicly demanded that the next edition of the journal publish the name of the essay's author. They also called on the journal to cease publishing articles on religion or politics. On November 16, 1950, the secretary of the Military Club received a letter signed by various officers, including Gen. Edgar Facó, the minister of the supreme military tribunal. These commanders stated that the journal lacked the right to present this article as the thought of the club. They insisted that the essay's author take responsibility for his writing.[56]

Despite this criticism, the Military Club defended the article. Not only did these leaders have a sense of loyalty to the officer who had written the article, but also his argument embodied many of their beliefs. An increasingly xenophobic note had entered this factions' thought. Whereas in 1948 Horta Barbosa had only referred to the threat of U.S. trusts, in 1950 Estillac's supporters openly referred to the imperialist pretensions of the United States itself. On October 23, Estillac stated that he refused to censor military thought. On November 17, 1950, Sodré presented a written defense of the article to the directory of the Military Club. The directory approved his arguments. The following week, Estillac stated that the article was "inopportune, inconvenient, subject to varied interpretations and sophisms that come to create the impression, espoused in the press throughout the country, that whoever is not with the article is against Communism, and that who is with the article is with Communism."[57]

This statement did not discourage criticism. The directory of the Military Club released a note to the press on November 26, 1950, reaffirming their commitment to their election program. The directory argued that the military needed to remain united in order to obtain a new law of wages and privileges for the army. As for the article on Korea, the directory restated its commitment to free speech. This last statement particularly infuriated their enemies because the journal refused to publish both their protests and their articles. After releasing this note to the press, the Military Club launched an energetic defense. A petition began to circulate in high military schools, calling on officers to support their club and their journal.[58]

The club's efforts failed to halt the firestorm of protest sweeping the army. Furious officers sent to the Military Club a note of protest that had been signed by 130 officers of the general staff, 40 members of the Andrade Neves Regiment, all the officers in the Regimental Artillery School, all the officers in the Regimental Infantry School, 60 officers of the Recife garrison, many officers in the Fifth Military Region, and approximately 100 officers in the Second Military Region. As Sodré described, the Military Club was flooded with letters, telegrams, and phone calls. Nonetheless, the Military Club continued to defend the article. It issued a statement expressing its solidarity with both the journal and Estillac, but this note made no mention of the Korea article. Estillac himself stated that he disapproved of the article, but he respected the author's opinion.[59]

In late October, the Chinese intervened in the Korean conflict, and U.S. forces once again were thrust to the south. To many observers, this moment seemed to mark the start of the third world war they had been dreading. The article on Korea became a major issue in Brazilian politics. João Neves da Fontoura, who soon afterwards became Vargas's foreign minister, wrote the future president that the question of absolute majority had ended but that a new danger had emerged from the international scene. The article on Korea favored the communists. In the atmosphere of fear, João Neves da Fontoura said, the attitude of the Military Club might furnish Vargas's opponents with a reason to impede his inauguration. The press criticized the Military Club in increasingly vitriolic terms.[60]

The general staff (and the leadership of the Fourth and Fifth Military Regions) organized intense attacks upon the Military Club. On December 1, 1950, ten officers demanded a convocation of the Military Club's members, unless the deliberative council of the Military Club explained why it had ignored a previous letter of criticism. On December 8, Congress approved the law of wages and privileges, but during the crisis this victory gained little support for the club. On December 12, the club's opponents published a manifesto, which 600 officers had signed, including 10 army Generals. The club's opponents had collected the signatures in five days. The petitioners blamed their opponents for bringing the issue to the press. They were furious that the club's journal had refused to publish critiques of the Korea article, and they accused the club's directory of being a Fifth Column. The following day the Military Club published a petition signed by 705 officers. This document did not specifically mention the Korea article; rather it spoke of the need for military unity, and it expressed support for the Military Club.[61] The two sides had reached a stalemate.

Public debate could not resolve the controversy. Consequently, the minister of war sanctioned the directory of the club. All of the members of the Military Club responsible for producing the edition of the journal with the article on Korea were posted to garrisons outside of Rio de Janeiro. The second vice-president of the Military Club (and a former member of the FEB) Maj. Tácito Lívio de Freitas was transferred to São Luis do Maranhão; the director of the recreational department, Joaquim Pessoa Miranda de Andrade was sent to Fortaleza; and the head of the journal, Maj. Humberto Freire de Andrade, was sent to Aracaju. Many other members of the club's directory were scattered throughout Brazil: "There, as I was saying, they were decapitated. They were liquidated in the Military Club. They were sent to places far away. Tácito was a major, if I am not mistaken, and at this time went to Maranhão. Others went to Matto Grosso, Goiás and I don't know where else. They scattered. It was the diaspora of the nationalist officers. This is the truth."[62] Nelson Werneck Sodré was pressured to resign from the Command School of the general staff. Various members of the general staff sought out Sodré to persuade him to take another position. After he refused these proposals, Sodré was transferred to the southern frontier, where he spent five years. Sodré believed that the head of the general staff and the minister of war ordered the transfers because they intended to impede Vargas's inauguration and needed to remove nationalist officers to do so. Sodré may have been correct. It is also possible, however, that Canrobert wanted to punish the club's members before losing his position.[63]

Between the repression of the hierarchy and the criticism of the press, the position of the Military Club had become untenable. The club's directory held a meeting, attended by Estillac. He wanted the directory to vote on whether to censure the club's journal, but nationalist officers believed this decision would betray their peers. Instead, the directory temporarily halted the journal's publication in order to prevent "diverse interpretations" of its the material. Many officers accepted this decision only reluctantly. The secretary of the Military Club, Capt. Paulo Eugenio Pinto Guedes, stated that the club had refused to renounce the article on Korea. The directory had ceased publishing the journal instead of changing its orientation, and the Military Club's decision had little effect. The December edition of the journal had already been printed and circulated freely amongst both civilians and officers. Typically, this edition contained a provocative article entitled "Foreign Capital dominates the National Economy." The critics of the Military Club were not mollified.[64]

An editorial in the newspaper *Correio da Manhã* stated that the club's journal had transformed itself into an organ of Soviet propaganda. The directory of the Military Club wanted only to buy more time by suspending the journal's publication. Most of the Military Club's enemies probably agreed with this analysis, but the hierarchy also knew that there was little to be gained from further struggle. The conflict had made the army's divisions public, which the hierarchy hated, and by mid-December it had become clear that Vargas would succeed to the presidency. There was no longer a purpose for attacking Vargas's military allies. On December 18, a declaration was published by a "considerable portion" of the members of the Military Club. These officers were not satisfied that the *Revista do Clube Militar* had stopped circulating. They wanted to change, not destroy, the journal. Nonetheless, they had decided to consider the issue closed. Despite their displeasure, they did not want an "inglorious struggle" that would damage the army's prestige. By late December there were no longer discussions of the Military Club in the press, to the relief of Vargas's supporters. On December 17, 1950, João Neves da Fontoura had written Vargas: "The question of the Military Club was a little calmed with the suspension of the journal, but we do not delude ourselves, Dutra, Canrobert, and others will go to the end trying to impede your investiture. For they don't care with what sauce they chew you. Any one will serve. What is important is that they satisfy themselves at political cannibalism."[65] Notwithstanding this graphic imagery, the resolution of the crisis benefited both Vargas and Estillac. Yet the army's internal struggles continued, away from the public eye.

The Changing Terms of the Struggle

The terms of the debate between the two factions had changed during the period from 1948 to 1951. Both sides had always attempted to define the struggle on their terms, to attract support, and to thwart attacks. By making the issue petroleum rather than economic defense, Horta Barbosa had defeated the hierarchy. One can hear the frustration in his opponent's voice: "The problem is that the things are never presented with the aspect of Communism. One speaks of the problem of petroleum, of nationalism, I don't know what. They are sound ideas, when they don't pass certain limits. The false nationalism is a danger. On that occasion, then, there was a crazy false nationalism."[66] As the Cold War continued, however, the debate came to take place less over petroleum development than over international relations, and this shift placed Estillac's faction at a disadvantage, as Nelson Werneck Sodré later argued.

In 1950, Sodré stated, the Military Club's program had attracted support from people with different views. But when the Military Club defended the Korea article, it opened itself to intense criticism from both the army and the press. The Military Club became a major political issue in Brazil—the subject of countless articles, editorials, and interviews—because the debate was framed by the Cold War. In this environment the hierarchy no longer had to argue the merits of its program: "And they didn't address the question. Even in the case of Korea. They didn't state, for example, that it was necessary to send troops to Korea. They only stated the following: 'They are Communists, they are Communists'—this was the refrain. So they didn't enter into the merit, but they situated the signboard. And we helped them! We helped with our errors."[67] Sodré believed that a needless position had harmed the career of numerous officers, including Estillac. Henrique Miranda agreed: "It was an imprudence beyond telling! Because they delivered themselves to the re-actionaries!"[68] Without this error, Miranda told an interviewer, it would have been far harder for Estillac's enemies to have defeated him. Nonetheless, it was not the article that made foreign relations the new focus of conflict. As the Cold War increasingly shaped officers' perception of the world, this trans-formation was inevitable.

Vargas Chooses His Minister of War

As Vargas approached his inauguration, he had to choose his minis-ter of war. The decision was of grave importance. Vargas knew that a bad selection could endanger his presidency. He needed to take into account the changing nature of the army, the formation of new factions, the new issues debated within the institution, and the personal loyalty of the man he chose. During late October and early November 1950, Caio Miranda had met with the most important military leaders, all of whom he asked the same question: "Who should be the next Minister of War?" Vargas may have received his best advice from Cordeiro de Farias, whom Miranda described as a brilliant man. Cordeiro de Farias stated that the person Vargas chose should be a man who could unify the institution, rather than engaging in politics. He recom-mended Gen. Alvaro Fiúza de Castro, who would be an apolitical choice.[69]

Vargas needed someone who did not lead either faction; otherwise the minister of war would be too vulnerable to internal attacks to be effective. But Vargas had always liked to combine contradictory forces within his govern-ment. During World War II he had based his government on Eurico Gaspar Dutra and Oswaldo Aranha, two men with opposing visions of Brazil's role in the conflict. In 1945 Vargas had founded two parties, the PSD and the PTB, with opposing political views. This policy had always allowed Vargas room to maneuver and to arbitrate. Vargas followed the same ideal in 1950. Though he wanted to negotiate a military accord with the United States, he also wanted to reach out to the nationalist wing of the military. He chose João Neves da Fontoura, who was pro–United States, to be his minister of foreign relations and he wanted Estillac, who was anti–United States, to be his minister of war.

But the army Vargas commanded in 1950 was very different from the army he had manipulated in 1935. In the past, Vargas had controlled the army by orchestrating the ambitions of its leaders. But this policy could not work with an army divided into two factions based upon opposing ideologies. Vargas might either have taken an apolitical stance or allied with the more powerful faction. But it was difficult for Vargas to see what took place in the army, despite his excellent network of informers: "There were certain things that Getúlio did not observe well, mainly in the army, where it is more difficult to observe, because it is a very closed corporation; only with much diligence and goodwill [can it be understood]. And Getúlio was very much looking from above. . . . He thought that, naming Estillac, he would have a great support and he did not have it."[70] Estillac's supporters within the army understood the problem far more clearly than Getúlio Vargas, and Estillac's friends were not pleased by his appointment.

When Nelson Werneck Sodré learned that Estillac had taken the position, he immediately went to see him. The first question he asked Estillac was if he had the power to alter the high command. Estillac said that he did not. Sodré then replied that Estillac was committing suicide because the hierarchy opposed him. Estillac refused to listen, saying only that Vargas had given him assurances. Sodré knew that he was making an error, but he never again raised the subject with Estillac.[71] But as Sodré predicted, Estillac's appointment created resentment within the officer corps. This tension was heightened after Vargas also chose a problematic figure to be the minister of the air force. Every senior officer in the air force was offended by Vargas's appointment of Col. Nero Moura as their superior: "A Colonel to be Minister? He was in the war, he commanded an attack squadron very well, he was a brilliant officer, but he was a Colonel."[72] Vargas's decisions not only failed to strengthen his position but also may have weakened his allies.

Nonetheless, in January 1951 it seemed that the nationalist faction would impose its vision onto the army, despite every setback. Estillac was head of the Military Club, a post he had won in a free election among officers, and he was also the new minister of war. President Vargas was inaugurated on January 31, 1951. General Dutra retired, and General Canrobert lost his post. General Góes Monteiro returned to duty, as the new head of the general staff. But he did so at Vargas's behest, and he never regained his old power. The journal of the Military Club resumed publication, and it continued to discuss the need for state intervention in the economy to ensure the national defense. If the nationalist faction no longer led a civil-military alliance, it nonetheless possessed considerable support within the army. It acquired a following among the sergeants (which the hierarchy had always lacked) as well as among junior officers. The army had been polarized during an ideological struggle over development, defense, and the military's role. In January 1951, Estillac's faction seemed likely to win this contest.

Conclusion

Nelson Werneck Sodré later stated that two factors—the pressure of the Cold War and the question of Vargas's return—defined the army's factional struggle.[73] These questions influenced events within the army to an extent that cannot be overemphasized. As the terms of the debate came to be framed by foreign policy and nationalist rhetoric became increasingly suspect, officers' perception of the conflict changed. Some issues particular to Brazil (such as the question of Vargas's return) shaped the struggle. Despite the importance of these factors, however, changes within the Brazilian army must be understood as part of a larger process. New social pressures and international constraints forced armies throughout the continent to rethink the meaning of nationalism. The growing fear of communism shaped officers' debates over the army's role in society and development.

7

Betrayal, Torture, and Suicide
1951–1954

Estillac's inauguration could not end the contest between the two blocs of officers. Army factions resembled political parties in that they were defined by their programs for defense and development. Officers struggled to determine not only the dominant faction within the army but also the army's role in society. Estillac's supporters favored involving Brazil's army in economic oversight and state-led development in order to "emancipate" Brazil from its dependency on northern nations. In contrast, the hierarchy's faction wanted to ally with the United States to fight communism and to gain its financial support for liberal development. Both factions sought to win over neutral officers, who held the balance of power within the institution. Civilian elites watched this struggle carefully because of its importance to the government. The programs of both military factions required the army to influence Brazil's foreign relations and economic policy.

The two factions used different tactics to make the army adopt their program. Estillac's faction worked within the army, through conferences and the *Revista do Clube Militar*, to persuade officers that the army had to defend the nation's economy. For this reason, Estillac's faction came to view the struggle as a debate over free speech. To the hierarchy's faction, however, commanders' inability to enforce their authority proved that communists had infiltrated the institution. Accordingly, this faction shifted its attention outside the army, to eliminate not only Estillac's civilian allies but also his presidential backing. The hierarchy's faction, the internationalists, believed that outside groups had prevented it from eliminating its "communist" opponents.

The internationalist faction enjoyed some success with this strategy because Vargas wanted to recapture Brazil's wartime agreement with the United States. This arrangement entailed Brazilian support for the U.S. military in exchange for U.S. capital for Brazilian development. As Vargas could not send soldiers to Korea because of political pressures within Brazil, he attempted to substitute Brazilian resources for troops. To create this economic relationship, Vargas negotiated a military accord with the United States. This step forced Vargas both to distance himself from Estillac's supporters and to soften some of his nationalist rhetoric. To Estillac's faction it seemed that they had been betrayed. Instead of implementing their policy of economic defense, Vargas had exchanged Brazilian resources for developmental capital, a key idea of internationalist officers.

Although the military accord alienated nationalist officers who had supported Vargas, it did not endear the president to the army hierarchy. Instead, it sparked a vicious contest to control the Military Club, with important implications for Vargas's presidency. The electoral campaign for the club became a referendum not only on the army's role but also on two approaches to development. Internationalists sought to win over to their cause the majority of officers, many of whom remained neutral. Surprisingly, this conflict took place less than two years after Vargas had achieved a stunning election victory and acquired the support of the dominant military party. Yet even immediately after Estillac's appointment, internecine struggles had foreshadowed a crisis for both Vargas and his military allies.

Estillac's Problems

Upon assuming power, Gen. Newton Estillac Leal had to achieve balance between his duties as the minister of war and his loyalties as the head of a military party.[1] Canrobert's earlier decision to transfer several officers to remote garrisons greatly complicated Estillac's position. Estillac's party expected him to reverse these transfers, which had targeted his supporters. But the army hierarchy warned Estillac to uphold Canrobert's decision. Caught between these contending interests, Estillac made the disastrous decision to violate tradition by remaining as president of the Military Club. As a result, General Estillac attended a crucial session of the Military Club in February 1951.

At this emotional gathering, Gen. Djalma Polly Coelho blamed the officers' transfers upon the heat of the political moment and the actions of sectarian journalists. Gen. Estevão Leitão de Carvalho appealed to Estillac to reverse Canrobert's orders. Pressured by his supporters, Estillac publically stated that "the injustices will be mended."[2] Yet, against the will of both the army hierarchy and many civilian leaders, Estillac found it impossible to fulfill his promise. Ultimately, Estillac not only broke his promise but also treated his supporters disdainfully. In May 1951, for example, Nelson Werneck Sodré received an invitation to meet Col. Osvino Ferreira Alves in his cabinet. Canrobert had ordered Sodré to a remote garrison in Rio Grande do Sul. Speaking on behalf of Estillac, who was then traveling in the United States, Alves told Sodré that the officers Canrobert had transferred "should follow their destiny."[3] Alves also told Sodré to leave Rio de Janeiro before Estillac returned to Brazil. Estillac seemed more worried by the embarrassment these officers represented than with honoring the sacrifices they had made during his election campaign.

Estillac rapidly lost support within his own faction. In part, the military hierarchy damaged Estillac's popularity by appointing officers who opposed the Military Club to posts in Estillac's cabinet. Estillac also alienated many supporters by deciding to distance himself from his bloc. Still, Estillac's main problem was that as minister of war he had to take steps that his followers disliked. On May 5, 1951, for example, Estillac began a customary trip to the United States to review military installations. The Pentagon viewed his trip with displeasure, and ambassador Herschel V. Johnson had to lobby the State Department to prevent Estillac from being snubbed. Still, Estillac chose to visit the United States, even though his supporters believed that nation threatened Brazil's sovereignty. When Estillac met with the U.S. secretary of defense, General Marshall, and gave an enthusiastic statement to the press upon his return, the nationalists believed he had betrayed them. Some officers even began to whisper that Canrobert had ordered the transfers at Estillac's request. Estillac wanted to retire some officers who opposed him, but Vargas refused to permit this. Estillac began to lose his base of support within the institution. The nationalists learned that they could not expect Estillac to be both the minister of war and their unfailing advocate.[4]

Attacks on CEDPEN

The nationalist faction lost not only faith in its leader, but also much of its civilian following. The CEDP had been renamed the Center for the Study and Defense of Petroleum and the National Economy (CEDPEN) in order to recognize the broad range of issues it had come to address. On April 2, 1951, a number of CEDPEN's old leaders publically broke with the center, which had adopted a tone of xenophobic anti-Americanism. General Horta Barbosa, General Leitao de Carvalho, and other ex-presidents published a letter to CEDPEN which said that because the center addressed irrelevant issues, they could not continue to support it. The public dispute that followed greatly benefited the government's efforts to portray CEDPEN as a communist front. The chief of police in the federal district, Gen. Cyrio Rio Pardense de Rezende, even wrote to thank General Horta Barbosa for helping to unmask the center. Nevertheless, CEDPEN repeatedly wrote to these former leaders and Gen. Raimundo Sampaio, to inform them that they had again been elected honorary presidents of the center. When they declined their old posts, an angry Gen. Felicíssimo Cardoso accused his former friends of aiding the government. Yet, by June 1951, these officers had stopped replying to CEDPEN's plaintive letters. Although some officers still remained in CEDPEN, the generals had helped to destroy the remnants of a civil-military alliance. Not only did the nationalist party lose the support of these civilians, it also exposed its former allies to government violence.[5] The days when a military faction could use mass mobilization to challenge the army hierarchy were over.

In June 1951 the head of the Federal Department of Public Security proposed closing CEDPEN because it was a public front for the communist party. Maj. Hugo Bethlehem, of the Political and Social Police, argued that the ex-presidents' letter proved that communists commanded the center. The army hierarchy—which controlled the police's leadership—then systematically attacked CEDPEN. On June 23, 1951, the center had a party in the home of engineer Pedro Coutinho Filho. The police arrived at nine that night, entered the house, shut off the lights, and beat those present. The leaders of CEDPEN went to Congress two days later to protest the attack, but they received little aid. The center's leadership therefore decided to discuss the mounting repression in a national convention. On July 5, 1951, Gen. Felicíssimo Cardoso began this convention at the headquarters of UNE (União Nacional de Estudantes), the students' organization. But when he began to speak, a provocateur stood up, fired a shot into the air, and yelled "Police!" Armed policemen then burst into the room, fired shots into the ceiling, and yelled "Communists!" One man broke his leg attempting to jump through the window, and another man suffered a fractured skull. Yet, the police allowed everyone to return home after the violence ended. They did not want to arrest the people present, but rather sought to create an atmosphere of terror. Without massive public support or the leadership of prominent generals, Brazilian institutions could not prevent the hierarchy's repression.

In this case, the political repercussions were more serious than they had been during the earlier attack at the engineer's house. Vargas ordered his minister of justice to report to Congress about the incident, and he called the chief of police to the presidential palace. This man, Gen. Cyrio Rio Pardense de Rezende, claimed that the conflict broke out at the event and that police had arrived only in response to the organizers' call for help. Although all the witnesses contradicted his version of events, no political group had enough power to punish him or the army commanders he represented.[6] The withdrawal of military support from CEDPEN allowed the army hierarchy to attack its civilian opponents with impunity.

The Journal of the Military Club

The turmoil within the nationalist party and its loss of civilian allies, did not prevent this bloc from advancing its vision of economic defense within the military. In March 1951 the *Revista do Clube Militar* resumed publishing after a two month hiatus. Despite the previous controversy, the journal continued to critique the hierarchy's call for an alliance with the United States. In April 1951 General Horta Barbosa published an article that argued that the United States might not want to develop Brazilian petroleum and that the U.S. government could not control American trusts. The nationalists believed that the United States wanted to maintain Brazil as an economic dependency, as Col. Salvador Corrêa de Sá e Benevides made clear: "Thus the interest of the United States, or better, of the international trusts that dominate the internal and foreign policy of the great nation to the north, is in retarding as much as possible the industrialization of Brazil."[7] Colonel Benevides went on to argue that the agents of the international trusts had used the article on Korea to attack the Military Club because they wanted to continue Brazil's economic slavery. The fact that the journal continued to attack the United States and to depict its military opponents as servants of Standard Oil infuriated internationalist officers beyond endurance.[8]

To internationalist officers, it seemed obvious that the Military Club had become a hotbed of communism. Early in June 1951 several colonels formed an executive committee to force the directory of the Military Club to call an assembly at which officers could vote to keep the journal from discussing controversial issues. The committee began circulating a petition that several generals immediately signed. These commanders also criticized the Military Club in public. On June 10, 1951, General Etchegoyen attacked the Military Club in a letter to General Horta Barbosa, who had become president after Estillac resigned. Two weeks later Gen. Zenóbio da Costa condemned the Military Club in the press. The hierarchy intended to silence its opponents.[9]

The Military Club refused to compromise before these attacks. In a special meeting on June 28, 1951, the directory of the club drafted a note for the public. This letter stated that the journal could not discuss questions of sectarian politics but that it would examine national issues. In what later proved to be a critical statement, General Horta Barbosa also announced that the *Revista da Clube Militar* would keep its editorial policy unless a general assembly of the club ordered it to change. Given the earlier conflict over the journal, this decision took courage. But the nationalists could not compromise. Because most of this faction's officers were retired, only the Military Club's journal allowed these officers to influence their peers. They could not abandon their most effective tool in their struggle to define the army's role.[10]

The United States, Korea, and the Amnesty Bill

By pursuing this policy the nationalist faction risked angering its most important supporter, Vargas, who hoped to gain critical aid from the United States. On February 12, 1951, Vargas had made General Góes Monteiro the new army chief of staff. Although both old and ill, Góes Monteiro had left for Washington on July 24, 1951, to attempt to use the Korean conflict to Brazil's advantage. The United Nations had appealed for additional troops on June 22, 1951, and the United States wanted Brazil to send a token contingent of soldiers. Although Brazilian troops could not have influenced the course of the war, they might have helped the U.S. propaganda effort. In Brazil, however, all political parties and the entire officer corps opposed the dispatch of troops. Vargas therefore gave Góes Monteiro a most difficult mission. Góes Monteiro had to make vague promises of Brazilian troops being deployed at some unclear point in the future, while attempting to revise existing treaties to Brazil's advantage. The entire effort depended upon maintaining the United States' expectation of Brazilian troops without committing to send them. Accordingly, General Góes Monteiro frustrated his U.S. counterparts, who wondered if he had arrived without an agenda. Nonetheless, Góes Monteiro handled a difficult assignment with consummate skill.

General Góes Monteiro revealed his goals to Estillac in a letter he wrote from Washington. Góes Monteiro stated that he wanted to revise previous U.S.–Brazil accords because otherwise Brazil would lose the financial aid it needed. Economic issues were his first priority, followed by questions of hemispheric defense. The U.N. resolution calling for more troops for Korea remained his least important concern. Accordingly, the interests of Brazil and the United States were difficult to reconcile, as General Góes Monteiro described: "At the end our drama with the United States can be summarized as the following: 'for them, without the question of Korea being given the highest priority in terms of the sending of troops, nothing interests them; and we, without economic-financial aid that permits the gradual development of our economy, above all transportation, hydro-electric energy, etc. . . . nothing more also interests us.' "[11] Vargas wanted to repeat the bargain of World War II without paying the price in troops. Accordingly, Góes Monteiro returned to the United States in October 1951 without any clear achievements, but he may have had more success than he realized. His U.S. counterparts mistakenly believed that he wanted to send a Brazilian division to Asia, and Góes Monteiro had lain the groundwork for a later military accord.[12]

Yet, while the Vargas administration negotiated with the United States in Washington, the nationalists vehemently criticized the United States' influence in Brazil. Even more disturbing to the government, Estillac fought to pass a bill to amnesty the officers involved in the 1935 communist uprising. In 1945 Vargas had passed a law that amnestied officers involved in earlier coup attempts. This legislation had allowed commanders like Prestes to return to politics. The bill that Estillac backed, however, permitted these men not only to return to the military but also to obtain the same rank and pay as if they had remained in service. Estillac's support for the bill shocked his fellow officers, who believed that fanatics could contaminate the armed forces.

Although Estillac's support for this bill weakened his authority, his core supporters backed this legislation. Indeed, the bill had been approved by the Commission on National Security, which included Artur Bernardes and a number of Estillac's supporters. These officers shared with the communists a desire for state-led development and the belief that the United States threatened Brazil's security. Accordingly, nationalist officers tolerated the few communists within the armed forces. Estillac held the political spotlight in coming months as he supported the amnesty bill.

Vargas understood the political risks Estillac's effort entailed. Vargas's 1945 amnesty had contributed to the military discontent that ended with his overthrow, and he did not wish to repeat that experience. Conservative politicians and the União Democrática Nacional (UDN) were outraged by the amnesty proposal. Army leaders claimed that in 1935 communist soldiers had killed their commanders while they slept. The Recife garrison telegraphed one senator who favored the amnesty to say that they hoped he would be present to help control the "Reds" when they returned to the barracks. The political costs made it dangerous for Vargas's government to approve the measure in the name of "social peace," especially because of international pressures. The controversy deeply worried some members of Vargas's administration, who feared it might damage Brazil's relationship with the United States at a crucial juncture. Vargas could not gain U.S. aid by promising to combat communism, while returning communist rebels to the ranks.[13]

Estillac's proposal encouraged internationalist officers to believe not only that the Military Club had been suborned by communism but also that communism cost the nationalist party the support of many officers who had participated in the petroleum campaign. Estillac's actions helped internationalist commanders gain the signatures they needed to force the Military Club to call an assembly. By this means, many internationalist officers hoped to silence the club's pronouncements on political questions.

An Assembly?

By August 13, 1951, a group of internationalist officers had collected over 2,000 signatures on a petition. This document called for a general assembly of the club to alter the journal's editorial policies. Yet many parties to the struggle had a reason to avoid an assembly. The hierarchy wanted to avoid a public clash that might damage the institution's image, the Military Club did not know if it could win a vote of the club's members, and many neutral officers wished to avoid further conflict. Accordingly, throughout August, neutral officers worked to prevent their peers from delivering the petition to the Military Club. On August 16, 1951, General Etchegoyen met with the club's vice-president, Artur Carnaúba. Their discussion went well. General Estillac then met the petition's organizers to suggest that the club's journal should be closed unless it changed its policies. Estillac asked the committee to delay delivering the petition. In the meantime, he suggested, the journal could announce key policy changes. It seemed that a painful clash might be averted and a facade of unity maintained.[14]

Yet the nationalist faction could not abandon its institutional voice. The Military Club never announced the expected policy changes. Instead, it waited in silence until the internationalists' committee delivered its petition to the club's president on August 27, 1951. The following day the press published the petition's demand that the club's journal cease its propaganda. Artur Carnaúba responded by publishing a note stating that the club would continue to defend both Brazil's natural resources and officers' right to free speech. The assembly was tentatively scheduled for September 10, 1951.[15] The president of the Military Club, General Horta Barbosa, decided to avoid the upcoming struggle. He had been gradually withdrawing from his duties as the club's president while the crisis approached. He turned the presidency over to Artur Carnaúba before embarking on an extended European vacation. Carnaúba delivered the club to its most radical members, who looked forward to the upcoming struggle.[16]

Carnaúba and his supporters believed that they were fighting to defend

Brazil's economy. The Military Club even published a handbill to argue that the club's critics attacked the nationalists in order to deliver Brazil to foreign trusts: "Its [the Club's] intransigent activity in defense of our sources of energy against the lusts of international organizations and its fidelity to the traditions of our Club, have drawn upon it the hatred of elements foreign to our class and bad Brazilians, interested in our economic enslavement and in the suppression of public liberties—civilian and military—which are inseparable from true national sovereignty."[17] In the handbill, the Military Club argued that the state should develop petroleum, monazite sands, and other strategic minerals. The club also condemned Hiléia Amazônica, a research center promoted by the United Nations. The Military Club claimed that wealthy nations wished to use this center to seize Brazilian resources in the Amazon. As the guarantor of the nation's independence, the army had to ensure Brazil's economic sovereignty. When the hierarchy attacked the Military Club, it did so to impose a liberal vision of development onto the nation, relegating Brazil to economic slavery. The question of free speech was at the core of the dispute.

The internationalists, however, stated that they wanted only to stop the Military Club from speaking on political themes in order to free the government from military pronouncements. The internationalists believed that the *Revista do Clube Militar* had been taken over by communists. According to internationalist officers, the Military Club had adopted the Soviet ideal of national liberation, which led it to organize the petroleum campaign and to attack the United States. The internationalists believed that the Brazilian army needed to ally with the United States to ensure hemispheric defense and to welcome the foreign capital Brazil needed. Still, the assembly was not a referendum on petroleum policy, despite Carnaúba's statements. The internationalists mainly wanted to maintain military discipline.[18]

At the core of the dispute were two opposing visions of defense. The nationalists viewed the United States and its powerful corporations as the main threats to Brazil. In particular, they feared an international presence in the Amazon and the economic domination of Brazil. These officers believed that a rational defense policy would focus less on tanks and planes than on petroleum refineries and other key resources. In contrast, the internationalists believed that international communism posed a grave threat to Brazil, as proven by the 1935 revolt. They wished to ally with the United States in hemispheric defense, which would not only generate ample foreign capital to develop the economy but also provide the army hierarchy with the resources it needed to create a powerful conventional army. In this sense, the two factions had radically different interpretations of the meaning of defense.

Although both blocs prepared feverishly for the upcoming assembly, Carnaúba had more success. Because the directory of the Military Club could organize the assembly, it could decide the meeting's agenda. Carnaúba intended to turn the meeting into a public affair—to transform it into a referendum upon national issues and a debate over the army's role. This was not what the club's opponents had intended, and they realized they had been outmaneuvered. On September 6, 1951, the internationalists adopted a conciliatory tone in a public note. They claimed that they intended the assembly only to change the editorial policies of the club's journal, not to make the work of the current directory more difficult. The commission wanted to meet with the club's president to discuss the assembly's agenda. Behind the scenes, neutral officers struggled to reconcile the opposing parties.[19]

Yet the Military Club did not intend to compromise. Instead, Carnaúba asked local radio stations to broadcast the upcoming debate. The Military Club also began attaching loudspeakers to the outside of its building to carry the assembly to the public. Carnaúba had arranged for three of the club's opponents to speak against fifteen of its supporters. These preparations received international attention, especially in the United States. The army hierarchy realized that even if it won, the assembly would be a disaster for the institution. The hierarchy had to cancel the gathering.[20]

The pressure upon President Vargas to resolve the crisis became intense. Indeed, many officers blamed Vargas for the conflict because they believed he could have defused the crisis months earlier. Commanders thought that Vargas encouraged the struggle because he wanted to keep the army too divided for a coup. Angered by the president's inactivity, high commanders such as General Zenóbio warned Vargas to end the confrontation. Realizing the gravity of the situation, Vargas met with Estillac on September 12, 1951 and told him to end the crisis. Estillac attempted to find enough signatures to delay the assembly, while rumors circulated that Vargas intended to replace him as minister of war. Yet Estillac remained at his post the night before the assembly, which had been rescheduled for September 20, 1951. Two thousand officers had flocked to Rio de Janeiro from the furthest corners of the nation. Inside the Military Club, officers frantically worked to finish stringing wires to loudspeakers on the outside walls. Carnaúba had announced that fifty officers would speak for the Military Club, for as long as twenty-five hours.[21]

The Postponement of the Assembly

On the night of September 19, 1951, Vargas called Estillac to the presidential palace for an hour-long private conference, Vargas ordered Estillac to resume the presidency of the Military Club and to end the agitation within the military. Estillac replied that he would resign if Vargas blocked the assembly. Vargas then forced Estillac to choose between delaying the assembly while he took action against communists or leaving his post as minister of war. Estillac chose to remain in the government, and Vargas gave him thirty days to resolve the crisis. Estillac then went to the Military Club and postponed the assembly for a month. The directory asked him to delay returning to the presidency for two days. Estillac refused and instead proposed closing the club. The conflict that followed was bitter and ended with Estillac's victory.[22]

On September 20, 1951, Estillac met with the club's most powerful opponents, such as General Etchegoyen, Gen. Zenóbio da Costa, Gen. Cordeiro de Farias, and Gen. Canrobert da Costa. Estillac told these commanders that the directory of the Military Club had betrayed him twice. Together, these leaders decided that Estillac would replace the directory of the *Revista do Clube Militar*, remain as president of the club, reverse Carnaúba's policies, and issue a note to the public. Estillac then sent a recommendation to the cultural department of the Military Club, asking that the journal not accept articles concerning sectarian politics or religious issues. He also ordered all officers to refrain from public statements about national or international questions. Finally, Estillac ordered the journal's editor, Maj. Humberto de Andrade, to complete his transfer to a remote state in the north as Canrobert had ordered. Notwithstanding his earlier argument with Vargas, Estillac tried to change the Military Club.[23]

Yet Estillac still tried to balance between being the head of a military faction and being the minister of war. He came to appear indecisive because he never made a clear break with his old supporters. On September 25, 1951, the internationalist faction expected Estillac to appear at a meeting of the deliberative council of the Military Club. The event required Estillac's full authority because Artur Carnaúba refused to resign his post as the hierarchy demanded. Estillac failed to attend the meeting, which then took place under Carnaúba's direction. The Military Club also published its journal, despite Estillac's clear promise that this would not take place. Internationalist commanders believed that Estillac had deceived them, and they gathered the next day to discuss the situation. Amongst those present was Estillac's brother, who commanded the Fourth Military Region and sympathized with the internationalist faction. Estillac had alienated his closest allies.[24]

There followed an extended struggle as both factions attempted to bend the minister of war to their will. Neither bloc succeeded, and each faction believed that Estillac had betrayed it. On October 4, 1951, the Military Club sent Estillac a lengthy letter welcoming him back to the presidency. In this letter the Military Club argued that the president's support for economic nationalism should have ended the struggle over the *Revista do Clube Militar*:

"We understand that, after the pronouncement of the chief of the government, in his speech of September 7th, pointing to imperialism as the enemy of economic independence, and given the highly responsible authority which gave this opinion, the differences that led some high military chiefs and other members to condemn the journal are outdated."[25] Yet many internationalist officers believed that Estillac would act decisively against the club's directory the next day, after a meeting with high commanders.

Estillac found himself in an impossible position, trapped between two blocs. After four days passed without action, however, Estillac met with Gen. Fiuza de Castro. This commander told him how the internationalists believed he should act to resolve the crisis. On October 9, 1951, Estillac met with Vargas before taking a proposal to end the conflict to the Military Club. Estillac forced a lengthy and bitter debate on his proposal. A vote found the directory to be evenly divided. When Estillac left the building he was too tired and worried to speak to the waiting reporters. Internationalist generals assumed an open tone of confrontation with Estillac as they pressured him to make a public statement against the club. Yet on October 16, 1951, Estillac canceled the upcoming assembly, which he had earlier postponed.[26] His declaration represented a complete victory for the Military Club. Not only had its opponents failed to win a vote in an assembly, but also the club's journal continued to publish articles advocating a vision of economic defense. Early in November, General Horta Barbosa returned from Europe and returned to his old post as the club's president. The Military Club's victory had united the nationalist faction. Estillac had decided to stop satisfying both parties, and he had turned his back on the army hierarchy.

Vargas and Development

In the end, the nationalists' victory may have helped to create a crisis by persuading these officers that they had the strength to fight Vargas. The president had campaigned and won on a platform of economic nationalism. While president, however, political reality compelled Vargas to make political compromises, even on sensitive issues such as petroleum development. During the first week of October 1951, while the struggle over the Military Club still raged, Vargas announced his intention to create a mixed company under national control to develop petroleum. Vargas received support from some famous members of the petroleum campaign, such as Artur Bernardes and General Horta Barbosa. The latter clearly recognized that a mixed corporation might be the best solution Brazil could achieve because of Brazilians' sympathy for these bodies. Yet when Vargas introduced his plan to

Congress on December 6, 1951, it met with cries of protest not only from conservative politicians but also from nationalist organizations. Many civilians and officers believed that the president's proposal left Brazil defenseless before the international trusts, which could invest in a mixed company.[27]

Yet Vargas remained reluctant to adopt a state-led approach to the petroleum industry, despite his rhetoric of economic nationalism during his election campaign. Vargas wanted to recapture the wartime arrangement that Brazil had enjoyed with the United States during the 1940s. Vargas knew that he could not send troops to fight in Korea. Yet given the demands of the U.S. war economy, Vargas believed that he could exchange raw materials in return for development capital. This arrangement, which Vargas conceived of as "economic reciprocity," was phrased in terms of defense concerns. The United States would demand resources because of its military requirements, while Brazil would receive special treatment because of its support for hemispheric defense. Consequently, Vargas favored the idea of a military accord because it would define the economic relationship between the United States and Brazil.[28]

The Military Accord

Although Vargas had appointed a staunch nationalist to be his minister of war, he had chosen a minister of foreign relations who was sympathetic towards the United States. João Neves da Fontoura had worked with General Góes Monteiro for months to lay the groundwork for a military accord. On August 22, 1951, General Góes Monteiro had telegraphed the administration that the United States had proposed such an agreement according to Brazilian priorities: first, to ensure internal security; second, to guarantee continental defense; and third, to prepare a force for Korea. In December the National Security Council discussed a possible accord during a meeting. No one had invited Estillac. The minister of war then caused a crisis by publishing a letter of protest he wrote to Vargas. In the letter Estillac protested any accord with the United States that might send troops to Korea. Still, on December 24, 1951, Fontoura wrote Vargas that he planned to begin negotiating with the U.S. ambassador on "a military accord and the sale of manganese, uranium, and monazite sands."[29] The army hierarchy and the government intended to fix Brazil into the military and economic relationship the nationalist faction most feared. Estillac dropped all pretense of neutrality in a desperate effort to prevent the accord.

On January 3, 1952, Brazil began formal talks with the United States to reach a military accord. Two days later President Vargas attended the traditional armed forces lunch for the president, where Estillac spoke in favor of a policy of economic defense and against greater co-operation with the United States. The minister of war became so emotional during his speech that he had to repeat passages because he stumbled over the words. Estillac even stopped in the midst of his speech to apologize for the vehemence with which he spoke. Estillac condemned those who wished to receive foreign loans and to increase Brazil's dependency, saying, "We are against all forms of colonialism." And he implied that the armed forces would not permit Brazil's economic policies to change: "It will not be with our consent that parts of the national sovereignty will be given away, nor that our hopes for a vigorous future will be frittered away."[30] Yet the audience of officers received his speech coolly. Vargas then spoke without making any reference to Estillac. Nonetheless, Vargas skillfully rebutted Estillac's speech by discussing Brazil's commitment to hemispheric defense and its international obligations. The 600 officers present awarded the president with warm applause. This moment marked a public break between the president and the nationalist faction. The Vargas administration ceased discussing military affairs with Estillac.[31]

The nationalist faction also faced political pressure because of the public's rising concern with communist infiltration within the army. The army hierarchy skillfully manipulated this fear to its own advantage. During the first week of February 1952, the Brazilian air force arrested eight sergeants who plastered an air base in Porto Alegre with communist slogans. Among those arrested was Lt. Hilton Bergman, an air force officer. This incident sparked a discussion in the senate over communist infiltration of the armed forces. But officers worried less about events at the base than over Bergman's escape from custody. Officers managed to recapture Bergman, only to find that he escaped a second time. Army commanders believed that collaborators within the armed forces had freed Bergman. Communist newspapers helped to feed a growing public hysteria, by claiming that "fascist" generals wanted to create a dictatorship in Brazil with the FBI's aid. On March 13, 1952, police in Rio de Janeiro arrested a communist mimeographing propaganda leaflets. According to the police, he had a list of the names of 500 officers and soldiers. Brazilian newspapers carried editorials calling for action and invoking the memory of the 1935 uprising. The issue received international attention. This political atmosphere set the stage for a wave of "anticommunist" repression, which allowed one military party to attack its opponents. The appearance of communist infiltration later enabled the hierarchy to impose its vision of the army's role by eliminating the vocal advocates of nationalism.[32]

Still the army hierarchy could not act while Estillac remained as minister of war. Yet Estillac's position became precarious after Vargas signed the U.S.–Brazil military accord on March 16, 1952. Earlier that year Ecuador and Cuba had signed similar accords that exchanged raw materials for military aid: "Its provisions are almost identical with those of the Ecuador agreement, covering first and foremost United States aid in arms, equipment, and technical skills in exchange for access to raw materials and the promise of armed support, if needed, in common defense of the hemisphere."[33] In the Brazilian case, the economic clauses of the accord prevented the access of communist nations to key resources, while obliging Brazil to sell manganese, uranium, and monazite sands to the United States at a fixed price. These provisions outraged nationalist officers, but the specific details were less important than the vision of defense and development that this accord defined. Although Vargas had campaigned on a program of economic nationalism, as president he accepted the hierarchy's view of the army's role. The accord created an economic and legal structure to translate the internationalists' vision of defense and development into government policy.[34]

The Military Club believed that it had been betrayed. Estillac and his supporters had helped to guarantee the president's inauguration because they thought that he supported their vision of defense. Yet Vargas had not returned Brazil's army to the role in economic oversight that it had held during the Estado Novo. Instead, Vargas had cemented Brazil's economic and military relationship with the United States according to the hierarchy's wishes. In the months before the signing of the accord, the club's journal had reflected the growing disillusionment and anger of these officers. The journal published articles calling for Brazilians to defend petroleum and atomic minerals. The journal also harshly criticized the president's proposal for a mixed corporation in petroleum, as well as his support for the military accord.[35]

General Zenóbio's Resignation

Criticizing the military accord, attacking the president's petroleum policy, and publishing xenophobic articles, the Military Club became a liability for Vargas. The army hierarchy had been unable to unleash repression against its opponents while the president had supported these officers and Estillac remained minister of war. Yet by March 1952 Estillac had come to loath Vargas: "In recent conversations with groups of generals, Leal has been reported to use harsh, even obscene language in referring to the President."[36] The internationalist faction, which controlled the hierarchy, moved to take advantage of the tension between the president and his minister of war. Generals Góes Monteiro and Canrobert, acting on the behalf of other generals, told President Vargas that he had to clean out his administration to save his government. Yet Vargas refused to bend before these threats directed at

Estillac. Instead, General Zenóbio created a crisis two days after the signing of the U.S.–Brazil military accord. Acting on his own initiative and not for the hierarchy, General Zenóbio wrote President Vargas to complain of the communist infiltration of the army. Angry that the "communists" had launched Estillac's name for reelection as the president of the Military Club, and, horrified by rumors that Vargas intended to accept his candidacy, Zenóbio offered the president his resignation. Zenóbio delivered his letter through the minister of war, following accepted procedure. Because of Zenóbio's serious accusations, Estillac also gave Vargas his own letter of resignation when he met the president, in the firm belief Vargas would refuse to accept it. Instead, Vargas took no action. Both commanders remained at their posts while the atmosphere of crisis heightened. While all Brazil waited for Vargas to choose between the two factions, rumors circulated of an impending coup.[37]

The Foundation of the Democratic Crusade

In making his decision, Vargas needed to consider not only the programs of these factions but also the power of their followings. During the previous election for the Military Club, Estillac's faction had acquired an extensive organization that many of Brazil's civilian parties might well have envied. In contrast, the hierarchy had run a disorganized campaign because it believed it could win based on its ideas alone. Many internationalist officers believed that their disorganization had cost them the election. Accordingly, in late September 1951, internationalist generals decided to form a political party within the armed forces to contest the May elections in the Military Club. The final impetus to organize this party came on February 14, 1952, when the Military Club held a conference to discuss the petroleum question. At this meeting, members of the nationalist faction stated that the directory of the Military Club remained "faithful to the high objectives of shaping public opinion."[38] They also claimed that an "army of salvation," composed of civilians and officers, had its "command post" in the Military Club. The hierarchy believed that the nationalists' control of the Military Club challenged their authority within the armed forces. To wrest control of the club from their opponents, they needed to organize.

In March 1952 internationalist officers issued a manifesto to create the Democratic Crusade, a military party to contest the upcoming elections. To this end, internationalist officers launched the candidacies of Gen. Alcides Etchegoyen, for the club's president, and Gen. Nelson de Mello, for vice-president. These two leaders, well known for their pro–United States views, promised to remove the club from questions of sectarian politics. The party quickly set up a complex organization, which included a formal hierarchy, civilian liaisons, and a fund-raising department. By mid-April, when Eduardo Gomes became the party's honorary president, internationalist officers had formed a formidable party. The foundation of the Democratic Crusade ended a long process through which particular leaders had become less important than the programs they advocated. The army had been polarized between two factions, which in many respects resembled political parties and that together defined military politics.[39]

The Two Factions

The internationalist faction, which had formed the Democratic Crusade, controlled the general staff. Its support was drawn from active-duty officers, most of whom commanded troops. Its base lay among infantry, artillery, and cavalry officers, and a few senior febianos. These officers had ties to civilian elites, who would fund their campaign, and with the UDN. They opposed Vargas because of his rhetoric of economic nationalism and his use of public mobilization. These commanders had never worked in the state corporations created during the Estado Novo. This party favored the United States and wanted to ally with that nation in hemispheric defense; they believed that the United States in return would not only strengthen the armed forces but also provide funds for Brazilian development. These officers did not favor unrestricted foreign investment because they believed that the government had to manage development to prevent it from creating challenges to the state. Yet for practical reasons they believed that Brazil's development depended upon its northern ally. These officers justified these policies by referring to the Cold War and the army's duty to prevent communist subversion within Brazil. Their vision of the army's role, originally created as a pragmatic calculation of military interests, had become a clear doctrine through the work of military intellectuals at ESG.

The nationalist faction drew its strength from engineers, older officers, and nationalists. It had few members from core services such as infantry. Almost all of its leadership had retired from active duty in order to escape the rules of discipline. leaving the faction with little power within the army, where its members were unable to promote their supporters, protect them from reprisals, or influence their training. Still, this faction retained considerable support among the youngest officers on active duty and many former febianos. The conservative journalist Carlos Lacerda had even claimed that, with the FEB's return, the communists had begun to infiltrate the army under the pretext of fighting for veterans' rights. This process culminated in 1950 when the Communist Party, working with some members of the Associação dos Ex-combatentes (the veterans' association), seized control of the Military Club.[40] Although Lacerda's comments were inaccurate and misleading, they illustrated the extent to which war veterans formed the dedicated core of the nationalists' membership.

While both the internationalists and the nationalists believed that security and development were linked, they differed on how to translate this belief into a political and economic policy. Nationalist officers remained dedicated proponents of a program designed to defend Brazil's economy from foreign infiltration. They perceived the United States, and the trusts they believed controlled it, to be Brazil's greatest threat. Old trends in military thought also influenced these officers. When Lobo Carneiro attempted to describe this party, he stated that he disliked calling it positivist—as not all its members espoused this philosophy—but that all these officers had been influenced by the famous positivist Benjamin Constant. According to positivism, a small, technocratic elite could promote the nation's progress. This vision accorded with the nationalists' belief that the army had to ensure the economic defense of the nation by managing a program of state-led development. In essence, these officers wanted to return the army to the role it had held during the Estado Novo. Although they distrusted Vargas, they had supported him in the past for this reason.[41]

In some respects, both factions resembled political parties in that they each sought to articulate a detailed program for national politics. And as with any political party, not every follower agreed with every aspect of the party's platform. For example, some commanders were sympathetic to the state development of petroleum but disliked the anti-American rhetoric of the nationalists. Other officers were dedicated nationalists but disliked Vargas or held right-wing views that clashed with the overall thought of the nationalist faction. It was also a risky move for any officer to become politically active if their superior held opposing views.[42] For all these reasons, an important bloc of officers, mainly mid-level troop commanders, did not belong to either wing of the army. Whichever military party could win the allegiance of these officers could control the army.

This struggle was an ideological contest. Bruce Farcau has argued that military factions in Latin America may adopt ideological positions to legitimate themselves but that these contests are really more about partisan advantage. Indeed, Farcau lists "Ideology" under the heading "Nonfactors" in his book: "It is my view that the ideology of a faction is determined largely by the charismatic leader of that faction."[43] Certainly, personal ties, shared experiences, regional loyalties, and many other factors shaped officers' allegiances.

But as the Brazilian army had professionalized during the twentieth century, its factions had increasingly formed along ideological lines. While the army sought to define its position in the international arena during the Cold War, ideological factors had begun to overshadow other claims on officers' allegiances. The character of the nationalist and internationalist factions indicated this fact. No one would have ever accused General Etchegoyen of being a "charismatic" leader, and many nationalists remained loyal to their faction in spite of, not because of, General Estillac. In the struggle between these factions, officers on both sides needed to persuade neutral officers of the ideological merits of their cause.

In 1950 Estillac's supporters had convinced these officers that the election was a referendum on petroleum. To win in 1952, the Democratic Crusade had to prevent this same perception from defining the campaign. Neutral officers wanted to concentrate on their specific duties instead of debating what they viewed as political questions. These leaders were deeply disturbed by the army's polarization and the public display of military conflict. Yet these commanders also worried about what they perceived as communist infiltration of the armed forces. The hierarchy realized that it could manipulate this fear to gain their support, provided it could defuse petroleum as an issue.

The Hierarchy's Tactics

The Democratic Crusade strove to remove petroleum as a campaign issue by having a series of high-ranking officers proclaim their desire for a state monopoly in petroleum. In March 1952, the front page of the newspaper *Jornal de Debates* captured the rhetorical struggle between the two military parties. A large picture of Generals Horta Barbosa and Estillac had the caption: "The slate launched by the officers of our armed forces who favor a state petroleum monopoly."[44] On the same page the paper reprinted a letter from General Dutra, who emphasized the importance of defending Brazil's petroleum reserves. Dutra's statements formed part of a carefully orchestrated campaign. When Juarez Távora stated that he planned to vote for the Democratic Crusade, he also stressed that the party did not share his views on petroleum. Indeed, he emphasized that the "democrats" would continue to struggle for a state monopoly in petroleum exercised through a mixed corporation. The conservative UDN (União Democrática Nacional, or National Democratic Union) came out in favor of a state monopoly of petroleum on May 10, 1952. The timing of this announcement and the ties this party had with the Democratic Crusade made it probable that the UDN made this deci-

sion to influence the election in the Military Club. These declarations persuaded many officers that Brazil's petroleum would be safe if they voted for
the Democratic Crusade.[45]

The hierarchy also manipulated the fear of communist infiltration that it
had begun to cultivate in February. When General Zenóbio proffered his
resignation, he had also ordered his men to arrest any officers they believed to
be communists. This order marked the onset of savage repression against the
nationalist party, as one of its members later remembered: "In March of 1952,
on the eve of the election—the election is in May—there was unleashed an
anti-communist trial in the armed forces. It was tremendous! Including bar-
barous tortures! You don't know! More than a thousand people were arrested,
between officers and civilians. They were arrested and faced trial, accused of
being Communists. . . . This was all done with two objectives: to get the
Communists and to influence the election. The political world accepted this
as a cleaning out of the armed forces."[46] A secret intelligence service within
the general staff tracked the activities of nationalist officers. The hierarchy
particularly targeted those soldiers forging ties between the enlisted ranks
and the nationalist party.

Bruce Farcau has argued that in Latin American armies only the officer
corps is politically engaged because poorly trained short-term conscripts lack
a sense of unity and purpose: "Consequently, it is the officer corps that has its
own political agenda to fulfill, and the inexperience and youth of the enlisted
troops has historically made them amenable to following the officers wherever they lead."[47] In fact, in Brazil the enlisted ranks have long taken part in
political contests. It would not be until after the 1964 coup that terror and
purges would end their political activity. Until that time, the enlisted men—
and in particular the sergeants—were an integral part of the military's factional conflicts. For example, on March 21, 1952, the army hierarchy arrested
several sergeants whom it accused being communists. In reality, the military
police arrested these men because they were leaders of a social club, the Casa
do Sargento. The nationalist party had used this organization to give talks on
economic development and to carry out propaganda among the enlisted men.
By arresting the president and the directory of the club, the Democratic
Crusade wanted to end the sergeants' support for the nationalists.[48]

The President's Choice

Vargas may have been the only man who could have halted this
repression, yet the president had to worry about his own position. Acting on
behalf of Vargas, Caio Miranda met a series of generals in March 1952, as he

had done before Vargas's inauguration. During one meeting, Gen. Cordeiro de Farias told Miranda that Estillac could not remain as minister of war because he had allowed the crisis to occur. Ominously, Cordeiro de Farias stated that Vargas's choice of Estillac and Nero Moura had cost him the support of the armed forces. In Brazil, the general stated, no one could govern without the military's backing. The president had to be either very sick or very tired not to see this crisis.[49] Yet Vargas could still surprise even those generals who had known him longest. Unable to accept either resignation without offending a military party, Vargas instead relieved both commanders from their posts. Vargas then named his own military aid, Gen. Ciro Espírito Santo Cardoso, to be minister of war. Although he was not a member of either military party, Santo Cardoso favored close ties to the United States. Estillac seemed to accept his demotion calmly. Nonetheless, the army hierarchy expected a backlash from their opponents, and troop commanders prepared for violence.[50]

The Campaign

Without Estillac as minister of war, the nationalist faction desperately needed to win the May elections in the Military Club. Estillac Leal initially refused to run, but the nationalists lobbied Estillac until he finally announced his candidacy on April 8, 1952. In his press release Estillac stated that he was campaigning to defend Brazil's natural resources from foreign interests. All Brazilians needed to unite to defend the national patrimony. The anticommunist campaign was only a smokescreen to give away Brazil's natural wealth.[51] These statements outraged internationalist officers because Estillac seemed to accuse the Democratic Crusade of betraying Brazil. The hierarchy also did not want to describe the contest as a debate over economic defense and development. Accordingly, General Etchegoyen published a note to the press on April 13, 1952, in response to what he called Estillac's grave accusations. Etchegoyen proposed creating a tribunal of honor, composed of members of parliament, to determine which military party was truly nationalist. Incredibly, the Democratic Crusade invited civilian arbitration of a military dispute. Yet Estillac refused to take this step.[52]

Estillac found that his post as minister of war had placed him in an impossible position. Although members of the nationalist faction had persuaded him to campaign, the party was divided. Some of Estillac's supporters had wanted him to leave the government when Vargas began negotiating a military accord. When Estillac decided to remain, he lost their backing, as one officer later described: "Estillac did not support us, and we did not support

Estillac."[53] Angered by their disdain, Estillac played only a minor role in the campaign. The contest was not focused on personalities but rather on ideology.

Both sides had created organizations that in some respects resembled powerful political parties in that they sought to rally the support of both officers and civilians to their cause. This similarity did not hold true in all respects. Neither faction's leaders ran for public office. The Democratic Crusade (sometimes called the "UDN in uniform") relied on its civilian allies to advance its cause in Congress. Nor did either party in this contest create the kind of grass-roots mobilization in 1952 that the nationalists had achieved in 1948. But the machinery of both factions resembled political parties, as they raised funds, lobbied civilians, published propaganda, collected intelligence, and conducted polls. In the space of five years, military factions had been transformed into much more organized structures, which endured long after the election. Ernâni do Amaral Peixoto described these factions as complex organizations with a sophisticated infra-structure of support staff and offices: "In the second election, there was a true General Staff on the two sides, spending a lot of money with trips, and offices placed close to the Military Club. The slate opposed to Etchegoyen had an office at the side of the Hotel OK, and they had rooms at the hotel at the disposition of officers that came from the interior. They ordered officers to travel constantly to visit garrisons obtaining support."[54] Both factions needed to campaign throughout the entire nation because the previous year the Military Club had changed its regulations to let officers in the interior vote. No longer was the contest confined to Rio de Janeiro; officers in the most remote garrisons found themselves drawn into the struggle.[55]

Officers could not have created such sophisticated organizations without both political expertise and money. The nationalist party had created its organization with the aid of civilian leaders such as Artur Bernardes and the funds it raised from civilians during the petroleum campaign. Yet, in 1952 this party retained only the support of ardent nationalists, who lacked the funds for an effective campaign. The Democratic Crusade, in contrast, used all the resources the UDN could command. A complex web of ties bound this civilian party to its military counterpart. Eduardo Gomes, the honorary head of the Democratic Crusade, had twice run for the presidency for the UDN. Juarez Távora, another key member of the Crusade, would run for president in 1955 with the UDN's backing. These leaders turned to the UDN for advice and funds. Nelson de Mello, the vice-presidential candidate of the Democratic Crusade, said that this aid greatly strengthened his campaign. Even many elites who opposed the UDN gave the Democratic Crusade money because they believed

Estillac to be a socialist. The Democratic Crusade also found support in the navy and the air force, traditionally conservative services. The air force allowed the Democratic Crusade to use its planes to carry to the interior both its representatives and its propaganda. The hierarchy's authority, the elites' money, and the air forces' aid all served to create an impressive electoral machine as Nelson de Mello noted: "With the campaign the Crusade reorganized itself, it strengthened itself, and it obtained money. That's no joke! To send someone to Rio Grande do Sul to carry out the campaign money is necessary. . . . We ordered agents to all the interior of Brazil, to all the garrisons. Cordeiro didn't conduct this campaign. It was done only in Rio de Janeiro. But after the [1950] defeat every-one created a great force; my God in Heaven! They went to all the garrisons, they obtained people from aviation, the air-force with planes, [and] money."[56] The Democratic Crusade had the money and the means to run a sophisticated campaign, which their opponents could not match.

Still, as the election approached, in April and May 1952 the leaders of the Democratic Crusade worried about their opponents' strength. The president and vice-president of the Democratic Crusade (Gen. Alcides Etchegoyen and Gen. Nelson de Mello) both had led the federal police during the Estado Novo, a time when political terror was widespread. This experience gave them contacts with the police and an understanding of how to manage an intelligence service. These men decided to use terror to make assurance doubly sure.

Terror

As it grew clear that the election would be decided outside of the capital, internationalist officers targeted nationalist commanders laboring in the interior, raising funds from civilians, meeting the enlisted ranks, and lobbying officers. The army hierarchy arrested these officers, held them incommunicado, and used torture.[57] Word of these events reached the press and the Brazilian public, but the army's leadership persuaded civilians that brutality was necessary to root communists out of the military. For this reason, there was little popular protest when soldiers were beaten on their genitals, burned with cigarettes, and confined to toilet stalls.[58]

Soldiers working for the nationalist campaign were arrested throughout Brazil in April and May of 1952.[59] For example, air force major Sebastião Dantas Loureiro was arrested on April 7, 1952, while traveling to interior garrisons on the nationalists' behalf. The military police seized and kept

dozens of ballots he had brought with him, all of which favored the nationalist slate. Loureiro was not alone. Dozens of his compatriots were also arrested
and held incommunicado.[60] Moreover, many officers claimed that the military tortured them, an accusation that attracted press attention for years to
come.[61] This violence may have reflected the desperation of internationalist
officers, who feared that despite their organization the nationalists might win
the impending election.[62]

This violence was hard to conceal. Prisoners showed visible signs of mistreatment.[63] Tortured officers and their families sent a document to the General Assembly of the United Nations that described prisoners' sufferings.[64]
Congressmen denounced the abuse of prisoners.[65] In 1953 nationalist soldiers
published a book which described their torture, *Depoimentos esclarecedores
sóbre os processos militares*. As the newspaper *Correio da Manhã* reported, the
Brazilian people quickly purchased thousands of copies of this work.[66] Yet this
publicity failed to stop the violence. The naval base on Snake Island (Ilha das
Cobras) was the site of torture, as it once had been after the Revolt of the
Whip in 1910 and would be again after the 1964 coup.[67]

Brazilian society was aware that an atmosphere of terror existed within the
armed forces. Yet most people accepted the hierarchy's assertion that imprisoned soldiers were communists as a justification for torture.[68] This toler-
ance permitted a coordinated effort by the armed forces and the police to
eliminate military dissidents.[69] In practice, the participation of all three military services and the civilian police in the repression was seamless. As the
manifesto of the Brazilian Association in Defense of Human Rights made
clear, sailors could be arrested by "the Special Police," then transported to a
naval prison, where they would be tortured by military officers.[70] Air force,
navy, and army officers also led Military Police Inquiries (IPMs) attacking
dissident officers in their services.[71] While the factional conflict had begun
within the army, by 1952 all branches of the armed forces witnessed the use of
terror. In the days before the election, this repression overcame the nationalists' political organization. Many nationalist officers assigned to bring ballot
boxes to Rio de Janeiro disappeared. Fear silenced the enlisted ranks, which
had become politically active.[72] The nationalist party found that its organization collapsed in the days before the election. The internationalist party had
created an apparatus for intelligence-gathering and for torture which would
continue to haunt Brazil for decades to come.

Estillac Leal was well aware of what was happening. In early April 1952 the
U.S. embassy believed that the nationalist candidate, General Estillac, would
win. Yet on April 25, 1952, in the midst of the election campaign, Estillac fled
the capital for Porto Alegre. At the airport, Estillac Leal told baffled reporters

that he was leaving because he wished to hunt and fish. Estillac also discussed Etchegoyen's call for a tribunal of honor. He believed that the two parties had divided over economic and cultural issues and that the debate should take place before a school or philosophy faculty. However, that same day Estillac published a letter rejecting the idea of a tribunal. Estillac realized that the dispute would not be ended by a philosophical debate. A principled man, Estillac did return to the capital a few days before the election to give an impassioned speech before the Military Club: "If more than a century ago we proclaimed our political independence, the moment has arrived for us to construct with energy and firmness the economic independence of our country."[73] But Estillac knew that his faction was being destroyed.

The Election

On election day, May 21, 1952, a lengthy line of officers formed early before the Military Club opened its doors at nine that morning. Once inside, officers had to pass through a long hall filled with the screaming supporters of both parties. On the left-hand side, nationalist officers leaned over their tables, as they attempted to stuff their ballots into officers' hands. On the opposite side, young members of the Democratic Crusade yelled to drown out their opponents' cries. Estillac was one of the first officers to enter this pandemonium, followed soon afterwards by Etchegoyen. Despite the conflict of the prior two months, both men embraced and smiled before the cameras. Gen. Correia Lima, a retired officer who had taught both of these commanders, then approached his former students. "I just want to see what these children are fighting about," he told one reporter.[74] Never had so many officers appeared to vote. Reporters photographed one general—too ill to walk without aid—as two officers helped him up the steps. Although Lt. Col. Miguel Travassos was 108 years old, he arrived to vote for the Democratic Crusade. The minister of war also cast his ballot for the hierarchy's party. A picture of Etchegoyen—short, fat, and wearing a bad tie—showed him standing with the Democratic Crusade's leadership: Mascarenhas de Morais, Eduardo Gomes, Canrobert Pereira da Costa, Cordeiro de Farias, and Juarez Távora. The generals looked relaxed and confident.

The voting stopped at nine that evening, and by 10:30 vote counters announced that Etchegoyen was in the lead. Officers applauded and set off rockets in Cinelândia plaza, where police had attacked the petroleum gathering in September 1948. The final results were announced at two in the morning. Etchegoyen and Nelson de Mello had received 8,288 votes, while Estillac and

Horta Barbosa had received only 4,489 votes. When Etchegoyen left the building, one reporter asked him how the army would handle petroleum after the election. The general replied that he "was elected by eight thousand members that don't want any more discussion about this question in the Club."[75] Indeed, the army hierarchy wanted to erase all memory of its painful struggle and the violence it had entailed. The day after the election, Etchegoyen met with reporters in his apartment. Before taking questions, Etchegoyen warned the journalists, "I am ready to answer only the questions that are about subjects after the elections. I forgot everything before the vote. I have a poor memory."[76] Collective amnesia has remained the army's official policy ever since.

Debutantes' Balls and Hidden Repression

On June 26, 1952, the Democratic Crusade officially took control of the Military Club. The nationalist party insisted that its subcommittees should continue to work on national problems. But the Democratic Crusade refused to allow its opponents into the Military Club, even for charity work. The Democratic Crusade intended to convert the Military Club into a symbol of the army's innocent social life. In late August the new directory celebrated its inauguration with a debutantes' ball, attended by thirty-six young women. These teenagers passed the night dancing with old military men, including General Etchegoyen, while photographers snapped their pictures. The entire evening formed part of a carefully crafted public relations effort, in which reporters played a willing part: "Between the dances, they [the debutantes] heard the greeting of General Etchegoyen who spoke of his emotion at the beautiful encounter—and truthfully the debutantes were a garland of human roses that crowned with purity and touching poetry the splendid victory of the Democratic Crusade. A victory for Brazil and therefore for its youth."[77] The new directory adopted a busy agenda of social activities, which included cooking classes for officers' wives and a book-reading club for their husbands. At the same time, the army hierarchy continued its ruthless efforts to purge its opponents from the institution. At the end of June, the commander of the First Military Region presented the minister of war with evidence of the "Bolshevik infiltration" of the army. This marked a renewed wave of repression through mass arrests that lasted until November 1952.

The internationalists wanted to eliminate not only all trace of opposition but also all memory of the struggle. Yet, the prisoners' families refused to let the fate of their loved ones disappear from public attention. By late June the officers arrested during the campaign had been held incommunicado for sixty to eighty days, during which many of them had been cruelly mistreated. Their mothers and wives began to come forward and to write heart-wrenching letters to the capital's press. Because almost all of the prisoners were war heroes, the families' accusations received coverage. The prisoners included Maj. Leandro Figueredo, who had seen combat in Italy; Capt. Joaquim Miranda de Andrade, whose unit had helped to take Monte Castelo; and Maj. Fortunato Câmara de Oliveira, who was a great hero of the air force. These mens' spouses described in graphic detail how their husbands were held in cells without light by guards with fixed bayonets, and given little chance to see their families. These women all proclaimed their pride in their imprisoned loved ones because they believed they had been arrested for defending the Brazilian economy. Like a hundred other officers, one women stated, her husband had been the victim of an injustice; a true nationalist, his only crime had been to work for Estillac's campaign because he wanted to protect Brazil's national riches.[78]

Fearful of further publicity, the internationalists also used threats and accusations of communism against the military judiciary to ensure that nationalist commanders remained imprisoned. In July 1952 Amador Cisneiro do Amaral, one of the prosecutors trying the military prisoners, protested that it was illegal to hold prisoners incommunicado for more than three days. This led him into a dangerous clash with the head of the military police inquiry, Col. Amauri Kruel. Such pressure ensured that many nationalist officers were not freed until July 1954. By then the army and navy to which they returned had changed, and new mechanisms were evolving to ensure the control of internationalist officers such as Gen. Nelson de Mello and Gen. Alcides Etchegoyen.[79]

On May 25, 1953, Vargas approved a report submitted to him by the National Security Council. The law gave the hierarchy the power to punish reserve officers who carried out "subversive activities" or showed "disrespect for their superiors." In describing those whom this law targeted, Gen. Aguinaldo Caiado de Castro said: "They are in the majority former colonels, including some from the services, promoted to be generals on entering the reserve. They join campaigns of Communist origin such as 'the petroleum is ours' or the 'peace' [campaign], etc. and they systematically attack the United States. They have fought the Military Agreement by every method, and in general have shown themselves to be very active."[80] The new legislation allowed the hierarchy to attack the commanders who had retired to escape the bonds of discipline. The internationalist officers forced their most brave and vocal opponents to leave the institution. Predictably, the Democratic Crusade easily won the 1954 election in the Military Club.

The Democratic Crusade and Politics

The campaign had been a referendum between two visions of the army's role, which defined the army's strategy for defense, development, and foreign affairs. Estillac himself described the contest in this manner, and even biased foreign observers understood that the parties had not clashed over communists in the military. Accordingly, the Democratic Crusade interpreted its victory as a mandate for its program. The election did not end the polarization of the military between two parties, but no longer could the nationalist faction so successfully present an alternative vision of defense from within the institution itself. The victory of the Democratic Crusade changed the army as a political actor.

The Democratic Crusade's victory had important implications for Brazil's economic policies. When Cordeiro de Farias had told Caio Miranda that no president could hope to govern Brazil without the armed forces' support, he had described Brazil's political reality. The military, therefore, influenced the government's policy even on such sensitive issues as petroleum, as the foundation of Petrobrás proved. Immediately after the Democratic Crusade's victory, the army hierarchy had attempted to avoid any military discussion of petroleum because it remained an explosive issue. Still, the president of the Democratic Crusade continued to state that his party had a sincerely nationalist attitude towards Brazil's natural riches. Accordingly, the army hierarchy did not intervene the following year as civilian groups lobbied for a state petroleum monopoly which would ban foreign participation in petroleum development. On October 3, 1953, President Vargas signed the decree into law that created this state monopoly, called Petrobrás. Yet the army hierarchy ensured that Petrobrás challenged neither military interests nor its vision of development. Understanding the army's concerns, Vargas appointed Juraci Magalhães, the former head of the UDN, to be Petrobrás' first president. Magalhães had close ties to the military leadership of the Democratic Crusade. His successors as president were almost all internationalist officers, such as Idálio Sardenburg, one of the founders of ESG. One can hear the disillusionment in the voice of Nelson Werneck Sodré: "And I make a statement that you could confirm: Petrobrás never had a nationalist president! None of the groups that ran the Petrobrás campaign, the campaign for the thesis of a state monopoly, was integrated into the organization of Petrobrás's leadership."[81] After Vargas's death the internationalist officers worked to ensure Petrobrás's survival. No longer was Petrobrás associated with economic nationalism, mass mobilization, and anti-Americanism. Petrobrás had mattered because of a larger struggle about Brazil's position within the international system, not because senior officers had a fierce opposition to state-led development in key sectors of the economy. Once the internationalists believed that they were victorious, Petrobrás no longer appeared threatening. Instead, the army hierarchy controlled the state monopoly to make it a useful instrument for petroleum development and a sinecure for internationalist officers.

The Democratic Crusade's concern with economic issues and their newfound power within the army created a dangerous situation for President Vargas. Internationalist officers had opposed Vargas's inauguration in 1950, and they believed that Vargas had encouraged the army's divisions in 1951. Their resentment made it difficult for Vargas to resolve a number of political paradoxes, described by a U.S. National Intelligence Estimate in December 1953. To obtain a majority in Congress, Vargas needed the support of conservatives. Yet these politicians distrusted Vargas, whom they perceived as an opportunist. Any concessions to conservatives angered the working-class, who formed the core of his constituency. Yet Vargas needed foreign capital to provide the economic growth to satisfy working class demands: "Vargas is politically committed to maintain a high rate of economic development, which can be accomplished only with substantial amounts of foreign capital. Substantial foreign investment is precluded by the prevalent nationalistic attitude towards such investment and by the uncertainty of the economic outlook."[82] These contradictions made it difficult for Vargas to govern without a strong political party to implement his political and economic agenda. Because of the weakness of the Brazilian party system, Vargas needed the army's support, much as he had during the Estado Novo. Yet by this point the military was dominated by a faction hostile to Vargas.

Vargas adopted an approach to economic development that accorded with many of the army hierarchy's ideals. Yet the internationalist officers so distrusted the president that even his minor concessions to nationalist sentiment created grave resentment. Francisco Teixeira described what the Democratic Crusade's victory meant to Vargas: "It was finished. So, from there on, Getúlio governed with a tremendous military opposition, tremendous! It was not secret, it was not a silent crisis, no it was public."[83] Vargas could have finished his term with good luck and his old energy, but in the end Vargas had neither. In August 1954 a presidential bodyguard attempted to assassinate one of the president's harshest critics, the conservative journalist Carlos Lacerda. The attempt failed, but the assassin killed an air force officer who had been guarding Lacerda. The air force swiftly traced the plot back to the presidential palace. Vargas probably had been ignorant of the plot, but the military demanded his resignation and threatened a coup. No longer could Vargas call on an organized and powerful military party to support him against the hierarchy. The coalition Vargas had created to ensure his inauguration had collapsed. New ties had formed between internationalist officers and the civilian elites who opposed Vargas. It had been no coincidence that Lacerda had enjoyed an air force bodyguard. Military leaders—all members of the Democratic Crusade—insisted that Vargas leave the presidency. Instead, on August 24, 1954, Vargas first wrote a note to the public, then turned a revolver on himself.[84]

The new president, João Café Filho, immediately turned to the Democratic Crusade's leadership to consolidate his power. As Nelson de Mello has described, internationalist officers gave their full support to the new president. Juarez Távora became the head of Café Filho's military cabinet. Eduardo Gomes—who had been honorary president of the Democratic Crusade—became the minister of the air force. Zenóbio da Costa, who had never been a member of the Democratic Crusade, lost his post as minister of war. To restore unity to the military, Távora recommended Henrique Lott, well known for his apolitical views, to be the next minister of war. Henrique Lott later removed Estillac from his command in São Paulo, after ensuring Café Filho that no unrest would result. The nationalist party survived and would continue to struggle against the hierarchy. Nonetheless, Estillac's defeat marked the end of an era. Vargas's downfall had proved that a president needed the support of the army's dominant party in order to govern. His suicide not only served as a warning to future leaders but also illustrated the Democratic Crusade's ability to define military politics. In this sense, Vargas's suicide brought the parting of the waters to an end.[85]

Conclusion

The victory of the Democratic Crusade reshaped the army's role in society. Officers acquired a clear program that involved the army in the struggle against communist infiltration and advocated development in alliance with foreign capital. This political and economic program was legitimated by an official ideology that had the support of the dominant party within the military, and this agenda had meaning to officers because they had forged it during internecine struggles. A series of ideals that commanders had originally adopted to satisfy military interests now defined the identity of the party controlling the army.

This change altered the army's nature as a political actor. During the petroleum struggle in 1948, nationalist officers had called mass protests that had brought tens of thousands of Brazilians into the street. By 1954 the nationalists had few civilian allies, and there were no large public protests against the mistreatment of nationalist officers. No longer could a military faction use mass mobilization as a tool to defeat the army hierarchy. Instead, the army hierarchy had changed the terms of the contest with its opponents. The nationalists were not defeated until 1964, and some of their economic ideals were later appropriated by another bloc, the duros (a faction of the far right), after the coup. But 1954 represented a political watershed because the informal structures that later laid the groundwork for military government already existed. Many policies and beliefs that had an immense impact on Brazil during authoritarian rule can be traced to this period.

8

The Foundations of Military Rule

The struggle between the internationalists (which after 1952 came to be called the blues) and the nationalists (the yellows) did not end in 1952 with the wave of terror that accompanied the Military Club's elections or in 1954 with the suicide of Vargas. Because both blocs had created powerful loyalties among officers, only a radical purge of the institution could ensure either party's final victory. This purge began in 1964, when the Brazilian armed forces overthrew the president and began twenty-one years of authoritarian rule. The Democratic Crusade played a crucial role in organizing the coup and in eliminating nationalists from the army.

Of course, the army was only one actor among many that combined to end Brazilian democracy, and it was never a unified power, neither before the coup nor in the years that followed it. Factional strife continued, although the issues in the struggle had often changed. Yet 1954 represents a watershed in Brazilian history, not because of the victory of the internationalists—as that conflict would not be decided for another decade—but rather because by this point the informal structures—the alliances, the beliefs, and the patterns—that later shaped the character of authoritarian rule already existed.

The military contained a powerful faction, united behind a clear ideology, which dominated the hierarchy. This faction was allied with conservative civilians, a bond that was strengthened by long-standing corruption, which officers used to distribute rewards to their followers. This faction had the support of the dominant power in the hemisphere, the United States, based on their shared anticommunism, and the internationalists had also created an informal intelligence service within the army. Within this organization they had placed men willing to use terror against their opponents. On this basis, the culture of fear that later shaped authoritarian rule emerged. Finally, as José Murilo de Carvalho has argued, the army underwent a process of "whitening" at "exactly the moment in which the institution would assume a central role in the politics of the country."[1] This process altered an older tradition in which people of color more readily gained entrance to the officer corps. These informal structures, including racial beliefs, colored military rule after the coup of April 1964.

The Enduring Struggle

Throughout the late 1950s and early 1960s, Brazilians became increasingly polarized as the political system lurched from one crisis to another. A complex series of factors combined to weaken Brazilian democracy. Along with the military, many actors—the political left, traditional elites, the Church, the United States, business interests, and conservative parties— shared responsibility for undermining the political system. Other scholars have carefully described these events, and this history lays outside the scope of this book.[2] Still, it is worth noting that the Democratic Crusade played an important role in preparing the military for the coup.

The contest between nationalists and internationalists lasted for more than a decade after Estillac Leal's defeat in 1952. In May 1954 the Democratic Crusade again won control of the Military Club. Gen. Canrobert Pereira da Costa became the club's president, while Gen. Juarez Távora became its vice-president. But the Democratic Crusade was defeated by a narrow margin in 1956, when Gen. João de Segadas Vianna won the presidency of the Military Club. In 1958 Gen. Humberto de Alencar Castello Branco ran for the presidency of the Military Club on behalf of the Democratic Crusade and lost. But this experience formed an enduring alliance between two key officers: "The campaign brought Castello into daily contact with Colonel Golberi do Couto e Silva, coordinator of the effort of the Democratic Crusade."[3] Golberi stated that Castello Branco (who became Brazil's first military president after the 1964 coup) was embittered by his defeat. Castello Branco even accused his opponents of using informers and damaging the careers of their opponents.[4] Internationalist officers realized that no electoral victory could ensure their permanent dominance. Only a complete purge of the institution could achieve this goal. Internationalist officers eventually turned to Golberi do Couto e Silva to prepare an organization of intelligence and terror for this purpose.[5]

The Terror before the Coup

Then Lt. Col. Golberi do Couto e Silva had entered the Escola Superior da Guerra in March 1952, where he remained until 1955.[6] The army hierarchy (especially Gen. Canrobert Pereira da Costa) had created this school as an instrument of internal propaganda to indoctrinate officers with the views of the Democratic Crusade. In this position, Golberi's opposition to "liberal" politicians endeared him to influential generals. Golberi was imprisoned for eight days in November 1955 after he sought to prevent Juscelino Kubitschek's inauguration as president. He also tried and failed to prevent the inauguration of João Goulart, the vice-president and leader of the left-wing Partido Trabalhista Brasileiro (PTB), in September 1961. That month, Golberi left his position as the head of the National Security Council and retired to the reserves, where he received the rank of general.[7] His retirement did not end his involvement in civilian affairs.

The general staff had planned a coup in late August and early September 1961, which failed in part because of nationalist sergeants and their civilian allies.[8] Afterwards, the Democratic Crusade believed that for a coup to succeed, it needed to silence military nationalists first by breaking their ties to civil society. Gen. Nelson de Mello, one of the Democratic Crusade's founding members, was at this time minister of war. Golberi moved to organize the military's informal system of intelligence in order to expand its reach into civilian society. In November 1961, Golberi helped to create the Instituto de Pesquisas e Estudos Sociais (Institute for Research and Social Studies, IPÊS), with the aid of conservative elites. For the next three years, Golberi would serve as the research chief of IPÊS.[9] He used his experience managing the intelligence work of the National Security Council under President Quadros to create an "efficient intelligence service" within this civil-military body.[10] From his office in Rio de Janeiro, General Golberi's team monitored over three thousand phones with secret recording devices. Based on this information, Golberi sent special reports to high commanders. These analyses argued that military discipline was collapsing because union leaders had formed dangerous alliances with nationalist sergeants. This information helped internationalist officers persuade key generals to support a coup in order to protect the institution from internal rebellion.[11] By March 1964, internationalist officers seized upon a political crisis to rally the military against the government.

General Golberi took part in planning the 1964 coup.[12] He first organized a wave of terror in which hundreds of soldiers were seized. Officers were retired, transferred, imprisoned, and deprived of all political rights. Dissident officers despaired as their families received death threats, colleagues were seized in their homes, and soldiers were tortured.[13] Officers went underground but with slight chance of escape.[14] The lower ranks faced even more savage repression. This terror eliminated opposition within the armed forces and enabled the coup to succeed. Golberi's organization then used terror against civilians to silence political dissent. In the aftermath of the coup, perhaps 7,500 men were purged from the armed forces, and perhaps 30,000 soldiers and civilians were imprisoned.[15]

On June 13, 1964, the army institutionalized General Golberi's organization, which became the Serviço Nacional de Informações (SNI), and made Golberi its first leader. Golberi fondly referred to the SNI as the "Ministry of Silence."[16] His organization was only one institution of terror among many.[17] The navy had played an active role in the repression surrounding the coup, and the holdings of CENIMAR (Centro de Informações da Marinha), the naval intelligence service, retained a fearsome reputation throughout military rule.[18] Still, the SNI played the major role in projecting terror into civilian society. Golberi (a man much respected as the army's best thinker) would later lament that he had unintentionally created a monster.[19] In fact, his organization resulted from years of careful planning and work with civilian organizations.[20] His men were not renegade officers who tortured nationalist commanders without the knowledge of army leaders. Internationalist officers had first used terror to control the army in 1952. After 1964 members of the Democratic Crusade adapted this same system to ensure the army's control over civil society.

The Basis of Military Government

The 1964 coup represented the ultimate triumph of officers linked to the Democratic Crusade, many of whom took senior positions in the new government. Gen. Augusto César Moniz de Aragão, the head of the Democratic Crusade, had at first refused to conspire, but the Democratic Crusade continued its work without his direction, and he finally changed his position. Indeed, after the coup Moniz de Aragão nominated Gen. Castello Branco to be the first president of the authoritarian regime.[21] Brazilian officers, such as Lt. Col. Octávio Costa, clearly perceived the coup to be a triumph of the Democratic Crusade and a result of the long struggle that preceded 1964:

And there was . . . a movement in place in the Military Club. . . . I already discussed the two clear tendencies: one nationalist, statist, characterized by those who voted for the "yellow slate," and the other (blue) of the Democratic Crusade. . . . The movement returned with the contest over successive elections in the Military Club; the Crusade was the central focus from which spread the revolutionary thought of 1964, uniting [officers], activating them, creating contacts. People went from Rio [de Janeiro] to the interior in order to meet people who served in distant places. Driven almost personally by Figueiredo [General João Figueiredo was one of the Democratic Crusades' leaders], it was a center of organization that unleashed the movement of '64."[22]

Of course, democratic government did not collapse solely because of the work of the Democratic Crusade. Alfred Stepan and John W. F. Dulles have shown how a combination of factors served to undermine the Brazilian political system.[23] But the army's decision to retain power—and the policies that it imposed—had its roots in the experience of the preceding decades.

The Informal Structures That Shaped Military Rule

Many key structures that laid the groundwork for military rule existed by 1954, including the Democratic Crusade. The character of military factions had changed considerably since the early twentieth century. The positivists, the Young Turks, and the tenentes had held the loyalty of only a minority of officers, many of whom came from the lowest ranks of the organization. It was for this reason that the tenentes acquired their name. The Democratic Crusade not only controlled the hierarchy but also attracted officers from all the ranks. Both the Democratic Crusade and its opponents were more carefully organized and less reliant on personalities than many past factions. In the 1930s, many factions had been named after their leaders. In contrast, by 1952 Estillac could disappear during the closing stage of the campaign within the Military Club, but the nationalists (many of whom despised Estillac) continued the struggle. Although personal loyalties remained important, both the nationalists and the Democratic Crusade had created a sophisticated structure (with presidents, vice-presidents, secretaries, and membership lists) that could endure past the departure of any one man. As officers sought to define the meaning of military rule, new factions would quickly emerge after 1964. But the character of military factions had permanently changed.

The military had also become ideologically polarized after World War II. In the past, isolated groups had acquired programs for the institution, but these programs were not always truly military; for example, the positivists were defined by a civilian ideology. Other factions had a purely military vision, which did not entail a large-scale program for society. This was the case of the Young Turks. Even those factions that did seek to create a vision for society only did so in the most vague terms, which proved to be the weakness of the tenentes. After 1930 the tenentes had come to a position of considerable power within Vargas's new regime, which represented an opportunity to put their beliefs into practice. But when tested, this faction proved to be so ideologically divided that it splintered between the left and right. The tenentes shared a vague ideology but not a clear program. This division helps to explain why all these factions had difficulty institutionalizing their beliefs.

In contrast, both the nationalists and the Democratic Crusade had a carefully articulated agenda. After 1954, the Democratic Crusade proved to be increasingly successful in translating this ideology into an official doctrine, National Security Ideology (NSI). Internationalist officers had codified this school of thought and ensured that officers were indoctrinated at the Escola Superior da Guerra (ESG). Other factions, such as the Young Turks, had never been able to impose their thought onto the institution as a whole because they had not controlled the hierarchy. National Security Ideology was not only a powerful trend in military thinking; it also represented a program for rule. When the military seized power in 1964 (despite many differences of thought within the institution), it had a sophisticated plan to alter Brazilian politics, economics, society, and culture. Between 1945 and 1954 ideology acquired new importance in military politics, a trend that endured.

To ensure ideological conformity within the institution, the Democratic Crusade had turned to military terror. During the campaign for the Military Club in 1952, officers and their men had been held incommunicado, and some had undergone unspeakable tortures. This structure of terror survived. When the military seized power in 1964, it used fear as a political instrument to intimidate both its military and its civilian opponents. What is striking about the military's use of terror is its scale and its professionalism. Military terror did not suddenly appear from nowhere. The military had used organized fear to uphold the social, political, and racial order ever since the colonial period. What had changed was the regularization and organization of terror, so that specific institutions (such as SNI) not only collected intelligence but also used systematic violence to quell opposition. Thoughtful and educated men had slowly laid the basis for these organizations after World War II, as these officers took part in a fierce ideological conflict within the military.

Terror alone, however, would not have been enough for the military to have seized and retained power. The army also needed civilian allies. During the factional conflict after World War II, both the nationalists and the Democratic Crusade had formed powerful alliances with civilians. Indeed, in not only their organization but also their ability to rally civilians to their cause, both factions had begun to resemble political parties. The nationalists had mobilized hundreds of thousands of people so efficiently that in 1948 they had defeated both the army hierarchy and the president. The movement that they created was truly national in scope, but it also had some telling weaknesses. The nationalists failed to fully integrate unions into their cause, perhaps because of long-standing tension between the army and labor, perhaps because nationalist officers feared a backlash from the army hierarchy. This decision meant that they could never create as effective or as powerful a civil-military movement as Peron had created in Argentina. In addition, the nationalists also never reached out to Afro-Brazilians. Theirs was a mass movement, but it was largely confined to whites, which weakened this faction in its long struggle.

To some extent, the victory of the internationalists indicated both the inherent weakness of the popular sector in Brazil and the enduring power of conservative elites. The internationalists never sought to rally the masses in the same manner. Instead, they relied on their control of the official lines of power within the institution and carefully crafted alliances with business elites. Internationalist officers' careful work with the UDN and their experience in ESG created ties to civilians that brought crucial expertise and support to their project. In 1952 these ties brought powerful advantages to the Democratic Crusade, which proved to be far wealthier than its opponents.

The ties between the Democratic Crusade and conservative business interests were bolstered by an evolving pattern of military corruption. By this means commanders not only rewarded their followers but also raised funds for political purposes.[24] In the early twentieth century, military corruption had served as an instrument to bind senior military leaders' loyalty to the government. By the 1940s this situation had changed. As the army became increasingly involved in regulating the economy, officers found opportunities to influence economic decisions in return for financial rewards. This circumstance created new ties between military leaders and the business class, which undermined officers' allegiance to the government. In 1952 support from civilians and greater financial resources had enabled the Democratic Crusade to outspend the nationalists in the campaign to control the Military Club. After this victory, officers such as Golberi do Couto e Silva still needed funds to create organizations of intelligence and terror. They gained these funds from civilian allies, who shared a multiplicity of interests with military leaders.

The internationalists had also managed to obtain international support because they framed the contest with their opponents as being one between democracy and communism. It was true that some of their opponents were communists, but the vast majority were positivists or nationalists. Nor were the internationalists any more committed to democracy than their opponents, as the future would reveal. Nonetheless, the xenophobic rhetoric and anti-American ideals of the nationalist faction played into the hands of the internationalist faction, as the conflict between the superpowers became increasingly intense with the start of the Korean War. By 1952 many Brazilians accepted the purge and isolation of nationalist officers as a necessary part of an anticommunist campaign. Nor were their international protests. The United States viewed the internationalist wing of the armed forces as their natural allies, both in 1952–54 and in 1964.

Lastly, the Brazilian army had undergone a racial evolution during the period from 1889 to 1954. While never free of racist ideals, the officer corps had included significant numbers of nonwhites since the Paraguayan War. Generally black people were restricted to the rank of captain and below, but some nonwhites reached higher levels of service. This would be less common a half-century later. The change began with the onset of obligatory military service, which (although in many ways a failure) had drawn more whites into the lower ranks of the army. With the closing of the Escola de Sargentos in 1931 and the end of promotions for sergeants in 1934, followed by the exclusionist military rules of the Estado Novo, the army had whitened.[25] Much more study needs to be done on the topic of race and the military in Brazil. Currently there are few good statistics on the racial makeup of the army. Other sources, such as officers' genealogies, memoirs, and anecdotes are painfully inadequate. Still, any historian perusing hundreds of old photos in archival holdings, old books, and military magazines must be struck by the extent to which officers in the 1940s and 1950s appeared to be white, probably even more so than in 1900. This change affected the army in many ways. Peter Beattie quotes Gen. Cordeiro de Farias, who said: "[In] the miscegenation of races and peoples that constitute the substratum of Brazil's race we find that always the European element dominates in this melting pot which in the past brought us a European culture and carries us toward a North-American culture today."[26] Although the army would not acknowledge this fact, such racial beliefs influenced military thought and policy after 1964.

The army's informal structures shaped how officers perceived the army's role in politics, and later set the parameters for authoritarian government. A history of the military from 1964 to 1985 lies outside the scope of this book. But it is worth noting that factional conflict did not disappear from within the institution during this period. The more involved in politics the army was, the more politicized it became. After an initial period of success, economic recession and political exhaustion began to undermine the army's authority. The army, however, was not forced from power in 1985. Rather it chose to return to the barracks because it believed that doing so was in its own interest. With new sources becoming available, it is an exciting time for scholars to study this period, and the next few years promise to bring major surprises.

Conclusion

When the Brazilian military seized power in 1964, it looked very different from the army of 1889. When a minority of officers acted to overthrow the emperor in 1889, the army lacked a clear political program, an official ideology which appealed to other branches of the armed forces, a powerful civil-military alliance, a system of intelligence and terror to repress dissent, an assurance of strong international support, or a clearly dominant party (the positivists were always a minority of officers) to shape the institution's politics. Given this reality, it is remarkable that the military retained power for as long as it did after 1889. In contrast, by the time the 1964 coup took place, the army had acquired all these structures, which bolstered and strengthened the military regime. For all its divisions and internal conflicts, the army in 1964 was a far more powerful institution than it had been under Deodoro da Fonseca.

Of course, these changes do not explain why the military was able to seize and retain power from the 1960s to the 1980s. Since the foundation of the Republic, Brazil had undergone a profound process of social, economic, and political change. But an understanding of the differences between the two periods does give us a richer description of the military and its motivations, which allows us to move beyond simplistic stereotypes of the military as a tool of the elites, an instrument of the middle class, a creature of the United States, a force for modernization, a haven for reactionaries, or a monolith with an identity crisis. One key to understanding the military is to examine the informal structures that shaped power within the institution. From this perspective, it is possible to see the complex history and cultural factors that affected the army and its enduring involvement in Brazilian society. In the context of current democratization, this approach also allows us to more successfully challenge the fear and the forgetting through which the Brazilian military has sought to shape its own memory.

Epilogue

In February 1993 I sought to gain access to the military archive at army headquarters in Rio de Janeiro. The officer I met with told me that the archive was officially closed but that he would make an exception in my case. I should return the next day. When I did so I sat for three hours on an uncomfortable chair outside the door to the archive. It never opened. I finally found one soldier who told me that headquarters was in a state of disorder because of a special meeting that day. I might have better luck returning tomorrow. I did not learn until later the cause of the confusion.[1]

Army headquarters had been in turmoil because of a factional conflict within the armed forces. Dissident officers under the leadership of Brig. Gen. Nilton de Albuquerque Cerqueira had seized control of the Military Club. Under his direction, the Military Club decided that it would hold an assembly on March 10, 1993 to discuss "the concession of special powers to its president" to press for "concrete measures to preserve the Nation and the Armed Forces."[2] This decision deeply concerned the minister of the army, Gen. Zenildo Lucena. He chaired a meeting in Rio de Janeiro on February 14, 1993, which ostensibly had the purpose of discussing lack of resources and low salaries within the armed forces. In reality, the meeting brought together the high command with thirty retired generals to try to resolve the political issues raised by the Military Club.[3] They failed to settle the conflict.[4]

As Wendy Hunter has convincingly and correctly argued, the Brazilian army's power in society and politics has slowly eroded since 1985.[5] Despite ongoing tensions with the army's leadership, the Military Club lacks the considerable power it had held in the past. Nor do Brazilian factions any longer closely match the old divisions between nationalists and internationalists. Nonetheless, certain patterns have persisted within the military, such as a desire to identify the nation and its history with the armed forces, the discomfort that many officers feel about identifying too closely with a regional hegemon, factional struggles over political issues, and the role of the Military Club as a voice of internal dissent. As this story suggests, these factors can be seen in recent factional conflicts within the Brazilian military.

The army high command wishes to focus on external defense. It is willing to take part in social programs if provided with adequate funding. But the army's leadership has reservations about its involvement in efforts to "police" the nation.[6] The internationalist faction that controls the army high command is generally pro–United States, outward looking, and economically liberal. Unlike their predecessors, however, they usually wish to keep the army out of the nation's internal affairs.

They have been opposed by an "authoritarian" faction that fears that the state is collapsing, in part because of the power of organized crime. They believe that the armed forces must strengthen the state to prevent the "destruction of Brazil."[7] This faction also holds xenophobic beliefs that lead it to oppose the United States. For this reason, it also fears globalization and neoliberalism, which it claims are instruments that the United States is using to destroy Latin American militaries and thereby seize control of the region. To authoritarian officers, these international forces are committing a "national genocide." They condemn the impositions of "international hegemons" that continue "humiliating and enslaving entire populations."[8] Authoritarian officers blame Brazilian elites for surrendering the nation to foreign forces, and they claim that an angry nation will ultimately react against these traitors.[9] They believe that Brazil is under siege by the combined forces of criminals, separatist movements, the international media, nongovernmental organizations, the environmental movement, native peoples, and the rural landless.[10]

This faction entertains doubts about the current trend towards democracy, which it fears will seriously weaken the state: "Redemocratization has come to be synonymous with the destruction and dismantlement of structures, organizations, programs, entities, services, procedures, and methods that have proven effective. The iconoclastic furor will not be placated until all that remains are ruins and shadows."[11] These views are not completely marginalized within the army. With the election of Gen. Hélio Ibiapina Lima in 1996 and 1998, the position of the Military Club has become even more extreme, xenophobic, anti-American, and anti-democratic.[12] Since that time the Military Club has harshly criticized President Fernando Henrique Cardoso and defended the armed forces' involvement in politics.[13]

This faction remains too weak to seize control of the army's leadership. But these tendencies matter because the army has not lost all public support. In 1993 Jair Bolsonaro, a Brazilian congressman and former soldier, strode before the Chamber of Deputies to call for an immediate return to military rule. He stated unequivocally, "I am in favor of a dictatorship. We will never resolve serious national problems with this irresponsible democracy."[14] Horrified, the president of the chamber tried to strip Bolsonaro of his mandate, but the president had to back down when Congressman Bolsonaro received an upsurge of popular support. Middle-class Brazilians wrote polite letters to the editor in Brazilian newspapers, while slum residents posted banners saying "Armed Forces, Take Over."[15] A large part of Bolsonaro's appeal came from his insistence that this course of action would end the political corruption that had horrified Brazilians, especially after President Fernando Collor de Mello was impeached for corruption in 1992.[16] Bolsonaro's speech certainly did not represent the views of most Brazilian officers. But the civilian response to his speech illustrated that the army still had some legitimacy.

Of course, this event happened in the early 1990s, and much has changed in Brazil since that time. But in late May 1999 Bolsonaro was once again in the news for having advocated the closure of Congress and the shooting of President Fernando Henrique Cardoso. Bolsonaro did not lose his mandate, although he did send a letter of apology to Michel Temper, the president of Congress. Brazilian newspapers printed letters to the editor in praise of Bolsonaro: "The statements of congressman Jair Bolsonaro, who proposed closing Congress and the shooting of 30,000 corrupt officials [corruptos], is an accurate expression of the sense of indignation that rules Brazil."[17]

In May 1999 a poll of youth living in Rio de Janeiro found that 21 percent of young, working-class people favored a dictatorship, 36.6 percent did not know which political system was best, and 35.5 percent preferred a democracy.[18] This is not an isolated result. Another public opinion poll found that 56 percent of Brazilians considered themselves to be democrats, while 44 percent preferred authoritarianism. A different poll found that 82 percent of all Brazilians have a positive image of the armed forces. The military carefully follows the results of these polls and finds comfort in them.[19] This reality may explain why politicians have continued to call on the military to play a larger role fighting crime, a position very popular with the Brazilian public.[20] The fact is that civilians in many Latin American nations still perceive that the army has legitimate reasons to intervene in politics.

The army remains engaged in society through many different structures. Some of these structures are formal, such as the military's intelligence institutions, which continue to collect information on Brazil's internal affairs. When the government asked the military to invade the favelas (shantytowns) in 1994, the armed forces revealed that they had longstanding espionage system already functioning in the favelas under the leadership of CIEX (Centro de Informaçes do Exército).[21] More recently, Gen. Alberto Cardoso, the chief of President Cardoso's "Casa Militar," was involved in a major political scandal after the Brazilian Intelligence Agency (Agência Brasileira de Inteligência) illegally tapped phone lines to follow the privatization of Telebrás.[22] The military remains involved in Brazilian politics.

Many other structures that shape the armed forces' involvement in society are informal, such as the networks of corruption that continue to ally a small minority of officers with civilians both within Brazil and without. For example, between October 1997 and April 1999, Brazilian air force flights smuggled drugs into the Canary islands on at least five occasions. In 1999 an air force Hercules C-130 carrying thirty-three kilos of cocaine was intercepted by the federal police in Recife. Allegedly, the airmen involved had connections to the ex-president of Suriname.[23] Corruption still binds a minority of officers together, while worrying other commanders. What is relatively new is the more international character that military corruption has acquired.

I wish to overemphasize neither the military's remaining power nor the threat to Brazilian democracy. Brazil has made remarkable progress towards democratization, but the military has not disappeared as a political actor. Scholars need to understand the complicated factors and culture that have shaped the institution's involvement in society. This effort entails escaping the military's own depiction of itself and its past. Major changes have not entirely erased the old patterns and relations that intertwined military interests with civilian affairs.

Conclusion

Recent democratization has eroded the military's power, while the end of the Cold War has undermined the political beliefs that legitimated its rule. In this circumstance, the Brazilian army has been forced to rethink its role in politics and society. Indeed, the current period resembles that after World War II, in which international economic and political forces and domestic social changes compelled Latin American armies to debate the meaning of defense. By formal measures, most of Latin America is politically democratic. But many informal structures that supported military rule remain. Regional armies are still powerful institutions, capable of challenging the democratic system. Latin American governments are vulnerable to currency crises, internal unrest, economic downturns, or the popular perception of political corruption. The extent to which democracy can weather these upheavals will depend in part upon events and trends within these militaries.

The armed forces' involvement in politics is a complex problem related to social and political issues. It is not the mere result of a lower stage of development that can be resolved with rapid economic growth and technocratic changes. Many separate issues need to be addressed in not only Brazil but also Latin America: military ties to the police, the existence of death squads, the culture of fear, military corruption, and the nature of civil-military alliances. The armed forces cannot simply restrain themselves from political action by the conscious choice of a few leaders. Regional armies are deeply involved in society because of a lengthy historical process. Recent democratization and changes in the formal structures of power are positive developments. But much more work needs to be done before Latin American political systems can be considered thoroughly democratic and regional armies can be declared apolitical.

NOTES

Abbreviations for Archival Collections

Brazil

AE
Arquivo do Exército

AE, AGM
Arquivo do Exército, Arquivo Goés Monteiro

AN
Arquivo Nacional, Rio de Janeiro

AN, AGM, AP 51
Arquivo Nacional, Rio de Janeiro, Arquivo Goés Monteiro

AN, FSN, CDEN
Arquivo Nacional, Rio de Janeiro, Fundo Secretaria da Presidência da República,
Commissao de Defesa da Economia Nacional

APERJ
Arquivo Publico do Estado do Rio de Janeiro

CFa, CPDOC/FGV
Fundação Getúlio Vargas, Archive of Cordeiro de Farias

CFA, DESPS
Arquivo Publico do Estado do Rio de Janeiro, Catálogo de Folhetos Apreendidos pela
Delegacia Especial de Segurança Política e Social

CPDOC/FGV
Fundação Getúlio Vargas, Centro de Pesquisa e Documentaçao de História
Contemporânea do Brasil

CPDOC/FGV–História Oral
Fundação Getúlio Vargas, The Oral History Project of Fundação Getúlio Vargas

CPDOC/FGV–SERCOM/Petrobrás
Fundação Getúlio Vargas, Joint interviews between CPDOC and Petrobrás

DESPS
Arquivo Publico do Estado do Rio de Janeiro, Delegacia Especial de Segurança
Política e Social

FGV
Fundação Getúlio Vargas

FM, CPDOC/FGV
Fundação Getúlio Vargas, Archive of Filinto Muller

FSC, CG, CPDOC/FGV
Fundação Getúlio Vargas, Archive of Fernando Setembrino de Carvalho,
Papers from the Correspondência Geral files

FSC, CONT, CPDOC/FGV
Fundação Getúlio Vargas, Archive of Fernando Setembrino de Carvalho,
Papers from the Contestado campaign

FSC, CPDOC/FGV
Fundação Getúlio Vargas, Archive of Fernando Setembrino de Carvalho

GV, CPDOC/FGV
Fundação Getúlio Vargas, Archive of Getúlio Vargas

HB, CPDOC/FGV
Fundação Getúlio Vargas, Archive of Horta Barbosa

JP, CPDOC/FGV
Fundação Getúlio Vargas, Archive of José Pessoa

NM, CPDOC/FGV
Fundação Getúlio Vargas, Archive of Nero Moura

United States of America
NA-USA
National Archives
RG
National Archives, Record Group

Introduction

1. For evidence of this effort by the Argentine military, see McSherry, *Incomplete Transitions*, 60, 79, 85–87, 90, 97–101, and "Military Power and Guardian Structures in Latin America," 87; Feitlowitz, *A Lexicon of Terror*, 7–8.

2. For some examples of this argument in the Brazilian case, see Skidmore, *Politics in Brazil, 1930–1964*; Alfred Stepan, *Military in Politics*; Dulles, *Unrest in Brazil*.

3. For Brazil's size, see Page, *Brazilians*, 3–4; Hansis, *Latin Americans*, 3–4. For Brazil's population, see Central Intelligence Agency, *World Fact Book, 1997*, 64; *Globo*, December 22, 2000, 23. For the relative population of Guatemala and São Paulo, see Page, *Brazilians*, 3. For information on the size of the Brazilian and Argentine armed forces, see U.S. Arms Control and Disarmament Agency, *World Military Expenditures and Arms Transfers, 1996*, 5, 36. For Brazil's GDP in 1996 dollars, and that of the nine Spanish-speaking countries in South America, see U.S. Central Intelligence Agency, *World Fact Book, 1997*, 20, 57, 65, 96, 104, 137, 369, 371, 492, 498. For Brazil's economic importance, see *the Christian Science Monitor*, October 28, 1998, 12; October 26, 1998, 1, 15; October 16, 1998, 1, 11.

4. See, for example, Kraay, " 'As Terrifying as Unexpected.' "

5. Hunter, *Eroding Military Influence in Brazil*.

6. For example, the records of the social and political police (DESPS) are now open at the public archive of Rio de Janeiro. Among the records held at this archive are the political pamphlets and works targeted for destruction by the government, some pertaining to the armed forces; see APERJ; CFA, DESPS. For more on censorship, see Smith, *A Forced Agreement*.

7. For an example of new resources available elsewhere in Latin America, see Nickson, "Paraguay's Archivo del Terror."

8. In particular, officers have discussed geopolitics at length. For an extensive bibliography of this literature, see Kelly, *Checkerboards and Shatterbelts*, 217–32.

9. Alfred Stepan, "The New Professionalism," 255. Of course, ideology is an important topic. Some scholars (such as Frank McCann and Frederick Nunn) have critically studied the changing character of military thought with considerable insight. McCann, "Origins of the 'New Professionalism' of the Brazilian Military," "The Brazilian Army and the Problem of Mission, 1939–1964," and "The Formative Period." Nunn, "Military Professionalism and Professional Militarism in Brazil, 1870–1970," and *Yesterday's Soldiers*.

10. Sodré, *História militar do Brasil*; Hilton, *Brazil and the Soviet Challenge, 1917–1947*.

11. Coelho, *Em busca da identidade*.

12. Hayes, *Armed Nation*.

13. Waack, *Camaradas*; Pinheiro, *Estratégias da ilusão*, 18.

14. For a discussion of the role factions play in the military, see Farcau, *Transition to Democracy in Latin America*, 53–86.

15. Rouquié, "Processes politiques dans les partis militaires au Brésil." Peixoto, "Clube militar." Manor, "Factions et idéologie."

16. Potash, *The Army and Politics in Argentina, 1928–1945*, *The Army and Politics in Argentina, 1945–1962*, and *The Army and Politics in Argentina, 1962–1973*. Dulles, *Unrest in Brazil*.

17. *Jornal do Brasil*, December 9, 1969, 13. Morel, *Revolta da Chibata*, 45–46, 185, 190–91, 255–56.

18. *Cruzeiro*, June 7, 1952, 108.

19. For a brief introduction to the scholarship that examines the coups, see Alfred Stepan, *Military in Politics*. Nun, "A Latin American Phenomenon: The Middle Class Military Coup." O'Donnell, *Modernization and Bureaucratic Authoritarianism*. Valenzuela, *The Breakdown of Democratic Regimes*. For a discussion of remaining problems in the literature, see Valenzuela, "A Note on the Military and Social Science Theory."

20. McCann, "The Military," 47.

21. For a discussion of civil-military relations in the region and current optimism about democratization, see McSherry, "Military Political Power and Guardian Structures in Latin America." See also Ruhl, "Changing Civil-Military Relations in Latin America." For a positive appraisal of civil-military relations in Brazil, see Wendy's Hunter's thoughtful work, *Eroding Military Influence in Brazil*. Interestingly, scholars of Mexico (where the armed forces have long abstained from direct involvement in politics) seem to take a dim view of current trends in that country; see Serrano, "The Armed Branch of the State: Civil-Military Relations in Mexico."

22. This extralegal violence is so severe as to cause some scholars to question the extent to which democratization has actually taken place. Huggins, "Introduction: A Look South," in *Vigilantism and the State in Modern Latin America*, 3.

Chapter One

1. Graham, "Free African Brazilians and the State in Slavery Times," 35.
2. Sodré, *História militar do Brasil*, 128–32, 144–45; Beattie, "The House, the Street, and the Barracks," "Conscription versus Penal Servitude," and "Transforming Enlisted Army Service in Brazil," 33. Meznar, "The Ranks of the Poor." Rouquié, *The Military and the State in Latin America.* 88, 92. João Quartim de Moraes has argued that the elites distrusted the army as an instrument of the central state outside their control. João Quartim de Moraes, *A esquerda militar no Brasil.*
3. For Pedro I's manipulation of the military's fears, see Hayes, *Armed Nation*, 48–49.
4. Kraay, "Slavery, Citizenship, and Military Service." For more information on the army's relationship with slaves, see Kraay, "The Shelter of the Uniform." For a discussion of contemporary friction between the army and people of color in Brazil, see José Murilo de Carvalho, *Pontos e bordados*, 340–42.
5. Sodré, *História militar do Brasil*, 177–84.
6. Carone, *República velha*, 1:153–58.
7. See the minister of war's report, Estado Unidos do Brasil, Ministério da Guerra, *Relatorio do anno de 1831*, 5, 7.
8. Ibid., 8. See Beattie, "Transforming Enlisted Army Service in Brazil," 58.
9. Ibid., 8. The government put down these military revolts with great brutality. Sodré, *História militar do Brasil*, 112.
10. João Quartim de Moraes, *A esquerda militar no Brasil*, vol. 1, 28.
11. Fausto, *Concise History of Brazil*, 88; Sodré, *História militar no Brasil*, 117–35; João Quartim de Moraes, *A esquerda militar no Brasil*, vol. 1, 29–31; José Murilo de Carvalho, "As forças armadas," 191–92; Rouquié, *The Military and the State in Latin America*, 68–69. For the black perception of the National Guard, see Kraay, " 'As Terrifying as Unexpected' " 514.
12. José Murilo de Carvalho, *Pontos e bordados*, 166, 236. During the Sabinada in Bahia the rebels declared their independence. Kraay, " 'As Terrifying as Unexpected,' " 505. This list of rebellions is not comprehensive.
13. Fausto, *Concise History of Brazil*, 77; José Murilo de Carvalho, *Pontos e bordados*, 161.
14. Sodré, *História militar do Brasil*, 115; Fausto, *Concise History of Brazil*, 93.
15. Kraay, " 'As Terrifying as Unexpected,' " 502. See also 508, 509.
16. Ibid., 510.
17. Ibid., 515.
18. Ibid., 520.
19. Sodré, *História militar do Brasil*, 124; Fausto, *Concise History of Brazil*, 87.
20. Fausto, *Concise History of Brazil*, 136
21. For the size of the army during this period, see Sodré, *História militar no Brasil*, 135. Sodré, an old army officer himself, subtitled his section on this period "The Struggle against the Army." Ibid., 127.
22. Sodré, *História militar no Brasil*, 113.
23. Fausto, *Concise History of Brazil*, 120–24.
24. Whigham and Potthast, "The Paraguayan Rosetta Stone," 185.
25. Skidmore, *Brazil: Five Centuries of Change*, 61.
26. Kraay, "Slavery, Citizenship and Military Service," 228–29, 245–46, 248–49.

27. Sodré, *História militar do Brasil*, 134, 141–43; Moraes, *A esquerda militar no Brasil*, 1:46; Fausto, *Concise History of Brazil*, 126.

28. The Brazilian government had clear evidence that war with Paraguay was coming but failed to prepare. Simmons, *Marshal Deodoro*, 27. It took two years for an effective general—Luis Alves Lima e Silva, the Duke of Caxias—to take control of Brazilian forces because of his political views. Ibid, 32. For the army's growing political power disturbing civilian politicians, see ibid., 45.

29. For the reduction in the army's enlistment after the Paraguayan War, see João Quartim de Moraes, *A esquerda militar no Brasil*, vol. 1., 32; see also Nunn, *Yesterday's Soldiers*, 61. An excellent source of information on the army's recruitment and expenses during the Empire is Coelho, *Em busca de identidade*, 40–41. For the government's unwillingness to modernize the military, see Castro, *Militares e a república*, 101. For how the politicians' neglect of the army created dangerous resentments within the institution, see Simmons, *Marshal Deodoro*, 35.

30. For the army's perception of itself as the nation's savior, see Hayes, *Armed Nation*; Hayes, "Formation of the Brazilian Army and the Military Class Mystique." For the Brazilian army's perception of the state, see Cardoso, "Dos governos militares a Prudente-Campos Sales," 30.

31. For a discussion of this topic, see Castro, *Militares e a república*, 85–103. Simmons discusses the issue from a pro-military point of view. Simmons, *Marshal Deodoro*, 41–56.

32. Rouquié, *The Military and the State in Latin America*, 69–70; João Quartim de Moraes, *A esquerda militar no Brasil*, 1:42.

33. In 1887 Capt. Serzedelo Corrêa gave a speech arguing that the military had to take a leading role in national politics, because the government was run by incompetents. Castro, *Militares e a república*, 127.

34. Military abolitionism did not begin with the Paraguayan War, as had been argued in the past. Instead, it seems to have emerged among junior officers in the postwar period. These officers pressured their commanders to adopt an abolitionist position. Castro, *Militares e a república*, 77, 129, 131–32; Kraay, "Slavery, Citizenship, and Military Service," 228–56. For the army's refusal to capture escaped slaves, see Simmons, *Marshal Deodoro*, 64–65.

35. The question of why the monarchy's influence entered into decline is too complex to fully address. For a richer discussion of this topic, see Costa, *The Brazilian Empire*, 202–33.

36. Sodré, *História militar do Brasil*, 144. Costa, *The Brazilian Empire*, 213–14. Moraes describes the army's major grievances in detail. João Quartim de Moraes, *A esquerda militar no Brasil*, 1:32–33.

37. Castro, *Militares e a república*, 91, 153; João Quartim de Moraes, *A esquerda militar no Brasil*, 1:46, 53–54. Viscount Ouro Preto not only strengthened the police in Rio de Janeiro but also organized a National Guard for that city in order to weaken the military's influence on the government by creating a powerful counterweight. Simmons, *Marshal Deodoro*, 101–2. For a nearly comic example of the friction between the Rio de Janeiro police and the military, see ibid., 90–91; in the weeks before the coup the republicans warned—falsely—that the government would weaken the army by scattering its units throughout the empire. Ibid., 114.

38. June Hahner, "The Brazilian Armed Forces and the Overthrow of the Monarchy,"

172; João Quartim de Moraes, *A esquerda militar no Brasil*, 1:53–54. Civilian republicans were surprised by the success that their propaganda had within the military. Simmons, *Marshal Deodoro*, 111.

39. For Edmundo Campos Coelho's argument that elite hostility to the army helped to bring the Empire to an end, see Coelho, *Em busca de identidade*, 45–46. For rumors that the government would arrest Deodoro da Fonseca and Benjamin Constant, see June Hahner, "Officers and Civilians," 42; Castro, *Militares e a república*, 179. The military's fear of being replaced or destroyed played an important role in turning the institution against the government at this moment. Ibid., 164–65.

40. For Deodoro's complex motivations, see Castro, *Militares e a república*, 189–90. Gen. Almeida Barreto joined Deodoro—a man he disliked—because he feared that the government intended to destroy the army. Simmons, *Marshal Deodoro*, 124.

41. This faction formed the most ideologically coherent bloc that the Brazilian army possessed until after World War II. For a careful examination of this faction and the role it played in the fall of the Empire, see Castro, *Militares e a república*.

42. For the fact that the republicans did not represent more than a fifth of the officer corps, see Viscount Ouro Preto's comments in ibid., 193; for the navy's support as an afterthought, see Benjamin Constant's comment to Deodoro in ibid., 189.

43. For officers' confusion about the meaning of the coup, see João Quartim de Moraes, *A esquerda militar no Brasil*, 1:48. For Deodoro's desire to preserve the monarchy, see Castro, *Militares e a república*, 190; Simmons, *Marshal Deodoro*, 128–29. For the fact that some officers who overthrew the government thought that they acted only against the cabinet, see ibid., 121.

44. According to Edmundo Campos Coelho, the military "lacked any clear idea, either of the regime that would replace the monarchy, or of the role of the army in post-monarchical society." Coelho, *Em busca de identidade*, 68.

45. Topik, *Trade and Gunboats*, 70, 77; Simmons, *Marshal Deodoro*, 151; Hahner, "Officers and Civilians," 62–63; Mercadante, *Militares e civis*, 124; Hayes, *Armed Nation*, 82.

46. For the composition of the Constituent Assembly, see Cardoso, "Dos governos militares a Prudente-Campos Sales," 40.

47. Hahner, "The Brazilian Armed Forces and the Overthrow of the Monarchy," 174. For Deodoro and Floriano Peixoto's political opposition to each other, see Hayes, *Armed Nation*, 85.

48. Topik, *Trade and Gunboats*, 62, 69.

49. Hahner, "The Brazilian Armed Forces and the Overthrow of the Monarchy," 176. For June Hahner's belief that the army united only when under attack, see ibid., 174. Historians have argued that the army believed that it held a civilizing mission or that it had inherited the emperor's moderating power. But this was a vague program, and most of the officers who advocated the first role were positivists, a minority within the military. For more on how the army perceived its role during this period, see Hahner, "Officers and Civilians," 103–33; McCann, "The Formative Period," and "The Origins of the 'New Professionalism' of the Brazilian Military." José Murilo de Carvalho, "As forças armadas," 211–15; Coelho, *Em busca de identidade*, 69.

50. As Topik has noted, Brazil ultimately gained an ally in the United States. Initially, however, most nations disapproved of the coup because they feared that it would lead to political chaos that would undermine their financial interests in Brazil. Topik, *Trade and Gunboats*, 61.

51. For Deodoro's courting of northeastern planters, see Topik, *Trade and Gunboats*, 71; the northeastern planters had been losing political power for decades before the fall of the empire. Simmons, *Marshal Deodoro*, 19; for decentralization as one of the key goals of republicans, see Topik, *Trade and Gunboats*, 7.

52. João Quartim de Moraes, *a esquerda militar no Brasil*, 1:55.

53. Rouquié, *The Military and the State in Latin America*, 68. Fausto, *Concise History of Brazil*, 149. For civilian politicians' wish to keep the central state weak, see João Quartim de Moraes, *A esquerda militar no Brasil*, 1:51.

54. For example, Eduardo Prado, a liberal monarchist, predicted the dissolution of Brazil. João Quartim de Moraes, *A esquerda militar no Brasil*, 1:58–59.

55. For the profound division of the military at the time of the coup, see Topik, *Trade and Gunboats*, 64.

56. Topik, *Trade and Gunboats*, 92; Simmons, *Marshal Deodoro*, 156–58.

57. Floriano Peixoto, *Mensagem dirigida ao Congresso Nacional pelo Marechal Peixoto*, 5.

58. Topik, "Economic Nationalism and the State in an Underdeveloped Country," 72–73; see also João Quartim de Moraes, *A esquerda militar no Brasil*, 1:65–66.

59. Topik, *Trade and Gunboats*, 155–77; for the loss of thousands of lives in this conflict, see ibid., 122; the foreign press supported the rebels. Ibid., 129.

60. Hayes, *Armed Nation*, 87.

61. For the Paulistas' strategy to regain control of the government, see June Hahner, "The Paulistas' Rise to Power." For the atmosphere of chaos, see Topik, *Trade and Gunboats*, 122.

62. Floriano Peixoto, *Mensagem dirigida ao Congresso Nacional pelo Marechal Peixoto*, 11–12. For a history of the rebellion, see ibid., 4–8.

63. Euclides da Cunha, *Os sertões*; Levine, *Vale of Tears*; João Quartim de Moraes, *A esquerda militar no Brasil*, 2:14–18; see also the special issue of Brazil's national magazine: *Veja*, September 3, 1997, 64–87.

64. For a history of the Contestado, see Diacon, *Millenarian Vision, Capitalist Reality*.

65. Hayes, *Armed Nation*, 90.

66. Jeffrey D. Needell, "The Revolta Contra Vacina of 1904," 179; Hayes, *Armed Nation*, 96–98. For more information on Sodré see Beattie, "Transforming Enlisted Army Service in Brazil," 226.

67. For information on the army's discrimination during the 1940s, see Sodré, *História militar do Brasil*, 282; Frank McCann, "The Military," 64; Beattie, "Transforming Enlisted Army Service in Brazil," 509.

68. Meade, *"Civilizing Rio,"* 92.

69. Ibid., 97.

70. Martins, *Revolta dos marinheiros*, 197; for information on the revolt, see Needell, "The Revolta Contra Vacina of 1904," 155–94; Ministério da Guerra, *Relatorio do ano de 1904*, 8–10.

71. Martins, *Revolta dos marinheiros*, 166; Meade has argued that the military rebels were opportunists who chose to rebel only at the height of popular protest. Meade, *"Civilizing Rio,"* 109.

72. Ministério da Guerra, *Relatorio do ano de 1904*, 4.

73. Ibid., 5.

74. João Quartim de Moraes, *A esquerda militar no Brasil*, 1:80.

75. Coelho, *Em busca de identidade*, 34.

76. For numerical information on the army's enlistment and budget, see José Murilo de Carvalho, "As forças armadas," 228.

77. Ibid., 201.

78. Skidmore, *Politics in Brazil, 1930–1964*, 3.

79. For information on the state militias, see José Murilo de Carvalho, "As forças armadas," 230–31.

80. McCann, "The Nation in Arms," 216 and "The Formative Period," 741; Manuel Domingos Neto, "L'influence étrangère," 59.

81. For a discussion of the army's efforts to begin mandatory conscription, see McCann, "The Nation in Arms," 211–44 and Beattie, "Transforming Enlisted Army Service in Brazil," 202–300. For more information on compulsory military service throughout Latin America during this period, see Rouquié, *The Military and the State in Latin America*, 94–97. For the debate over national conscription in Argentina, see Cantón, *La politica de los militares argentinos*, 136–42.

82. The army lacked the resources to train conscripts adequately. Hayes, *Armed Nation*, 126.

83. José Murilo de Carvalho, "As forças armadas," 190–91; McCann, "The Formative Period," 747; Carone, *República velha*. 1:354–55.

84. Beattie, "Conscription versus Penal Servitude," 80–113.

85. Hayes, *Armed Nation*, 127.

86. Costa, *The Brazilian Empire*, 234–46.

87. For background information on race, see Kraay, "Soldiers, Officers, and Society."

88. For Góes Monteiro's critique of racist thought, see Estados Unidos do Brasil, Estado-Maior do Exército, *Relatório do Ministerio da Guerra, 1935*, 28–32. For the army's discrimination during the 1940s, see Sodré, *História militar do Brasil*, 282; McCann, "The Military," 64; José Murilo de Carvalho, "Armed Forces and Politics in Brazil," 205–6. See especially notes 29 and 30 for further information on the discriminatory regulations, as well as the army's ideological justification for racism, ibid., 205–6. Beattie's work is a helpful source on race and the Brazilian army; see Beattie, "'And One Calls this Misery a Republic?,'" 13, 20–24. For the ideological basis of racism, see Nancy Stepan, *The Hour of Eugenics*.

89. For literature on the uprising, see Morel, *Revolta da chibata*; Carone, *República velha*, 2:256–63; Manor, "Un prolétariat en uniforme." João Quartim de Moraes, *A esquerda militar no Brasil*, 1; Martins, *Revolta dos marinheiros*; Heitor Xavier Pereira da Cunha, *Revolta na esquadra brasileira*; Paulo, *Revolta de João Candido*; José Carlos de Carvalho, *Livro de minha vida*; Freyre, *Order and Progress*; Sodré, *História militar do Brasil*, 190–92.

90. For the recruitment of naval officers from the elites, see José Murilo de Carvalho, "As forças armadas," 224; Carone, *República velha*, 1:367.

91. Morel, *Revolta da chibata*, 16–19. Only 10 percent of all sailors were considered white or "almost white." The navy took many of its sailors straight from prison. José Murilo de Carvalho, "As forças armadas," 190. For the number of sailors forcibly recruited during particular years, see ibid., 191. For popular fear of service in the navy, see Beattie, "Conscription Versus Penal Servitude," 93.

92. Faced with sailors' protests, the navy hierarchy had agreed to limit whippings to five hundred blows. Paulo, *Revolta de João Candido*, 6. For whipping as a cause of the rebellion, see *New York Times*, November 28, 1910, 3. For how racism led to violence by sailors, see Paulo, *Revolta de João Candido*, 14, 16.

93. For more on the planned uprising, see Martins, *Revolta dos marinheiros*, 73. For information on João Candido, see de José Murilo de Carvalho, *Pontos e bordados*, 15–33.

94. *O Estado do São Paulo*, December 9, 1969, 8. See also Morel, *Revolta da chibata*, 57.

95. Almost all sailors remaining on the ships were Afro-Brazilians. Morel, *Revolta da chibata*, 132; the army had also experienced rebellions caused by officers' use of violence. Carone, *República velha*, 1:357.

96. *Correio da Manhã*, November 23, 1910, 2nd ed., 1; Manor, "Un prolétariat en uniforme," 75–77.

97. *Correio da Manhã*, November 25, 1910, 1; November 26, 1910, 1; November 27, 1910, 1; Martins, *Revolta dos marinheiros*, 123.

98. Carone, *República velha*, 2:260.

99. *Correio da Manhã*, November 29, 1910, 1. Paulo, *Revolta de João Candido*, 54; Morel, *Revolta da chibata*, 148; *Correio da Manhã*, November 30, 1910, 1; Paulo, *Revolta de João Candido*, 54.

100. Anonymous, *Política versus marinha*. For quotations from this work, see the following: João Quartim de Moraes, *A esquerda militar no Brasil*, 1:97–98; Evaristo de Moraes Filho, "Prefácio," in Morel, *Revolta da chibata*, 22–23; Carone, *República velha*, 1:370; Freyre, *Order and Progress*, 400–401; for officers' perception of sailors and race, see Manor, "Un prolétariat en uniforme," 94–95.

101. João Quartim de Moraes, *A esquerda militar no Brasil*, 1:96; Paulo, *Revolta de Joao Candido*, 57–58. For the government's desire for a confrontation, see also Carone, *República velha*, 2:261.

102. *Correio da Manhã*, December 10, 1910, 1; December 12, 1910, 1.

103. Martins, *Revolta dos marinheiros*, 190. Morel, *Revolta da chibata*, 154. *O Estado de São Paulo*, January 14, 1911, 4.

104. Martins, *Revolta dos marinheiros*, 192.

105. *O Estado de São Paulo*, January 14, 1911, 4.

106. Morel, *Revolta da Chibata*, 181–82. *O Estado de São Paulo*, January 14, 1911, 4; January 15, 1911, 3; Paulo, *Revolta de João Candido*, 63. Carvalho says that the prisoners were placed in a cell recently cleaned with water and lime, that is, whitewash. José Murilo de Carvalho, *Pontos e bordados*, 21.

107. João Quartim de Moraes, *A esquerda militar no Brasil*, 1:96.

108. *Correio da Manhã*, January 16, 1911, 3; Carone, *República velha*, 2:262–63.

109. Barbosa, *Obras completas*, vol. 38, sec. 1; Manor, "Un prolétariat en uniforme," 87–89; Beattie, "Transforming Enlisted Army Service in Brazil," 273. For the number of sailors aboard the ships, see Martins, *Revolta dos marinheiros*, 193; Morel, *Revolta da chibata*, 163. Brazil had long used its interior to punish rebel soldiers and political dissidents. Pinheiro, *Estratégias da ilusão*, 87–104. Beattie, "Conscription versus Penal Servitude," 96–97; Hardman, *Trem fantasma*.

110. Martins, *Revolta dos marinheiros*, 193–95, 198; Morel, *Revolta da chibata*, 161, 167. For the reputation of Santo Antônio do Madeira, see Barbosa, *Obras completas*, 23. Many former sailors died from malaria. Morel, *Revolta da chibata*, 167, 174–75. The navy abandoned some prisoners on the banks of a river, to be claimed as slave labor by rubber tappers. Carone, *República velha*, 2:263. Although later and at a different location, the experience of men exiled in the 1920s may give us some understanding of what awaited people in 1910. The army exiled enlisted men (but not officers) after the 1922 and 1924 rebellion of the tenentes. In this case the mortality rate quickly reached over 50 percent. See Pinheiro, *Estratégias da ilusão*, 103.

111. Morel, *Revolta da chibata*, 161, 163. For a copy of this document, see ibid., 164.

112. Martins, *Revolta dos marinheiros*, 195–97; Barbosa, *Obras completas*, 11, 13–17; João Quartim de Moraes, *A esquerda militar no Brasil*, 1:96.

113. Morel, *Revolta da chibata*, 188; Martins, *Revolta dos marinheiros*, 192.

114. Barbosa, *Obras completas*, 123–27; Evaristo de Moraes Filho, "Prefácio," in Morel, *Revolta da chibata*, 31.

115. Barbosa, *Obras completas*, 88, 113–15.

116. See the following press coverage: *Correio da Manhã*, January 17, 1911, 1; January 16, 1911, 3; *O Estado de São Paulo*, January 14, 1911, 4.

117. Barbosa, *Obras Completas*.

118. João Quartim de Moraes, *A esquerda militar no Brasil*, 1:97.

119. *O Paiz*, January 19, 1911, 1. Most civilian politicians did not sympathize with the rebels; see Carone, *República velha*, 2:260.

120. Morel, *Revolta da chibata*, 171. For other cartoons, see Djata, "Viva a Liberdade," 53; Marcos Antonio da Silva, *Caricata república*. For race as a cause of the rebellion, see ibid.

121. Anonymous, *Política versus marinha*. For information on race in Brazil, see Butler, *Freedoms Given, Freedoms Won*; Kraay, *Afro-Brazilian Culture and Politics*.

122. Manor, "Un prolétariat en uniforme," 85.

123. Violence failed to end the discontent in the navy. Sailors rebelled in 1911–12, 1915, and 1917. Carone, *República velha*, 1:372.

124. Morel, *Revolta da chibata*, 182; Martins, *Revolta dos marinheiros*, 192.

125. *Jornal do Brasil*, December 9, 1969, 13; Morel, *Revolta da chibata*, 185, 190–91; José Murilo de Carvalho, *Pontos e bordados*, 22.

126. Paulo, *Revolta de João Candido*, 64. Candido usually refused to discuss the rebellion in future decades. *Jornal do Brasil*, December 9, 1969, 13; *O Estado de São Paulo*, December 9, 1969, 8.

127. *Jornal do Brasil*, December 9, 1969, 13; Morel, *Revolta da chibata*, 45. For more information on this incident, see Dulles, *Brazilian Communism*, 42–42. This story has modern parallels elsewhere in Latin America. See, for example, Feitlowitz, *A Lexicon of Terror*, 254–55.

128. For censorship during the Estado Novo, see *Jornal do Brasil*, December 9, 1969, 13; Morel, *Revolta da chibata*, 45. For Adão Manuel Pereira Nunes's use of the pseudonym Benedito Paulo, see Morel, *Revolta da chibata*, 123; Martins, *Revolta dos marinheiros*, 127. Nunes's work may be found in the following archive: APERJ, CFA, DESPS, entry 228.

129. Morel, *Revolta da chibata*, 255–56.

130. For example, Hayes's study of the military makes no reference whatsoever to this event. Hayes, *Armed Nation*. Djata's work is the best study in English of the rebellion. Djata, "Viva a Liberdade," 39–56.

131. Ministério da Marinha, *Relatorio do Ano de 1910*, 32. This report also contains detailed information on the revolt.

132. Sodré, *História militar do Brasil*, 186, 190.

133. The salvations have generated considerable controversy, and authors disagree even over key facts and dates. For more information on this topic see João Quartim de Moraes, *A esquerda militar no Brasil*, 1:99–113; Keith, "Armed Federal Interventions." Hayes, *Armed Nation*, 103–7; for the anti-elite nature of the interventions, see José Murilo de Carvalho, "As forças armadas," 219.

134. For General Mena Barreto's statement that the army intended to intervene in São Paulo, see Silva, *Luta pela democracia*, 165–66. For General Mena Baretto's decision to run for governor in Rio Grande do Sul, see Hayes, *Armed Nation*, 105. Hayes's version of events is contradicted by João Quartim de Moraes, *A esquerda militar no Brasil*, 1:107.

135. For Pinheiro Machado's ultimatum, see Hayes, *Armed Nation*, 104–5. For the government's crackdown on the Military Club, see José Murilo de Carvalho, "As forças armadas," 219.

136. Rouquié, *The Military and the State in Latin America*, 69; João Quartim de Moraes, *A esquerda militar no Brasil*, 1:83–84.

137. There has been considerable debate about the extent to which the Young Turks wanted to create an apolitical institution. McCann correctly stressed that the Young Turks viewed the army as an instrument of national transformation. McCann, "The Formative Period," 749–56. Moraes argued that the Young Turks saw their reform of the military as part of a larger reform of society. João Quartim de Moraes, *A esquerda militar no Brasil*, 1:86–88. Nonetheless, the Young Turks were characterized by their calls for an apolitical institution. Manuel Domingos Neto, "L'influence étrangère," 54; Coelho, *Em busca de identidade*, 78–79; Nunn, *Yesterday's Soldiers*, 134; José Murilo de Carvalho, "As forças armadas," 212–13. For the backlash against the army's ambitious role in society, see Hayes, *Armed Nation*, 116.

138. For information on the French mission, see Manuel Domingos Neto, "L'influence étrangère."

139. For the army's opposition to the French mission, see Hayes, *Armed Nation*, 133. For the influence of the French military mission in Brazil, see Nunn, *Yesterday's Soldiers*, 192–98; José Murilo de Carvalho, "As forças armadas," 199.

140. Azevedo, *Militares e a Política*, 60. For a description of the author and this work, see Hayes, *Armed Nation*, 142.

141. For more information on the political impact that corruption had on the Brazilian military, see Smallman, "Shady Business." For how corruption shaped military loyalties during the crisis in 1922, see Hayes, *Armed Nation*, 139.

142. See the transcript of the confrontation in João Quartim de Moraes, *A esquerda militar no Brasil*, 1:141–47; Sodré, *História militar no Brasil*, 202–8. For the original, see Azevedo, *Discurso pronuciado no Clube Militar*. For another discussion of the army's moral failings, and how civilian politicians took advantage of this situation, see Azevedo, *Militares e a política*, 33–34.

143. Sodré, *História Militar do Brasil*, 204–7. The troops in the Contestado did experience severe financial difficulties. See the telegram of Lt. Col. Vespasiano Gonçalves de Albuquerque to Gen. Setembrino de Carvalho, October 8, 1914, FSC 14.10.08/1 CONT, CPDOC/FGV. R. Bonjean's telegrams to Setembrino de Carvalho, FSC 15.03.29/2 CONT; FSC 15.03.31/3 CONT; FSC 15.04.03 CONT, CPDOC/FGV. José Caetano de Faria's telegram to Setembrino de Carvalho, April 24, 1915, FSC 15.04.24 CONT, CPDOC/FGV. Examples of corruption related to provisioning were not confined to Brazil, as Sater and Herwig's study of the Prussian mission to Chile makes clear. Sater and Herwig, *The Grand Illusion*, 132–202.

144. For the belief that the government promoted incompetent army commanders for immoral reasons, see Azevedo, *Militares e a política*, 55–59; Azevedo argued that presidents and politicians had so corrupted senior officers that they had weakened military obedience. Ibid., 60–62.

145. José Murilo de Carvalho, "As forças armadas," 221.

146. For the reduction in the army's enlistment, see Nunn, *Yesterday's Soldiers*, 205.

147. As chief of the army general staff, General Setembrino maintained close contact with Bernardes before he became president. See General Fernando Setembrino de Carvalho to Artur Bernardes, August 29, 1922, FSC 22.08.29 CG, CPDOC/FGV.

148. João Quartim de Moraes, *A esquerda militar no Brasil*, vol 1; Comblin, *A ideologia da segurança nacional*, 153; Borges, *Tenentismo e revolução brasileira*. For an introduction to this literature, also see Alexander, "The Brazilian Tenentes after the Revolution of 1930." Macaulay, *The Prestes Column*; Drummond, *O Movimento tenentista*. Some authors have argued that the tenentes represented the political voice of the middle class. Rosa, *O Sentido do Tenentismo*. Forjaz, *Tenentismo e política*.

149. The major military factions during the Old Republic all wanted political centralization in order to weaken the power of rural elites and state governments. José Murilo de Carvalho, "As forças armadas," 232. See also McCann, "The Formative Period," 764.

150. For Távora's role as the spokesperson for the tenentes, see José Murilo de Carvalho, "As forças armadas," 211.

151. See the letter of Juarez Távora to Luís Carlos Prestes, from mid 1930, in Távora, *Uma vida e muitas lutas*, 1:359; see also João Quartim de Moraes, *A esquerda militar no Brasil*, 2:121–22.

Chapter Two

1. See the letter from Gen. Góes Monteiro to Getúlio Vargas of January 4, 1934, GV 34.01.04, CPDOC/FGV; "Conselho de justificação do Coronel Octavio de Alencastro: depoimento do General Góes Monteiro," AN, AGM, 12 (9), 16; "Reflexos da crise político-militar na 3a R.M: suas causas e consequencias," Cabinet of the Ministry of War, Rio de Janeiro, 1934, AN, AGM, 10 (95), 3.

2. Protógenes Guimarães et al. to Getúlio Vargas, May 2, 1931, p. 6, GV 31.05.02/1, CPDOC/FGV; see also João Quartim de Moraes, *A esquerda militar no Brasil*, 2:103.

3. See the interview with José Américo de Almeida, 1979, CPDOC/FGV–História Oral, 94.

4. Estados Unidos do Brasil, Ministério da Guerra, *Relatório apresentado ao presidente . . . em Maio de 1935*, 23. For general information on this period, see José Murilo de Carvalho, "Armed Forces and Politics in Brazil."

5. For information on sergeants' rebellions, see Vanda Ribeiro Costa, "Com rancor e com afeto." Costa uses a psychological perspective to explain the relations between different ranks in the army. Costa then examines the sources of the sergeants' discontent during 1935–40, the efforts that outside parties made to manipulate this dissatisfaction, and the common characteristics of these revolts.

6. Ibid., 272–74.

7. José Murilo de Carvalho, *Pontos e bordados*, 341. For the frequency and bitterness of rebellions among the sergeants, see Vanda Ribeiro Costa, "Com rancor e com afeto," 260–91. After the Paraguayan war a considerable number of blacks and people of mixed race had entered the Brazilian officer corps. Sodré, *História militar do Brasil*, 134.

8. Camargo and Góes, *Meio século de combate*, 197–99. Artur Levy, an army officer, said that these divisions took five to ten years to heal. Artur Levy, 1988, CPDOC/

FGV–SERCOM/Petrobrás, 52; see also Augusto do Amaral Peixoto's interview, 1982, CPDOC/FGV–História Oral, 124; Hayes, *Armed Nation*, 161.

9. Senior commanders were united in their desire to end the power of the tenentes. See the letter from Juraci Magalhães to Getúlio Vargas, November 26, 1931, GV 31.11.26/2, CPDOC/FGV.

10. For information on the club and its foundation, see José Americo de Almeida's interview, CPDOC/FGV, 112; the interview with Augusto do Amaral Peixoto, CPDOC/FGV, and the interview with Ernâni do Amaral Peixoto, 1985, CPDOC/FGV–História Oral; José Murilo de Carvalho, "The Armed Forces and Politics in Brazil."

11. The man who did much of the work to create a program for the club was Estênio de Albuquerque Lima; see José Americo de Almeida's interview, CPDOC/FGV, 112.

12. Távora asked Vargas to promote members of the Liberating Alliance. See Maj. Juarez Távora to Vargas, April 1931, GV 31.04.13, CPDOC-FGV. The tenentes probably benefited less from political promotions than the hierarchy, but most officers perceived that the tenentes had advanced unfairly. See Henrique Teixeira Lott's interview, 1982, CPDOC/FGV–História Oral, 62.

13. Even many members of the October 3 Club thought that the organization had grown too radical and too disorganized. José Americo de Almeida's interview, CPDOC/FGV, 114–15. In April 1932 Góes Monteiro and several key leaders not only left the club but also disassociated themselves from its policies. See Góes Monteiro's unpublished history, AN, AGM, AP 51, 8 (1), 121. For information on the tenentes, see Alexander, "The Brazilian Tenentes after the Revolution of 1930," and John Wirth, "Tenentismo in the Brazilian Revolution of 1930."

14. See Góes Monteiro's history, AN, AGM, AP 51, 8 (1), 61.

15. Family relationships also defined structures of power within the military. The army largely consisted of soldiers' relatives because military academies granted them preference. See the interview with Henrique Teixeira Lott, CPDOC/FGV, 49. Within the ranks, family relationships created influence and aided promotion, as demonstrated by the many family ties among generals.

16. See Ernâni do Amaral Peixoto's interview, CPDOC/FGV, 312–13.

17. Farcau, *Transition to Democracy in Latin America*, 77.

18. Ibid., 77. He also suggests that Latin American armies have a higher "percentage of insecure, obsessive personalities" than armies in the United States, Britain, or France. Ibid., 58.

19. Ibid., 69.

20. Ibid., 54.

21. Depoimento de Góes Monteiro, "Conselho de justificação do General Octavio de Alencastro," AN, AGM, 12 (9), 4.

22. In 1935 Góes Monteiro wrote a detailed history to prove that the governor of Rio Grande do Sul conspired to undermine the military. In this work, he described the atmosphere of chaos in the army during the early 1930s. See Góes Monteiro's history, AN, AGM, AP 51, 8 (1). Monteiro also described military disorder at length during an army hearing in July 1935, where he answered the accusations of Col. Alvaro Octavio de Alencastro. AN, AGM, AP 51, 12 (9). For an excellent study of how the army's discipline collapsed after the revolution, see José Murilo de Carvalho, "Armed Forces and Politics in Brazil."

23. See Góes Monteiro's history, AN, AGM, AP 51, 8 (1), 55, and the undated telegram from Flores da Cunha to Getúlio Vargas, GV 34.04.05, CPDOC/FGV.

24. For how Vargas played key officers against each other, see the interview with Ernâni do Amaral Peixoto, CPDOC/FGV, 154; Coutinho, *General Góes depõe*, 372.

25. See the telegram from Olegário Maciel and Artur Bernardes to Getúlio Vargas, n.d., GV 31.00.00/4, CPDOC/FGV.

26. See Estevão Leitão de Carvalho, *Dever militar e politica partidaria*.

27. Goés Monteiro to Vargas, August 18, 1931, GV 31.08.18, CPDOC/FGV. Senior officers protested vehemently because Goés Monteiro fought to favor revolutionary officers in promotions. See Góes Monteiro to Vargas, August 13, 1931, GV 31.08.13/2, CPDOC/FGV.

28. See the interview with Ernâni do Amaral Peixoto, CPDOC/FGV, 92–93.

29. This issue has generated considerable controversy in the literature. For a discussion of this question, see João Quartim de Moraes, *A esquerda militar no Brasil*, 2:107–13.

30. Borges, *Tenentismo e revolução brasileira*, 184. The tenentes wished the period of exception to continue in order to carry out the reforms opposed by traditional elites. They attacked rallies calling for a return to constitutional government, which frightened the Paulistas. See Ernâni do Amaral Peixoto's interview, 93.

31. For the reasons behind this state's discontent see Skidmore, *Politics in Brazil, 1930–1964*, 15–16.

32. See José Américo de Almeida's interview, CPDOC/FGV, 137, and McCann, "The Brazilian Army and the Problem of Mission, 1939–1965," 115.

33. This fact undermined São Paulo's entire strategy for the conflict. São Paulo's military forces decided against a rapid military strike upon Rio de Janeiro, the federal capital. They correctly believed that this attack would be more effective coming from Rio Grande do Sul. See Cortés, "Armed Politics in Rio Grande do Sul," 125. For the São Paulo rebellion and its failure, see João Quartim de Moraes, *A esquerda militar no Brasil*, 2:133–40.

34. Skidmore, *Politics in Brazil, 1930–1964*, 17.

35. Ibid.

36. The army had proved unprepared for this conflict. See Góes Monteiro's secret memorandum to President Vargas, August 1932, GV 32.08.09/1, CPDOC/FGV.

37. Vavy Pacheco Borges analyzes this period skillfully through the experience of one particular officer in the São Paulo State Força Pública. Borges, *Memória paulista*.

38. For the 1932 rebellion strengthening discipline within the army, see "Conselho de justificação do Coronel Octavio de Alencastro: depoimento do General Góes Monteiro," AN, AGM, 12 (9), 3; Góes Monteiro's history, AN, AGM, AP 51, 8 (1), 92.

39. Góes Monteiro's history, AN, AGM, 8 (1), 5.

40. Góes Monteiro to Gen. José Maria Franco Ferreira, February 27, 1934, 3–4. This document is part of Ferreira's diary entitled "Copias dos documentos relativos aos fatos que determinaram a minha transferéncia para a 5a Região Militar," AE, AGM, 9 (1). For more on this theme, see also the letter from Góes Monteiro to Getúlio Vargas of January 4, 1934, GV 34.01.04, CPDOC/FGV.

41. See Góes Monteiro's history of the army during the early 1930s: AN, AGM, AP 51, 8 (1), 58–59. For more on the struggle between the army and a regional leader, see Cortés, "Armed Politics in Rio Grande do Sul."

42. Letter from Góes Monteiro to Gen. José Maria Franco Ferreira, February 27, 1934, HB 34.02.22 1–2 vp, CPDOC/FGV. For a sophisticated discussion of civil-military alliances in Brazil, see Peixoto, "Armée et politique au Brésil," 25–40.

43. "Conselho de justificação do Coronel Octavio de Alencastro: depoimento do General Góes Monteiro," AN, AGM, 12 (9), 16. See Góes Monteiro's rhetoric in ibid., 17; see also Estados Unidos do Brasil, Ministério da Guerra, *Relatorio apresentado ao presidente . . . em maio de 1935*, 20–21.

44. "Conselho de justificação do Coronel Octavio de Alencastro: depoimento do General Góes Monteiro," AN, AGM, 12 (9), 16, 29.

45. Góes Monteiro's history, AN, AGM, AP 51, 8 (1), 1, 5–6, 56–59.

46. Ibid., 79.

47. For more information on this period, see the following work, originally published in 1933: Rosa, *O sentido do tenentismo*, 93–101.

48. For Góes Monteiro's memorandum, see Monteiro to Vargas, n.d., GV 34.01.04, CPDOC/FGV. For José Murilo de Carvalho's description of this document, see Carvalho, "The Armed Forces and Politics in Brazil," 220; for Góes Monteiro's belief that the nation had to be changed to permit the creation of a strong military, see McCann, "The Brazilian Army and the Problem of Mission, 1939–1964," 114.

49. See Góes Monteiro's history, AN, AGM, AP 51, 8 (1), 126. For Góes Monteiro's earlier refusal to become minister of war because Vargas had not accepted his program, see Góes Monteiro to Vargas, January 18, 1934, GV 34.01.18/2, CPDOC/FGV.

50. See Gen. Góes Monteiro's circular "Idéas gerais da reorganização judiciara militar," February 22, 1934, HB 34.02.22 vp 1-1, CPDOC/FGV. For Góes Monteiro's influence on the 1934 Constitution, see José Murilo de Carvalho, "Forças armadas e política, 1930–1945," 130. For opposition to Góes Monteiro's reforms, see Góes Monteiro to Gen. Angelo Mendes de Moraes, March 18, 1944, AE, AGM, 8 (2), 3.

51. For information on how the governor prevented the minister of war's efforts to change promotion regulations, see Góes Monteiro's 1935 deposition, AN, AGM, AP51, 12 (9), 13. See also General Monteiro's letter to Gen. Andrade Neves, "1934: Correspondência do Ministro da Guerra com o Ministro Naval e a chefia do EME," January 27, 1934: AN, AGM, 12, folder: "1934: Correspondêcia," 1. In April 1934 the governor surrounded a naval air squadron in Porto Alegre with provisional troops, including pilots, who were prepared to take over the planes. The naval minister transferred this unit to Sao Paulo to protect it. See Góes Monteiro's history, AN, AGM, AP 51, 12 (9), 23.

52. See "Conselho de justificação do Coronel Octavio de Alencastro," AN, AGM, AP 51, 12 (9), 6.

53. Valdomiro Castilho Lima's memorandum, May 1934, HB 34.02.22 vp I-22, CPDOC-FGV.

54. For Gen. José Maria Franco Ferreira's interpretation of the memorandum, see Ferreira to Gen. Valdomiro Castilho Lima, June 16, 1934, HB 34.02.22 vp 1-16, 2, CPDOC/FGV. For the same argument by another general, see Gen. Pedro Cavalcanti to Gen. Góes Monteiro, May 31, 1934, HB 34.02.22 vp I-13a, CPDOC-FGV. For Góes Monteiro's ambitions, see Juraci Magalhães' interview, 1981, CPDOC/FGV–História Oral, 111–12.

55. Estados Unidos do Brasil, Ministério da Guerra, *Relatório apresentado ao presidente . . . em maio de 1935*, 20.

56. For more on this role, see McCann "The Formative Period." See also José Murilo de Carvalho "Forças armadas e política 1930–1945," 126.

57. Anonymous, *Política versus marinha*. See the selections in João Quartim de Moraes, *A esquerda militar no Brasil*, 1:97–98; see also Evaristo de Moraes Filho, "Prefácio," in Morel, *Revolta da chibata*, 22–23. See also Carone, *República velha*, 1:370.

58. For changes that influenced how elites perceived race, see Costa, *The Brazilian Empire*, 244–45.

59. Estados Unidos do Brasil, Ministério da Guerra, *Relatório apresentado ao presidente . . . em maio de 1935*, 28–32.

60. Ibid., 25–27. For Góes Monteiro's thoughts on education and the army, see ibid, 34–40.

61. Coelho, *Em busca de identitade*, 99. See also Hayes, *Armed Nation*, 166–67.

62. Sodré, *História militar do Brasil*, 282. McCann, "The Military," 64.

63. See "Conselho de justificação do Coronel Octavio de Alencastro," AN, AGM, AP 51, 12 (9), 4, 9–10. For the extent of military indiscipline, see Sodré, *Intentona comunista*, 73.

64. For information on Góes Monteiro's forced resignation, see Carvalho, "Forças armadas e política, 1930–1945," 141, 146. See also Aspásia Camargo et al., *Golpe silencioso*, 78–79. For Góes Monteiro's plan, see his military circular, GV 35.04.09/3, CPDOC/FGV. For reaction to Góes Monteiro's proposal, see Gen. José Pessoa to Monteiro, April 11, 1935, GV 35.05.09/3, CPDOC/FGV. For Góes Monteiro's meeting with Vargas, see AN, AGM, AP 51, 12 (9), 18–19. For President Vargas's thoughts on military salary adjustments, see Vargas to Flores da Cunha, April 20, 1935, GV 35.04.09/3, CPDOC/FGV.

65. For information on the rebellion's leadership, plans, and motivation, see an undated and unsigned study titled "Exposição," probably written by Filinto Muller in late 1934, AN, AGM, AP 51, 14 (10). See also Filinto Muller's report of December 1935, "O golpe de vista retrospetivo," GV 35.12.03/3, CPDOC/FGV.

66. See the telegram from Getúlio Vargas to Flores da Cunha, April 20, 1935, GV 35.04.09/3, CPDOC/FGV.

67. Góes Monteiro's 1935 deposition, AN, AGM, AP 51, 12 (9), 10.

68. "Exposição," AN, AGM, AP 51, 14 (10), 24–25.

69. For information on Olga Benario, see Waack, *Camaradas*, 92–108. See also Fernando de Moraes, *Olga*. João Quartim de Moraes presents a very favorable picture of Prestes's involvment in the uprising; see Moraes, *A esquerda militar no Brasil*, 2:145–93. Moraes's depiction of Prestes has become untenable since the publication of Waack's work. Waack, *Camaradas*.

70. Filinto Muller, "O golpe de vista retrospetivo," GV 35.12.03/3, CPDOC/FGV, 3.

71. Ibid., 7.

72. Ibid., 6.

73. For why the rebellion failed, see Hilton, *Brazil and the Soviet Challenge, 1917–1947*, 53.

74. For the navy's support for military repression, see ibid., 75.

75. Ernâni do Amaral Peixoto's interview, CPDOC/FGV, 322–23. Dulles, *Brazilian Communism*, 42–43.

76. Dulles, *Brazilian Communism*, 43–44. Latin American navies have historically played a special role in military terror. For example, the Argentine navy was the service most implicated in terror during the Dirty War. Feitlowitz, *Lexicon of Terror*, 172–74, 193, 195–97, 226. Verbitsky, *The Flight*. For the reputation of CENIMAR (the Brazilian naval intelligence service), see Hunter, *Eroding Military Influence in Brazil*, 34.

77. Hilton, *Brazil and the Soviet Challenge, 1917–1947*, 75.

78. Ibid., 71.

79. Ibid., 72.

80. Ibid., 75; Camargo et al., *Golpe silencioso*, 55–56.

81. Waack, *Camaradas*, 300; Sodré, *Intentona comunista*, 101.

82. Waack, *Camaradas*, 261; Sodré, *Intentona comunista*, 100; Hilton, *Brazil and the Soviet Challenge, 1917–1947*, 102–3; Dulles, *Brazilian Communism*, 7, 85. For biographical information on Arthur Ernst Ewert, see Pinheiro, *Estratégias da ilusão*, 313.

83. Sodré, *Intentona comunista*, 101. Dulles also describes how Ewert's wife was tortured before him. Dulles, *Brazilian Communism*, 31. For Ewert's loss of reason, see Waack, *Camaradas*, 343; Hilton, *Brazil and the Soviet Challenge, 1917–1947*, 152–53. Two British women imprisoned during this period (Lady Marian Cameron and her sister-in-law) also alleged that a prisoner's wife was beaten before him. *Times* (London), July 10, 1936, 12. Hilton, *Brazil and the Soviet Challenge, 1917–1947*, 110–11.

84. Minna Ewert's letter, *Times* (London), July 18, 1936, 8. For the Ewert's (aka Berger) claims of torture, see Dulles, *Brazilian Communism*, 16–17. For Minna Ewert's efforts to save her brother, see Dulles, *Brazilian Communism*, 70–74.

85. Sodré, *Intentona comunista*, 102; Waack, *Camaradas*, 341. The Brazilian police had an accord with the Gestapo. Cancelli, *Mundo da violencia*, 87–92.

86. Hilton, *Brazil and the Soviet Challenge, 1917–1947*, 81–82; Dulles, *Brazilian Communism*, 10.

87. Waack, *Camaradas*, 300; Hilton, *Brazil and the Soviet Challenge, 1917–1947*, 81–82.

88. Hilton, *Brazil and the Soviet Challenge, 1917–1947*, 104.

89. Waack, *Camaradas*, 300; Sodré, *Intentona comunista*, 95; Dulles, *Brazilian Communism*, 16. Another prisoner died similarly. Hilton, *Brazil and the Soviet Challenge, 1917–1947*, 83, 104.

90. *New York Times*, April 3, 1936, 19.

91. *New York Times*, March 26, 1936, 24.

92. Waack, *Camaradas*, 92–93, 341. The Gestapo worked closely with Brazilian police. Hilton, *Brazil and the Soviet Challenge, 1917–1947*, 116–20.

93. Waack, *Camaradas*, 258, 280. For more on torture during this period, see Hilton, *Brazil and the Soviet Challenge, 1917–1947*, 81–84. The "special police" were founded in 1933. Cancelli, *Mundo da violencia*, 65. For the climate of terror, see Camargo et al., *Golpe silencioso*, 64.

94. Waack, *Camaradas*, 252, 280; see also *Times* (London), July 10, 1936, 12. For other instances of torture, see Dulles, *Brazilian Communism*, 37, 68–70.

95. Waack, *Camaradas*, 284, 300, 334.

96. Camargo et al., *Golpe silencioso*, 70–71.

97. Ibid, 52.

98. Waack, *Camaradas*, 146; Sodré, *Intentona comunista*, 99–102. For more on this climate, see Camargo et al., *Golpe silencioso*, 63.

99. *New York Times*, Nov. 29, 1935, 13. See also Sodré, *Intentona comunista*, 99.

100. Anonymous (probably Filinto Muller), "Exposição," AN, AGM, AP 51, 14 (10), 7–8, 10.

101. D'Araújo et al., *Visões do golpe*, 77; Camargo et al., *Golpe silencioso*, 52.

102. "Exposição," AN, AGM, AP 51, 14 (10), 15, 24.

103. Ibid., 7, 8, 15, 22.

104. Camargo et al., *Golpe silencioso*, 41.

105. Of course, the military officers who began the conspiracy were eager to conceal their involvement. For example, Gen. Valdomiro Castilho de Lima was an original conspirator. "Exposição," AN, AGM, AP 51, 14 (10), 15. Yet after the uprising he was

horrified by the revolutionary nature of the rebellion, and he pushed for harsh laws to punish rebel soldiers. Beloch and Abreu, *Dicionário histórico-biográfico brasileiro, 1930–1983*, 3:1869.

106. Pinheiro, *Estratégias da ilusão*, 18; Waack, *Camaradas*.

107. Sodré, *Intentona comunista*, 107; Pinheiro, *Estratégias da ilusão*, 303–5; João Quartim de Moraes, *A esquerda militar no Brasil*, 2:186. For the military's rhetoric concerning the uprising, see Hilton, *Brazil and the Soviet Challenge, 1917–1947*, 168. Other Latin American militaries have also used imaginary "atrocities" to justify repression. For example, Argentina's military government accused the guerrillas of attacking schools, school buses, and day care centers, which never happened. Feitlowitz, *A Lexicon of Terror*, 42.

108. Hilton, *Brazil and the Soviet Challenge, 1917–1947*, 78; Goés Monteiro's papers contain an undated and unsigned copy of a speech to the society "Amigos Alberto Torres," presumably by Goés Monteiro himself. The speech described how the "Jewish peace" of the Weimar Republic had led to German suffering "until the day when the nation recovers by the victory of national socialism." The speech continued to say that the calculated impoverishment of the German people could also happen in Brazil because of the "Satanic policy of corrupt internationalism." Speech to society "Amigos Alberto Torres," AE, AGM, 1.

109. Camargo et al., *Golpe silencioso*, 54. Anti-Semitic attitudes were widespread within the army. After the head of the secret police, army captain Afonso Miranda Correia, toured Gestapo facilities in Germany, the Germans noted that he shared their anti-Semitic attitude. Hilton, *Brazil and the Soviet Challenge, 1917–1947*, 118. See also Levine, *Father of the Poor*, 63–64.

110. For example, during the Argentine Dirty War, General Jorge Rafael Videla said that the "repression is directed against a minority we do not consider Argentine." Feitlowitz, *Lexicon of Terror*, 24, 106; see also 44, 90, 98. For anti-Semitism as a justification for military terror, see McSherry, *Incomplete Transition*, 92. For information on anti-Semitism in Brazil's military, see Lesser, *Welcoming the Undesirables*, 11, 135–36, 138.

111. For the armed forces' interests during this period, see Carvalho, "The Armed Forces and Politics," 193–223.

112. See Ernâni do Amaral Peixoto's interview, CPDOC/FGV, 315.

113. Camargo et al., *Golpe silencioso*, 13. For the army's desire to close itself to society, see Carvalho, "Armed Forces and Politics in Brazil," 204–5.

114. Camargo et al., *Golpe silencioso*, 203–9. This work provides an excellent history of the coup.

115. Coutinho, *General Góes depõe*, 281.

116. See the interview with Augusto do Amaral Peixoto, CPDOC/FGV, 287. See also Camargo et al., *Golpe silencioso*, 214–16. Skidmore suggested that the Brazilian fascist party, the integralistas, forged the document. Skidmore, *Politics in Brazil: 1930–1964*, 27; for more information on the possible author of the Cohen plan, see Silva, *General Olympio Mourão Filho*.

117. Hilton, *Brazil and the Soviet Challenge, 1917–1947*, 129.

118. Bertonha, "Between Sigma e Fascio," 93–105.

119. Camargo et al., *Golpe silencioso*, 11–12.

120. Skidmore, *Politics in Brazil, 1930–1964*, 6. For a history of the Catholic Church in

Brazil from 1916 to 1955, see Scott Mainwaring, *The Catholic Church and Politics in Brazil, 1916–1985*, 25–42.

121. Serbin, *Secret Dialogues*. Based on extensive interviews and new primary sources, Serbin examines secret talks held between the military and the Catholic Church during authoritarian rule.

122. Fausto, *Concise History of Brazil*, 141; Sodré, *História militar do Brasil*, 163.

123. Vargas also made it clear that he would advance military interests. See Nunn, "Military Professionalism and Professional Militarism in Brazil, 1870–1970," 50.

124. For the tenentes' opposition to the Estado Novo, see Nelson de Mello's interview, 1983, CPDOC/FGV–História Oral, 173. For officers' acceptance of events, see Ernâni do Amaral Peixoto's interview, CPDOC/FGV, 317.

125. For Dutra's ability to take control of the military, see Ernâni do Amaral Peixoto's interview, CPDOC/FGV, 154.

126. Sodré, *História militar do Brasil*, 282.

127. See the undated and unsigned "Comunicação," 1. This document, written on army general staff paper was probably created shortly before the foundation of the Estado Novo. AE, AGM, 9 (A). Muller still tapped Góes Monteiro's phone for Vargas. Levine, *Father of the Poor*, 52.

128. Eurico Gaspar Dutra to Filinto Muller, August 14, 1940, FM 33.02.09, chp/ad, I 1939, document 80, CPDOC/FGV.

129. Sodré, *História militar do Brasil*, 282. José Murilo de Carvalho, "Armed Forces and Politics in Brazil," 205–6. Beattie, " 'And One Calls this Misery a Republic?,' " 23–24. For Dutra's intelligence system, see ibid., 281–82.

130. As Frank McCann has pointed out, until 1984 the army filled the ranks of the capital guard units with "tall, blue-eyed, blond German descendants called up from Santa Caterina and Paraná." McCann, "The Military," 64.

131. José Murilo de Carvalho, *Pontos e bordados*, 340–41.

132. For information on political torture during the Estado Novo, see Maspero, *Violence militaire au Brésil*, 18–20.

133. For information on the police, see Cancelli, *Mundo da violencia*. For Miranda Correia as an army officer, see Hilton, *Brazil and the Soviet Challenge, 1917–1947*, 118.

134. The army's control over the military police was total. See the interview with Ernâni do Amaral Peixoto, CPDOC/FGV, 150. Similarly, after the 1964 coup the military controlled Brazil's police to promote state terror. America's Watch, *Police Abuse in Brazil*.

135. Mota, *História vivida*, 2:111.

136. Hilton, *Brazil and the Soviet Challenge, 1917–1947*, 162. Such irregular sources of funding may explain how the army funded an intelligence service within the general staff, despite Vargas's reservations. Ibid., 160–61.

137. Hilton, *Brazil and the Soviet Challenge, 1917–1947*, 181. Dutra relied on Muller to inform him of sentiment in the army. See the letter from Minister of War Eurico Gaspar Dutra to Filinto Muller, August 14, 1940, Arquivo Filinto Muller, FM 33-02-09 chp/ad I, 1939, document 80, CPDOC/FGV. Officers' careers depended on their political reliability. Sodré, *História militar do Brasil*, 279–80, n. 423; 282.

138. Beloch and Abreu, *Dicionário histórico-biográfico brasileiro, 1930–1983*, 2:1207, 3:2192.

139. Hilton, *Brazil and the Soviet Challenge, 1917–1947*, 126.

140. Ibid., 181; Cancelli, *Mundo da violencia*, 36.

141. Cancelli, *Mundo da Violencia*, 37.

142. For a discussion of memory and violence, see Coronil and Skurski, "Dismembering and Remembering the Nation."

143. For censorship during the Estado Novo, see *Jornal do Brasil*, December 9, 1969, 13; Morel, *Revolta da chibata*, 231, 237.

144. Morel, *Revolta da chibata*, 45–46.

145. Hilton, *Brazil and the Soviet Challenge, 1917–1947*, 135.

146. Ibid, 135.

147. Maspero, *Violence militaire au Brésil*, 10.

Chapter Three

1. For Salgado's motives for the coup attempt, see Plinio Salgado to Getúlio Vargas, January 28, 1938, GV 38.01.28, CPDOC/FGV. The integralistas had particular support within the navy. The minister of the navy, Admiral Guilhem, arrived at one naval ceremony in an integralista uniform. Ernâni do Amaral Peixoto's interview, 1985, CPDOC/FGV–História Oral, 322–25. Still, the party had considerable support within the army. Gen. Newton Cavalcanti resigned as head of the First Infantry Brigade in December 1937 because he believed that Vargas had betrayed the integralistas. See Cavalcanti to Vargas, December 2, 1937, GV 37.12.02, CPDOC/FGV. The military response to the coup may have been slow because of the collaboration of senior officers. Ernâni do Amaral Peixoto's interview, CPDOC/FGV, 365–70. For conflicting accounts of the attempted coup, see Peixoto, *Getúlio Vargas, meu pai*, 177–95; Leite and Novelli, *Marechal Eurico Gaspar Dutra*, 289–319; Camargo and Góes, *Meio século de combate*, 261–66.

2. Pinheiro, *Estratégias da ilusão*, 105–31.

3. Leite and Novelli, *Marechal Eurico Gaspar Dutra*, 269–71.

4. Solberg, *Oil and Nationalism in Argentina*, 29, 83–85.

5. This story appeared in countless interviews with Brazilian officers. See Júlio Caetano Horta Barbosa's speech on September 17, 1948, HB 47.02.10 vp 4–21, CPDOC-FGV. Even civilians in Brazil knew the anecdote. See the interview with Drault Ernanny, 1988, CPDOC/FGV–SERCOM/Petrobrás, 38–40. Solberg makes no mention of this "event" in his work. Solberg, *Oil and Nationalism in Argentina*, 88.

6. Few questions have been as carefully studied as the linkage between security and development in the thought of Latin American militaries. For a brief introduction to this extensive literature, see Wirth, *Politics of Brazilian Development*; McCann, "The Formative Period." Hilton, "Military Influence on Brazilian Economic Policy," and "The Armed Forces and Industrialists in Modern Brazil." Solberg, *Oil and Nationalism in Argentina*; Maria Ana Quaglino, "O exército e seus técnicos." Smith, *Oil and Politics in Modern Brazil*.

7. For Argentine officers' wish for state intervention in the economy, see Solberg, *Oil and Nationalism in Argentina*, 76, 85. For information on Mosconi's influence on other South American militaries, see ibid., 180–81.

8. Senior officers in Brazil believed that the nation was threatened both by economic dependency and military force. Coutinho, *General Góes depôe*, 234. See also José

Pessoa's autobiography, JP 53.00.00 dv IX, chap. 8, 6, CPDOC/FGV. For the problem of arms, see Henrique Teixeira Lott's interview, 1982, CPDOC/FGV–História Oral, 90; Canton, *La política de los militares argentinos*, 47.

9. Solberg, *Oil and Nationalism in Argentina*, 181.

10. Wirth, *Politics of Brazilian Development*, 135.

11. Ibid., 9, 95, 103.

12. *Tribuna da Imprensa*, August 8, 1951, 8.

13. Many authors have argued that Brazil's military adopted a new role overseeing development; see Wirth, *Politics of Brazilian Development*. Nonetheless, some scholars have disagreed with this argument. See Tronca, "O exército e a industrialização." See also Hilton, "Military Influence on Brazilian Economic Policy."

14. Wirth, *Politics of Brazilian Development*, 6–9; Coelho, *Em busca da identidade*, 107–8.

15. Coelho, *Em busca da identidade*, 153; McCann, "The Brazilian Army and the Problem of Mission, 1939–1964," 113.

16. For the army's concern with these ideals, see Góes Monteiro's secret memorandum of 1932, GV 32.08.09/1, CPDOC/FGV.

17. McCann, "The Brazilian Army and the Problem of Mission, 1939–1964," 114.

18. For further information on the army engineer's role in creating a new military program, see Quaglino, "O exército e seus técnicos."

19. General Horta Barbosa became a positivist while in school, as did many engineering officers. He later had close ties to the famous military positivist, Marshal Candido Rondon, for whom he worked for years. For positivism's influence on army engineers see João Quartim de Moraes, *A esquerda militar no Brasil*, 1:76–80.

20. Augusto do Amaral Peixoto's interview, 1982, CPDOC/FGV–História Oral, 103, 198–202.

21. Trinidade, "Integralismo," 305.

22. The navy also approved of this development approach because of its long-standing concern with industrialization. Ministério da Marinha, "Problema siderúrgico e construção naval," in *Relatorio ao Exmo. Sr. Chefe do Govêrno Provisorio, Dr. Getúlio Dornelles Vargas*, 84–87.

23. For how a broadened concept of national defense augmented the military's power, see José Murilo de Carvalho, "Armed Forces and Politics in Brazil," 221.

24. Topik, "Economic Nationalism and the State," 298–99.

25. For example, the former tenente Juarez Távora advocated the "socialization" of petroleum as minister of agriculture in 1934. He then became the best known spokesperson for opening Brazilian petroleum to foreign investment in the 1940s. In a similar manner, air force brigadier Eduardo Gomes had a nationalist reputation, but he favored American investment in petroleum during the 1940s. What had changed was not the men's character, but their perception of the military's interests. For Távora's views on petroleum, see Távora, *Petróleo para o Brasil*; Peter Smith, *Oil and Politics in Modern Brazil*, 49–53.

26. Estados Unidos do Brasil, Ministério do Exército, *História do Estado-Maior do Exército*, 80.

27. As José Murilo de Carvalho has argued, officers who wished for straightforward military reforms were also pleased after the coup, which strengthened the army's leadership. Carvalho, "Forças armadas e política, 1930–1945," 142. For an officer's

view, see Nelson de Mello's interview, 1983, CPDOC/FGV–História Oral, 234. For information on the 1937 constitution and the National Economic Council, see Leite and Novelli, *Marechal Eurico Gaspar Dutra*, 289–95.

28. The term "defense institutes" comes from Pedro Malan's work. For more on these bodies, see Malan et al., *Política econômica externa e industrialização no Brasil, 1939–1952*, 352–53.

29. For more information on the major oil companies, see Tanzer, *The Political Economy of International Oil and the Underdeveloped Countries*.

30. See the memo of Júlio Caetano Horta Barbosa to Eurico Gaspar Dutra, January 30, 1936, Estados Unidos do Brasil Câmara dos Deputados, *Documentos Parlamentares— Petróleo*. vol. 2, 3–7. For a history of Horta Barbosa's involvement with petroleum issues see Wirth, *Politics of Brazilian Development*, 133–59.

31. Euzébio Rocha's interview, 1988, CPDOC/FGV–SERCOM/Petrobrás, 3.

32. For the military's concerns about Brazil's fuel reserves see Moura, *Campanha do petróleo*, 23–24; for information on how Horta Barbosa manipulated Góes Monteiro's proposals, see Henrique Miranda's interview, 1992, CPDOC/FGV–História Oral, 3; for the military's influence within the Federal Council on Foreign Trade, see Drault Ernanny's interview, CPDOC/FGV, 169–71.

33. Drault Ernanny's interview, CPDOC/FGV, 47, 85; Martins, *Pouvoir et développement economique*, 288–301. For information on the CNP's organization, see decree law 538 of July 7, 1938. This legislation is reproduced in Carlos de Araújo Lima, *Processo do petróleo*, 183–89.

34. Wirth, *Politics of Brazilian Development*, 150. For Col. Artur Levy's statements about the military's power within the organization, see Artur Levy's interview, 1988, CPDOC/FGV–SERCON/Petrobrás, 84–90. Moura stated that the CNP was essentially a military organization in terms of its creation and outlook. Moura, *Campanha do petróleo*, 24–25.

35. For an extensive discussion of military corruption in Brazil, see Smallman, "Shady Business," 39–62.

36. See Memorandum One, "Sobre a situação do paiz," December 1936, AE, AGM, 7 (9), 2; see also Góes Monteiro to Dutra, September 23, 1939, AE, AGM, 9 (A). The British blockade evoked memories of previous conflicts in the minister of war's mind. Dutra cited Britain's blockade of Brazil's slave trade as an example of aggression. Leite and Novelli, *Marechal Eurico Gaspar Dutra*, 377–78. The minister of war was so angry that he proposed declaring war upon Britain. Sodré, *História militar do Brasil*, 278.

37. McCann, *Brazilian-American Alliance, 1937–1945*, 140–203.

38. Ibid., 188. McCann discussed how the army overcame its anti-imperialist thinking to become involved in the war. McCann, "The Brazilian Army and the Problem of Mission, 1939–1954," 117.

39. See Góes Monteiro's report to Dutra, June 2, 1941. Leite and Novelli, *Marechal Eurico Gaspar Dutra*, 428.

40. McCann, *Brazilian-American Alliance*, 240.

41. Leite and Novelli, *Marechal Eurico Gaspar Dutra*, 422.

42. See Dutra's speech on the fifth anniversary of the foundation of the Estado Novo, on November 11, 1942. In this speech he celebrated the state intervention in the economy that had begun under the Estado Novo. Leite and Novelli, *Marechal Eurico Gaspar Dutra*, 573.

43. See "The Report on the Attitude of Brazil towards the Establishment of Naval

and Air Bases by the United States on Brazilian Territory," November 21, 1941, U.S. State Department, *O.S.S. and State Department Intelligence Reports*, part 14, reel 6, 2–3.

44. Ibid., 4.

45. For information on the foundation of Volta Redonda, see Moura, *Sucessos e ilusões*, 12–21. For Vargas's use of the situation to acquire the goods Brazil needed, see the interview with Ernâni do Amaral Peixoto, CPDOC/FGV, 334–35.

46. Nelson de Mello's interview, CPDOC/FGV, 239–40, 244; McCann, "The Brazilian Army and the Problem of Mission, 1939–1964," 117; and Ricardo Neto, *Nossa segunda guerra*, 31.

47. Nelson de Mello's interview, CPDOC/FGV, 239. For the cheers of Dutra's family, see McCann, *Brazilian-American Alliance*, 256.

48. Quaglino, "O exército e seus técnicos," 51.

49. Interview with Alcy Demillicamps, 1987, CPDOC/FGV–SERCOM/Petrobrás, 33. See also the interview with Mário Bittencourt Sampaio, 1988, CPDOC/FGV–SERCOM/Petrobrás, 16.

50. Luciano Martins, *Pouvoir et développment économique*, 310–24.

51. Joaquím Eulálio to President Vargas, July 5, 1942, AN, FSN, 451, CDEN, 1942.

52. Góes Monteiro to Canrobert da Costa, November 1942, AN, AGM, 13 (1).

53. McCann, "The Brazilian Army and the Problem of Mission, 1939–1964" 117. See also the interview with Nelson de Mello, CPDOC/FGV, 241–44.

54. For Vargas's reasons for creating the Brazilian expeditionary force (FEB), see Moura, *Sucesos e ilusões*, 6, 15–20. For popular reluctance to send troops to fight in Europe, see Nelson de Mello's interview, CPDOC/FGV, 246–47. For Britain's opposition to Brazil's participation in the war, see Ernâni do Amaral Peixoto's interview, CPDOC/FGV, 394–95.

55. McCann, "The Brazilian Army and the Problem of Mission, 1939–1964," 117.

56. Camargo and Góes, *Meio século de combate*, 168, 309, 347–48. Within Brazil the delays were generally blamed on the influence of Nazi fifth columnists. From this perspective, the mere fact that the FEB departed for Europe at all was seen as a victory by many Brazilians. McCann, "The Brazilian Army and the Problem of Mission, 1939–1964," 118.

57. Ricardo Bonalume Neto, *Nossa segunda guerra*, 129–30.

58. Ernâni do Amaral Peixoto's interview, CPDOC/FGV, 392.

59. For how Góes Monteiro and Dutra rigorously weeded out Communists from the FEB, see Nelson de Mello's interview, CPDOC/FGV, 243.

60. Alzira Vargas do Amaral Peixoto's interview, 1981, CPDOC/FGV–SERCOM/Petrobrás, 80.

61. Alzira Vargas do Amaral Peixoto's interview, ibid., 80–81; Coutinho, *General Góes depõe*, 390–91; Camargo and Góes, *Meio século de combate*, 361. Mascarenhas de Morais had been a cadet with Vargas in 1901. McCann, *Brazilian-American Alliance*, 426.

62. Camargo and Góes, *Meio século de combate*, 326–56.

63. Ricardo do Bonalume Neto, *Nossa segunda guerra*, 129.

64. Alzira Vargas argued that her father did not interfere in the selection of the febianos (expedition members). Alzira Vargas do Amaral Peixoto's interview, CPDOC/FGV, 81. But Juraci Magalhães claimed to have seen written proof that Vargas prevented his departure with the FEB. Juraci Magalhães's interview, 1981, CPDOC/FGV–História Oral, 197–205. Unlike the officers, the enlisted men were not carefully vetted. Indeed, the government forcibly recruited most of them. Silveira, *Duas guerras*, 13.

65. For an excellent annotated bibliography of the literature on the FEB, see Mc-Cann, *Brazilian-American Alliance*, 497–500. See also Ricardo Bonalume Neto's discussion of the historiography. Neto, *Nossa segunda guerra*, 10–16. For differing views of the FEB's wartime performance see Waack, *Duas faces da glória*; McCann, "The Força Expedicionária Brasileira in the Italian Campaign."

66. For comments by officers and their support by scholars, see Stepan, *Military in Politics*, 242–46; Peixoto, "Clube Militar," 75–78; Farcau, *Transition to Democracy in Latin America*, 88–90, and Ricardo Bonalume Neto, *Nossa segunda guerra*, 217.

67. Antonio Carlos Peixoto states that the focus of opposition to Vargas's regime came from FEB officers. Peixoto, "Clube Militar," 75. Joel Silveira argues that the FEB fought two enemies, both the German army in Italy and Vargas's regime in Brazil. Silveira, *Duas guerras*, 29. Ricardo Bonalume Neto asserts that the FEB supported democratic ideals, which led Vargas to fear this force. Neto, *Nossa segunda guerra*, 14–15, 217. For an extended discussion of the FEB's thought, see Alfred Stepan, *Military in Politics*, 239, 242–47.

68. Umberto Peregrino Seabra Fegundes argues that the FEB played an important role in overthrowing Vargas and imbuing the army with democratic ideals. See Mota, *História vivida*, 2:105–7. Marcio Moreira Alves suggests that although the febianos believed in the infallibility of North American democracy, it was the 1964 coup that consumated their rise to power. See his introduction in Silveira, *Duas guerras*, 5–6. See also Silveira's comments, ibid., 11, 32. Stepan maintains that the experience of the FEB shaped military government after the 1964 coup. Alfred Stepan, "The New Professionalism," 255.

69. Smallman, "The Official Story."

70. For the communication difficulties between the United States and Brazilian soldiers, see McCann, *Brazilian-American Alliance*, 406–25. See also Waack, *Duas faces da glória*, 154.

71. Waack, *Duas faces da glória*, 152. For criticism by U.S. officers, see ibid., 117. For Brayner's resentment, see Brayner, *Verdade sôbre a FEB*. Neto commented on Brayner's bitterness: "Resentment towards the Americans is a constant in the book." Ricardo Bonalume Neto, *Nossa segunda guerra*, 36. Brayner also had personal reasons to be disgruntled. See McCann, *Brazilian-American Alliance*, 499.

72. Nelson de Mello's interview, CPDOC/FGV, 275. For biographical information on this commander, see Beloch and Abreu, *Dicionário histórico-biográfico brasileiro, 1930–1983*, vol. 3, 2191–94.

73. João Baptista Mascarenhas de Moraes, *Brazilian Expeditionary Force by Its Commander*, 230–31.

74. Silveira, *Duas guerras*, 61–62. For the fact that the FEB was ignorant of political trends in Brazil, see Nelson de Mello's interview, CPDOC/FGV, 275–77; Camargo and Góes, *Meio século de combate*, 358; and Silveira, *Histórias da pracinha*, 47.

75. McCann, *Brazilian-American Alliance*, 462.

76. For an example of the press coverage surrounding the FEB, see McCann, *Brazilian-American Alliance*, 461–62.

77. For information on military conspirators during the Estado Novo, see Juraci Magalhães's interview, CPDOC/FGV, 193–94. Despite Magalhães's statements, he seemed to maintain cordial relations with Vargas during this period. For information on the Military Club, see Bijos, *Clube Militar e seus presidentes*. For Pessoa's endless

struggle with the hierarchy, see his unpublished autobiography, JP 53.00.00 dv IV, 4, CPDOC/FGV. For information on Pessoa, see Câmara, *Marechal José Pessoa*.

78. José Pessoa's unpublished autobiography, JP 53.00.00 dv VII, 1–2, CPDOC/FGV. For how Pessoa's victory challenged the army's leadership, see Nelson Werneck Sodré's interview, 1988, CPDOC/FGV–SERCOM Petrobrás, 6–7.

79. Alzira Vargas do Amaral Peixoto's interview, CPDOC/FGV, 82–83, 85, 90. Levine, *Father of the Poor*, 73.

80. The FEB's return created great enthusiasm in Brazil. Moraes, *Brazilian Expeditionary Force by Its Commander*, xx, 227. For Vargas's use of parades greeting the FEB to gain support for his government, see Coutinho, *General Góes depõe*, 420–39. For an example of a pro-Vargas officer disturbing his comrades with his statements at a rally for the FEB, see Juarez Távora, *Uma vida e muitas Lutas*, vol 2, 192–93. For army leaders' fear that Vargas might use the FEB to retain power, see Moura's comments in Valentina da Rocha Lima, *Getúlio*, 216–17. Frank McCann argued that the FEB overwhelmingly opposed Vargas. McCann, *Brazilian-American Alliance*, 468. Nonetheless, he also noted that Vargas seemed to enjoy the victory parades that showed his popularity. Vargas even talked of taking the leader of the FEB into his cabinet. Ibid., 466.

81. For officers' concern that communists were infiltrating the army, see the minutes of the seventh meeting of the generals, September 28, 1945, AE, AGM, 11, 13.

82. Ricardo Bonalume Neto, *Nossa segunda guerra*, 129.

83. The febianos raised 10,000 cruzeiros to aid Prestes's daughter. Silveira, *Histórias*, 280. After the war Prestes turned to a febiano major who searched for Prestes's wife. She was dead. Dulles, *Brazilian Communism*, 214.

84. Secret, Secretario Geral do Ministério da Guerra, Gabinette S.S.I., Relatório no. 18, Sept. 1945, AE, AGM, 11, 3.

85. Secret, Secretario Geral do Ministério da Guerra, Gabinette S.S.I., Relatório no. 18, Sept. 1945, ibid., 4.

86. McCann, *Brazilian-American Alliance*, 440. The FEB viewed Dutra as an enemy and opposed his presidential ambitions. Silveira, *Duas guerras*, 11–12, 31–32. The first troops did not return from Italy until July 18, 1945. Ibid., 23. Later effort by febianos to organize politically were ruthlessly repressed by the government. For example, the government quickly closed the "Associação dos Ex-combatentes da F.E.B.," a veterans' club that returning soldiers created in the state of Pará. See Sodré, *História militar do Brasil*, 296.

87. Waack, *Duas faces da glória*, 216.

88. McCann, "The Brazilian Army and the Problem of Mission, 1939–1964," 120; McCann noted the army's fears about the FEB, even during the war. McCann, *Brazilian-American Alliance*, 426.

89. For the febianos' lack of influence in the future, see Juraci Magalhães's interview, CPDOC/FGV, 246. See also Augusto do Amaral Peixoto's comments in Valentina da Rocha Lima, *Getúlio*, 221.

90. Henrique Miranda's interview, 1992, CPDOC/FGV–História Oral, 1. For Horta Barbosa's resignation letter, see Victor, *Batalha do petróleo nacional*, 143. For information on Barreto's appointment, see Mario Bittencourt Sampaio's interview, CPDOC/FGV, 14; Victor, *Batalha do petróleo brasileiro*, 157.

91. For the minutes of the meetings, see AE, AGM, 11. Góes Monteiro stated at the first meeting that he had called his fellow generals together to learn their thoughts.

Record of the first meeting of the generals, AE, AGM, 11, 1. As the political situation deteriorated, these meetings gave Góes Monteiro a means to sound out his peers about the army's involvement in politics. For a list of the generals who attended the September 28, 1945 meeting, see AE, AGM, 11.

92. For Góes Monteiro's speech upon becoming minister of war, see AE, AGM, 5 (1). For Góes Monteiro's arguments during the first meeting of the generals see the minutes of August 10, 1945, AE, AGM, 11, 1–9.

93. Quaglino, "O exército e seus técnicos," 74.

94. A good overview of events within the military during the end of the Estado Novo can be gained from Cordeiro de Farias's statements. Camargo and Góes, *Meio século de combate*, 383–400. See also French, "The Populist Gamble of Getúlio Vargas." For Prestes's support for Vargas, see Alzira Vargas's interview, CPDOC/FGV, 86. See also Skidmore, *Politics in Brazil, 1930–1964*, 61–62. For the military concerns about Vargas's communist support, see Távora, *Uma vida e muitas lutas*, 2:192. For Vargas's attempt to use "social reform" to derail "democratic restoration," see Moura, *Successos e ilusões*, 51. Vargas is a complex figure. For a good study of his political life, see Levine, *Father of the Poor*.

95. In Argentina Peron managed to make both the army and the unions pillars of his regime, although in the end this strange alliance could not be sustained. Rouquíe, "Adhesión militar." For Góes Monteiro's belief that Peron influenced Vargas, see Coutinho, *General Góes depõe*, 429–30. In the early 1960s the Brazilian military greatly feared that the unions "might displace the armed forces as the most powerful group in Brazilian politics." Skidmore, *Politics in Brazil, 1930–1964*, 209.

96. See the minutes of the ninth meeting of the generals on October 11, 1945. AE, AGM, 11, 3.

97. The minutes of the tenth meeting of the generals, AE, AGM, 11, 7.

98. Ibid., 17.

99. For the reasons why Brazil turned to the United States, see Martins, *Pouvoir et développement économique*, 310–23. For how the war conditioned the government and military expectations for the U.S.-Brazil relationship, see Wirth, *Politics of Brazilian Development*, 158.

100. For more information on the overthrow of Vargas, see Vale, *General Dutra e a redemocratização de 45*. See also José Americo de Almeida's interview, 1979, CPDOC/FGV–História Oral, 148–50, 277. For officers' presidential ambitions, see Alzira Vargas do Amaral Peixoto's interview, CPDOC/FGV, 82.

101. Moura, *Campanha do petróleo*, 37.

102. For information on the personal followings of generals, see Ernâni do Amaral Peixoto's interview, CPDOC/FGV, 399–400. General Dutra gave key appointments to men in his confidence. See the anonymous document, GV 42.08.13/2, CPDOC/FGV.

103. José Murilo de Carvalho, "Armed Forces and Politics in Brazil," 223.

Chapter Four

1. Dutra gained prestige commanding a cavalry unit against the Paulistas in 1932. Nelson de Mello's interview, 1983, CPDOC/FGV–História Oral, 230. See also Henrique Lott's interview, 1982, CPDOC/FGV–História Oral, 101. For the death of Dutra's aid in 1935, see ibid., 44. I have been unable to find any material confirming that this

incident happened. For Dutra's injury in 1938, see Alzira Vargas do Amaral Peixoto, *Getúlio Vargas, meu pai*, 188. Despite his injury, Alzira Vargas had doubts about Dutra's role in these events.

2. For Dutra's removal of men he distrusted from positions of command, see José Soares Maciel Filho to Vargas, May 8, 1946, GV 46.03.08/2, CPDOC/FGV. For Dutra's ruthless efforts to destroy his enemies, see Estevão Leitão de Carvalho, *Memórias de um general reformado*, 64–71.

3. Gen. José Pessoa said that Canrobert was the favorite "disciple" of Góes Monteiro and Dutra. See Pessoa's unpublished autobiography, JP 53.00.00 dv XIV, 3, CPDOC/FGV.

4. Dutra won the election largely because he had Vargas's support. Nelson de Mello's interview, CPDOC/FGV, 140, 302. For Dutra's difficulties with public speaking, see Augusto do Amaral Peixoto's interview, 1982, CPDOC/FGV–História Oral, 225.

5. Moura, *Campanha do petróleo*, 27–28; Wirth, *Politics of Brazilian Development*, 164–65; Malan et al., *Política econômica externa industrialização no Brasil: 1939–1952*, 28–31. Peter Seaborn Smith noted that the corporatism of Horta Barbosa had gone out of fashion. Smith, *Oil and Politics in Modern Brazil*, 40.

6. See U.S. chargé d'affaires Daniels to the secretary of state, May 10, 1946, U.S. State Department, *Foreign Relations of the United States*, 1946, 11:544. See also Daniels to the U.S. secretary of state, May 14, 1946; May 31, 1946; June 7, 1946; and October 8, 1946. Ibid., 544–47, 550–52. For how government censorship and repression influenced Brazil's constitution, see Sodré, *História militar do Brasil*, 296.

7. See Artur Levy's interview, 1988, CPDOC/FGV–SERCOM/Petrobrás, 155. For information on Távora's involvement in the committee's work, see ibid., 114, 116, and 154–55. See also the letter from Juarez Távora to President Dutra dated April 14, 1947, JT 1946.10.04 dpf PI, 1-17, CPDOC/FGV. For information on the committees, see Victor, *Batalha do petróleo brasileiro*, 191.

8. Levy later led the campaign against the statute he had helped to draft, although in the 1980s he denied this to be the case. See Artur Levy's interview, CPDOC/FGV, 105, 100. Levy probably signed the document because it was, in effect, the creation of the army general staff.

9. See Moura, *Campanha do petróleo*. For more information on how Brazil struggled with the question of petroleum, see Getúlio Pereira Carvalho, "Petrobrás." Cohn, *Petróleo e nacionalismo*.

10. See the copy of Távora's speech to the National Congress in 1951. Estados Unidos do Brasil, Câmara dos Deputados, *Documentos Parlamentares—Petróleo*, 5:207.

11. Estevão Leitão de Carvalho, 27.

12. Estados Unidos do Brasil, Câmara dos Deputados, *Documentos Parlamentares—Petróleo*, 5:207.

13. Fernando Luiz Lobo Barbosa Carneiro, a nationalist engineer, said that Távora agreed with many of his points but always justified a liberal policy by referring to the war he believed was inevitable. See Fernando Luis Lobo Brabosa Carneiro's interview, 1988, CPDOC/FGV–SERCOM/Petrobrás, 23–24. For more on the hierarchy's beliefs, see Estavão Leitão de Carvalho, *Petróleo*, 23–24.

14. Távora, *Petróleo para o Brasil*, 35. For copies of Távora's speeches, see Estados Unidos do Brasil, Câmara dos Deputados, *Documentos Parlamentares—Petróleo*, 2:324–86. See also JT 1946.10.04 dpf PV, 5-22, CPDOC/FGV. For a copy of Távora's speech to

the naval club, see JT 1946.10.04 dpf PII, 2-2, CPDOC/FGV. For Távora's acknowledgment of the advantages of a state monopoly in petroleum, see Estados Unidos do Brasil, Câmara dos Deputados, *Documentos Parlamentares—Petróleo*, 2:373. For a description of Távora's speeches, see Smith, *Oil and Politics in Modern Brazil*, 49–53.

15. Fernando Luiz Lobo Barbosa Carneiro's interview, CPDOC/FGV, 24.

16. Wirth, *Politics of Brazilian Development*, 144.

17. Drault Ernanny's interview, CPDOC/FGV, 127. For a genealogy of Horta Barbosa's family, see HB 27.08.09, dp 1-23, CPDOC/FGV.

18. Estados Unidos do Brasil, Câmara dos Deputados, *Documentos Parlamentares—Petróleo*, 2:387–486. These speeches are also available at Horta Barbosa's archive at Fundação Getúlio Vargas. For the first speech, see HB 47.02.10, vp I-2, CPDOC/FGV; for the second speech, see HB 47.02.10, vp I-21, CPDOC/FGV; see also JT 1946.10.04, dpf, PI, I-45, CPDOC/FGV; JT 1946.10.04, dpf, PI, I-47, CPDOC/FGV; see also the copy of the speech Horta Barbosa gave to engineers in São Paulo on October 16, 1947, HB 47.02.10 vp 2–27, CPDOC/FGV. For his old fear of economic imperialism, see Horta Barbosa's memo to Dutra, January 30, 1936, Estados Unidos do Brasil, Câmara dos Deputados, *Documentos Parlamentares—Petróleo*, 2:3–7.

19. For Horta Barbosa's description of how petroleum corporations threatened national governments, see his speech to the Educational Institute of Belo Horizonte on July 3, 1948, HB 47.02.10 vp 4-1, CPDOC/FGV. For his version of Mosconi's experience, see HB 47.02.10 vp 4-21, CPDOC/FGV. For his fear that trusts might dominate Brazil's economy, see Estevão Leitão de Carvalho, *Petróleo*, 128. For his mistrust of the United States, see Horta Barbosa's memo to Dutra, October 20, 1942, Estados Unidos do Brasil, Câmara dos Deputados, *Documentos Parlamentares—Petróleo*, 2:321. For other officers' perception that anti-americanism drove the petroleum campaign, see Tavares, *Brasil de minha geração*, 306–7.

20. For Paul Manor's description of what he called the "nationalist" faction, see Manor, "Factions et idéologie," 561–62. See also Hayes, "Military Club and National Politics," and Antonio Carlos Peixoto, "Clube Militar," 71–73.

21. Lobo Carneiro described how some integralista officers in the navy supported a state monopoly in petroleum. Fernando Luiz Lobo Barbosa Carneiro's interview, CPDOC/FGV, 32. See also "O problema do petróleo nacional," a conference held by Adm. Juvenal Greenhalgh at the Naval Club on May 12, 1948, a transcript of which may be found in Estados Unidos do Brasil, Câmara dos Deputados, *Documentos Parlamentares—Petróleo*, 2:508–30. Sergeants and enlisted men took an interest in the petroleum campaign. See the memo of November 14, 1946, "Setor trabalhista," APERJ, DESPS, N 46, "Casa do Sargento do Brasil." Paul Manor described the basis of military support for what he called the liberal and nationalist factions. Manor, "Factions et idéologie," 565. For the support Horta Barbosa received from Argentine officers, see Gen. Isidoro I. Martini to Horta Barbosa, September 5, 1947, HB 47.02.10 vp 2–7, CPDOC/FGV.

22. For Pessoa's criticism of the legislation and the conflict it created with the minister of war, see JP 53.00.00 dv XIV, CPDOC/FGV, pp. 3–33.

23. For the immense influence of the United States in Brazil after World War II, see Bandeira, *Presença dos Estados Unidos no Brasil*, 310–11. See also Haines, *Americanization of Brazil*. For xenophobia and the campaign, see Smith, *Oil and Politics in Modern Brazil*, 60–61. Wirth argued that petroleum and nationalism became a political issue because of Brazil's international marginalization after World War II. Wirth, *Politics of Brazilian Development*, 168–69.

24. Solberg, *Oil and Nationalism in Argentina*, 119–20.

25. Moura, *Campanha do petróleo*, 62.

26. Roberto Gusmao's interview, 1988, CPDOC/FGV–SERCOM/Petrobrás, 22. For why Argentine students supported economic nationalism, see Solberg, *Oil and Nationalism in Argentina*, 118. For anti-Americanism among the students, see Roberto Gusmão's interview, 1988, CPDOC/FGV–SERCOM/Petrobrás, 17–18.

27. Roberto Gusmão's interview, CPDOC/FGV, 18.

28. Ibid., 15; Távora struck the table during a radio interview with Euzébio Rocha. Euzébio Rocha's interview, 1992, CPDOC/FGV–História Oral, 19. For information on the debates around petroleum during this period, see Cohn, *Petróleo e nacionalismo*.

29. For how Prestes's statement was reported in the United States, see *New York Times*, March 20, 1946, 3. For the anticommunist sentiment that swept Brazil, see the "CIA Research Report, Brazil," 13. See also the memo of the U.S. Army Staff, March 26, 1948, RG 319, Entry 57, Box 12, NA-USA. For a broad (though poorly written) history of the Communist Party, see Chilcote, *Brazilian Communist Party*. For Prestes' evasion of Magalhães's question and the latter's meeting with the generals, see Juraci Magalhães' interview, 1981, CPDOC/FGV–História Oral, 42–43. Magalhães did two series of interviews with the oral history project of Fundação Getúlio Vargas. The second series of interviews formed part of a joint project with Petrobrás. All citations for Magalhães' interview are from the former series. I saw an early transcript of this interview, and page numbers may differ from the final transcript.

30. Gerson Moura described the events surrounding the banning of the Communist Party. See Moura, *Sucessos e ilusões*, 88–89. For the revocation of the congressmen's mandates, see the interview of Juraci Magalhães, CPDOC/FGV, 43–44, 255–56. For the rumors of revolt in Rio Grande do Sul, see *New York Times*, January 8, 1948, 1.

31. See, respectively, *New York Times*, January 4, 1948, 17, and January 9, 1948, 17.

32. For the burning of the infantry barracks, see the records of the U.S. Military Attache to CSGID, January 23, 1948, NA-USA, RG 319, Entry 57, Box 6. *New York Times*, January 18, 1948, 40. For the rumors of a communist revolt in São Paulo, see *New York Times*, April 1, 1948, 6. For the explosion at the army arsenal, see the memo from the U.S. Embassy to the State Department, April 19, 1948, NA-USA, RG 319, E57, Box 6. *New York Times*, April 17, 1948, 5.

33. For the discovery of the plan to blow up the oil tanks, see *New York Times*, April 24, 1948, 8. For Prestes' flight to Uruguay, see *New York Times*, April 25, 1948, 1.

34. For a summary of the statute's key provisions, see Maria Augusta Tibiriçá Miranda, *Petróleo é nosso*, 32–33. For the comments of Herbert Hoover Jr. and Arthur A. Curtice, see Estados Unidos do Brasil, Câmara dos Deputados, *Documentos Parlamentares—Petróleo*, vol. 3, 392–412. Herbert Hoover Jr. had helped to draft petroleum legislation for both Peru and Colombia. Bandeira, *Presença dos Estados Unidos no Brasil*, 316–17.

35. Three books that describe the foundation and organization of this institute in depth are Maria Augusta Tibiriçá Miranda, *Petróleo é nosso*; Estevão Leitão de Carvalho, *Petróleo*; and Victor, *Batalha do petróleo brasileiro*.

36. For the role the Positivist Club played in CEDP's foundation, see Estevão Leitão de Carvalho, *Petróleo*, 169–70; to read the Club's manifesto, see Victor, *Batalha do petróleo brasileiro*, 205–6.

37. The best single document to describe the history of the center's foundation is a letter that the Anti-Fascist League of Tijuca sent to the press in January 1949. See

"Documento da Liga Anti-Fascista da Tijuca" *Diário de Noticias*, January 21, 1949, 5; see also Henrique Miranda's interview, 1992, CPDOC/FGV–História Oral, 17–18; Fernando Luiz Lobo Barbosa Carneiro's interview, CPDOC/FGV, 18; "Liga Antifascista da Tijuca," APERJ, DPS, N52, Box 397.

38. Solberg, *Oil and Nationalism in Argentina*, 141. For an example of how army officers acted as spokesmen for the center, see the articles of Horta Barbosa, Raimundo Sampaio, and Estevão Leitão de Carvalho in the *Jornal de Debates*, October 20, 1948, 1. Maria Augusta Tibiriçá Miranda mentions the close ties between military men and the club. See Maria Augusta Tibiriçá Miranda's interview, 1988, CPDOC/FGV–SERCOM/Petrobrás, 110; Henrique Miranda's interview, CPDOC/FGV, 22. Although the communists were important to the center's formation, according to Henrique Miranda it was the center that drew them into the struggle. Ibid. Military men formed a small fraction of the center's membership. For a list of CEDP's membership, see HB 47.02.10 vp 3–17, CPDOC/FGV. Family relationships were important to the center's growth, and one can find many examples where related officers worked together. For example, Col. Felicíssimo Cardoso's brother, Gen. Leonidas Cardoso, later became the president of the CEDP in São Paulo. See Fernando Luiz Lobo Barbosa Carneiro's interview, CPDOC/FGV, 45.

39. As quoted by Henrique Miranda. See Henrique Miranda's interview, CPDOC/FGV, 22. See also Maria Augusta Tibiriçá Miranda's interview, CPDOC/FGV, 89.

40. For CEDP's desire to include Artur Bernardes in the campaign, see Henrique Miranda's interview, CPDOC/FGV, 26. For more information on Bernardes's speech, see the U.S. Embassy telegram to the U.S. State Department, April 9, 1948, NA-USA, RG 59, 832.6363/4-948.

41. Fernando Luiz Lobo Barbosa Carneiro's interview, CPDOC/FGV, 30.

42. For the center's efforts to draw Bernardes into the campaign, see Henrique Miranda's interview, CPDOC/FGV, 24. The officer with whom I spoke was in Bernardes's house during this meeting. At the time he was a junior officer very involved in the petroleum campaign.

43. See Maria Augusta Tibiriçá Miranda's interview, CPDOC/FGV, 109–10.

44. For more on officers' retiring to the reserve, see Henrique Miranda's interview, CPDOC/FGV, 37. For Carvalho's comments, see Estevão Leitão de Carvalho, *Petróleo*, 6.

45. See Juarez Távora, "Problema brasileiro do petróleo," *Defesa Nacional*, 411 (August 1948): 117–36.

46. For the support of small farmers for CEDP, see Maria Augusta Tibiriçá Miranda's interview, CPDOC/FGV, 25. For the role municipal councils played in spreading the campaign, see ibid., 43–44. For UDN participation in CEDP, see ibid., 69. For the role of women's movements in the organization, see ibid., 98. For the role of neighborhood organizations, see ibid., 98. For the work of Mattos Pimenta, see ibid., 24. For the broad support for the campaign, see ibid., 17, and Henrique Miranda's interview, CPDOC/FGV, 21. For the fact that unions gave little support to the campaign, see ibid., 66.

47. José Murilo de Carvalho, *Pontos e bordados*, 341.

48. See the memo from the American consulate-general in São Paulo to the secretary of state, June 17, 1948, RG 59, 832.6363/6-1748, NA-USA. For references to Carnaúba's, travels see Maria Augusta Tibiriçá Miranda, *Petróleo é nosso*, 50–52, 69. See also *Emancipação*, March 2, 1951, 10.

49. See the memo from the American consulate-general in São Paulo to the secretary of state, June 17, 1948, RG 59, 832.6363/6-1748, NA-USA.

50. See Pessoa's unpublished autobiography, JP 53.00.00 dv, xi, 12, CPDOC/FGV.

51. Moura, *Sucessos e ilusões*, 59.

52. Wirth, *Politics of Brazilian Development*, 173. For communists' participation in the movement, see José Soares Maciel Filho to Getúlio Vargas, October 1948, GV 48.10.00/4, CPDOC/FGV. Roberto Gusmão stated that the students used the structure of the Communist Party to spread the petroleum movement. Roberto Gusmão's interview, CPDOC/FGV, 15; for more information on communists in the campaign, see Euzébio Rocha's interview (CPDOC/FGV), 6–7; Victor, *Batalha do petróleo brasileiro*, 195–96; Fernando Luiz Lobo Barbosa Carneiro's interview, CPDOC/FGV, 16–17; Wirth, *Politics of Development*, 173–74; Maria Augusta Tibiriçá Miranda's interview, CPDOC/FGV, 17–18; Henrique Miranda's interview, CPDOC/FGV, 9–10, 22. For the fact that Fernando Luiz Lobo Barbosa Carneiro was a communist, see Roberto Gusmão's interview, CPDOC/FGV, 45.

53. See Mattos Pimenta to Luíz Hildebrando B. Horta Barbosa, July 17, 1948, HB 47.02.10 vp 4–19, CPDOC/FGV.

54. For an example of how Pimenta included a weekly section on the CEDP in his paper, see *Jornal de Debates*, April 30, 1948. This small paper circulated almost solely in Rio de Janeiro; see Nelson Werneck Sodré's interview, CPDOC/FGV–SERCOM/ Petrobrás, 3. The *Jornal de Debates* often carried anti-American articles. See for example *Jornal de Debates*, May 7, 1948, 10. For the response to Pimenta's letter see Luíz Hildebrando de B. Horta Barbosa to Mattos Pimenta, August 21, 1948, HB 47.02.10 vp 4–18, CPDOC/FGV.

55. See Henrique Miranda's interview, CPDOC/FGV, 25. Bernardes's comments were so funny because Miranda was a communist himself.

56. For Dutra's overtures to the communists, see Alzira Vargas do Amaral Peixoto's interview, 1981, CPDOC/FGV–História Oral, 86. For the dispersal of street demonstrations by students, see the U.S. State Department Memo, April 26, 1948, RG 59, 832.6363/4-2648, NA-USA. See also *Jornal de Debates*, April 23, 1948, 10. For the government's use of repression in May, then its reluctance to continue this policy in June, see the American Embassy to the U.S. State Department, June 28, 1948, RG 59, 832.6363/ 6-2848, NA-USA. For the arrest of soldiers watching a petroleum rally, see the memo of July 1, 1948, "Sr. chefe do setôr trabalhista, in "Dossie sobre o Centro de Estudos e Defesa do Petróleo s/documentação," APERJ, DPS, D186, 428. For the meeting in Amazonas, see Miranda Braga's telegram to Júlio Caetano Horta Barbosa, HB 47.02.10 vp 4–6, CPDOC/FGV. For Dutra's call to Professor Sá, see Fernando Luiz Lobo Barbosa Carneiro's interview, CPDOC/FGV, 43–44.

57. For the U.S. State Department's belief that no loans should be given for petroleum production until the legislation had been altered, see Daniels to Lawson, January 6, 1948, RG 59, 832.6363/1-248, NA-USA. For the State Department's thought about contacts with army officers, see Daniels to Lawson, January 5, 1948, RG 59, 832.6363/1-248, NA-USA.

58. For Távora's comments, see the memorandum of conversation, July 26, 1948, RG 59, 832.6363/7-2648, NA-USA. In this document the chief of the general staff is referred to as General Tabora [*sic*]. For the U.S. perception that communists lay behind the movement, see the consul general of São Paulo, Cecil Cross, to David McKey, the

acting U.S. chargé d'affaires in Rio de Janeiro, April 15, 1948, RG 59, 832.6363/4-1548, NA-USA.

59. "CIA Research Report, Brazil," 30.

60. For the garrison of Santa Maria's telegram to Horta Barbosa, see *Jornal de Debates*, July 30, 1948, 1. This telegram was reprinted in a work by Colonel Carnaúba titled (in translation) "The Army and the Defense of Petroleum." This work was sold at CEDPEN meetings, as the police carefully noted. See the memo "Setor trabalhista" of August 5, 1948, APERJ, DPS, D186, box 428, "Dossie sobre o Centro de Estudos e Defesa do Petróleo s/documentação." For information on the August petition by officers, see *Jornal de Debates*, August 13, 1948, 6.

61. For the history of the events of that night, see the police deposition of Gen. Júlio Caetano Horta Barbosa, September 27, 1948, HB 47.02.10 vp 4–36, CPDOC/FGV; Euzébio Rocha's interview, CPDOC/FGV, 24–25; Maria Augusta Tibiriçá Miranda, *Petróleo é nosso*, 141–42; Moura, *Campanha do petróleo*, 7–11; *Correio da Manhã*, September 24, 1948, 3. For Fernando Luiz Lobo Barbosa Carneiro's description of these generals as men influenced by Benjamin Constant, see Fernando Luiz Lobo Barbosa Carneiro's interview, CPDOC/FGV, 42. For the fact that Carnaúba, although often described as a positivist, was a marxist, see Henrique Miranda's interview, CPDOC/ FGV, 14. For the statements of Gen. Lima Câmara, the chief of police, see *Globo*, September 24, 1948, 1. For the earlier use of rhetoric involving Floriano Peixoto during the petroleum campaign, see Estevão Carvalho, *Petróleo*, 168.

62. For the fact that General Horta Barbosa's son called the army, see Fernando Luiz Lobo Barbosa Carneiro's interview, CPDOC/FGV, 42. For what Horta Barbosa's son said, see General Câmara's interview, *Globo*, September 24, 1948, 1, column 1. For the crowds' applause of the soldiers, see Maria Augusta Tibiriçá Miranda's interview, CPDOC/FGV, 20. For the arrest of the wounded policeman, see *Correio da Manhã*, September 24, 1948, 3.

63. For pictures of the policemen who were wounded that night, see *Globo*, September 24, 1948, 5. For the records of other injured people and a description of events at the hospital, see the *Jornal de Debates*, October 8, 1948, 5. For the confrontation between the policemen and General Horta Barbosa, see *Correio da Manhã*, September 24, 1948, 3.

64. For Carvalho's belief that Dutra sanctioned the attack, see Estevão Carvalho, *Memórias de um general reformado*, 124. For Dias Medronha's resignation, see Victor, *Batalha do petróleo brasileiro*, 270. For General Câmara's meeting with Carvalho and Horta Barbosa, see *Correio da Manhã*, September 25, 1948, 3. José Pessoa, who had participated in the event, said that he deplored the attack but that he was outraged by the agitation that surrounded the issue of petroleum. *Globo*, September 24, 1948, 1.

65. For Canrobert's circular, see the U.S. Embassy dispatch, October 21, 1948, RG 59, 832.6363/10-2148, NA-USA; Maria Augusta Tibiriçá, *Petróleo é nosso*, 87.

66. See Henrique Miranda's interview, CPDOC/FGV, 114.

67. For the situation in the military, see Euzébio Rocha's interview, CPDOC/FGV, 24. For the telegram signed by the officers of the First Military Region, see the *Jornal de Debates*, October 15, 1948, 6. For the attendance of the president of the Veteran's Association at this gathering, see Maria Augusta Tibiriçá Miranda, *Petróleo é nosso*, 149. For the fact that most officers supported Horta Barbosa, see Nelson Werneck Sodré's interview, CPDOC/FGV, 14.

68. For Dutra's proposed changes to the SALTE plan, see Victor, *Batalha do petróleo*

brasileiro, 273. For Dutra's October seventh decree, see the memo of Harold M. Midriff, October 7, 1948 in *Foreign Relations of the United States*, 1948, 9:364. Euzébio Rocha and others stated that France was reluctant to sell refinery equipment to Brazil because of pressure from the United States. Only after the Brazilian government threatened to turn to Czechoslovakia was the sale was permitted. See Euzébio Rocha's interview, CPDOC/FGV, 16. For more on the purchases and the public relations campaign Dutra launched, see the U.S. Embassy message, October 21, 1948, RG 59, 832.6363/10-2148, NA-USA. For more on the public relations campaign, see Fernando Luiz Lobo Barbosa Carneiro's interview, CPDOC/FGV, 22; Estevão Leitão de Carvalho *Petróleo*, 206. For Dutra's visit to Salvador, see the *Jornal de Debates*, December 24, 1948, 8.

69. For the fact that Dutra may have made petroleum purchases to strengthen Canrobert, see the U.S. Embassy message, October 21, 1948, RG 59, 832.6363/10-2148, NA-USA. Ernâni do Amaral Peixoto stated that Dutra did not support Canrobert for the presidency. Ernâni do Amaral Peixoto's interview, CPDOC/FGV, 525. But the records of the time indicate otherwise. For how Vargas monitored Canrobert's candidacy, see Duarte Anibal to Getúlio Vargas, September 7, 1948, GV 48.12.07, CPDOC/FGV. In this document Anibal discussed the list of Canrobert's supporters circulating amongst officers. See also Napoleão de Alencastro Guimarães to Getúlio Vargas, December 12, 1948, GV 48.12.17, CPDOC/FGV.

70. See Maria Augusta Tibiriçá Miranda's interview, CPDOC/FGV, 90; Smith, *Oil and Politics in Modern Brazil*, 1–2. Peixoto argues that the true issue for the military was economic development. See Antonio Carlos Peixoto, "Le Clube Militar." See also Ronning, "The Military," 208–9, 214–15.

Chapter Five

1. Coelho argued that the army acquired an ideology during the Estado Novo, but it did not institutionalize this doctrine until the foundation of the Escola Superior da Guerra in 1946. Coelho, *Em busca da identidade*, 153.

2. Alfred Stepan, *Military in Politics*, 172–87; Alfred Stepan, "The New Professionalism," 47–65.

3. For Pimenta's meeting with Canrobert, see *Jornal de Debates*, January 28, 1949, 1. For Távora's comments, see *Jornal de Debates*, February 25, 1949, 1. For statements by CEDP's leaders that anticommunist rhetoric cost the movement support, see, *Emancipação*, March 16, 1949, 2.

4. For more information on Moraes Filho's arrest, see *Emancipação*, February 9, 1949, 3; see also the center spread of this edition; Miranda, *Petróleo é nosso*, 171–73, 188.

5. For Domingo Vellasco's speech see *Emancipação*, April 6, 1949, 6. For acts of government violence against the campaign, see Maria Augusta Tibiriçá Miranda, *Petróleo é nosso*, 202–5.

6. See the U.S. Embassy in Rio de Janeiro dispatch to the secretary of state, December 24, 1948, RG 59, 832.6363/12-2448, NA-USA; Oliveira's article, *Diário de Noticias*, October 26, 1948, 4. Pimenta also criticized the center. *Jornal de Debates*, December 17, 1948, 10. For the problems Henrique Miranda's anti–United States statements created, see Wirth, *Politics of Brazilian Development*, 177.

7. See Henrique Miranda's interview, 1992, CPDOC/FGV–História Oral, 44.

8. On January 21, 1949 the Anti-Fascist League of Tijuca described how they had

founded the CEDP. The letter was signed by several people, including Felicíssimo Cardoso and Henrique Miranda. *Diário de Noticias*, January 21, 1949, 5. Mattos Pimenta critiqued this letter in an article the following day. *Diário de Noticias*, January 22, 1949, 5.

9. For Pimenta's publication of both his letter to Luís Hildebrando Horta Barbosa and the reply he received, see *Diário de Noticias*, February 1, 1949, 5. For Oliveira's belief that the question at issue was the center's involvement in an international struggle, see *Diário de Noticias*, January 23, 1949, 5.

10. For the creation of a commission to question Mattos Pimenta, see Henrique Miranda's interview, CPDOC/FGV, 45. For the expulsion of Pimenta and Oliveira from the campaign, see *Jornal de Debates*, February 25, 1949, 1. Professor Hileo Lacerda wrote General Horta Barbosa on May 19, 1950. In this plaintive letter he said that he had resigned from the São Paulo branch of CEDP because of the "sectarianism" of communists. He had decided not to fight publicly because he did not want to hurt the movement. See Lacerda to Horta Barbosa, May 19, 1950, HB 47.02.10 vp 5-14, CPDOC/FGV. For the weakening of the campaign, see the U.S. Embassy to the State Department, February 8, 1949, RG 59, 832.6363/2-849, NA-USA.

11. For *Emancipação's* distribution see Henrique Miranda's interview, CPDOC/FGV, 33. See also Maria Augusta Tibiriçá Miranda's interview, 1988, CPDOC/FGV–SRCOM/Petrobrás, 46. For a description of the magazine and its role, see Manor, "Factions et idéologie," 561.

12. For information on the magazine's membership, see *Emancipação*, February 2, 1949, 1.

13. See *Emancipação*, February 9, 1949, 1. For the magazine's description of its purpose, see *Emancipação*, February 2, 1949, 3.

14. See Horta Barbosa's article, "A política colonial à luz do positivismo," *Emancipação*, February 9, 1949, 2; see also *Emancipação*, March 16, 1949, 2.

15. See the U.S. Embassy dispatch to the secretary of state, December 24, 1948, RG 59, 832.6363/12-2448, NA-USA. See also *Diário de Noticias*, October 26, 1948, 4.

16. For Raimundo Sampaio's meeting with the generals, see *Jornal de Debates*, February 18, 1949, 9. For more on the transfer of the executive presidency see *Emancipação*, February 16, 1949, center spread, 1–2. For more on the inauguration, see Maria Augusta Tibiriçá Miranda, *Petróleo é nosso*, 174–76. For Sampaio's criticism of the role of communists in the campaign, see *Jornal de Debates*, February 18, 1949, 9.

17. For officers' abandonment of CEDP, see Wirth, *Politics of Brazilian Development*, 177. For officer's embarrassment over military ties to CEDP, see Smith, *Oil and Politics in Modern Brazil*, 76. For the continued attendance of officers at CEDPEN's meetings, see *Emancipação*, July 1949. For a list of army leaders in CEDPEN in January 1951, see Maria Augusta Tibiriçá Miranda, *Petróleo é nosso*, 226–27.

18. Smith, *Oil and Politics in Modern Brazil*, 76.

19. For a description of this faction's thought, see Antonio Carlos Peixoto, "Le Clube Militar," 73–77. Peixoto has used the term "antinationalist" to describe this faction, yet this word is problematic. Although this faction believed Brazil would benefit from its alliance with the United States, its officers perceived themselves to be the "true" nationalists.

20. Antonio Carlos Peixoto has referred to the old mission officers as the "nationalist" faction. He argued that their ideology was not "specifically military" but rather was adapted from civilian groups. In Peixoto's words, this faction "never produced an

elaborated doctrine." See Antonio Carlos Peixoto "Le Clube Militar," 80. I believe Peixoto's argument to be incorrect. Horta Barbosa's speeches addressed specific military concerns. First in *Emancipação*, then in *Revista do Clube Militar*, this faction articulated a clear ideology, quite distinct from the vision of their civilian allies. The faction used nationalist rhetoric to gain civilian support, but the core of their ideology was a vision of state development some nationalists disliked.

21. For more information on Peru's CAEM (the Center for Higher Military Studies), see Einaudi, "Revolution from Within?," and Villanueva, *El CAEM y la revolucion de la fuerza armada*.

22. For an example of how authors have overemphasized the foreign influence on ESG, see Hayes, *Armed Nation*, 196. For U.S. participation in the school, see Camargo and Góes, *Meio século de combate*, 412–17. For the argument that ESG was the intellectual child of the febianos, see Antonio Carlos Peixoto, "Le Clube Militar," 78; Farcau, *Transition to Democracy in Latin America*, 89; McCann, "The Brazilian Army and the Problem of Mission, 1939–1964," 123; Silviera, *Duas guerras*, 25. Alfred Stepan has also stressed the role of the FEB in creating ESG. See Alfred Stepan, *Military in Politics*, 172–87. Cordeiro de Farias argued that ESG was the creation of the FEB. See Comblin, *Ideologia da segurança nacional*, 155.

23. See Camargo and Góes, *Meio século de combate*, 417.

24. Because of the military's influence, most scholars have described the FEB as a democratic and internationalist force that opposed Vargas. See McCann, *Brazilian-American Alliance*, 442; Antonio Carlos Peixoto, "Le Clube Militar," 75; Silveira, *Duas guerras*, 29; Ricardo Bonalume Neto, *Nossa segunda guerra*, 14–15, 217. For an extensive discussion of the FEB's thought, see Alfred Stepan, *Military in Politics*, 239, 242–47; Alfred Stepan, "The New Professionalism," 255. For a critique of these arguments, see Smallman, "The Official Story."

25. Smallman, "The Official Story," 232, 254–56.

26. See Ernâni do Amaral Peixoto's interview, 1985, CPDOC/FGV–História Oral, 312. For more about the ESG and its role in creating a new ideology, see Oliveira, *Forças armadas*, 15–22. For Stepan's arguments see Alfred Stepan, *Military in Politics*, 172–87.

27. For a critique of Stepan's arguments, see Markoff and Baretta, "Professional Ideology."

28. For how Cordeiro de Farias came to head the school, see Camargo and Góes, *Meio século de combate*, 409–10. The schools' character was shaped not only by design, but also by the course of the factional struggle. In December 1950, when Canrobert learned an nationalist officer would replace him as minister of war, he placed his allies in safe positions. Cordeiro de Farias took two of Canrobert's followers into ESG to shield them. See Antônio Carlos Murici's comments in Valentina da Rocha Lima, *Getúlio*, 226

29. Antonio Carlos Peixoto, "Le Clube Militar," 80.

30. See Idálio Sardenburg's comments in Mota, *História Vivida*, 2:363. See also ibid., 364; Camargo and Góes, *Meio século de combate*, 411, 416.

31. For more information on NSI, see Alves, *State and Opposition*, 13–28. Comblin has argued that this doctrine was imported from the United States. Comblin, *Ideologia da segurança militar*, 23, 103–4. For Edmundo Campos Coelho's arguments, see Coelho, *Em busca da identidade*, 167. Daniel Masterson has described how CAEM also built upon old beliefs within the Peruvian military. Masterson, "Peruvian Armed Forces in Transition," 256–57.

32. Sardenburg wrote these regulations as the director-general of the commission that drafted them. See Mota, *História Vivida*, 2:363. See Camargo and Góes, *Meio século de combate*, 419. For more on the association of development with security in the Brazilian military, see Hilton, "The Armed Forces and Industrialists in Modern Brazil," 666. Also important is Nunn, "Military Professionalism and Professional Militarism in Brazil, 1870–1970."

33. Nelson de Mello's interview, 1983, CPDOC/FGV–História Oral, 318.

34. For the new concept of security, see the comments of Umberto Peregrino Seabra Fagundes in Mota, *História vivida*, 2:114. For the inevitability of the alliance with the United States, see Schooyans, *Destin du Brésil*, 57–58. For more on the ideology, see ibid., 47–58. Army intellectuals also used geopolitics to justify their old perception that the state and the nation were indivisible. Comblin, *Ideologia da segurança nacional*, 28.

35. See McCann, "The Brazilian Army and the Problem of Mission, 1939–1964," See also Coelho, *Em busca da identidade*, 166–67 and Comblin, *Ideologia da segurança nacional*, 54.

36. Joseph Comblin has argued that the association of development with security was first made by Robert McNamara during a speech in Montreal in 1967. Latin American nations then followed the U.S. lead and adopted this ideal. See Comblin, *Ideologia da segurança nacional*, 64–68. Comblin overlooked the fact that this idea had existed within continental militaries since the turn of the century. What was new was that this ideal had been adapted to the Cold War era, in most countries through the use of anticommunist rhetoric. Comblin also denied the autonomy of regional militaries. Comblin believed that NSI was the creation of the United States, which used this doctrine to influence satellite nations. See ibid., 103–4. Yet Peruvian officers adapted the same ideals—taught in similar schools—to create an ideology specifically designed to limit the economic and political power of the United States. Ibid., 165–77.

37. Goldwert, *Democracy, Militarism, and Nationalism*, xvii–xix. For another description of Argentine factions, see Perina, "Raíces históricos."

38. Luigi Einaudi described the Peruvian military's perception of national sovereignty in this manner: "Specifically, this is defined as an obligation to increase Peru's capacity for maneuver vis-á-vis the outside world, and specifically the United States." Einaudi, "Revolution from Within?" 76.

39. Comblin, *Ideologia da segurança nacional*, 64–68, 155. Alves, *State and Opposition*, 13–28; Alfred Stepan, *Military in Politics*, 172–87.

Chapter Six

1. See Epitacio Pessoa Albuquerque to Getúlio Vargas, March 24, 1949, GV 49.03.24/1, CPDOC/FGV. Albuquerque also discussed Dutra's plans for Canrobert in this letter. For a copy of José Pessoa's bulletin, see *Estado do São Paulo*, March 23, 1949, 3. For the history of events, see José Pessoa's autobiography, JP 53.00.00 dv XIV,, 50–57, CPDOC/FGV. For public speculation about why José Pessoa acted, see *Estado do São Paulo*, March 24, 1949, 3.

2. For information on CEXIM, see Beloch and Abreu, *Dicionário histórico-biográfico brasileiro, 1930–1983*, 1:664. For discussions of the Banco do Brasil and CEXIM, see Estados Unidos do Brasil, Câmara dos Deputados, *Anais da Câmara dos Deputados*, 43

(November 14–17, 1952) 54, 296–97. On the functionary's confession, see *Jornal de Debates*, June 20, 1952, 3. See also *Globo*, June 14, 1952, 3. For Gen. Rio Pardense's imposition of censorship on police reporting, see *Jornal de Debates*, July 18, 1952, 3.

3. Smallman, "Shady Business."

4. José Pessoa knew the identity of the author of this note, but his handwritten notation (made years later) is illegible. The author did not sign his name. See JP 48.08.11 vp/A, CPDOC/FGV. For more on this illegal transaction, see José Pessoa's unpublished autobiography, JP 53.00.00 dv XIII, CPDOC/FGV.

5. JP 53.00.00 dv XIII, 17–25, CPDOC/FGV.

6. For the correspondence between José Pessoa and the hierarchy, see JP. 53.00.00 dv XIII, 1–25, CPDOC/FGV. See also GV 48.08.11 vp, CPDOC/FGV.

7. In 1946 Brazilian generals purchased U.S. wheat with the aid of Vieira Machado, the exchange director of the Bank of Brazil. Most of the wheat later rotted when the United States refused to grant Brazil the necessary export contracts. Grave irregularities in this purchase then prompted a government investigation, which emphasized the role of the minister of war, Canrobert Pereira da Costa. See José Pessoa's unpublished autobiography, JP 53.00.00, dv XIII, 22–23. For background on the purchase, see the memo of April 30, 1946 in the records of the U.S. Army staff in Rio de Janeiro, RG 319, Entry 57, Box 12, NA-USA. See also U.S. State Department, *Foreign Relations of the United States: the American Republics, 1947*, 8:475–80.

8. For José Pessoa's desire to have an inquiry, see José Pessoa's autobiography, JP 53.00.00 dv XIII, 22, CPDOC/FGV. For Canrobert's participation in the illegal wheat sale, see ibid., 22–23. Canrobert conducted a public correspondence with the director of the inquiry through which much of this material became public; see *Globo*, November 22, 1952, 1, 4. See also *Globo*, November 24, 1952, 1. The Bank of Brazil report became a major question in 1952, as political parties debated whether to publish it. I can find no record that it was ever released to the public. It contained embarrassing information on military leaders such as Gen. Ângelo Mendes, who had been found with an unexpectedly large amount of money in his personal account. See Estados Unidos do Brasil, Congresso Federal, *Anais da Câmara dos Deputados*, 1952, vol. 43, sessions of November 18, 19, 20, 84. Miguel Teixeira de Oliveira, Canrobert's friend, later became the head of the Bank of Brazil.

9. José Monteiro Ribeiro Junqueira to Getúlio Vargas, September 6, 1949, GV 49.09.06/2, CPDOC/FGV. For Canrobert's continued plans to run for the presidency, see José Soares Maciel Filho to Getúlio Vargas, n.d. GV 49.00.00/16, CPDOC/FGV. Canrobert petitioned the minister of war, asking for a statement of confidence in his person. Gen. Santo Cardoso obliged. JP 53.00.00 dv XIII, 22, CPDOC/FGV.

10. For General Góes Monteiro's continued support for Canrobert, see Gashipo Chagas Pereira to Getúlio Vargas, 1950 (probably March), GV 53.03.01/3, CPDOC/FGV. For Dutra's wish to replace Canrobert, see Miguel Teixeira to Getúlio Vargas, April 12, 1950, GV 50.04.12/1, CPDOC/FGV and João Neves da Fontoura to Getúlio Vargas, April 26, 1950, GV 50.04.26/2, CPDOC/FGV.

11. *New York Times*, January 3, 1950, 14.

12. See Erwin Keeler to the U.S. State Department, March 14, 1950, RG 59, 732.551/3-1450, NA-USA.

13. Juraci Magalhães' interview, 1981, CPDOC/FGV–História Oral, 350.

14. See Candida Ivete Vargas Martins to Getúlio Vargas, April 4, 1950, GV 50.04.30, CPDOC/FGV.

15. See Ernâni do Amaral Peixoto's interview, 1985, CPDOC/FGV–História Oral, 527.

16. Ibid.

17. General Nelson de Mello said that all officers more or less opposed Vargas's return. See Nelson de Mello's interview, 1983, CPDOC/FGV–História Oral, 309. But he told Lourival Fontes at the time that only a minority within the army opposed free elections. See Lourival Fontes to Getúlio Vargas, probably March 1950, GV 50.03.00/8, CPDOC/FGV. For Vargas's influence within the army, see the cryptic letter of Maj. Bruno Ribeiro to Getúlio Vargas, January 25, 1949, GV 49.01.25, CPDOC/FGV. Lt. Col. Anamelino Vargas spoke to Candida Ivete Vargas Martins of the resistance to the coup within the army. For Canrobert's desire to guarantee the election, and the possibility of a coup, see Candida Ivete Vargas Martins to Getúlio Vargas, April 4, 1950, GV 50.04.30, CPDOC/FGV. New York Times, January 3, 1950, 14. For Canrobert's announcement that he would not run for the presidency, see Tribuna da Imprensa, April 3, 1950, 1. For Canrobert's meeting with Viriato Dornelles Vargas, see GV 50.04.00/8, CPDOC/FGV.

18. For a history of the struggle within the Military Club, the best single source is Sodré, Do estado novo à ditadura militar. See also Sodré, História militar do Brasil. For a theoretical discussion of the role the Military Club played, see Antonio Carlos Peixoto, "Le Clube Militar," 65–69. For the history of the Military Club during this period, see ibid., 81–88. Peixoto suggested that the conflict emerged in 1950 because both factions needed a forum for their debate; see ibid., 67. For Rouquié's statement that these elections were nearly as important as those for the presidency, see Rouquié "Processus politiques dans les partis militaires au Brésil," 13. Sodré contradicted him on this point. He believed that the Estado Novo had nearly destroyed the Military Club. See Nelson Werneck Sodré's interview, 1988, CPDOC/FGV–SERCOM/Petrobrás, 15. For the increased prestige and membership the Military Club acquired during the petroleum struggle, see Antonio Carlos Peixoto, "Le Clube Militar,"85.

19. See João Neves da Fontoura to Getúlio Vargas, March 1950, GV 50.05.00/13, CPDOC/FGV. For Sodré's magnificent description of Estillac, see Sodré, Do estado novo à ditadura militar, 61–63. For more information on Estillac, see his biography written by an anonymous U.S. military attache on February 9, 1951, RG 319, Entry 47, Box 81, NA-USA.

20. Sodré stated that Estillac marked the appearance of a new military "component." See Sodré, História militar do Brasil, 304. But Estillac drew his support from the nationalist faction, which had become increasingly radical.

21. See Teixeira's comments in Valentina da Rocha Lima, Getúlio, 223–24. See also the comments of Cordeiro de Farias, ibid., 224. For Estillac's candidacy, see his election handbill, GV 50.01.17/1, CPDOC/FGV.

22. For the friendship of Estillac and Cordeiro de Farias, see Valentina da Rocha Lima, Getúlio, 224. See also Estillac's comments, O Estado de São Paulo, February 26, 1950, 3. For the contradictory statements Estillac made about military divisions, see his election handbills, GV 50.01.17/1, CPDOC/FGV, and GV 50.01.25/2, CPDOC/FGV. For Oliveira's comments, see Jornal de Debates, March 3, 1950, 4; Paulo Pinto Guedes stated that the candidacy of Estillac and Horta Barbosa polarized the army. Valentina da Rocha Lima, Getúlio, 223.

23. Nelson Werneck Sodré's interview, CPDOC/FGV, 14. Cordeiro de Farias later

said of the campaign: "The division in the army was really clear." See Camargo and Góes, *Meio século de combate*, 436. But he contradicted himself later in the same interview, in which he said that there were no major themes to the campaign. Ibid., 437–38. For the fact that the election had become a national event, see *O Estado de São Paulo*, February 26, 1950, 3. See also *Jornal de Debates*, March 3, 1950, 4.

24. See Nelson de Mello's interview, CPDOC/FGV, 307. Speaking of the 1952 elections within the Military Club, John Wirth said: "Ironically, petroleum was not the real issue, for both groups were in fact nationalist." See Wirth, *Politics of Brazilian Development*, 203. For the fact that Cordeiro de Farias represented the military hierarchy, see Sodré, *História militar do Brasil*, 305. Paul Manor described Cordeiro de Farias as the head of the "liberal" faction, see Manor, "Factions et idéologie," 569. For the question of state industries and petroleum in the campaign, see Nelson Werneck Sodré's interview, CPDOC/FGV, 4–5.

25. See Valentina da Rocha Lima, *Getúlio*, 224. Antônio Carlos Murici stated that the "democrats" who supported Cordeiro de Farias were convinced that they could win based on an idea alone. See ibid. For the fact that officers were suffering from inflation, see Manor, "Factions et idéologie," 570. For Estillac's campaign literature, see HB 49.12.06 vp 1–9, CPDOC/FGV. According to Carlos Lacerda, the governor of São Paulo helped Estillac's campaign. See *Tribuna da Imprensa*, November 29, 1950, 5. For the anti-Dutra nature of Estillac's campaign slate, see Nelson Werneck Sodré's interview, CPDOC/FGV, 16.

26. For the percentage of officers who voted, see Antonio Carlos Peixoto, "Le Clube Militar," 85. On July 26, 1950 Gen. Estillac Leal formally became the president of the Military Club.

27. *Tribuna da Imprensa*, September 21, 1951, 4. For a discussion of the communist leanings of the Associação dos Ex-combatentes and how army leaders responded to this challenge, see Dulles, *Castello Branco*, 185–89.

28. For the participation of febiano Emygdio da Costa Miranda in Estillac's campaign, see ibid., 191.

29. João Neves da Fontoura to Getúlio Vargas, May, 1950, GV 50.05.00/13, CPDOC/FGV. According to Nelson Werneck Sodré, Estillac's supporters within the Military Club feared that they would be identified as the group supporting Vargas's candidacy. Sodré believed that their support for Vargas was lukewarm: "Possibly the majority of those who were part of the Estillac-Horta current preferred Vargas, would prefer him without passion. Because Vargas was anti-Dutra. The problem was to be anti-Dutra." See Nelson Werneck Sodré's interview, CPDOC/FGV, 17.

30. This party was similar to the English labor party of the period and different from the modern Brazilian workers' party, Partido Trabalhista Brasileira.

31. See Ernâni do Amaral Peixoto's interview, CPDOC/FGV, 660.

32. *Tribuna da Imprensa*, September 1, 1950, 1.

33. See *Diário de Noticias*, August 29, 1950, 5. For information on the Casa do Sargento do Brasil, see the memorandum of João Martinho Netto to Senhor Chefe do S. Iv (Serviço de Investigaçoes) of May 31, 1951, APERJ, DESPS, N 46, "Casa do sargento do Brasil."

34. See *Tribuna da Imprensa*, August 29, 1950, 1. See also *Tribuna da Imprensa*, August 30, 1950, 1, all columns.

35. Caio Miranda met with the most important military commanders during late

October and December, 1950. His reports provide a priceless record of these officers' thoughts and personalities. See Caio Miranda's reports to Getúlio Vargas, late
October–November 1950, GV 50.10.18/1, CPDOC/FGV.

36. Smith, *Oil and Politics in Brazil*, 76.

37. See "Discurso do Gen. Estillac Leal na cerimônia de posse da nova diretoria."
Revista do Clube Militar 107 (July 1950): 5–11.

38. See Raimundo Sampaio, "Em defesa dos minerais radiativos, fontes de energia
atômica," *Revista do Clube Militar* 107 (July 1950): 12–21. Artur Bernardes, "A questão
da Hiléa Amazonica: um discurso do Dr. Arthur Bernardes na Camara dos Deputados," *Revista do Clube Militar* 109 (September 1950): 129–32. Colonel X, "Prefácio ao
relatorio juin," *Revista do Clube Militar* 110 (October 1950): 66–67.

39. Clarence C. Brooks to "Dick", June 28, 1949, RG 59, 832.6363/6-2849, NA-USA.

40. Henrique Teixeira Lott's interview, 1982, CPDOC/FGV–História Oral, 114.

41. Nelson de Mello's interview, CPDOC/FGV, 312.

42. See Colonel X, "Cronica internacional: considerações sobre a guerra a Coréia,"
Revista do Clube Militar 107 (July 1950): 75–80. For a reprint of the original article, see
Emancipação, January 13, 1951, 11. Sodré also reprinted selections from the article.
Sodré, *Do estado novo à ditadura militar*, 23–24. For a history of the conflict caused by
this article, see Manor, "Factions et idéologie." Manor traced the struggle only until
January 1951, although it continued into 1952. For the delay in the magazines' publica-
tion, see ibid., 574. For the resignation of three members of the magazine before the
article was published, see *Tribuna da Imprensa*, November 29, 1950, 5.

43. The author must have known that the article would create a fierce response or he
would not have remained anonymous. In the past, no articles had appeared without
credit. Colonel X also used extensive quotations from a French newspaper to make his
point, which enabled his supporters to argue that he only offered commentary on
another author's writings.

44. For the note of protest to the press, see Sodré, *Do estado novo à ditadura militar*,
27. See also Manor, "Factions et idéologie," 576.

45. See the record of Caio Miranda's meeting with General Cordeiro de Farias on
November 2, 1950, GV 50.10.18/1, CPDOC/FGV. See also the record of Caio Miranda's meeting with General de Menezes on October 21, 1950, GV 50.10.18/1, CPDOC/
FGV. General Menezes told Miranda that the army did not question the election
results.

46. See the letter of Danton Coelho to Getúlio Vargas, NM 51.05.16m, 1 (3a),
CPDOC/FGV.

47. See Ernâni do Amaral Peixoto's interview, CPDOC/FGV, 791–92. For the fact
that Estillac worked for Vargas's inauguration, see Sodré, *História militar do Brasil*, 314.
For a copy of Estillac's speech to the Military Club on November 15, 1950, see GV
50.11.15/1, CPDOC/FGV. For reaction to his speech, see *Correio da Manha*, November
18, 1950, 1. See also, *Tribuna da Imprensa*, November 17, 1950, 1.

48. For General Zenóbio's bravery, see Henrique Teixeira Lott's interview, CPDOC/
FGV, 61. In January 1951, the vice president of the National Council of Veterans Associations, N. Pithan e Silva, wrote to President Vargas. This man had founded the veterans'
associations in Rio de Janeiro and Rio Grande do Sul, and he had twice been elected to
the presidency of the latter body. Speaking on behalf of the febianos, he stated that
General Zenóbio had been an unpleasant commander in Italy and that he had opposed
the febianos' requests after the war. The former members of the FEB wished to prevent

Gen. Zenóbio da Costa from becoming the minister of war: "Any other commander will always be a better choice than General Zenóbio da Costa." See Danton Coelho to Getúlio Vargas, January 21, 1951, NM 51.05.16m, 1 (3A), CPDOC/FGV.

49. See Ciro Rio Grandense de Resende to Getúlio Vargas, November, 1948, GV 48.11.16, CPDOC/FGV. See also Viriato Dornelles Vargas to Getúlio Vargas, August 1, 1949, GV 49.08.01, CPDOC/FGV.

50. Caio Miranda met with Zenóbio on November 17, 1950. See Caio Miranda to Getúlio Vargas, November 1950, GV 50.10.18/1, CPDOC/FGV.

51. Perhaps it was during this meeting that a famous exchange took place. According to Ernâni do Amaral Peixoto, at one point Zenóbio told Dutra that he could not count on his aid to prevent Vargas's inauguration. Dutra denied that he was intending to do so. Zenóbio replied: "But your friends are thinking of doing it." See Ernâni do Amaral Peixoto's interview, CPDOC/FG, 791. See José Monteiro Ribeiro Junqueira to Getúlio Vargas, September 6, 1949, GV 49.09.06/2, CPDOC/FGV. Caio Miranda to Getúlio Vargas, November 1950, GV 50.10.18/1, CPDOC/FGV. For the fear of a coup, and the will to react against it, see Napoleão de Alencastro Guimarães to Getúlio Vargas, December 1950, GV 50.12.00/1, CPDOC/FGV.

52. See Napoleão de Alencastro Guimarães to Getúlio Vargas, December 1950, GV 50.12.00/1, CPDOC/FGV. For Zenobio's comments to the press, see *Tribuna da Imprensa*, November 17, 1950, 1.

53. Ernâni do Amaral Peixoto's interview, CPDOC/FGV, 794. For the belief of many commanders that the elections had to be respected, see Caio Miranda's reports to Getúlio Vargas, November 1950, GV 50.10.18/1, CPDOC/FGV.

54. Nelson Werneck Sodré's interview, CPDOC/FGV, 23.

55. Nelson de Mello stated that the Korea article was favorable to communism. See Nelson de Mello's interview, CPDOC/FGV, 313.

56. For the protests to the Military Club, see Sodré, *Do estado novo à ditadura militar*, 27–33. Sodré believed that the attacks on the Military Club had been carefully orchestrated. Manor's article provides an excellent history of this struggle. See Manor, "Factions et idéologie." For Capt. Antônio Joaquim Figueiredo's letter, see *Tribuna da Imprensa*, November 10, 1950, 5. For the commanders' demand that the anonymous author accept responsibility for his article, see *Tribuna da Imprensa*, November 23, 1950, 10.

57. See *Diário de Noticias*, November 24, 1950, 4. For Estillac's earlier comment that it was not his task to censor military thought, see Manor, "Factions et idéologie," 579. For Sodré's presentation of a written defense of the article, see Sodré, *Do estado novo à ditadura militar*, 36–38.

58. For the Military Club's note to the press, see *Diário de Noticias*, November 26, 1950, 4. For Estillac's continued refusal to censure the journal, see Carlos Lacerda's editorial in *Tribuna da Imprensa*, November 27, 1950, 4. For a copy of the petition circulating among officers in defense of the Military Club, see *Tribuna da Imprensa*, November 29, 1950, 5.

59. For the note of protest, see *Tribuna da Imprensa*, November 29, 1950, 5. For Estillac's comments on the article, see ibid.

60. See João Neves da Fontoura to Getúlio Vargas, December 1, 1950, GV 50.12.03, CPDOC/FGV. For press criticism of the Military Club, see *Correio da Manhã*, December 7, 1950, 1. For the vitriolic rhetoric of the club's opponents, see Sodré, *Do estado novo à ditadura militar*, 38.

61. For the demand for a convocation of the Military Club's members, see Manor, "Factions et idéologie," 580. For the manifesto of the Military Club's opponents, see Tribuna da Imprensa, December 12, 1950, 1. For a copy of the petition, see Correio da Manhã, December 12, 1950, 1. For the manifesto in support of the club, see Tribuna da Imprensa, December 14, 1950, 1. Sodré quotes at length from this document. See Sodré, Do estado novo à ditadura militar, 41.

62. See Henrique Miranda's interview, 1992, CPDOC/FGV–História Oral, 63. See Antonio Carlos Peixoto, "Le Clube Militar." See also Sodré, Do estado novo à ditadura militar, 60.

63. For Sodré's perception of why Canrobert ordered these transfers, see Sodré, Do estado novo à ditadura militar, 59. These transfers meant that Artur Carnaúba, a leader in CEDP, automatically became the second vice-president of the Military Club. This fact soon became critical. For the bureaucratic struggle to force Sodré from his position at the general staff school, see Nelson Werneck Sodré's interview, CPDOC/FGV, 21–22; Sodré, Do estado novo à ditadura militar, 57.

64. For the suspension of the Military Club's journal, see Tribuna da Imprensa, December 16–17, 1950, 1. For Estillac's wish to hold a vote on whether to censure the magazine, see Valentina da Rocha Lima, Getúlio, 229. For Captain Guedes' comments, see Correio da Manhã, December 16, 1950, 1. For the fact that the December edition of the journal still circulated, see Manor, "Factions et idéologie," 582.

65. See João Neves da Fontoura to Getúlio Vargas, December 17, 1950, GV 50.12.17, CPDOC/FGV. For the continued criticism of the Military Club's journal, see Correio da Manhã, December 16, 1950, 1. For the declaration of the club's opponents, see Tribuna da Imprensa, December 18, 1950, 5.

66. See the comment of Antônio Carlos Murici in Lima, Getúlio, 224. For a discussion of the issues the military debated during this period, see Antonio Carlos Peixoto, "Le Clube Militar," 69–81.

67. See Nelson Werneck Sodré's interview, CPDOC/FGV, 11–12. See also ibid., 9–10, 13–14. Sodré later stressed the overwhelming importance of the Cold War to the factional struggle. Sodré, Do Estado Novo à ditadura militar, 45. For more on the relationship between the factional struggle and foreign relations, see Manor, "Factions et idéologie," 585–86.

68. See Henrique Miranda's interview, CPDOC/FGV, 61. For the fact that another strategy would have made it more difficult for the hierarchy to attack Estillac, see ibid., 63.

69. Caio Miranda to Getúlio Vargas, November 1950, GV 50.10.18, CPDOC/FGV.

70. Nelson de Mello's interview, CPDOC/FGV, 317. Nelson de Mello also spoke about the contradictions inherent in Vargas's choice of Estillac: "The man was so. During the war didn't Getúlio have Dutra, who was a Germanophile, decorated by Hitler [sic], and did he not have Oswaldo Aranha. A contradiction, right? Getulismo was this." See ibid., 316. For Vargas's reasons for choosing a leftist member of the military, see Nelson Werneck Sodré's interview, CPDOC/FGV, 20.

71. Zenóbio had a very different reaction. He had been assured by the Governor of São Paulo, Adhemar de Barros, that Vargas had intended to make him the next minister of war. But Zenóbio had then committed a number of thoughtless acts that were widely perceived to be ridiculous. Vargas chose Estillac, to the fury of Zenóbio who continually repeated that he had been "betrayed, miserably betrayed." See the anonymous report of February 13, 1950, GV 51.02.13, CPDOC/FGV. For Sodré's meeting

with Estillac, see Nelson Werneck Sodré's interview, CPDOC/FGV, 10–11. Sodré later said: "Estillac committed other errors. But that he should have accepted the function of Minister of War without forces to exercise it appears to me the fundamental error." See ibid., 11. For Estillac's meeting with Vargas see Augusto do Amaral Peixoto's interview, 1982, CPDOC/FGV–História Oral, 397.

72. See Nelson de Mello's interview, CPDOC/FGV, 317.

73. Nelson Werneck Sodré's interview, CPDOC/FGV, 3, 22.

Chapter Seven

1. For the contradictions inherent in Estillac's position as minister of war, see Antonio Carlos Peixoto, "Le Clube Militar," 88–89.

2. See Sodré, *Historia militar do Brasil*, 317. For conflicting versions of the following events, see ibid., 314 and Antonio Carlos Peixoto, "Le Clube Militar," 87.

3. For this history, see Sodré, *Do estado novo à ditadura militar*, 68–69.

4. Estillac's cabinet was composed of officers who opposed the directory of the Military Club. Sodré, *Do estado novo à ditadura militar*, 66. Some officers believed that Canrobert had transferred these officers at Estillac's request, see ibid., 67–68. Estillac wanted to retire some officers who opposed him. See Euzébio Rocha's interview, 1988, CPDOC/FGV–SERCOM/Petrobrás, 41–42. For the diplomatic maneuvering concerning Estillac's visit to the United States, see U.S. ambassador Herschel V. Johnson to Randolph A. Kidder, April 23, 1952, RG 59, 033.3211/4-2351, NA-USA; and Randolph A. Kidder to Miller, April 27, 1951, RG 59, 033.3211/4-2751, NA-USA. For Estillac's statement to the press upon his return, see Eldred D. Kuppinger to the State Department, June 6, 1951, RG 59, 033.3211/6-651, NA-USA.

5. See Horta Barbosa et al. to the directory of CEDPEN, April 2, 1951, HB 47.02.10 vp 5–21, CPDOC/FGV; Gen. Cyro Rio Pardense de Razende to General Horta Barbosa, April 7, 1951, HB 47.02.10 vp 5–22, CPDOC/FGV; Nilo da Silveira Werneck to General Horta Barbosa, April 30, 1951, HB 47.02.10 vp 5–24, CPDOC/FGV; Gen. Felicíssimo Cardoso to Arthur Bernardes et al., April 27, 1951, HB 47.02.10 vp 5–25, CPDOC/FGV; Gen. Felicíssimo Cardoso to Arthur Bernardes et al., June 17, 1951, HB 47.02.10 vp 5–28, CPDOC/FGV.

6. For General Rezende's defense of the police, see *Ultima Hora*, July 10, 1951, 1. For Maj. Hugo Bethlehem's description of CEDPEN as a communist front, see *A Noite*, June 16, 1951, 1–2. For the attack on the party at Coutinho Filho's house, see *Emancipação*, July 1951, 4. For CEDPEN's decision to hold a convention because of gathering pressure against the organization, see Maria Augusta Tibiriçá Miranda's interview, 1988, CPDOC/FGV–SERCOM/Petrobrás, 35. For her memory of the police attack on the convention, see ibid., 95. See also *Tribuna da Imprensa*, July 6, 1951, 1, 6. For the political repurcussions of the attack, see *Última Hora*, July 9, 1951, 1.

7. See Col. Salvador Corrêa de Sá e Benevides, "Defendemos o Brasil," *Revista do Clube Militar* 112 (April 1951): 61–66. See also Gen. Júlio Caetano Horta Barbosa, "O problema do petróleo," *Revista do Clube Militar* 112 (April 1951): 35–45.

8. The June–July edition of the journal reprinted an article from the newspaper *Diário de Noticias*, in which Rafael Corrêa de Oliveira had defended the author of the Korea article. See Rafael Corrêa de Oliveira, "O Clube e a guerra na Coréia," *Revista do Clube Militar* 114 (June–July 1951): 45–47. Colonel Benevides continued to make savage

attacks on the Military Club's opponents. See Col. Salvador Corrêa de Sá e Benevides, "Os trustes estrangeiros e a Revista do Clube Militar," *Revista do Clube Militar* 114 (June–July 1951): 48–52.

9. For the circulation of the petition, see *Tribuna da Imprensa*, June 6, 1951, 6. For General Etchegoyen's letter to Horta Barbosa, see *Tribuna da Imprensa*, June 10, 1951, 1. For General Zenóbio's public comments, see *Tribuna da Imprensa*, June 21, 1951, 1.

10. For the club's note defending the journal, see *Tribuna da Imprensa*, June 29, 1951, 1, 10. See also the U.S. military attache in Rio de Janeiro to the State Department, June 30, 1951, RG 319, Entry 57, Box 10, NA-USA; and *Emancipação*, July 1951, 2.

11. See General Góes Monteiro to João Neves da Fontoura, September 1, 1951, AN, AGM, AP 51, 15 (6). For General Góes Monteiro's description of his priorities in the negotiations see Góes Monteiro to Estillac, August 3, 1951, AN, AGM, AP 51, 15 (6). For the opposition of Brazil's officers corps to the dispatch of troops, see Henrique Teixeira Lott's interview, CPDOC/FGV, 115. For Vargas's strategy with the negotiations, see Bandeira, *Presença dos Estados Unidos no Brasil*, 330–33. For Vargas's discussion with the U.S. ambassador, see Herschel V. Johnson to the secretary of state, July 5, 1951, U.S. State Department, *Foreign Relations of the United States*, 1951, 2:1203.

12. See Miller to U.S. ambassador Herschel V. Johnson, October 23, 1951, U.S. State Department, *Foreign Relations of the United States*, 1951, 2:1229–31.

13. For more on the amnesty bill, see *Última Hora*, August 1, 1951, 1; August 10, 1951, 3. For a U.S. perspective, see *New York Times*, February 25, 1952, 9. For the situation in the officers corps, see Viriato Dornelles Vargas to Getúlio Vargas, August 9, 1951, GV 51.08.09/3, CPDOC/FGV. For the administration's concern that the controvery might damage Brazil's relationship with the United States, see João Neves da Fontoura to Goís Monteiro, August 6, 1951, AN, AGM, AP 51, 14, (8).

14. For events surrounding the petition's delivery and Carnaúba's reaction, see *Última Hora*, August 13, 1951, 2; August 16, 1951, 1; *Tribuna da Imprensa*, August 16, 1951, 6; August 18–19, 2.

15. See *Tribuna da Imprensa*, August 28, 1951, 10; *Diário de Noticias*, August 28, 1951, 3; *Emancipação*, September 1951, 1, 2; *Última Hora*, August 31, 1951, 1.

16. See Francisco Teixeira's comments in Valentina da Rocha Lima, *Getúlio*, 227. For General Horta Barbosa's departure, see *Tribuna da Imprensa*, November 5, 1951, 6. See also the anonymous history in Vargas's personal records. Undated history, GV 51.09.09, CPDOC/FGV.

17. See the handbill "Em marcha para a assembleia," 1951 (no month), GV 51.09.09, CPDOC/FGV. For the two factions' vision of development, see Antonio Carlos Peixoto, "Le Clube Militar," 60–81.

18. See the anonymous history in the papers of President Vargas. N.d., GV 51.09.09, CPDOC/FGV; see also *Correio da Manhã*, September 19, 1951, 2.

19. See *Tribuna da Imprensa*, September 3, 1951, 8; September 1–2, 1951, 4. For how the Military Club intended to use the assembly, see Sodré, *Do estado novo à ditadura militar*, 76; *Tribuna da Imprensa*, September 6, 1951, 3. For the petition in favor of the Military Club, see *Última Hora*, September 18, 1951, 4.

20. For the preparations for the assembly, see *Tribuna da Imprensa*, September 19, 1951, 10.

21. For the orders Estillac received from Vargas on September 12, 1951, see *Tribuna da Imprensa*, September 20, 1951, 1. For rumors that Vargas intended to replace Estillac as minister of war, see U.S. ambassador Herschel V. Johnson to the secretary of state,

September 14, 1951, RG 319, Entry 57, Box 10, NA-USA. For how the last minute preparations were described by U.S. journalists, see *Time*, October 1, 1951, 34. For the number of officers expected at the assembly, see *Correio da Manha*, September 21, 1951, 1. For the number of speakers, see *Tribuna da Imprensa*, September 21, 1951, 1.

22. For the history of these events, see U.S. ambassador Herschel V. Johnson to the secretary of state, September 21, 1951, RG 319, Entry 57, Box 10, NA-USA; *Tribuna da Imprensa*, September 20, 1951, 1, 10; September 21, 1951, 1.

23. The delay threw the Military Club's opponents into confusion. See the telegram of the U.S. Army attaché to the State Department, September 21, 1951, RG 319, Entry 57, Box 10, NA-USA. The postponement of the assembly displeased Gen. Cordeiro de Farias, see *Tribuna da Imprensa*, September 21, 1951, 1. For Estillac's meeting with the generals, see *Tribuna da Imprensa*, September 21, 1951, 10. For Estillac's note to the cultural department of the Military Club see "Resolução," GV 51.09.09, CPDOC/FGV. For the transfer of Maj. Humberto Andrade, see *Última Hora*, September 26, 1951, 1. See also U.S. ambassador Herschel V. Johnson to the Secretary of State, September 30, 1951, RG 319, Entry 57, Box 10, NA-USA.

24. For Estillac's failure to attend the meeting, see *Tribuna da Imprensa*, September 26, 1951, 1. For the meeting of internationalist commanders the following day, see *Tribuna da Imprensa*, September, 27, 1951, 2.

25. *Correio da Manhã*, October 5, 1951, 8.

26. For expectations that Estillac would act decisively against the Military Club, see *Tribuna da Imprensa*, October 6–7, 1951, 1. For Estillac's meeting with Gen. Fiuza Castro, see *Tribuna da Imprensa*, October 9, 1951, 1, 10. For the confrontation in the Military Club, see *Tribuna da Imprensa*, October 11, 1951, 1. See also *Correio da Manhã*, October 11, 1951, 3. For pressure on Estillac, see *Tribuna da Imprensa*, October 15, 1951, 10. For the cancellation of the assembly, see *Correio da Manhã*, October 17, 1951, 4. See also U.S. ambassador Herschel V. Johnson to the secretary of state, October 19, 1951, RG 319, Entry 57, Box 10, NA-USA.

27. For the telegrams of congratulation, see Artur Bernardes to Getúlio Vargas, October 5, 1951, GV 51.11.07/4, CPDOC/FGV, and Horta Barbosa to Getúlio Vargas, October 7, 1951, GV 51.11.07/4, CPDOC/FGV. For General Horta Barbosa's belief that a mixed company might be the only possible answer, see Horta Barbosa's memo, December 12, 1951, HB 47.02.10 vp 5–30, CPDOC/FGV. For CEDPEN's belief that Vargas had changed his stance, see Maria Augusta Tibiriçá Miranda's interview, CPDOC/FGV, 72.

28. See Moniz Bandeira for more on Vargas's developmental strategy and how it involved the United States. Bandeira, *Presença dos Estados Unidos no Brasil*, 320–28.

29. João Neves da Fontoura to Getúlio Vargas, December 24, 1951, GV 51.12.24/2, CPDOC/FGV. For General Góes Monteiro's telegram announcing the United States' desire to negotiate the accord, see Gen. Góes Monteiro to João Neves da Fontoura, August 22, 1951, AN, AGM, 15 (6). For Estillac's letter of protest, see the telegram of the U.S. Army attaché to the State Department, December 1, 1951, RG 319, Entry 57, Box 10, NA-USA. The United States needed monazite sands, a phosphate of cerium metals and thorium, for its nuclear program.

30. For a transcript of Estillac's speech, see Eldred D. Kuppinger to the State Department, January 7, 1952, RG 59, 732.5/1-1452, NA-USA. See also NM 51.05.16, 1 (11), CPDOC/FGV. For a description of the two speeches and their reception, see William A. Wieland to the secretary of state, January 7, 1952, RG 59, 732.5 MSP/1-752, NA-USA.

31. When Fontoura wanted to discuss the military accord and the sale of Brazilian resources, he went to Gen. Ciro Espírito Santo Cardoso, not to Estillac. See João Neves da Fontoura to Getúlio Vargas, February 16, 1952, GV 52.02.16, CPDOC/FGV.

32. For how the events in Porto Alegre were portrayed in the United States, see *New York Times*, February 14, 1952, 9, and February 25, 1952, 9. For communist papers' criticism of the army, see *New York Times*, February 24, 1952, 9.

33. *New York Times*, March 16, 1952, 31. Much of the United States' military aid came in the form of the "loan" of supplies that Brazil never returned. See Ernâni do Amaral Peixoto's interview, 1985, CPDOC/FGV–História Oral, 746.

34. For information on the economic clauses of the accord and their implications, see Bandeira, *Presença dos Estados Unidos no Brasil*, 335–37. See also Nelson Werneck Sodré, *História militar do Brasil*, 324.

35. The Military Club published its study of petroleum on May 13, 1952. The club's commission condemned Vargas's proposals as a step backward. See "Paracer da commissão de estudo do petróleo do Clube Militar," *Revista do Clube Militar* 120 (March, April, May 1952): 135–47.

36. See William A. Wieland to the State Department, April 3, 1952, RG 59, 732.55/4-352, NA-USA. Also see this document for the hierarchy's pressure upon President Vargas.

37. For the history of events surrounding Zenóbio's letter of resignation, see William A Wieland to the State Department, April 3, 1952, RG 59, 732.55/4-352, NA-USA; U.S. ambassador Hershel Johnson to the secretary of state, March 19, 1952, RG 59, 732.551/3-1952, NA-USA. For General Zenóbio's letter of resignation, see Gen. Zenóbio da Costa to Getúlio Vargas, March 18, 1952, GV 52.03.15, CPDOC/FGV.

38. See *O Estado de São Paulo*, May 17, 1952, 3. In this article Estillac described events at a meeting held the previous day by the Democratic Crusade. For more on the nature of military parties, see Alain Rouquié, "processus politiques dans les partis militaires au Brésil."

39. For Eduardo Gomes' appointment to be the honorary president of the Democratic Crusade, see *Diário Carioca*, April 20, 1952, 1, 8.

40. For the fact that most of the nationalists' leadership had retired, see Nelson de Mello's interview, 1983, CPDOC/FGV–História Oral, 320. He stated that because this party had so many retired personnel that their victory in the 1950 election for the Military Club could be explained only by the hierarchy's carelessness. The vulnerability of retired officers in the Military Club was captured in a cartoon in the club's journal. See *Revista do Clube Militar* 117 (November–December 1951): 55. For Carlos Lacerda's comments, see *Tribuna da Imprensa*, September 21, 1951, 4. The febianos had voted to have General Horta Barbosa take a leading role in their veterans' organization. *Emancipação*, May 26, 1950, 1. Peter Seaborn Smith and Antonio Carlos Peixoto have argued that the febianos allied with the hierarchy's party. See Antonio Carlos Peixoto, "Le Clube Militar," 89. Smith, *Oil and Politics in Modern Brazil*, 58.

41. For the influence of positivism on these officers, see Fernando Luiz Lobo Barbosa Carneiro's interview, 1988, CPDOC/FGV–SERCOM/Petrobrás, 42. For anti-Americanism as a component of this party's thought, see Nelson Werneck Sodré's interview, 1988, CPDOC/FGV–SERCOM/Petrobrás, 23.

42. For the reasons why officers may remain outside of military factions, see Farcau, *Transition to Democracy in Latin America*, 54.

43. Ibid., 69.

44. See *Jornal de Debates*, March 21, 1952, 1.

45. For the original printing of Dutra's letter to Mario Sampaio concerning petroleum, see *Diário Carioca*, March 16, 1952, 1, 8. For Juarez Távora's comments, see *O Estado do São Paulo*, May 17, 1952, 3. For Estillac's efforts to stress the importance of petroleum to the campaign, see *Jornal de Debates*, May 16, 1952, 2.

46. See Francisco Teixeira's comments in Valentina da Rocha Lima, *Getúlio*, 230.

47. Farcau, *Transition to Democracy in Latin America*, 54.

48. For the fact that amongst those arrested were the president and directory of the *Casa do Sargento*, see U.S. ambassador Herschel V. Johnson to the secretary of state, March 24, 1952, RG 59, 732.55/3-2452, NA-USA; Maria Augusta Tibiriçá Miranda said that these arrests hit the *Casa do Sargento* especially hard. See Maria Augusta Tibiriçá Miranda's interview, CPDOC/FGV, 89. On October 13, 1951, Gen. Stenio de Albuquerque Lima had given a conference on petroleum at the Casa do Sargento. See *Emancipação*, November 1951, 2. On February 13, 1952, Gen. Valerio Braga had held a similar conference at the same location. See *Emancipação*, March 1952, 2. The international press depicted the arrests as an attack on a well-organized communist conspiracy. *New York Times*, March 22, 1952, 4, and March 23, 1952, 24. For more information on the Casa do Sargento, see the Special Police Memorandum of March 31, 1952, "Setor trabalhista," APERJ, DESPS, N 46, "Casa do Sargento do Brasil." See also the letter from Pedro Paulo S. M. Mello Carvalho to "Ilm. Sr. Chefe do setor trabalhista" dated March 31, 1952, APERJ, DESPS, N 46, "Casa do Sargento do Brasil."

49. See Caio Miranda to Getúlio Vargas, n.d. GV 52.03.15, CPDOC/FGV. Gen. Cordeiro de Farias also emphasized that Zenóbio da Costa had acted on his own, not on behalf of the Democratic Crusade.

50. For evidence of the level of tension within the military, examine the uproar created when a nervous sentry fired at a shadow in April 1952. *Jornal de Debates*, April 11, 1952, 1.

51. *Emancipação*, April 1952, 9.

52. For General Etchegoyen's call for a tribunal of honor, see *Diário de Noticias*, April 13, 1952, 4.

53. See Francisco Teixeira's comments in Valentina da Rocha Lima, *Getúlio*, 229. For why Estillac lost support, see ibid.

54. Ernâni do Amaral Peixoto's interview, CPDOC/FGV, 655.

55. Ibid., 797.

56. See Nelson de Mello's interview, CPDOC/FGV, 310. For the support the Democratic Crusade received from the air force and navy, see ibid., 311. For the UDN's support for the Democratic Crusade, see Ernâni do Amaral Peixoto's interview, CPDOC/FGV, 656.

57. Maria Augusta Tibiriçá Miranda, *Petróleo é nosso*, 341–48; H. Miranda's interview, 1992, CPDOC/FGV–História Oral, 10; Maria Augusta Tibiriçá Miranda's interview, CPDOC-FGV, 19–20.

58. Anonymous, *Depoimentos esclarecedores*. Like other works that displeased the military, this book vanished from Brazilian libraries during military rule. Nelson Werneck Sodré, however, quoted this work at length. Sodré, *História militar do Brasil*, 331–33, nn. 464 and 465, as well as 342–43, nn. 471 and 472. For a contemporary reference to this book, see *Correio da Manhã*, July 2, 1955, 7. As early as the Estado Novo, the government burned material it disliked at the National Library. Levine, *Father of the Poor*, 56.

59. Maria Augusta Tibiriçé Miranda's interview, CPDOC/FGV, 94. The hierarchy targeted officers bringing ballots from the interior. Sodré, *História militar do Brasil*, 334–38. Many of the arrested officers had distributed a nationalist magazine called *Emancipação*. Henrique Miranda's interview, 62.

60. *Correio da Manhã*, July 2, 1955, section 1, 7.

61. Ibid.

62. Ibid. For a list of arrested soldiers, see Maria Augusta Tibiriçá Miranda, *Petróleo é nosso*, 343.

63. For example, one soldier lost over thirty pounds in under a month of captivity. *Última Hora*, July 5, 1954, 7.

64. Maria Augusta Tibiriçá Miranda, *Petróleo é nosso*, 342. See also the document that fifteen prisoners smuggled out of military prison, ibid., 349.

65. *Correio da Manhã*, July 2, 1955, section 1, 7.

66. Ibid. Anonymous, *Depoimentos esclarecedores*.

67. See the manifesto of the Brazilian Association in Defense of Human Rights. Maria Augusta Tibiriçá Miranda, *Petróleo é nosso*, 346.

68. The minister of war, Gen. Ciro Espírito Santo Cardoso, warned about communist activity in the armed forces on May 8, 1952. *New York Times*, May 9, 1952, 3.

69. *New York Times*, March 22, 1952, 4.

70. Maria Augusta Tibiriçá Miranda, *Petróleo é nosso*, 346.

71. For a list of the army, navy, and air force officers who led the Military-Police Inquiries, see Valentina da Rocha Lima, *Getúlio*, 230. For officers' arrests in all three services, see *New York Times*, April 17, 1952, 4; April 15, 1952, 3; March 30, 1952, 12.

72. The enlisted ranks had their own social organization, the Casa do Sargento. On March 21, 1952, the military police arrested the president and directory of the club, whom they claimed were communists. See the comments of U.S. ambassador Herschel V. Johnson to the secretary of state, March 24, 1952, RG 59, 732.55/3-2452, NA-USA; Maria Augusta Tibiriçá Miranda's interview, CPDOC/FGV, 89; *New York Times*, March 22, 1952, 4, and March 23, 1952, 24.

73. For Estillac's statements, see Sodré, *Do estado novo à ditadura militar*, 106. For the U.S. embassy's belief that Estillac would win the election, see William W. Wieland to the State Department, April 3, 1952, RG 59, 732.55/4-352, NA-USA. For Estillac's discussion with reporters on the airport tarmac before his departure, see *Jornal de Debates*, April 25, 1952, 1. For Estillac's letter speaking against the need for a tribunal of honor, see ibid., 7.

74. For the history of events that day, see *Cruzeiro*, June 7, 1952, 108, 114–20.

75. Ibid., 114.

76. Ibid., 108.

77. See ibid., August 23, 1952, 78. For the Military Club's reluctance to abandon control of its subcommittees, see *Globo*, June 19, 1952, 6.

78. A commission of six wives and mothers went to the newspaper *O Mundo* to speak of the difficulties they had faced. See *O Mundo*, June 17, 1952, 1. One man wrote to the minister of war to appeal him to remember Maj. Fortunato Câmara's war record. See N. Pithan de Silva to Nero Moura, July 19, 1952, NM 51.05.16m, 1 (4), CPDOC/FGV. For letters the wives and mothers wrote about the prisoners, see *Diário da Noticias*, June 6, 1952, 5; *Emancipação*, June 1952, 10; *Diário da Noticias*, June 14, 1952, 5. The issue was even discussed in Congress. See Estados Unidos do Brasil, Câmara dos Deputados,

Anais da Câmara dos Deputados (June 19–24, 1952): 368–71. For Daisy Costa Pessoa de Andrade's statement that her husband was only one of a hundred victims of an injustice, see *Diário da Noticias*, June 12, 1952, 5.

79. *New York Times*, July 13, 1952, 1; *Correio da Manhã*, July 3, 1952, 5; *Cruzeiro*, August 23, 1952, 36–42; *New York Times*, September 1, 1952, 2. For the thirty-eight officers absolved in July 1954, see *Última Hora*, July 5, 1954, 7. For the fact that some other officers' cases dragged on for years, see *Correio da Manhã*, July 2, 1955, 7. In the late 1950s Amauri Kruel created a death squad within the civil police. Huggins, *Political Policing*, 96, 136. We now know that prosecutor Amador Cisneiro do Amaral was not arrested during his 1952 contest with Kruel.

80. See the U.S. Embassy dispatch, June 3, 1953, RG 59, 732.551/6-353, NA-USA.

81. See Nelson Werneck Sodré's interview, CPDOC/FGV, 32. For Etchegoyen's refusal to speak of petroleum after his victory, see *Diário de Noticias*, June 5, 1952, 5. Gen. Manuel Henrique Gomes, the Democratic Crusade's president, stated that his party had a truly nationalist attitude towards Brazil's natural resources. *Diário de Noticias*, June 10, 1952, 5.

82. See the "National Intelligence Estimate," December 4, 1953, U.S. State Department, *Foreign Relations of the United States*, 1952–1953, 4:633–45. For the contradictions Vargas faced, see ibid., 637.

83. See Francisco Teixeira in Valentina da Rocha Lima, *Getúlio*, 230.

84. Vargas's suicide note was altered before publication. Levine, *Father of the Poor*, 131–32.

85. For the fact that the Democratic Crusade supported Cafe Filho, see Nelson de Mello's interview, CPDOC/FGV, 338. For Cafe Filho's concern to maintain military unity and the choice of Henrique Teixeira Lott as Minister of War, see Filho, *Do Sindicato ao Catete*, vol. 2, 385–87. For Estillac's demission, see ibid., 474–75.

Chapter Eight

1. José Murilo de Carvalho, *Pontos e bordados*, 341.

2. See for example, Alfred Stepan, *Military Politics in Brazil*.

3. Dulles, *Castello Branco*, 226. For Castello Branco's defeat, see ibid. Antonio Carlos Peixoto, "Clube Militar," 96; Valentina da Rocha Lima, *Getúlio*, 230. For information on earlier elections, see Dulles, *Castello Branco*, 201, 223–24.

4. Dulles, *Castello Branco*, 227.

5. For the fact that Golberi do Couto e Silva was one of the heads of the Democratic Crusade, see the comments of Paulo Eugênio Pinto Guedes in Valentina da Rocha Lima, *Getúlio*, 230.

6. For information on Golberi do Couto Silva, see Beloch and Abreu, *Dicionário histórico-biográfico brasileiro*, 4:3157–62; Schooyans, *Destin du Brésil*.

7. Beloch and Abreu, *Dicionário*, 4:3158.

8. Sodré, *Do Estado Nôvo à ditadura militar*, 240–50; Sodré, *História militar do Brasil*, 382–83.

9. Hepple, "Geopolitics, Generals, and the State in Brazil," 84. For information on IPÊS and the 1964 coup, see Dreifuss, *1964: A conquista do estado*.

10. Dulles, *Unrest in Brazil*, 189. For the organization's creation, see ibid., 172.

11. Beloch and Abreu, *Dicionário histórico-biográfico brasileiro*, 4:3158.

12. Alfred Stepan, *Military in Politics*, 97.

13. Sodré, *Do estado nôvo à ditadura militar*, 279–81.

14. Sodré, for example, fled to the countryside where he was captured. Ibid., 286–90.

15. See Hélio Silva, *Vez e a voz dos vencidos*; Comblin, *Ideologia da segurança nacional*, 77; Maspero, *Violence militaire au Brésil*, 10; Sodré, *Do estado nôvo à ditadura militar*, 245–349. Many senior commanders opposed the coup, which encouraged lower rank-ing officers to continue the purge. Alfred Stepan, *Military in Politics*, 223–25; Sodré, *Do Estado Nôvo à ditadura militar*, 295.

16. For Golberi's leadership of SNI (and his term for the organization), see Beloch and Abreu, *Dicionário histórico-biográfico brasileiro*, 4:3158–59; see also Lagoa, *SNI*.

17. See, for example, D'Araújo, et al. *Os anos de chumbo*. For more information on military repression after the coup, see Contreiras, *Militares*.

18. Maspero, *Violence militaire au Brésil*, 50–51; Hunter, *Eroding Military Influence*, 34; Zirker, "Democracy and the Military in Brazil," 592.

19. Alfred Stepan, *Rethinking Military Politics*, 16.

20. For the funding of IPÊS, see Beloch and Abreu, *Dicionário histórico-biográfico brasileiro*, 4:3158. SNI was also made up of both military men and civilians. Alfred Stepan, *Rethinking Military Politics*, 17. For information on ties between civilians and soldiers, see Alfred Stepan, *The Military in Politics*, 186, n. 38, 175–77, 186, 246.

21. Dulles, *Castello Branco*, 357, 399; for the fact that the 1964 coup represented a vic-tory for the Democratic Crusade, see Beloch and Abreu, *Dicionário histórico-biográfico brasileiro*, 2:1012.

22. D'Araújo, *Os anos de chumbo*, 91.

23. Alfred Stepan, *Military in Politics*; Dulles, *Unrest in Brazil*.

24. Smallman, "Shady Business."

25. José Murilo de Carvalho, *Pontos e bordados*, 340–42. For the restrictions placed on sergeants' careers, see Vanda Costa, "Com rancor e com afeto," 272–74. For the racist military policies of the Estado Novo, see Sodré, *História militar do Brasil*, 282. For the fact that there had been many people of color in the army after the Paraguayan War, see ibid., 134.

26. Translation by Peter Beattie. Beattie, " 'And One Calls this Misery a Republic?,' " 23. Beattie's reference (note 73) is "Speech text in Farias, CFa 44.09.20 tv, Fundação Getúlio Vargas/Centro de Pesquisa e Documentação, pasta I-22." Beattie's thesis pro-vides some statistics on the army's racial makeup during the Old Republic. Beattie, "Transforming Enlisted Army Service in Brazil," 417–18, 506.

Epilogue

1. The following day I gained access to the archive, where I was treated with great warmth and professionalism.

2. *Globo*, February 16, 1993, 7.

3. Ibid.

4. This issue continued to draw press attention the following month. *Globo*, May 14, 1993, 4.

5. Hunter, *Eroding Military Influence in Brazil*, and "Politicians against Soldiers."

6. *Globo*, May 14, 1993, 4.

7. Brig. Gen. Nilton de Albuquerque Cerqueira, "O preço da liberdade é a eterna vigilância," *Revista do Clube Militar* 314 (November–December 1993): 36; General Armando Patrício, "Opinão-autoridade e autoritarismo," *Revista do Clube Militar* 310 (March–April 1993):14–15.

8. Col. Althair Guedes, "Genocídio nacional," *Revista do Clube Militar* 329 (October 1996): 15. See also Col. Roberto Monteiro de Oliveira, "Ameaças atuais à integridade territorial do Brasil e à nossa soberania plena sobre a Amazônia," *Revista do Clube Militar* 325 (January–February 1996): 5–11; Col. Manuel Cambeses Júnior, "O Brasil diante do neoliberalismo," *Revista do Clube Militar* 327 (May–June 1996): 8–12; Col. Nilton de Freitas Guimarães, "A defesa," *Revista do Clube Militar* 356 (February 1999): 10.

9. Col. Althair Guedes, "Genocídio nacional," 15.

10. The best guide to this faction's thought can be gained from the *Revista do Clube Militar* from 1993 to 1999, which contains numerous articles on all these topics. For the danger posed to Brazil by separatist movements, see Wilson Choeri, "Separatismo-balcanização da América do Sul," *Revista do Clube Militar* 311 (May–June 1993): 6–8. For a fuller sense of this faction's perspective see Col. Roberto Monteiro de Oliveira, "Ameaças atuais à integridade territorial do Brasil e à nossa soberania plena sobre a Amazônia," *Revista do Clube Militar* 325 (January–February 1996): 5–11. Wilson Choeri, "O projeto rondon em nova dimensão," *Revista do Clube Militar* 315 (January–February 1994): 6–12.

11. Anonymous editorial, "O labirinto," *Revista do Clube Militar* 315 (January–February 1994): 4. For a harsh attack on Brazil's executive, judiciary, and legislature, see Col. Francisco Jander de Olveira, "Cegos, surdos, e mudos," *Revista do Clube Militar* 332 (January 1997): 6.

12. See Gen. Hélio Ibiapina Lima's inauguration speech, "Posse da nova diretoria," *Revista do Clube Militar* 328 (July, August, September 1996): 6–9.

13. Col. Ivan Carvalho, "A reeleiçao: um caso para o 'Procon,'" *Revista do Clube Militar* 333 (February 1997): 12. Anonymous editorial, "Síndrome do amor às forças armadas," *Revista do Clube Militar* 338 (August 1997): 3–4.

14. *New York Times*, July 25, 1993, section 4, 7.

15. Ibid.

16. For information on Collor's corruption and impeachment, see Weyland, "The Rise and Fall of President Collor," and Zirker, "The Political Dynamics of Presidential Impeachment."

17. *Globo*, May 26, 1999, 6, 13.

18. Ibid., May 25, 1999, 13.

19. Brig. Gen. Adriano Aulio Pinheiro da Silva, "Ainda sobre o todo-poderosa mídia," *Revista do Clube Militar* 332 (January 1997): 7. Gen. Sebastiao José Ramos de Castro, "As forças armadas e a opinião pública," *Revista do Clube Militar* 342 (December 1997): 13–14.

20. *Jornal do Brasil*, March 27, 1995, 14; *Folha de São Paulo*, November 13, 1994, 10, November 27, 1994, 1; McSherry, "Military Power and Guardian Structures in Latin America," 98.

21. *Folha de Sao Paulo*, November 3, 1994, sec. 3, 3.

22. *Jornal do Brasil*, May 29, 1999, 3. In December 2000, President Cardoso nomi-

nated a new director of ABIN (Agencia Brasileira de Inteligencia), after revelations that the agency spied on domestic figures, including the president's son. *Oregonian*, December 15, 2000, A33.

23. *Jornal do Brasil*, May 27, 1999, 6. An awareness of military corruption is important because a report created by a major inquiry into drug corruption in Brazil has called for the military to play a larger role in fighting the drug trade. *Oregonian*, December 15, 2000, A-33; *Christian Science Monitor*, December 14, 2000, 9. For more information on military corruption in Brazil, see Smallman, "Shady Business."

BIBLIOGRAPHY

Newspapers and Periodicals

Christian Science Monitor (United States)
Correio da Manhã (Rio de Janeiro)
O Cruzeiro (Rio de Janeiro)
Diário Carioca (Rio de Janeiro)
Diário de Notícias (Rio de Janeiro)
Emancipação (Rio de Janeiro)
O Estado de São Paulo (São Paulo)
A Folha de São Paulo (São Paulo)
O Globo (Rio de Janeiro)
Jornal do Brasil (Rio de Janeiro)
Jornal de Debates (Rio de Janeiro)
O Mundo (Rio de Janeiro)
New York Times (New York)
A Noite (Rio de Janeiro)
O Paiz (Rio de Janeiro)
Oregonian (Portland)
Revista do Clube Militar (Rio de Janeiro)
Time (United States)
Times (London)
Tribuna da Imprensa (Rio de Janeiro)
Última Hora (Rio de Janeiro and São Paulo)
Veja (Brazil)

Public Documents

Estados Unidos do Brasil. Congresso Nacional. Câmara dos Deputados. *Anais da Câmara dos Deputados*, 1952. Rio de Janeiro: Serviço Gráfico do Instituto Brasileiro de Geografia e Estatistica, 1953.

———. Congresso Nacional. Câmara dos Deputados. *Diário do Congresso*. Rio de Janeiro: Imprensa Nacional, 1953.

———. Congresso Federal. Câmara dos Deputados. *Documentos parlamentares—petroléo*. 12 vols. Rio de Janeiro: Imprensa Nacional, 1956–1959.

———. Departmento de ordem política e social do estado de São Paulo. *Atividades comunistas junto a campanha do petroleo*. São Paulo, 1949.

———. Inquérito Policial Militar no. 709. *O communismo no Brasil*. 4 vols. Rio de Janeiro: Biblioteca do Exército, 1966–1967.

——. Ministério de Exército. *Almanaque do exército.* annual. Rio de Janeiro: Imprensa Militar, 1930–52.

——. Ministério de Exército. *História do Estado-Maior do Exército.* Rio de Janeiro: Biblioteca do Exército, 1984.

——. Exército do Brasil. *História do Estado-Maior do Exército.* Brasilia: Exército do Brasil, 1984.

——. Ministério da Guerra. *Relatorio do anno de 1831 da administração do Ministério da Guerra apresentado na augusta câmara dos Senhores Deputados na sessão de 1832.* Rio de Janeiro: n.p., 1832. Accessed online June 16, 2000. http://www.crl-jukebox.uchicago.edu/bsd/bsd/u2182/000002.html

——. Ministério da Guerra. *Relatorio do ano de 1904 apresentado ao Presidente da República dos Estados Unidos do Brazil pelo Marechal Francisco de Paula Argollo em maio de 1905.* Rio de Janeiro: Imprensa Nacional, 1905. Accessed online June 16, 2000. http://www.crl-jukebox.uchicago. edu/bsd/bsd/u23322/000009.html

——. Ministério da Guerra. *Relatório apresentado ao Presidente da República dos Estados Unidos do Brasil pelo general de divisão, Ministro de Estado da Guerra, em maio de 1935.* (1934.) Rio de Janeiro: Imprensa do Estado-Maior do Exército, 1935.

——. Ministério da Marinha. *Almanaque da Marinha, 1911.* Rio de Janeiro: Imprensa Nacional, 1911.

——. Ministério da Marinha. *Relatorio do ano de 1910 apresentado ao Presidente da República dos Estados Unidos de Brazil pelo Vice-Almirante Joaquim Marques Baptista de Leão em maio de 1911.* Rio de Janeiro: Imprensa Nacional, 1911. Accessed online June 18, 2000. (http://www.crl-jukebox.uchicago.edu/bsd/bsd/u2145/00003.)

——. Ministério da Marinha. *Relatorio ao Exmo. Sr. Chefe do Govêrno Provisorio, Dr. Getúlio Dornelles Vargas pelo Contra-Almirante Pereira Guimarães, Ministro de Estado dos Negocios da Marinha.* Rio de Janeiro: Ministro da Marinha, 1932.

Peixoto, Floriano. *Mensagem dirigida ao Congresso Nacional pelo Marechal Peixoto, vice-presidente da Republica dos Estados Unidos do Brazil, por occasião de abrir-se a 1a sessão da 2a legislatura.* Rio de Janeiro: Imprensa Nacional, 1894. Accessed online June 18, 2000. http://www.crl-jukebox.uchicago.edu/bsd/bsd/u1282/000001.html

U.S. Arms Control and Disarmament Agency. *World Military Expenditures and Arms Transfers, 1996.* Washington, D.C.: Government Printing Office, 1997.

U.S. Central Intelligence Agency. "CIA Research Report, Brazil," November 1948. Frederick, MD: University Publications of America, 1982.

U.S. Central Intelligence Agency. *The World Fact Book, 1997.* Washington, D.C: Central Intelligence Agency, 1998.

U.S. State Department. "The Western Hemisphere." *Index of Papers of the Foreign Relations of the United States.* Washington, D.C.: Government Printing Office, 1946–1954.

——. *O.S.S. and State Department Intelligence Reports.* Washington, D.C.: University Publications of America, n.d.

General Works

Agüero, Felipe. "Debilitating Democracy: Political Elites and Military Rebels in Venezuela." In *Lessons from Venezuela,* edited by Louis W. Goodman, Johana Mendelson, Moisés Naim, and Joseph Tulchin, 136–62. Baltimore: John Hopkins University Press, 1995.

Albert, Bruce. "Indian Lands, Environmental Policy and Military Geopolitics in the

Development of the Brazilian Amazon: the Case of the Yanomami." *Development and Change* 23 (1992): 35–70.

Alexander, Robert. "The Brazilian Tenentes after the Revolution of 1930." *Journal of Inter-American Studies and World Affairs* 15:2 (1973): 221–48.

Allen, Elizabeth. "Calha Norte: Military Development in Brazilian Amazônia." *Development and Change* 23 (1992): 71–99.

Almeida, José Américo de. Preface to *A revolução de 30 e a finalidade política do exército*, by Pedro Aurélio de Góes Monteiro, 1–28. Rio de Janeiro: Adersen, n.d.

Alves, Maria Helena Moreira. *State and Opposition in Military Brazil*. Austin: University of Texas Press, 1985.

Alves, Márcio Moreira. *Torturas e torturados*. Rio de Janeiro: Livraria José Olympio, 1954.

America's Watch. *Police Abuse in Brazil: Summary Executions and Torture in São Paulo and Rio de Janeiro*. New York: America's Watch, 1987.

Andreas, Peter. "Profits, Poverty, and Illegality: the Logic of Drug Corruption." *NACLA Report on the Americas* 27:3 (1993): 22–28.

Anonymous. *Depoimentos esclarecedores sobre os processos dos militares*. Vol. 1. Rio de Janeiro: n.p., 1953.

——. *Política versus marinha*. Edited by J. Nachimovitch. Paris: n.p., 1911.

Argolo, José Amaral, et al. *A direita explosiva no Brasil*. Rio de Janeiro: Mauad, 1996.

Arruda, Antonio de. *ESG: História de sua doutrina*. Rio de Janeiro: Ediçoes GRD em convênio com o Instituto Nacional do Livro e Ministério da Educação e Cultura, 1980.

Azevedo, Asdrubal Gwaier de. *Discurso pronunciado no Clube Militar no dia 25 de junho de 1922*. Recife: n.p., 1932.

——. *Os militares e a política*. Barcelos: Companhia Editora do Minho, 1926.

Baer, M. Delal. "Mexico's Coming Backlash." *Foreign Affairs* 78:4 (1999): 90–104.

Baldessarini, Hugo. *Crônica de uma época: Getúlio Vargas e o crime de Toneleros* (São Paulo: Companhia Editora, 1957).

Bandeira, L. A. Moniz. *Presença dos Estados Unidos no Brasil*. Rio de Janeiro: Civilização Brasileira, 1973.

Barbosa, Rui. *Obras completas de Rui Barbosa: Discursos parlamentares*. Vol. 38 Rio de Janeiro: Fundação Casa de Rui Barbosa, 1977.

Barros, Alexandre de Souza Costa. "The Brazilian Military: Professional Socialization, Political Performance, and State Building." Ph.D. diss., University of Chicago, 1978.

Beattie, Peter. "'And Once Call this Misery a Republic?' Conscription, Public Health, and the Central State, 1890–1945." Unpublished paper.

——. "Conscription versus Penal Servitude: Army Reform's Influence on the Brazilian State's Management of Social Control, 1870–1930." *Journal of Social History* 32:4 (1999), 80–113.

——. "The House, the Street, and the Barracks: Reform and Honorable Masculine Social Space in Brazil, 1864–1945." *Hispanic American Historical Review* 76:3 (1996): 439–73.

——. "Transforming Enlisted Army Service in Brazil, 1864–1940: Penal Servitude versus Conscription and Changing Conceptions of Race, Honor, and Nation." Ph.D. diss., University of Florida–Coral Gables, 1994.

Beloch, Israel, and Alzira Alves de Abreu. *Dicionária histórico-biográfico brasileiro, 1930–1983*. 4 Vols. Rio de Janeiro: Ed. Forense-Universitária and FGV/CPDOC, 1984.

Bertonha, João Fábio. "Between Sigma e Fascio: An Analysis of the Relationship between Italian Fascism and Brazilian Integralism." *Luso-Brazilian Review* 37:1 (2000): 93–106.

Bijos, Gerardo Majella. *O Clube Militar e seus presidentes*. Rio de Janeiro: Revista de Química e Farmácia, 1960.

Borges, Vavy Pacheco. *Memória paulista*. São Paulo: Editora da Universidade de São Paulo (EDUSP), 1997.

———. *Tenentismo e revolução brasileira*. São Paulo: Editora Brasiliense, 1992.

Brayner, Floriano de Lima. *A verdade sôbre a FEB: Memórias de um chefe de Estado-Maior na campanha da Itália, 1943–1945*. Rio de Janeiro: Editora Civilização Brasileira, 1969.

Butler, Kim D. *Freedoms Given, Freedoms Won: Afro-Brazilians in Post-Abolition São Paulo and Salvador*. New Brunswick, N.J.: Rutgers University Press, 1998.

Câmara, Ten. Cel. Hiram de Freitas. *Marechal José Pessoa: A força de um ideal*. Rio de Janeiro: Biblioteca do Exército, 1985.

Camargo, Aspásia, and Walder de Goés, eds. *Meio século de combate: Diálogo com Cordeiro de Farias*. Rio de Janeiro: Editora Nova Fronteira, 1981.

Camargo, Aspásia, et al. *O golpe silencioso*. Rio de Janeiro: Rio Fundo, 1989.

Cancelli, Elizabeth. *O mundo da violencia: A polícia da era Vargas*. Brazil: Editora Universidade de Brasília, 1993.

Canton, Dario. *La política de los militares argentinos, 1900–1970*. Buenos Aires: Siglo XXI, 1971.

Caó, José. *Dutra*. São Paulo: Instituto Progresso Editorial, 1949.

Cardoso, Fernando Henrique. "Dos Governos Militares a Prudente-Campos Sales." In *História geral da civilizacão brasileira*, ser. 3, vol. 1, edited by Boris Fausto, 15–50. São Paulo: Difusão Européia do Livro, 1975.

Carli, Carlos Alberto de. *O escândolo rei: O SNI e a trama Capemi-Baumbarten*. São Paulo: Global, 1985.

Carone, Edgard.. *A quarta republica*. São Paulo: Difusão Européia do Livro, 1980.

———. *A república velha: Evolução política*. 2d ed. Vol. 2. São Paulo: Difusão Européia do Livro, 1974.

———. *A república velha: Instituições e classes sociais*. 2d ed. Vol. 1. São Paulo: Difusão Européia do Livro, 1972.

Carvalho, Estevão Leitão de. *Dever militar e política partidária*. São Paulo: Companhia Editora Nacional, 1959.

———. *Memórias de um general reformado*. Rio de Janeiro: Imprensa do Exército, 1967.

———. *Petróleo: Salvação ou desgraça do Brasil?* Rio de Janeiro: Editora do Centro de Estudos e Defesa do Petróleo e da Economia Nacional, 1949.

Carvalho, Getúlio Pereira. "Petrobrás: A Case Study of Nationalism and Institution Building in Brazil." Ph.D. diss., University of Connecticut, 1976.

Carvalho, José Carlos de. *O livro de minha vida: Na guerra, na paz, e nas revoluções, 1847–1910*. Rio de Janeiro: Jornal do Comércio, 1912.

Carvalho, José Murilo de. "The Armed Forces and Politics in Brazil: 1930–1945." *Hispanic American Historical Review* 62, 2 (1982): 193–223.

———. "As forcas armadas na primeira república: O poder desestabilizador." In *História geral da civilização brasileira, III: O Brasil republicano*. sec. 3, vol. 2, edited by Boris Fausto, 183–234. Rio de Janeiro: Difusão Européia do Livro, 1977.

———. "Forças armadas e política, 1930–1945." In *A revoluçao de 30: Semanário internacional*, 150–70. Brasília: Universidade de Brasília, 1983.

———. *Pontos e bordados—Escritos de história e política*. Belo Horizonte: Ed. UFMG, 1998.

Castello Branco, (Lt. Colonel) Manoel Thomaz. *O Brasil na II Grande Guerra*. Rio de Janeiro: Biblioteca do Exército, 1960.

Castro, Celso. *Os militares e a república: Um estudo sobre cultura e ação política*. Rio de Janeiro: Jorge Zahar Editora, 1995.

Chilcote, Ronald H. *The Brazilian Communist Party*. New York: Oxford University Press, 1974.

Coelho, Edmundo Campos. *Em busca de identidade: O exército e a política na sociedade brasileira*. Rio de Janeiro: Forense-Universitária, 1976.

Cohn, Gabriel. *Petróleo e nacionalismo*. São Paulo: Difusão Européia do Livro, 1968.

Collier, David, ed. *The New Authoritarianism in Latin America*. Princeton: Princeton University Press, 1979.

Comblin, Joseph. *A ideologia da segurança nacional: O poder militar na América Latina*. Rio de Janeiro: Editora Civilização Brasileira, 1980.

Contreiras, Hélio. *Militares: Confissoes-histórias secretas do Brasil*. 3d ed. Rio de Janeiro: Mauad, 1998.

Coronil, Fernando, and Julie Skurski. "Dismembering and Remembering the Nation: the Semantics of Political Violence in Venezuela." *Comparative Study of Society and History* 33, 2 (1991): 288–337.

Cortés, Carlos E. "Armed Politics in Rio Grande do Su." In *Perspectives on Armed Politics in Brazil*, edited by Henry H. Keith and Robert Ames Hayes, 51–78. Tempe: Arizona State University Press, 1976.

Costa, Emilia Viotti da. *The Brazilian Empire: Myths and Histories*. Belmont, Calif.: Wadsworth Publishing Company, 1988.

———. "Empire, 1870–1889." In *Brazil: Empire and Republic, 1822–1930*, edited by Leslie Bethell, 161–213. New York: Cambridge University Press, 1989.

Costa, Vanda Ribeiro. "Com rancor e com afeto: Rebeliões militares na década de 30." In *Ciencias socias hojé*, 260–91. São Paulo: ANPOCS, 1986.

Coutinho, Lourival. *O General Góes depõe*. Rio de Janeiro: Livraria Editôra Coelho Branco, 1955.

Cunha, Euclides da. *Os sertoes*. São Paulo: Alves, 1936.

Cunha, Heitor Xavier Pereira da. *A revolta na esquadra brasileira em novembro e dezembro de 1910*. Rio de Janeiro: Imprensa Naval, 1953.

D'Araújo, Maria Celina, et al. *Os anos de chumbo: A memória militar sobre a repressão*. Rio de Janeiro: Relumé-Dumará, 1994.

———. *Visões do golpe: A memória militar sobre 1964*. Rio de Janeiro: Relume-Dumará, 1994.

Dagnino, Evelina. "State and Ideology: Nationalism in Brazil; 1930–1945." Ph.D. diss., Stanford University, 1985.

Diacon, Todd. *Millenarian Vision, Capitalist Reality: Brazil's Contestado Rebellion, 1912–1916*. Durham, N.C.: Duke University Press, 1991.

Djata, Sundj. "Viva a Liberdade! The Brazilian Naval Revolt of 1910." *Journal of Caribbean Studies* 11:1/2 (1995–96): 39–56.

Dreifuss, René Armand. *1964: A conquista do estado: Ação política, poder, e golpe de classe*. Translated by Ayeska Branca de Oliveira Farias, et al. 5th ed. Petrópolis, Brazil: Editora Vozes, 1987.

Drummond, José Augusto. *O movimento tenentista: A intervencão política dos oficiais jovens, 1922–1935*. Rio de Janeiro: Graal, 1986.

Dulles, J. W. F. *Brazilian Communism, 1935–1945: Repression during World Upheaval*. Austin: University of Texas Press, 1983.

———. *Castello Branco: the Making of a Brazilian President*. College Station: Texas A&M Press, 1978.

———. *Unrest in Brazil: Political Military Crises, 1955–1964*. Austin: University of Texas Press, 1970.

Einaudi, Luigi. "Revolution from Within? Military Rule in Peru Since 1968." *Comparative International Development* 8:1 (1973): 71–87.

Farcau, Bruce. *The Transition to Democracy in Latin America: the Role of the Military*. Westport, Conn.: Praeger Publishers, 1996.

Faucher, Philippe. *Le Brésil des militares*. Montreal: Les Preses de l'Université de Montréal, 1981.

Fausto, Boris. *A Concise History of Brazil*. Translated by Arthur Brakel. New York: Cambridge University Press, 1999.

———. "Society and Politics." In *Brazil: Empire and Republic, 1822–1930*, edited by Leslie Bethell, 257–307. New York: Cambridge University Press, 1989.

Feitlowitz, Marguerite. *A Lexicon of Terror: Argentina and the Legacies of Torture*. New York: Oxford University Press, 1998.

Filho, João Cafe. *Do sindicato ao Catete*. Vol. 2. Rio de Janeiro: José Olympio, 1966.

Filho, João Martins, and Daniel Zirker. "The Brazilian Military and the New World Order." *Journal of Political and Military Sociology* 24:1 (1996): 31–55.

Forjaz, Maria Cecília Spina. *Tenentismo e política*. Rio de Janeiro: Paz e Terra, 1977.

Franko, Patrice. "De Facto Demilitarization: Budget Driven Downsizing in Latin America." *Journal of Inter-American Studies and World Affairs* 36:1 (1994): 37–74.

French, John D. "The Populist Gamble of Getúlio Vargas in 1945: Political and Ideological Transitions in Brazil." In *Latin America in the 1940s: War and Postwar Transitions*, edited by David Rock, 141–65. Berkeley: University of California Press, 1994.

Freyre, Gilberto. *Order and Progress: Brazil from Monarchy to Republic*. Translated by Rod W. Horton. New York: Alfred A. Knopf, 1970.

Geddes, Barbara, and Artur Ribeiro Neto. "Institutional Sources of Corruption in Brazil." *Third World Quarterly* 13:4 (1992): 641–61.

Goldwert Martin. *Democracy, Militarism, and Nationalism in Argentina, 1930–1966*. Austin: University of Texas Press, 1972.

———. "The Rise of Modern Militarism in Argentina." *Hispanic American Historical Review* 48,2 (1968): 189–205.

Goodman, Louis W., and Johanna S. R. Mendelson. "The Threat of New Missions: Latin American Militaries and the Drug War." In *The Military and Democracy: The Future of Civil-Military Relations in Latin America*, edited by Louis W. Goodman, Johanna S. R. Mendelson, and Juan Rial, 189–95. Lexington, Mass.: Lexington Books, 1990.

Graham, Richard. "Free African Brazilians and the State in Slavery Times." In *Racial Politics in Contemporary Brazil*, edited by Michael Hanchard, 30–58. Durham, N.C.: Duke University Press, 1999.

Hahner, June. "The Brazilian Armed Forces and the Overthrow of the Monarchy: Another Perspective." *The Americas* 26 (October 1969): 171–82.

———. "Officers and Civilians in Brazil, 1889–1898." Ph.D. diss., Cornell University, 1966.

———. "The Paulistas' Rise to Power: A Civilian Group Ends Military Rule." *Hispanic American Historical Review* 47 (May 1967): 149–65.

Haines, Gerald K. *The Americanization of Brazil: A Study of U.S. Cold War Diplomacy in the Third World, 1945–1954*. Wilmington, Del.: Scholarly Resources, 1989.

Hansis, Randall. *The Latin Americans: Understanding Their Legacy.* New York: McGraw-Hill, Inc., 1997.

Hardman, Francisco Foot. *Trem fantasma: A modernidade na selva.* São Paulo: Companhia das Letras, 1988.

Hayes, Robert. *The Armed Nation: The Brazilian Corporate Mystique.* Tempe: Arizona State University Press, 1989.

——. "Formation of the Brazilian Army and the Military Class Mystique." In *Perspectives on Armed Politics in Brazil,* edited by Henry H. Keith and Robert Hayes, 1–26. Tempe: Arizona State University Press, 1976.

——. "The Military Club and National Politics in Brazil." In *Perspectives on Armed Politics in Brazil,* edited by Henry Keith and Robert Hayes, 139–76. Tempe: Arizona State University Press, 1976.

Hepple, Leslie W. "Geopolitics, Generals, and the State in Brazil." *Political Geographical Quarterly* 5:4 (1986): 79–90.

Hilton, Stanley. "The Armed Forces and Industrialists in Modern Brazil: The Drive for Military Autonomy, 1889–1954." *Hispanic American Historical Review* 62:4 (1982): 629–73.

——. *Brazil and the Soviet Challenge, 1917–1947.* Austin: University of Texas Press, 1991.

——. "Brazilian Diplomacy and the Washington–Rio de Janeiro 'Axis' during the World War II Era." *Hispanic American Historical Review* 59:2 (1979): 201–31.

——. "Military Influence on Brazilian Economic Policy: 1930–1945." *Hispanic American Historical Review* 53:1 (1973): 71–94.

——. "The U.S., Brazil, and the Cold War, 1945–1960: End of the Special Relationship." *Journal of American History* 68:3 (1981): 599–624.

Huggins, Martha K. *Political Policing: The United States and Latin America.* Durham, N.C.: Duke University Press, 1988.

——, ed. *Vigilantism and the State in Modern Latin America.* New York: Praeger, 1991.

Hunter, Wendy. *Eroding Military Influence in Brazil: Politicians against Soldiers.* Chapel Hill: University of North Carolina Press, 1997.

——. "Politicians against Soldiers: Contesting the Military in Post-Authoritarian Brazil." *Comparative Politics* 27:4 (1995): 425–43.

Huntington, Samuel P. *The Soldier and the State.* Cambridge, Mass.: Harvard University Press, 1957.

——, ed. *Changing Patterns of Military Politics.* New York: Free Press of Glencoe, 1962.

Johnson, John J. *The Military and Society in Latin America.* Stanford: Stanford University Press, 1964.

——. *The Role of the Military in Underdeveloped Countries.* Princeton: Princeton University Press, 1962.

Keith, Henry H. "Armed Federal Interventions in the States During the Old Republic." In *Perspectives on Armed Politics in Brazil,* edited by Henry Keith and Robert Hayes, 51–77. Tempe: Arizona State University Press, 1976.

Kelly, Phillip. *Checkerboards and Shatterbelts: the Geopolitics of South America.* Austin: University of Texas Press, 1997.

Kraay, Hendrik. " 'As Terrifying as Unexpected': The Bahian Sabinada, 1837–1838." *Hispanic American Historical Review* 72:4 (1992): 501–27.

——. " 'The Shelter of the Uniform': The Brazilian Army and Runaway Slaves, 1800–1888." *Journal of Social History* 29:3 (1996), 637–57.

——. "Slavery, Citizenship, and Military Service in Brazil's Mobilization for the Paraguayan War." *Slavery and Abolition* 18:3 (1997): 228–56.

——. "Soldiers, Officers, and Society: the Army in Bahia, Brazil, 1808–1889," Ph.D. diss., University of Texas at Austin, 1995.

——, ed. *Afro-Brazilian Culture and Politics: Bahia, 1790s to 1990s*. Armonk, NY: M. E. Sharpe, 1998.

Lagoa, Ana. *O SNI: Como nasceu, como funciona*. São Paulo: Editora Brasiliense, 1983.

LaGuerre, Michel S. *The Military and Society in Haiti*. Knoxville: University of Tennessee Press, 1993.

Lanoue, Kenneth Callis. "An Alliance Shaken: Brazil and the United States, 1945–1950." Ph.D. diss., Lousiana State University and Agricultural and Mechanical College, 1978.

Leite, Mauro Renault, and Luiz Gonzaga Novelli Jr., eds. *Marechal Eurico Gaspar Dutra: O dever da verdade*. Rio de Janeiro: Nova Fronteira, 1983.

Lesser, Jeff. *Welcoming the Undesirables: Brazil and the Jewish Question*. Berkeley: University of California Press, 1995.

Levine, Robert. *Father of the Poor: Vargas and His Era*. New York: Cambridge University Press, 1998.

——. *Vale of Tears: Revisiting the Canudos Massacre in Northeastern Brazil*. Berkeley: University of California Press, 1992.

Lewis, Paul H. *Paraguay under Stroessner*. Chapel Hill: University of North Carolina Press, 1980.

Lieuwen, Edwin. *Arms and Politics in Latin America*. New York: Praeger, 1960.

Lima, Carlos de Araújo. *O processo do petróleo: Monteiro Lobato no banco dos réus*. Rio de Janeiro: Published by the author, 1977.

Lima, Valentina da Rocha. *Getúlio: Uma história oral*. Rio de Janeiro: Editora Record, 1986.

Loftus, J. *Latin American Defence Expenditures, 1938–1965*. Santa Monica: The RAND Corporation, 1968.

Loveman, Brian. *The Constitution of Tyranny: Regimes of Exception in Spanish America*. Pittsburgh: University of Pittsburgh Press, 1993.

——. *For la Patria: Politics and the Armed Forces in Latin America*. Wilmington, Del.: Scholarly Resources, 1999.

——. " '¿Misión cumplida?': Civil-Military Relations and the Chilean Political Transition." *Journal of Inter-American Studies and World Affairs* 33:3 (1991): 35–74.

——. " 'Protected Democracies' and Military Guardianship: Political Transitions in Latin America, 1978–1993." *Journal of Inter-American Studies and World Affairs* 36:2 (1994): 105–89.

Loveman, Brian, and T. Davis Jr., eds. *The Politics of Anti-Politics: the Military in Latin America*. 2d ed. Lincoln: University of Nebraska Press, 1989.

McCann, Frank. "The Brazilian Army and the Problem of Mission, 1939–1964." *Journal of Latin American Studies* 12:1 (1980): 107–26.

——. *The Brazilian-American Alliance 1937–1945*. Princeton: Princeton University Press, 1973.

——. "The Força Expedicionária Brasileira in the Italian Campaign, 1944–1945." *Army History: The Professional Bulletin of Army History* 26 (Spring 1993): 1–11.

——. "The Formative Period of Twentieth Century Brazilian Army Thought: 1900–1922." *Hispanic American Historical Review* 64:4 (1984): 737–65.

——. "The Military." In *Modern Brazil: Elites and Masses in Historical Perspective*, edited by Michael L. Coniff and Frank D. McCann, 47–80. Lincoln: University of Nebraska Press, 1989.

——. "The Nation in Arms: Obligatory Military Service during the Old Republic." In

Essays Concerning the Socio-Economic History of Brazil, edited by Dauril Alden and Warren Dean, 211–43. Gainsville: University Press of Florida, 1977.

——. "Origins of the 'New Professionalism' of the Brazilian Military." *Journal of Inter-American Studies and World Affairs* 21 (November 1979): 501–22.

Macaulay, Neill. *The Prestes Column: Revolution in Brazil*. New York: New Viewpoints, 1974.

MacLean, Ian S. *Opting for Democracy: Liberation Theology and the Struggle for Democracy in Brazil*. New York: M. Wien, 1999.

McSherry, J. Patrice. *Incomplete Transitions: Military Power and Democracy in Argentina.* New York: St. Martin's Press, 1997.

——. "Military Power, Impunity, and State-Society Change in Latin America." *Canadian Journal of Political Science* 25:3 (1992): 463–88.

——. "Military Political Power and Guardian Structures in Latin America." *Journal of Third World Studies* 12:1 (1995): 80–119.

Maingot, Anthony P. "Confronting Corruption in the Hemisphere: A Sociological Perspective." *Journal of Inter-American Studies and World Affairs* 36, 3 (1994): 49–74.

Mainwaring, Scott. *The Catholic Church and Politics in Brazil, 1916–1985*. Stanford: Stanford University Press, 1986.

Malan, Pedro, et al. *Política econômica externa e industrialização no Brasil: 1939–1952.* Rio de Janeiro: IPEA/INPES, 1977.

Mange, Roger de Carvalho. "Alguns problemas das pequenas frações de infantaria na F.E.B." In *Depoimento de Oficiais da Reserva Sôbre a F.E.B.*, edited by Berta Morais et al., 103–22. São Paulo: Instituto Progresso Editorial, 1949.

Manor, Paul. "Factions et idéologie dans l'armée brésilienne: 'nationalistes' et 'libéraux,' 1946–1951." *Revue d'histoire moderne contemporaine* 25 (October–December 1978): 556–86.

——. "Un prolétariat en uniforme et une révolution 'honnête.' " *Caravelle* 30 (1978): 63–108.

Manwaring, Max. "The Military in Brazilian Politics," Ph.D. diss., University of Illinois, 1968.

Markoff, John, and S. Duncan Baretta. "Professional Ideology and Military Activism: Critique of a Thesis of Alfred Stepan." *Comparative Politics* 17:2 (1985): 175–91.

Martins, Hélio Leônicio. *A revolta dos marinheiros, 1910*. Rio de Janeiro: Serviço de Documentação Geral da Marinha; São Paulo: Cia. Editora Nacional, 1988.

Martins, Luciano. *Pouvoir et développement economique*. Paris: Editions Anthropos, 1976.

Maspero, Francisco. *La violence militaire au Brésil*. Paris: Cahiers Libres, 1971.

Masterson, Daniel. "The Peruvian Armed Forces in Transition, 1939–1963: The Impact of National Politics and Changing Professional Perspectives." Ph.D. diss., Michigan State University, 1976.

Meade, Teresa A. *"Civilizing Rio": Reform and Resistence in a Brazilian City*. University Park: Pennsylvania State University Press, 1997.

Mecham, J. Lloyd. *The U.S. and Inter-American Security, 1889–1960*. Austin: University of Texas Press, 1965.

Mercadante, Paulo. *Militares e civis: A ética e o compromisso*. Rio de Janeiro: Zahar Editôres, 1978.

Meznar, Joan. "The Ranks of the Poor: Military Service and Social Differentiation in Northeast Brazil, 1830–1875." *Hispanic American Historical Review* 72:3 (1992): 336–51.

Millington, Thomas. *Colombia's Military and Brazil's Monarchy: Undermining the*

Republican Foundations of South American Independence. Westport, Conn.:
Greenwood Press, 1996.

Miranda, Carlos R. *The Stroessner Era: Authoritarian Rule in Paraguay*. San Francisco:
Westview, 1990.

Miranda, Maria Augusta Tibiriçá. *O petróleo é nosso: A luta contra a 'entreguismo' pelo
monopólio estatal*. Petrópolis, Brazil: Vozes, 1983.

Moraes, João Baptista Mascarenhas de. *The Brazilian Expeditionary Force by Its
Commander*. Washington, D.C: U.S. Government Printing Office, 1966.

Moraes, João Quartim de. *Da conspiração republicana à guerrilha dos tenentes*. Vol. 1 of
A esquerda militar no Brasil. São Paulo: Edições Siciliano, 1991.

——. *Da coluna à comuna*. Vol. 2 of *A esquerda militar no Brasil*. São Paulo: Editora
Siciliano, 1994.

Morais, Berta, et al. *Depoimento de oficiais da reserva sôbre a F.E.B*. São Paulo: Instituto
Progresso Editorial, 1949.

Morais, Fernando. *Olga: a vida de Olga Benario Prestes, judia comunista entregue a Hitler
pelo governo Vargas*. 6th ed. São Paulo: Editora Alfa-Omega, 1986.

Morel, Edmar. *A revolta da chibata*. Rio de Janeiro: Editôra Letras e Artes, 1963.

Mota, Lourenço Dantas. *A história vivida*. Vol. 2. São Paulo: O Estado do São Paulo,
1981.

Moura, Gerson. *A campanha do petróleo*. São Paulo: Editora Brasiliense S.A., 1986.

——. *Sucessos e ilusões: relações internaconais do Brasil durante e após a segunda guerra
mundial*. Rio de Janeiro: Editora Fundação Getulio Vargas, 1991.

Needell, Jeffrey D. "The Revolta Contra Vacina of 1904: The Revolt against
'Modernization' in Belle-Epoque Rio de Janeiro." In *Riots in the Cities*, edited by
Silvia M. Arrom and Servando Ortoll. Wilmington, Del.: Scholarly Resources,
1996.

Neto, Manuel Domingos. "L'influence étrangère et la formation des groupes et
tendances au sein de l'armeé brésilienee, 1889–1930." In *Les partis militaires au
Brésil*, edited by Alain Rouquié, 41–63. Paris: Presses de la Fondation National des
Sciences Politiques, 1980.

Neto, Ricardo Bonalume. *A nossa segunda guerra: os brasileiros em combate, 1942–1945*.
Rio de Janeiro: Expressão e Cultura, 1995.

Nickson, R. Andrew. "Paraguay's Archivo del Terror." *Latin American Research Review*
30:1 (1995):125–29.

Norden, Deborah. "Democracy and Military Control in Venezuela: From
Subordination to Insurrection." *Latin American Research Review* 33:2 (1998): 143–65.

——. *Military Rebellion in Argentina: Between Coups and Consolidation*. Lincoln:
University of Nebraska Press, 1996.

North, L. *Civil–Military Relations in Argentina, Chile and Peru*. Berkeley: Institute of
International Studies, University of California, 1966.

Nun, José. "A Latin American Phenomenon: The Middle-Class Military Coup." In
Latin America: Reform or Revolution?, edited by James Petras and Maurice Zeitlin,
146–85. Greenwich, Conn.: Fawcett Publications, 1969.

Nunn, Frederick. *Latin American Militarism in World Perspective*. Lincoln: University of
Nebraska Press, 1992.

——. "Military Professionalism and Professional Militarism in Brazil, 1870–1970:
Historical Perspective and Political Implications." *Journal of Latin American Studies*
4:6 (1972): 29–54.

——. "The South American Military and (Re)Democratization: Professional Thought and Self-Perception." *Journal of Inter-American Studies and World Affairs* 37:2 (1995): 1–56.

——. *Yesterday's Soldiers: European Military Professionalism in South America, 1890–1940.* Lincoln: University of Nebraska Press, 1983.

O'Donnell, Guillermo. *Modernization and Bureaucratic-Authoritarianism: Studies in South American Politics.* Berkeley: Institute of International Studies, University of California, 1973.

Oliveira, Eliézer Rizzo de. *As forças armadas: política e ideologia no Brasil, 1964–1969.* Petrópolis, Brazil: Editôra Vozes, 1976.

——. "Brazilian National Defense Policy and Civil-Military Relations in the Government of Fernando Henrique Cardoso." In *Conference Report: The Role of the Armed Forces in the Americas: Civil-Military Relations for the 21st Century,* edited by Donald E. Schulz, 31–70. Carlisle Barracks, Pa.: Strategic Studies Institute, U.S. Army War College, 1998.

Page, Joseph. *The Brazilians.* New York: Addison-Wesley, 1995.

Paulo, Benedito. *A revolta de João Candido.* Pelotas, Brazil: Editora Independencia, 1934.

Peixoto, Alzira Vargas do Amaral. *Getúlio Vargas, meu pai.* Rio de Janeiro: Editôra Globo, 1960.

Peixoto, Antonio Carlos. "Armée et politique au Brésil." In *Les partis militaires au Brésil,* edited by Alain Rouquié, 25–40. Paris: Presses de la Fondation Nationale des Sciences Politiques 1980.

——. "Le clube militar et les affrontements au sein des forces armées." In *Les partis militaires au Brésil,* edited by Alain Rouquié, 65–104. Paris: Presses de la Fondation Nationale Des Sciences Politiques, 1980.

Peregrino, Umberto. *História e projeção das instituições culturais do exército.* Rio de Janeiro: Editôra José Olimpio, 1967.

Perez, Louis A., Jr. *Army Politics in Cuba, 1898–1958.* Pittsburgh, Pa.: University of Pittsburgh Press, 1976.

Perina, Ruben. "Raíces históricos de la participación de los militares argentinos." *Mundo Nuevo* 3:7/8 (1981): 35–67.

Philip, George. *The Military in South American Politics.* London: Croom Helm, 1985.

Pinheiro, Paulo Sérgio. *Estratégias da ilusão: A revolução mundial e o Brasil, 1922–1935.* São Paulo: Companhia das Letras, 1991.

Pion-Berlin, David, and Ernesto López. "A House Divided: Crisis, Cleavage, and Conflict in the Argentine Army." In *The New Argentine Democracy: The Search for a Successful Formula* edited by Edward C. Epstein, 63–96. Westport, Conn.: Praeger, 1992.

Potash, Robert. *The Army and Politics in Argentina, 1928–1945.* Stanford: Stanford University Press, 1969.

——. *The Army and Politics in Argentina, 1945–1962: Perón to Frondizi.* London: Athlone Press, 1980.

——. *The Army and Politics in Argentina, 1962–1973: From Frondizi's Fall to the Peronist Restoration.* Stanford: Stanford University Press, 1996.

Quaglino, Maria Ana. "O exército e seus técnicos: O projeto do circulo de técnicos militares, 1937–1956." Master's thesis, Universidade do Rio de Janeiro, 1992.

Rabello, Manoel Henrique da Cunha. *Guia de legislação militar.* 2d ed. Rio de Janeiro: Irmaõs Di Giorgio & Cia, 1948.

Ronning, C. Neale. "The Military and the Formulation of Internal and External Policy in Brazil in the Twentieth Century." In *Perspectives on Armed Politics in Brazil*, edited by Henry H. Keith and Robert A. Hayes, 207–24. Tempe: Arizona State University Press, 1976.

Rosa, Virginio Santa. *O sentido de tenentismo*. 3rd ed. São Paulo: Alfa-Omega, 1976.

Rouquié, Alain. "Adhesión Militar y Control Político del Ejército en el Régimen Peronista: 1946–1955." *Aportes* 19 (January 1971): 74–93.

———. *The Military and the State in Latin America*. Translated by Paul E. Sigmund. Berkeley: University of California Press, 1989.

———. "Papéis e Comportamento Políticos das Forças Armadas na América Latina: 1930–1945." In *A Revolução de 30*, Seminario Internacional, 191–209. Brasília: Universidade de Brasília, 1983.

———. "Les processus politiques dans les partis militaires au Brésil." In *Les partis militaires au Brésil*, edited by Alain Rouquié, 9–24. Paris: Presses de la Fondation Nationale des Sciences Politiques, 1980.

Ruhl, J. Mark. "Changing Civil-Military Relations in Latin America." *Latin American Research Review* 33:3 (1998): 257–69.

Santos, Francisco Ruas. *Coleção bibliográfica militar*. Rio de Janeiro: Biblioteca de Exército, 1980.

———. *Fontes para a história da FEB*. Rio de Janeiro: Biblioteca do Exército, 1958.

Sater, William F., and Holger H. Herwig. *The Grand Illusion: The Prussianization of the Chilean Army*. Lincoln: University of Nebraska Press, 1999.

Scarry, Elaine. *The Body in Pain: The Making and Unmaking of the World*. New York: Oxford University Press, 1985.

Schooyans, Michel. *Destin du Brésil: La technocratie militaire et son idéologie*. Gembloux, France: Duculot, 1973.

Serbin, Kenneth P. *Secret Dialogues: Church-State Relations, Torture, and Social Justice in Authoritarian Brazil*. Pittsburgh: University of Pittsburgh Press, 2000.

Serrano, Mónica. "The Armed Branch of the State: Civil-Military Relations in Mexico." *Journal of Latin American Studies* 27:2 (1995): 423–48.

Shifter, Michael. "Colombia on the Brink." *Foreign Affairs* 78:4 (1999): 14–21.

Silva, Hélio. *General Olympio Mourão Filho: Memórias, a verdade de um revolucionario*. 6th ed. Porto Alegre, Brazil: L&PM Editores, 1978.

———. *Hermes da Fonseca*. São Paulo: Grupo de Comunicação Três, 1984.

———. *A luta pela democracia, 1911–1914*. São Paulo: Editora Tres, 1975.

———. *A vez e a voz dos vencidos*. Petrópolis, Brazil: Vozes, 1988.

Silva, Hélio, and Maria Cecília Ribas Carneiro. *O poder militar*. Porto Alegre, Brazil: L&PM Editores, 1984.

Silva, Marcos Antonio da. *Caricata república: Zé Povo e o Brasil*. 1st ed. São Paulo: Editora Marco, 1990.

Silveira, Joel. *As duas guerras da FEB*. Rio de Janeiro: Idade Nova Editôra, 1965.

———. *Histórias da pracinha: Oito meses com o FEB*. Rio de Janeiro: Edições de Ouro, 1967.

Simmons, Charles Wilson. *Marshal Deodoro and the Fall of Dom Pedro II*. Durham, N.C: Duke University Press, 1966.

Skidmore, Thomas E. *Brazil: Five Centuries of Change*. New York: Oxford University Press, 1999.

———. "Politics and Economic Policy Making in Authoritarian Brazil, 1937–1971." In *Authoritarian Brazil: Origins, Policy and Future*, edited by Alfred Stepan, 3–46. New Haven: Yale University Press, 1973.

——. *Politics in Brazil, 1930–1964: An Experiment in Democracy*. New York: Oxford University Press, 1967.

——. *The Politics of Military Rule in Brazil, 1964–1985*. New York: Oxford University Press, 1988.

Smallman, Shawn. "Military Terror and Silence in Brazil, 1910–1945." *Canadian Journal of Latin American and Caribbean Studies* 24:47 (1999): 5–27.

——. "The Official Story: The Violent Censorship of Brazilian Veterans, 1945–1954." *Hispanic American Historical Review* 78:2 (1998): 229–59.

——. "The Professionalization of Military Terror in Brazil, 1945–1964." *Luso-Brazilian Review* 37:1 (2000): 117–28.

——. "Shady Business: Corruption in the Brazilian Army before 1954." *Latin American Research Review* 32:3 (1997): 39–62.

Smith, Ann-Marie. *A Forced Agreement: Press Acquiescence to Censorship in Brazil*. Pittsburgh: University of Pittsburgh Press, 1997.

Smith, Peter Seaborn. *Oil and Politics in Modern Brazil*. Toronto: Macmillan of Canada, 1976.

Sodré, Nelson W. *Do estado novo à ditadura militar: Memórias de um soldado*. Petrópolis, Brazil: Editora Vozes, 1988.

——. *A história militar do Brasil*. Rio de Janeiro: Editôra Civilização Brasileira, 1967.

——. *A intentona comunista de 1935*. Porto Alegre: Mercado Aberto, 1986.

——. *Memórias de um soldado*. Rio de Janeiro: Editôra Civilação Brasileira S.A., 1967.

——. *A verdade sobre o ISEB*. Rio de Janeiro: Avenir Editora, 1978.

Solberg, Carl E. *Oil and Nationalism in Argentina: A History*. Stanford: Stanford University Press, 1979.

Sondrol, Paul C. "The Emerging New Politics of Liberalizing Paraguay: Sustained Civil-Military Control without Democracy," *Journal of Inter-American Studies and World Affairs* 34:2 (1992): 127–63.

Stepan, Alfred. *The Military in Politics: Changing Patterns in Brazil*. Princeton: Princeton University Press, 1971.

——. "The New Professionalism of Internal Warfare and Military Role Expansion." In *Armies and Politics in Latin America*, edited by Abraham F. Lowenthal, 47–65. New York: Holmes and Meier Publishers, 1976.

——. *Rethinking Military Politics: Brazil and the Southern Cone*. Princeton: Princeton University Press, 1988.

Stepan, Nancy Leys. *The Hour of Eugenics: Race, Gender and Nation in Latin America*. Ithaca, N.Y.: Cornell University Press, 1991.

Tanzer, Michael. *The Political Economy of International Oil and the Underdeveloped Countries*. Boston: Beacon Press, 1969.

Taussig, Michael. "Culture of Terror—Space of Death: Roger Casement's Putumayo Report and the Explanation of Terror." *Comparative Studies in Society and History* 26 (1984): 466–97.

Tavares, Aurélio de Lyra. *O brasil de minha geração*. Rio de Janeiro: Biblioteca do Exército, 1976.

Távora, Juarez do Nascimento Fernandes. *Petróleo para o Brazil*. Rio de Janeiro: José Olímpio Editora, 1955.

——. *Uma política de desenvolvimento para o Brasil*. Rio de Janeiro: Livraria José Olympio, 1962.

——. *Uma vida e muitas lutas*. 3 vols. Rio de Janeiro: José Olympio Editora, 1973–76.

Topik, Stephen Curtis. "Economic Nationalism and the State in an Underdeveloped Country: Brazil, 1889–1930." Ph.D. diss., University of Texas at Austin, 1978.

——. *Trade and Gunboats: The United States and Brazil in the Age of Empire*. Stanford: Stanford University Press, 1996.

Trinidade, Helgio. "Integralismo: Teoria e práxis política nos anos 30." In *História geral da civilização brasileira*, sec. 3, vol. 3. edited by Boris Fausto, 290–335. São Paulo: Difusão Européia do Livro, 1981.

Tronca, Italo. "O exército e a industrialização: Entre as armas e Volta Redonda." In *História geral da civilização brasileira*, sec. 3, vol. 3, edited by Boris Fausto, 338–60. São Paulo: Difel, 1981.

Vale, Osvaldo Trigueiro de. *O General Dutra e a redemocratização de 45*. Rio de Janeiro: Civilização Brasileira, 1978.

Valenzuela, Arturo, *The Breakdown of Democratic Regimes, Chile*. Baltimore: Johns Hopkins University Press, 1978.

——. "A Note on the Military and Social Science Theory." *Third World Quarterly* 7:1 (1985): 132–43.

Vargas, Getúlio. *A política nacionalista do petróleo no Brasil*. Rio de Janeiro: Tempo Brasileiro, 1964.

Verbitsky, Horacio. *The Flight: Confessions of an Argentine Dirty Warrior*. Translated by Esther Allen. New York: New Press, 1996.

Victor, Mário. *A batalha do petróleo brasileiro*. Rio de Janeiro: Civilização Brasileira, 1970.

Villanueva, Victor. *El CAEM y la revolución de la fuerza armada*. Lima: Instituto de Estudios Peruanos, 1976.

Waack, William. *Camaradas: nos arquivos de Moscou: A história secreta da revolução brasileira de 1935*. São Paulo: Companhia das Letras, 1993.

——. *As duas faces da glória: A FEB vista pelos seus aliados e inimigos*. Rio de Janeiro: Editora Nova Fronteira, 1985.

Wesson, Robert, ed. *The Latin American Military Institutions*. New York: Praeger, 1986.

Weyland, Kurt. "The Rise and Fall of President Collor and Its Impact on Brazilian Democracy." *Journal of Inter-American Studies and World Affairs* 35:1 (1993): 1–37.

Whigham, Thomas L., and Barbara Potthast. "The Paraguayan Rosetta Stone: New Insights into the Demographics of the Paraguayan War, 1864–1870." *Latin American Research Review* 34:1 (1999): 174–86.

Wirth, John D. ed. *Latin American Oil Companies and the Politics of Energy*. Lincoln: University of Nebraska Press, 1985.

——. *The Politics of Brazilian Development*. Stanford: Stanford University Press, 1970.

——. "Tenentismo in the Brazilian Revolution of 1930." *Hispanic American Historical Review* 44:2 (1964): 161–79.

Zirker, Daniel. "Democracy and the Military in Brazil: Elite Accomodation in Cases of Torture." *Armed Forces and Society* 14:4 (1988): 587–606.

——. "The Political Dynamics of Presidential Impeachment in Brazil." *Canadian Journal of Latin American and Caribbean Studies* 21:41 (1996): 9–29.

Zirker, Daniel, and Marvin Henberg. "Amazônia: Democracy, Ecology, and Brazilian Military Perogatives in the 1990s." *Armed Forces and Society* 20:2 (1994): 259–81.

INDEX